Know Thine Enemy

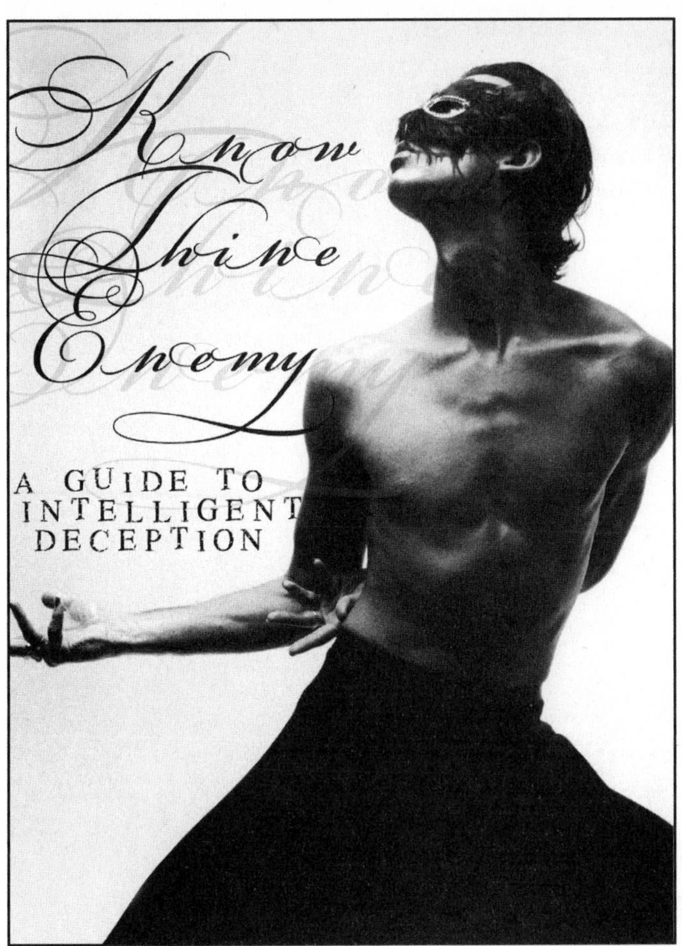

Understanding the Supernatural and the Paranormal within the Context of the Bible

C. A. HUFT

HIGHWAY
A DIVISION OF ANOMALOS PUBLISHING HOUSE
CRANE

HighWay
A division of Anomalos Publishing House, Crane 65633
 Published 2009
Printed in the United States of America

10 2

ISBN-10: 0982211929 (paper)
EAN-13: 9780982211922 (paper)

A CIP catalog record for this book is available from the Library of Congress.

Cover illustration and design by Steve Warner

Dedication

To my mom: I miss you, can't wait to see you again.
Thank you Jesus! Your word will not return void.

CONTENTS

PART I
The Supernatural

PART II
The Paranormal

PART III
The Abodes of the Dead: Hell and Heaven

Part One

The Supernatural

INTRODUCTION

But the Spiritual man tries all things (he examines, investigates, inquires into, questions, and discerns all things...)

—1 CORINTHIANS 2:15; AMP[1]

I wrote this book in obedience to God, but also out of a burning, searing, insatiable desire to know the truth about the mysteries of our world and the cosmos. From a small child I was enamored with the paranormal; with secret, hidden things. I wanted to know about aliens, and UFOs, ghosts, the Bermuda Triangle, angels, demons, and other mysterious forces in our world.

After having several sinister and ominous paranormal encounters, I wanted to know who, and what, was really behind these mysteries from a biblical standpoint, but I could not find any help or answers from the church. I had tried to investigate these things on my own, and ended up in a deep spiritual mess. So I decided to do a foolish thing; I asked God for the answers, and wouldn't you know it, he was only too pleased to answer my questions. After much trial and error, and deep spiritual soul searching, not to mention hours upon hours of scripture study and research, I finally have the answers to quench my burning questions, and yours—all from the Bible! Not from secular sources!

This is a timely read, no other time in our history has man been so bombarded with the paranormal through TV, Internet, books, magazines, and other medias. A 2005 Gallop Poll states three out of four people believe in some aspect of the paranormal. Is there a more sinister side to our God-given curiosity of the spiritual realms? Does the Bible talk about the paranormal, ghosts, UFOs, witchcraft, etc? Are we being groomed for the ultimate deception? This is not a spiritual warfare book; it is a tactical manual on our enemy and his modus operandi.

This book is a field guide on the very father of the paranormal: the Intelligent Deceiver, Satan, the father of the occult. Whether you are deeply involved in the occult, just dabbling, or have a vain curiosity of the spiritual, ethereal realm, or perhaps, you are a seasoned Christian who always had burning questions never answered in church, this book was written for you.

Maybe you have been tormented by spirits in your home or work place, maybe you saw a UFO, maybe you have "seen" things which did not add up in your logical mind, but you did not want to be labeled a "nut job."

God has brought me through, and made good on his promise: "Those who diligently seek, shall find" (Hebrews 11:6: KJV).[2] We are more than overcomers in Christ. The answer is yes, in Christ most all mysteries are revealed and discussed in the Bible, you just have to be trained and taught how to look for them and study them in our modern English.

This book was designed to be read from beginning to end, each chapter and section builds upon the information in the previous section. Holy scripture is quoted throughout the text. For ease I want my readers to know up front every emphasis in scripture, bold text, underlining, larger font size, was added by the author, to help better emphasize certain points throughout our lessons. Several Bible translations were also used to help the reader gain syntax and understanding of the text. The King James Version, the Amplified Bible, and the NIV Life Application Bible were quoted.

My prayer for you is that your deep burning questions will be satisfied and answered by our Lord Jesus, and that you can begin to walk in victory as we are all called to be soldiers in Christ's army.

Chapter One

AN IGNORANT CHRISTIAN

How did I get here? I asked myself. The anger, rage, and seething discontent enveloped me. With each step up the staircase I felt myself getting blacker. My very heart was black and rotting to the core. I felt such smothering heaviness on my shoulders, back, and neck, like a very large, wet, wool blanket, soaked and wrapped tightly around my entire body. I couldn't see past it. I just felt it. I couldn't remember ever feeling good about life or anything. Nothing would ever get better; this was life for me, now and forever. It would never, ever get better. I hated myself, I hated life, and, right now I HATED God! Why would you ever create me to be this way? Why would you allow this to happen to me, and where were YOU, anyway? I reached the top of the stairs. And I said it…yes, just blurted it out. "I hate you God! And I want absolutely nothing to do with you anymore! I DONT WANT YOU!" Immediately, at my core, I knew I had done something so wrong, so unforgivable—I almost took it back. But, NO! I put my foot down, like a spoiled child. I MEANT IT! EVERY WORD! The blackness permeated every cell in my body now.

My inner spirit and soul was as ash. Thick black tar pumped through my veins, and hatred and searing anger permeated my very being.

The ad read one hundred fifty bucks a month, basement room to rent, no lease, shared kitchen, separate entry. "Wow, this is just the break I needed," I thought to myself. My first year of college hadn't been going well. It was the beginning of my last quarter in my first year, January, 1990. I was almost twenty-one. I drove up the hill overlooking Missoula, Montana in my little beater, Ford Fiesta, which also cost me one hundred fifty dollars. It had been a good car, despite the glaring hole in the floor, and the white front panel on the yellow car. It was cold out, probably close to zero.

I parked in front of a modest tri-level suburban house in a tight-knit neighborhood, and started for the front door. I had no idea renting a room for the next five months would forever drastically change my life and its future course.

As I rang the doorbell an attractive blond woman answered the door. Most likely mid-thirties, she introduced herself with a title: Reverend. I thought to myself, "Cool, she must be a Christian to have a title of Reverend." But in my limited existence, I had never heard of a woman reverend. The most striking feature of this pretty woman was her eyes. They were huge—gray, crystal blue eyes. I can still recall the feeling I had when I met her eyes…Hypnotic. I felt like the cartoon, "Looney Tunes," when Sylvester the Cat got hypnotized, and his eyes were these huge black and white swirls, rotating inwards like a whirlpool. "How odd," I thought to myself. She showed me the room in the basement; it was perfect. There was a little shower outside the room, and I could use the upstairs bathroom and the kitchen.

As we walked through the house and went upstairs, she told

me that she was a clairvoyant and that she helped people get over addictions, counseled them, and also was helping the police solve unsolved crimes in the area. As we ascended the stairs there was a small room, with a closed door. A "Do Not Enter" sign graced the door. "Never, go into this room!" she said. Her tone had changed from conversational banter to a stern warning. "I do my *readings* in this room. This is my place of work, so I can't be disturbed, understand?" Okay lady, I thought to myself. The theme song from the Twilight Zone played in my head.

As we finished the tour, I was politely fascinated with her chosen profession. She had two young children, both under the age of five. Her husband seemed like a nice *normal* white-collar guy. He showed me newspaper articles about his wife helping the police solve a crime. "Wow, neat," I said.

"Yeah, we just moved up here from California last year," he said. "She used to work for Shirley McLane, you know, the actress, who wrote the book *Out on a Limb.* She was her top spiritual advisor and clairvoyant."

"Wow, that's pretty interesting. I have always been fascinated with the supernatural." We finished up the rent paperwork, and I moved in that week.

I was so excited to *not* have a roommate, and to have my own room. Now I could focus on my studies, and I was saving $100 per month. As a Christian, I knew that psychics and clairvoyants were wrong...I just didn't know why exactly. My folks had always said that it has to do with witchcraft, and the Bible condemned it. Yeah, yeah, whatever; nobody really believes in that stuff, do they? I mean, this lady was just a shyster, a whack-a-do, out on the fringes of society, right? After all, she was from California. Can anything good come out of California? This was the 1990s; things like witches didn't exist anymore.

I had always been thoroughly intrigued with the supernatural... life after death, aliens, the Bermuda Triangle, healings, ghosts. My absolutely favorite show was *Unsolved Mysteries*, and even as a small child, I would watch *In Search of...* hosted by Leonard Nimoy. I used to go to bed scared to death, but I was still fascinated by it. This whole psychic thing, maybe there was something to it, maybe she had a *gift*, like Nostradamus or Edgar Casey. Whatever, didn't really affect me anyway; I had school to think about.

Life seemed to progress downward for me after I rented that room. My little car's heater and defrosters went out the next week. I remember driving to work at 6:45 a.m., it was ten below zero, and the frost was so thick on the windshield, scraping it didn't help; it just made it frost up more. I had to roll the window down and drive through town to work with my head out the window, to the gas station where I was a checker and also worked in the deli. I had worked for this same company for three years, and then had transferred here to this store when I came to college. The boss didn't like me, and I couldn't figure out why. I was always a hard worker, very punctual, always did my work and then some. I was efficient, and flexible, and friendly to the customers. But, he just seemed to have it out for me. He was the type who liked to do nothing, and have people make him look good. He always brown-nosed the area manager whenever he came around. You know the type: shallow, blowhard, and lazy. Well, maybe, *I* didn't like *him*, and I certainly didn't cater to his flights of fancy. I did my job, collected my check, and kept telling myself in a couple of years I would be out of college and have my dream job. Making some real money, with a real car, with a real heater! And no hole in the floor! Yeah! Life would be good! After work, I'd go out to a friend's house and see my horse. My horse always made me feel better! I had to practice up for the weekend anyway. I was on the college rodeo team, and we had the Carpenter Winter Series Jackpot Rodeo that weekend. I would be running barrels with my best friend, my horse—Rye. I had gotten him when I was thirteen. Growing up in rural Montana, I didn't have electricity or a phone, and my nearest girlfriend was ten miles away. So I rode my horse. I spent every waking hour with that animal. He was my *everything*. I must have put over one hundred thousand miles on that critter over the previous eight years. At eleven years old, he was in his prime, and he loved to run! College Rodeo had been a dream of mine, and now I was doing it!

The weeks seemed to pass without end...My little room was my oasis from all of my troubles. Had someone moved my Bible? I wondered if my landlord ever came into my room. There were days when I felt like someone had been in my room, going through my things. Naw, why would she do that? I'm just being paranoid I told myself. Nighttime was always a bit freaky in the house. My bed was directly below the vent; I could hear right up to the kids' room on the second floor. Her girls always screamed themselves to sleep. This wasn't an "I don't want to go to bed" thing. It was creepy. They screamed and cried for hours! All the kids I had ever been around gave up and went to sleep after fifteen minutes. Not these kids. I would lay awake at night and wonder if spirits or demons were coming out of her *reading room* and tormenting those kids. It creeped me out, but the good reverend always had an explanation for me when I would see her. I never said anything...she must have used her ESP powers and sensed it. "Oh, sorry about the kids. Did they keep you up last night? The little one has bad dreams, and the other one has stomach problems."

"Oh, no biggy, I am a pretty sound sleeper. They don't bother me," I lied.

School was getting harder that quarter. I hated anthropology: what was the point of that class anyway? My major was radio/television communications. What did the study of monkeys turning into humans have to do with radio? And, then I had this cough. I couldn't sleep; I had this nagging, hacking cough all night. I had been to student health, and they said there was nothing wrong, maybe just a touch of bronchitis, stay away from smoke. Stay away from smoke? What, were they high? I wasn't around any smokers!

Then there was my beloved horse, Rye. He pulled up lame at the winter series rodeo, and he wasn't getting better. I couldn't afford to go to the vet. I barely had enough money to meet rent and buy a few groceries. Then the whole boyfriend deal, or lack of one I should say. I had lots of boy *friends*, but nobody ever asked me out. I wasn't ugly, was I? A little chunky, well, not even so much that, I was just really big-boned, and very muscular. It hurt; here I was twenty-one, and I had never been out on real date. No one ever asked me. All my girlfriends had to beat guys off with a stick. I guess I would just have to go get a stick and beat one, just to get him to go out with me...ha-ha. Oh well.

Then, the whole work situation went from marginal to worse; I had put in for a couple of days off months before, and was approved. It was my birthday, and my sister had gotten me tickets to go see Alice Cooper in concert in Spokane, Washington. I had never been to a concert before. It was my one bright spot in my gray little life. But, my boss decided to tell me two days before I left that he was short-handed in the deli and he needed me to work. I refused. I actually got mad! He told me if I didn't work, I would be fired. Fired? Me?! I left his office crying. I didn't understand; I followed procedure by the book. I needed this job. I couldn't find another one with my school schedule the way it was, and I made too much with my seniority to leave and start over somewhere else. I thought

I'd have to just swallow it and take it...Why didn't he like me? What did I ever do to him?

As the end of the school year approached, things went from bad to worse. I couldn't keep anything in life together. Was I that much of a failure? I was a good kid, I read my Bible, went to school, was paying my way, went to work on time, tried to be the best friend possible to my friends, took care of my horse; I was working really hard at my studies, and yet, I was failing at everything. Frustration over my life circumstances was mounting. Not to mention I didn't *feel* right in the head. I was subject to fits of crying and a feeling of hopelessness and such utter self-degradation. "I must just be a total, utter failure; I'm stupid, ugly, fat, and poor!" I thought. Couldn't get much worse than that right? And, I felt like there was something or someone in my room at night, and it would hide in the vent during the day.

I was flunking anthropology, I had a D, which would bring my grade point average way down, not that it was stellar: a couple of low Bs and Cs. But I had never had a failing grade before. I opted for more extra credit work to try to bring my grade up.

Then, the you-know-what hit the fan! My lovely boss had me be a shift leader at one of the other store locations—the one all the drunks and low-lifes frequented by the railroad tracks and biker bars. He was short-handed and sent me over there mid-shift! As a shift leader I was responsible for balancing the till and paperwork at the end of the night, and you guessed it—we were off, short fifty bucks! I stayed late, until 2:00 a.m., redoing all the figures; I checked everywhere, asked all of the employees if they had made a mistake when making change...nothing. I was called into the office the next day and accused of stealing the money. I had never felt so degraded in my life. I tried to reason with my boss. I was only shift leader for half the night, the other part of the night I couldn't be held accountable for! I had never stole even so much as a candy bar before, why after all of these years would I steal now? At the time of the accusation I didn't realize I was being set-up. They had been having *short* nights at that store for the past several weeks, since a certain new hire had come aboard, but they didn't have any proof, so here was my boss' chance to get rid of me once and for all. Revenge—because a couple of months earlier, when he made me cry in his office, the area manager came around the next day, and asked how things were going. I told him about my days off, which were approved and then denied. I was granted my time off from the senior manager, and when I returned from my trip, the buzz was, you could hear the area manager yelling at my boss from outside the store! Yeah, I guess payback was the order of the day for my boss. He said I was on probation, the money would be taken from my pay, and I would be suspended and demoted until they could *investigate* more. So in a fit of tears and complete frustration I quit! I could make it, financially...maybe. I only had a couple more weeks of school.

I called my mom at her work. My parents didn't have a phone because of their remote location. I cried, "Mom, I was accused of stealing!" She consoled me over the phone...then told me, "Get out of that house; she is a witch! You just need to move!" I tried to reason with her. It made no sense to me that my landlord would have anything to do with my problems. It was all *me*—I was the loser! "You come home when school is out. Go back to work at your old job in Helena, and figure out what you want to do with your life. But, come home for the summer and get out of that house!" she said.

Things got really tight. I had no money, and to make matters worse, I had decided I had to euthanize my precious horse. I had finally taken him to the vet after a strange incident at my girlfriend's house where I kept my horse. My girlfriend's stepfather was there when I went out to see my horse. Rye's lameness had gotten progressively worse. Her stepfather told me he couldn't keep up with the other horses in the pasture anymore and maybe I should think about putting him down. "He is in pain all the time, and nothing can be done for him." Then he creeped me out by hitting on me! Eeww! Yuck! He was twenty years my senior and my best friend's stepfather! Gross! I kept that to myself, since I didn't know what to say to my friend. Great, the only guy that asked me out was married and old. Yuck! And told me to kill my horse! What was up with that?

I took my horse to the vet. "Yep, looks like progressive rheumatoid arthritis. Nothing you can do for him except bute-em up and keep him as a pasture pet, or put him down." There was no compassion in his voice. I cried for days. I was miserable. "Lord, what is happening to me? My job, school, my horse! Not my horse—he is all I have in this world! He is the one good thing I have. Why is this happening to me? Am I going crazy?" I thought.

I felt like my world, my dreams, my hard work, were crashing in around me. I was imploding. I took my horse to the "canner sale" on Tuesday, April 10, 1990. A canner sale is a horse auction where the meat packers buy horses to be used for dog food and other products, thus the name "canner." I got $526.68 for my dear childhood friend. I felt like I had betrayed my closest friend…It was enough money to pay my rent and live on until school was out in May. I didn't know a human was capable of crying as much as I did.

Life became very dark for me after that.

I went home that summer in a fog. I felt disconnected, deeply depressed, and darkly disturbed. I don't remember if it was a beautiful Montana summer or not. I was consumed, fearful, bitter, enraged. I felt such self-loathing, and the best I can describe how I felt on the inside was red hot poker rage...like a huge rabid dog lived on the inside chained up, just waiting to get off his leash and kill whatever came into his path.

My parents lived in the tiny western town of Wolf Creek, Montana. We lived back in the mountains, a mile away from the nearest power lines, so we had no electricity, running water, or telephone. It was quiet, restful, beautiful. A small stream continually bubbled and gurgled and giggled its way down the mountain in front our log house. Our closest neighbors were half a mile away. I was surrounded by God's glorious creation. Ten thousand plus acres of state land surrounded our modest forty acres. Balmy breezes made their way off the ridges and into the creek bottoms, where tall, fragrant ponderosa pines swayed in the breezes and deer came down for a cool drink of water. It was paradise—my refuge, but now it felt like a prison. The mountains I used to ride my horse on, the paths, the roads all seemed to say, "You will never enjoy our pleasures again! You are trapped! Loser! You can't even make it through your first year of college on your own!" And if that were not bad enough...at night, when I had to go out to the outhouse in the dark, well...I just didn't anymore. Things, shadows, moved in the trees, darkness in darker corners moved. I had never been afraid of being outdoors at night before—never! And then, the nightmares started.

As I made my way upstairs to bed, in the poor light of the propane lamp, shadows again moved in my parents' large open closet. I could swear the clothes in the closet were rustling with an unseen force. I would shine my flashlight into the darkness of the closet: nothing there. I would turn off the propane lamp and scurry to bed, making sure my closet door was always shut, because lately I noticed that an eerie darkness now lurked in its depths, and at times when I shut the flashlight off to go to sleep, I thought for sure the same thing that inhabited my room in Missoula was coming out from the closet to move about the darkness. It was a presence. I couldn't "see" anything; I just "felt" it.

As I would drift off to sleep, I began to encounter a recurring dream…actually it wasn't a dream, it was a nightmare. It was the same every night, but it would progress every night. I would be walking down a pretty little dirt road, in the middle of nowhere in particular, and there would be a driveway leading down to an old white farmhouse, in a ravine or coulee, next to a creek with trees. As the dream progressed, everything would be green and leafed out, pretty, and as I got closer to the driveway and started my descent down to the house, I would begin to notice gut piles, from dead animals. Every night the dream got worse. As I would begin down the little road, the trees would be dead and naked of their foliage near the house. The gut piles would be strewn everywhere, gut piles upon gut piles. Big, little, gut piles from every kind of animal. This really appalled me because I loved animals. I understood raising and killing animals for food; I grew up on a farm. That was just how it was, but, somehow in the dream, these weren't being killed for food; they were being killed for fun. I don't recall the rotting smell so much from these nightmares as I do the grizzly sites. It was truly awful! And it got worse every night. Something would push me into the gut piles and laugh! I would see innocent farm animals of every kind by the farmhouse, bleating and bellering, petrified of the smell of death in their nostrils and something would swoop in and kill them. I never saw who or what they were, I just knew "they" were there…Death was everywhere! It enveloped me. I would be led farther and farther down the driveway every night, more and more gore, guts, flies, stench, entrails everywhere! Eviscerated animals everywhere I turned, and such sadness! The only way out of the dream was to wake up. I don't have nightmares. Never have…The only other nightmare I can ever recall was as a small child when I had scarlet fever. These were different. I no longer wanted to go to sleep.

I felt myself becoming more fearful of the night every day. I would awake to the sounds of the beautiful babbling stream out my window and the sunlight pouring into my room and I would tell myself to feel better today. But that never lasted for longer than a few fleeting moments. Most days I went to work in Helena. About an hour's drive from Wolf Creek, through a winding beautiful deep canyon carved by the Little Prickly Pear Creek, out onto the windy flats of Seiben Ranch Company and over the microwave pass to Helena, the Capital of Montana. I still drove my little beater Ford Fiesta, the one constant in my life I thought. But on more than one occasion I began to have thoughts of just turning my wheel ever so slightly into the cement pylon keeping me from certain death as the little car would go crashing into the side of the mountain and plummet into the Little Prickly Pear Creek below. I even had the perfect spot picked out. I noticed that I didn't smile anymore, I didn't laugh, and when I did it was purely to hide the inner hatred and terror and hopelessness I felt. I had always been taught that committing suicide was a sin, and that I would go to hell if I did. That thought scared me…Even though I felt I was in a living hell now, I innately knew the real hell had to be worse. Deep down I wasn't even sure if I believed I would go to hell, but I figured I had a fifty-fifty chance. What if I was wrong? Eternity, in hell, besides the thought of doing this to my parents and my family…No, I just couldn't. The way my luck was going I would mess it up too. Crash my car, and not kill myself, but end up as a paraplegic or a quadriplegic, and be a burden to my family for the next forty years. No, I wouldn't kill myself, but the thought never left. I thought about it all the time.

My mother was very concerned for me. She constantly asked,

"What is wrong?" I didn't know, but I did know…I thought I was going crazy. How do you tell your mother that you think you are going insane? She would ask if I wanted to go to church…Nope. God doesn't seem to be thinking of me much these days. She would beg me to go. Nope. I will go on my own terms, and after they would leave for church I would cry out to God. "JESUS! Where are you? What's wrong with me?" I began to feel very bitter towards God, I couldn't even pick up my Bible and read anymore. All happiness had left me. How do you tell your mother that you are pretty sure demons are living in your closet, and now *they*, it was no longer one, would come out at night and press in around your bed? I would pray to Jesus, every night to keep them away from me, and then I would fall asleep to be trapped by my "Guts-n-Gore" dream night after night.

I felt black, heavy, weighted, depressed. I couldn't tell my dad anything. He really didn't believe in this kind of stuff. He would probably say, "Oh, quit feeling sorry for yourself. Pull yourself up by your bootstraps and get on with life. That's life."

My mom came back from church. "Do you think that witch you lived with could have done this to you?"

"Ma, I dunno…" I said apathetically. "It was kind of creepy there, and her kids sure did cry and scream a lot…But she said she was a clairvoyant. Isn't that completely different from a witch?"

"No, not according to the pastor at church…that *is* witchcraft. He thinks you may be under some demonic oppression. I am very worried. I know your father doesn't believe in shrinks, and I don't have much faith in them either, but there is one I know of at work, I think you should go."

Great, just great. Now they were going to send me to a shrink. "Ma, you guys can't afford to send me to a shrink. I'll be fine."

"No, I am really concerned about you. You are too depressed;

you let me worry about paying for it. I may be able to get it covered by insurance."

Inside I felt worse. Now my mom thought I really was crazy. The pastor thought I had demons, which just scared me to death. What was I supposed to do?

As I took off my shoes after work the next day, my mom told me, "Steve came by while you were at work today."

"Oh, what did he want?"

"We had a nice talk."

Steve was living up the road and working for our neighbors. He was an ex-con, a friendly fellow. He looked pretty scruffy—beard, long hair. Kind of a cross between a hippy and a mountain man, he lived in a tipi in one of the meadows where I used to ride my horse. He was a strong born-again Christian…a real "Jesus freak." He wanted to become a pastor and go into prison ministry.

"He stopped by to tell me he has been praying for you."

"Why would he do that?" I snapped. "I don't even know the guy."

"He had some pretty interesting things to say. I don't even know what to make of it all. He said that God told him that you are under a witch's spell, and the witch you lived with cursed you!"

"Oh, Ma, would you get off my back already about that? I don't live there anymore! I get it! I will never live with a witch again!"

"No, listen, he said you are under severe demonic oppression, and he has seen the demons. He said two of them were in his tipi the other night, trying to come after him when he was praying for you!"

"He saw them?" In my mind I was thinking, "This guy lives in a tipi, yeah…He's crazier than I am!"

"Yes, he said you need to be delivered. You need to pray to God to help you and deliver you."

"Do you really think that's what this is Ma?" I was kind of hopeful.

"I don't know. I don't know how to help you," she said.

Things got worse. I felt blacker than ever, seething bitterness, hatred, discontentment, and self-loathing. How did I get here? I asked myself. The anger, rage, and seething discontent enveloped me. With each step up the staircase I felt myself getting blacker. My very heart was black and rotting to the core. I felt such smothering heaviness on my shoulders, back, and neck, like a very large, wet woolen blanket, soaked and wrapped tightly around my entire body. I couldn't see past it. I just felt it. I couldn't remember ever feeling good about life or anything. *Nothing would ever get better; this was life for me, now and forever. It would never, ever get better.* I hated myself, I hated life, and, right now I HATED God! Why would you ever create me to be this way? Why would you allow this to happen to me, and where are you, anyway? I reached the top of the stairs, and I said it…yes, just blurted it out. "I hate you God! And I want absolutely nothing to do with you anymore! I DONT WANT YOU!" I knowingly, on purpose, willfully DENOUNCED the Almighty. *Immediately, at my core I knew I had done something so wrong, so unforgivable…I almost took it back.* But, NO! I put my foot down, like a spoiled child. I MEANT IT! EVERY WORD! The blackness permeated every cell in my body now. My inner spirit and soul was as ash. Thick black tar pumped through my veins, and hatred and searing anger permeated my very being.

God had done what I asked him. He left me! I felt his protection go. It was the worst, darkest week I had ever experienced in my life. At night the demons came out in droves now from the closet. The nightmare was stepped up to a new level of visceral horror, and I blended into the blackness, there was no discernable light in me. I had been utterly impossible to live with since my decision to denounce and "get rid of" God. I continually snapped and snarled at anyone who spoke to me, even my boss and co-workers were now voicing concern. I was reprimanded for being rude to the customers. My world was unraveling as I drove home that night; I had to stay my hand from turning the wheel into my *special* suicide area of the canyon.

That night as I lay in bed, I awoke suddenly; it must have been around midnight. I wanted to turn the flashlight on, but I found I couldn't move. I was sweating, profusely. My heartbeat wasn't pounding in my ears; in fact my heart, I became aware, wasn't beating. I wanted to breathe, my lungs felt searing hot, like I had been holding my breath under water for a very long time, but, I couldn't breathe. I could not move my head, or any part of my body, just my eyes. This was so weird, frightening—I could see in the darkness. I thought to myself—panicked, "What is happening? I am paralyzed." The sudden thought came to my head. "You are dead, and we are coming to get you." The thought, decisive and profound, was in my head, but it wasn't my inner voice. I knew instantly what was happening. I was dead! But my spirit had not yet left my body. The demons that inhabited my closet started to come out and completely surround my bed. There must have been a dozen or more. I could "see" them, but I couldn't. Do you know how when you look directly at the sun for a few moments and you turn away and blink and still see the sun, like a negative image burned into your retina? That's how I "saw" them. Most of them were only about four feet high and hunched over, like imps. I saw no discernable features except *evil* and blackness. They were on the bed, over the bed, at my head, at my feet, at my arms, surrounding and hovering over me. I am quite certain a winged bat-like creature was flapping and hovering at the foot of my bed. I knew, that I knew, that I knew, that this was it…My parents were going to find my dead body lying on my back in bed in the morning with a horror grimace, and my eyes wide open dead and cold on the bed. I was dead! And I was going straight to hell! I felt I deserved this punishment; I had denounced my Lord! I had turned my back on him, and now I was going to get my everlasting judgment: eternity in hell. I wish I could describe it to you better, but I knew! The demons were pushy and insistent, it was time to go. I wanted to fight, to struggle, to run, but I was paralyzed. The only capacities I possessed were sight and the ability to think. It was instinctive…If I couldn't fight them, I knew who could. I screamed it in my head…as loud, as fast, as willful as I was capable. "Jesus! Save me!"

It was instantaneous. I heard a voice on the inside of me, like from an inner ear. I will never forget it. It said, "Hang on. Gabriel's coming!" That was it. "Hang on. Gabriel's coming!" I felt hope for the first time in six months. I instantly thought to myself, "Did he say Gabriel? Isn't that an archangel? Like a really, really important archangel, and he is coming for me? Who am I? A nobody, an insolent brat, who made the gravest of errors, denouncing God."

The demons were still there, but I felt instantly their power had been stripped from them. I felt they no longer had "a right" to me. They could make no claims, even though I felt I deserved it. I never saw Gabriel, but I had a deep sense he was flying through the air in heavy hand-to-hand combat, brandishing a sword. The very strange thing was, I felt the demons leave—scatter, run for their lives, and I fell asleep.

The following morning was different; I didn't feel so dark. I remembered everything. I felt like it was dream, but it wasn't. I didn't have my icky nightmare, I actually felt lighter, better. Not one hundred percent, but maybe fifteen percent better. I knew for sure the demons were gone. There was no presence in my room, and I no longer feared the closet, not even at night. I wanted to tell my mom, but I thought she would really think I was weird and crazy. After all, doesn't stuff like that only happen in the stories in the Bible, or in those silly horror movies? Why would that happen nowadays? No one ever talks about this stuff, and you never hear stories from *normal* people, having encounters such as this. I kept it to myself, for many, many years.

I eventually went to that shrink, a couple of weeks later. I only told him about the nightmares I was having, and I certainly didn't mention anything about suicidal thoughts, witches, demons, or archangels. Had I mentioned any of those things I know I would have been institutionalized immediately, put under suicide watch, and worked up for paranoid schizophrenia, with suicidal ideation, and hallucinations! Instead he called me a "maverick," said I had been severely depressed and saddened over the loss of my horse, and I was feeling severe symptoms of guilt and grief, and time would heal my emotional wounds for my beloved animal. I only went once. By the end of the summer, I was nearly back to my optimistic self and I successfully completed another year of college. I learned how to study and take college exams, and began to excel at my studies. After another year of radio and television communications, I switched my major to nursing and transferred to Montana State University. It wasn't the last time I encountered witches and demons. This was only the beginning…

After my insane ordeal, I found I had an insatiable desire to know what goes on in the spirit and unknown realms. I did not however, have the proper tools to help me find the answers I was looking for, and without the proper tools, I spent the next several years exploring every avenue I could think of to find answers, and I got into trouble. I knew God had the answers, but I didn't know how to access those answers, and I certainly wasn't aware I possessed a book that explained ALL of my burning questions. The Bible gave me the formula for victory over the enemy! I was under the false presumption what happened to me was a fluke of nature, it would not be repeated, I was one of the "weird ones" that had a unique encounter with "the outer world," and life would progress much the same as anyone else's. I was wrong! Dead wrong!

Seventeen years later, my quest has produced experience, knowledge, and Christian maturity (to an extent, I plan on maturing for quite some time, don't you?). My quest for knowledge and understanding has brought us here…to Intelligent Deception. Be prepared to learn, for our enemy prowls about as a roaring lion, seeking whom he may devour!

Many Christians and non-Christians alike have a natural God-given curiosity about Satan, angels, heaven and hell, and many other supernatural phenomena in our world. The problem is we get our information from the wrong places, leading us astray of the truth. We need to re-learn how to mine the depths of the Bible. The church has gotten away from preaching fire and brimstone, and the fear and stigmatization is if you talk about Satan and his evil ones too much, you will lead people away from the true message of Christ, and people will focus on the drama and macabre nature of these *myths* instead of our Lord.

I have found that to be a bunch of bunk! In fact it is unbiblical to NOT know and understand your enemy. Jesus came to teach us how to destroy the works of the devil. Let me give you an example; say you are planning a walk-about in Australia. Australia is known for its poisonous snakes, scorpions, and bugs; don't you think you would do a little research ahead of time regarding these dangerous, life-threatening creatures? Do you think you would take precautions, repellent, and even weapons to protect yourself? Now, I ask you a question: by learning about these despicable harmful creatures, did you glorify them? Did you give them more credit than they deserve? Did you become obsessed with them or merely aware and more careful of where you stepped and slept? Yeah, thought so. The Bible is one big book about our Lord—and our enemy! How is it *not* biblical to understand how a snake operates in our lives?

Likewise do you think our troops, normal men and woman in the reserves, just hopped on the nearest Army base and went to war with Iraq? Hardly! They actually had classes on the enemy; they learned how they operate, what they believe, what they looked like, how they fought, their culture, their hierarchy, etc. They even had demonstrations and drills, dressing up and role-playing as the enemy to prepare the soldiers to fight. Did you ever learn any of these skills in church when it came to our enemy? I hope you did, but I sure didn't, and I know I am not alone.

In my own walk, I have found the opposite to be true. When I didn't know where to look for answers, and I wanted so desperately for the church to answer my questions, I got a "don't touch" response! They kept telling me to "keep my hand out of the cookie jar"! I love cookies! If you tell me I can't have them, guess what, that's all I can think about! I will sneak in and eat the cookies! I sure as heck won't tell anyone what I am doing for fear of reprisal. Come on, now you know what I'm talking about. Christians need to step up and have intelligent, understanding, loving responses to today's inquisitive minds. Answers from the Word! We live in the Information Age and we haven't been taught how to disseminate this information! We are fearful, if we put our hand in the cookie jar we are going to get slapped and put into Satan's prison. But the Bible tells us a very different story—this is what this book is about. Understand the enemy; know how he operates. Once you know who he is and how he operates, he isn't so scary anymore! The enemy is then defeated on a daily basis, you walk in victory, in the will of God, and you draw ever closer to your savior! Come with me on this journey, we will travel into pre-history, explore our fears; the unknown, the mysteries, the ghosts, aliens, ESP, witchcraft, levitation, demonic possession, zombies, life-after-death, reincarnation, the zodiac, evolution, science, occultism, Mars, the depths of hell, the heights of heaven, angels, demons, giants, worm holes, and so much more! Prepare to have your deepest fears and questions answered. The realm of mysteries is about to be demystified!

Who is God? Who is Jesus?

Jesus replied, "Are you not in error because you do not know the scriptures, or the power of God?"

—Mark 12:24; NIV[3]

Who is God? Who is Jesus?

To answer that question, I draw upon my experience as a nurse. To understand what is diseased or abnormal you must know what is normal or healthy first. Then you can start to look for what is abnormal. As a Christian from youth, I was taught God is God, I am to serve him, become like him, and have a personal relationship with him. I read my Bible, went to church, tried to be a good Christian, but I believe my growth was stunted; I was a midget, vertically challenged in Christ, because I really didn't understand my savior. I feel as though I have been privileged to see glimpses, types, and shadows, but I didn't know this being who took my sins and died in my sted—why would he do that? This being actually thought me up—drew me—created me, every molecule, and then chose my parents, family, time in history, number of my days, and wrote, actually tattooed my name on his hands. *See, I have engraved you on the palms of my hand* (Isaiah 49:16; NIV). Wow, who is this "God" I serve? I know my friends, family, husband intimately, but who is God, the Christ? Who is he, really? Did I really know? *No*, I really didn't. How on earth do we become Christ-like, emulating who he is, living up to his ideals of who he is, if we do not know who he is?

So I set about this task—to find out who he is really—because I know who Satan is. In a conversation with my sister one day, we got into a discussion about our Lord and Satan. She said something rather profound. She said, "There have been so many times in my life when I question God's existence, but I have never once doubted the existence of Satan." Yep, been there many times myself. Sad that we have so much faith in the existence of evil instead of good. We know we can count on him to wreak havoc in our lives and in this world.

As I began my search to truly commune with Jesus, be his servant and friend, I realized I needed to know his character, his attributes, his will, mission, plan, likes and dislikes, his physical attributes. I know many Christians like me had heard about his great love, sacrifice, creation, etc. but hey, I'm a woman, I need details.

What I found strengthened my convictions and firmed my beliefs, cemented my hopes. There are no contradictions in the Bible, in Christ, God the Father, and the Holy Spirit. He doesn't create conflict and contradiction within us or our nature…someone else does, and he is very good at it. I realized I needed to get to know both of these entities so I would be able to recognize the attacks of the enemy versus the goodness of God.

Do you have trouble understanding the Bible? Do you think the

Old Testament is outdated and too harsh? And can't possibly apply to our times? Do you read the Bible and feel that your understanding is just as cloudy as it would be reading the original Hebrew and Greek? So many Christians are spiritually bereft due to lack of knowledge and training. It's like someone giving you a brand new piece of technology without an operating manual, without training you in its use or functions. I spent the better part of my Christian life this way; I didn't realize someone had given me a spiritual vehicle that would help my life tremendously and answer all of my questions. Don't get me wrong, I read through the Bible many times before my encounter; I read daily devotions, I asked questions. But I faced the same trouble I had in college: no one took the time to teach me how to study or prepare for exams. Once I learned how to study it correctly, how to unlock its secrets and mysteries, the impact was huge! Just as Jesus said, *Are you not in error because you do not know the scriptures, or the power of God?* (Mark 12:24; NIV).

As I write this, the *Da Vinci Code* is a huge success. It is brilliant fiction. People are buying the code-breaking books, following clues, enjoying a great game…but I submit to you the Creator of man's intellect has given us a book which defies natural laws of time and space and mathematical probabilities. It is so craftily woven together, so encrypted, but yet so plain. So historical, yet so prevailing—now, so futuristic. We just have to spend the time it takes to learn what it says, discover its clues, clues which take you from Revelation, back to Genesis, to the middle of the book of Isaiah. You have to learn how to put the whole thing together and then disseminate that information. We have been taught the Bible by stories, in increments, by chapter and verse. But once you realize that it was written by over forty-four different authors, spanning five-thousand-plus years, and is a library of sixty-six books that relay an integrated message telling the exact same story, why it's just mind-boggling, and it all fits! Something given in a dream two thousand years prior to it coming into being—and it happens exactly. That is a pretty cool code to decipher. It's fun! I have found the word of God to contain answers to every mystery, you just have to be a detective and decipher where it is leading you. So why is the Bible so mysterious? We will go into that in great depth later, but suffice it to say it is a spiritually discerned book, and without a certain element of the Trinity, you don't have the key to unlock its mysteries. This is why unsaved intellectuals can't possibly believe or understand it. To them it is truly Greek!

The Bible isn't just written by God. It is a piece of God, it's a "see it with your own eyes, hold it in your hands, embrace it with your mind, interpret it by the spirit, hear it with your ears" part of God. John tells us, *In the beginning was the Word, and the word was with God, and the Word was God* (John 1:1; NIV). So this scripture is telling us God equals the Word. Jesus sits at the right hand of the Father; he has been since the beginning. So Jesus *is* the Word, a *part* of God; he *is* God.

Jesus is telling us, we can hold him in our own hands, we can "read" him, we can read his thoughts. My Bible is God in printed form. What other book can make such a claim? So God speaks to us, instructs us, we just have to plug in and read and study what he says about our earth, bodies, lives, eternities.

When you cry out, "God where are you?" he is patiently waiting, sitting on your desk waiting for you to pick him up and pursue him. Hebrews tells us, *because anyone who comes to him must believe that he exists and that he rewards those who* ***earnestly*** *seek him* (Hebrews 11:6; NIV). I believe this will comfort many Christians who have a hard time believing God still speaks to his children. According to Vine's Dictionary "earnestly" (*spoudios*) is used to denote "active diligence."[4] The word diligently used in some translations gives us a better picture of what Jesus is talking about here. *Spoudios* has meaning corresponding to *hasten to do a thing, to exert oneself, endeavor, give diligence.* When was the last time you hurried-up and put some work into exerting yourself, (worked) and sought to know the Lord you serve? We spend more time learning about our jobs than we do about our eternal destinies—sad. We expect to have victory over an unseen, evil force with a few crumbs on Sunday. I don't know about you but I have to eat at least four to five times a day just to have the energy to get through the day. One spiritual meal on Sunday doesn't cut it for me to get through the week.

So the tools you will need on this spiritual dig are a good concordance, at least two to three different translations of the Bible so you can better understand syntax and meaning, a Bible dictionary, and a very good Bible study group to help sustain you, bounce questions off of, and give you a deeper meaning as it applies to each individual's life.

So before we begin to learn about the enemy, let's learn about our Supreme Leader, and Commander. This is a very important task because once we know what is right, what is normal, then we can recognize the *abnormal.*

The highest purpose of the Bible is to reveal God's Character: Come meet your God!

> Thus saith Jehovah, Let not the wise man glory in his wisdom, neither let the mighty man glory in his might, let not the rich man glory in his riches; But let him that glorieth glory in this, that he understandeth and knoweth me, that I am the LORD which exercise lovingkindness, judgment, and righteousness, in the earth: for in these things I delight, saith the LORD. (Jeremiah 9:23–24; KJV)

So God is saying that when we know and understand him that he is full of kindness, justice, righteousness, then we can tell everyone how great he is!

Many of us know of God, but we don't know him—take our president as an example. We know him by the way he talks, looks, his policies, etc. We would recognize him anywhere, but few of us actually know him as a person. If you knew the most powerful person in the free world, and you were his personal friend, do you think you may be privy to some special treatment? Know things the regular Joe Blow may not? Have access to some nice perks? Why yes, you would! This is what we can have with Jesus! How cool is that? And he gives us a very special guidebook, which gives us his likes and dislikes, his personality, his motivation, our special privileges, our perks! It's his own personal diary of sorts, and he even gives us the key to understanding it. Our special password if you will…a portion of his being…the Holy Spirit.

This special guidebook to the almighty tells us we are literally…*destroyed for lack of knowledge* (Hosea 4:6; NIV). That's a strong statement. The word for destroyed is *Shamad*; according to Vines it always expresses complete destruction, annihilation, extermination. So we can safely reword that to say, "We are annihilated, wiped out, killed, and squashed by our lack of familiarity and information regarding our Lord." Don't you feel like a bug on a windshield? Which reminds me of a joke my friend used to tell. When a bug would hit the windshield of her pick-up truck, she would giggle and say: "Betcha he won't have guts enough to do that again!" Well, are you tired of being splattered over the windshield of life? Not enough guts left to do anything of consequence? Read on—we have the solution to lack of guts.

This is how to get our "titanium backbone." To know God's immutable character, let's start off with the names of God. In

Hebrew, names were very graphic. They told a story. They were very literal. So when you named your baby, you were in effect prophesying that baby's future.

In *Rose's Book of Bible Charts, Maps, & Timelines,*[5] there is a list of the names of God in Hebrew. It is very easy to understand, and it paints a very clear picture of the Character of God.

- Adonai—The Lord, My Great Lord
- El—The Strong One
- El Elohe Yisrael—God, the God of Israel
- El Elyon—The God Most High
- Elohim—The All Powerful One, Creator
- El Olam—The Eternal God, the Everlasting God
- El Roi—The God Who Sees Me
- El Shaddai—The All Sufficient One, the God of the Mountains, God Almighty
- Immanuel—God with Us, "I Am"
- Jehovah—"I Am," the one who is the self-existent one
- Jehovah-Jireh—The Lord Will Provide
- Jehovah-Mekaddishkem—The Lord Who Sanctifies
- Jehovah-Nissi—The Lord is My Banner (Miracle)
- Jehovah-Rapha—The Lord Who Heals
- Jehovah-Rohi—The Lord is My Shepherd
- Jehovah-Sabaoth—The Lord of Host, The Lord of Armies
- Jehovah-Shalom—The Lord is Peace
- Jehovah-Shammah—The Lord is There, The Lord is My Companion
- Jehovah-Tsidkenu—The Lord Our Righteousness
- Yah or Jah—"I Am," the one who is the self-existent one
- YHWH—"I Am," the one who is the self-existent one

We can break these down into three categories: A military commander, characteristics, and personality.

Military Commander

- God of Israel
- My Great Lord (Leader)
- Lord of the Mountains (or in this case our problems, that seem like mountains)
- Hosts and Armies (of Heaven)

Characteristics

- Lord
- Strong one
- Most high
- All powerful one
- Creator
- Eternal & Everlasting
- Almighty
- I AM
- Self existent
- (is) Peace

Personal (as it relates to us)

- God who sees me
- All sufficient one
- God who is with us

- Provider
- Sanctifier (which means forgiveness, purification, make holy)
- My banner (a device emblematic of our faith)
- Healer
- Shepherd (provides guidance, protection)
- My companion, friend
- My righteousness

Get to know this list intimately; when you are under attack it will definitely be part of your arsenal. As a Christian I found I had to literally marinate, or soak-in, these concepts and facts. When you marinate a steak, it takes on the flavor of the marinade; when you marinate in the Word, your being is taking on the flavor, smell, and taste of our God. These truths start to become a part of you; you become seasoned by the Word. One way to marinate in the Word is to hear it, over and over and over again. The more times the better. I once heard you have to see or hear a commercial forty-plus times before you will actually act on it. So what does that tell you? Hearing one separate message at church isn't even going to season your steak. You wouldn't even know the ingredient went into your marinade. So, better beef up your spiritual recipe for victory. And get that word into you. *Faith comes from hearing the message, and the message through the word of Christ* (Romans 10:17; NIV).

God is also three-in-one. This will be very important for you to grasp when we get to understanding the enemy. The trinity is complicated; I don't think there is a human on this planet who can fully comprehend this mystery. You can really cook your noodle thinking about it, but here goes. I will make no grandiose theological claims here. When I buy a household cleaner, and it has the cleaning powers to clean, disinfect, and deodorize, then it's a three-in-one cleaner. One bottle, three separate and distinct functions. Now don't get me wrong, I am not comparing our Lord to a bottle of cleaner, but it does help my feeble mind to grasp the concept of the trinity.

Theologians use big words to describe Christ; Omniscient—all knowing, Omnipresent—all present everywhere all at the same time, Omnipotent—having infinite power. They also use words such as immortal, infinite, infallible, and incorruptible. I will show you how our Intelligent Deceiver tries to make us believe he is all that and a bag of chips, but he got gonged!

What Does God Look Like?

God does not give us a very good physical description of himself. He does tell us no man can see him and live. Why is that? The Bible alludes to God's immense power and glory, which emanate from him all the time. It is simply too strong for us to handle. Like a shock wave from a nuclear explosion, only multiplied by a gazillion. Moses asked God if he could see him; it's human nature to be curious about what your creator looks like. *Then Moses said, "Now show me your glory." And the Lord said, "I will cause my goodness to pass in front of you…" But he said, "You cannot see my face for no one may see me and live"* (Exodus 33:18–20; NIV).

We have a much more complete picture of Jesus however, because he came in human form. He actually had to cram all that Godness and glory into a human cavity or shell. He walked incognito among us.

Isaiah speaks to us about Jesus' physical appearance on earth: *He had no beauty or majesty to attract us to him, nothing in his appearance that we should desire him* (Isaiah 53:2; NIV). So he evidently was a pretty plain looking fellow; we wouldn't be attracted to his looks.

But Luke tells us he was tall and strong, and alludes to the fact he was very charismatic: *And the child grew and became strong; he was filled with wisdom and the grace of God was upon him,* (Luke 2:40; NIV), *and Jesus grew in wisdom, and stature and in favor with God and with men* (Luke2:52; NIV). He also had great oratory skills, as the Bible teaches us he spoke with great authority (see Mark 1:21–22).

I believe the reason the Bible doesn't focus on his looks is because throughout the ages humans have a tendency to equate physical beauty with power. Instead the language of the Bible focuses on word pictures which evoke strong character, will, personality, and title. The flip side to all of this is Satan, which we will describe in detail later. Satan's *beauty* was his downfall. God made sure it would not be the Christ's.

There are many strong references to Jesus' scars after his crucifixion and resurrection. *His appearance was so (For many the Servant of God became an object of horror)* ***disfigured*** *beyond that of any man and* ***his form marred beyond human likeness*** (Isaiah 52:14; AMP). When Mel Gibson's movie *The Passion* came out, there was a huge controversy over the blood, gore, and graphic violence portrayed. But again, go back to scripture. Remember the Bible was the word made flesh. So this is Jesus himself, describing what he looked like to Isaiah. In my opinion the movie wasn't graphic enough. I used to be an Emergency Room nurse. I have seen people mangled and disfigured, body parts you couldn't identify if you wanted to. The body can live through some pretty awful trauma. Isaiah is telling us, Jesus was beaten up so badly, he *didn't look human.* I don't mean to be gross, but I will be blunt, Jesus looked like human hamburger, and people were absolutely appalled, and grossed-out by the site. That kind of beating was the punishment for *our* sin.

Another verse often overlooked in Isaiah is: *I offered my back to those who beat me, my cheeks to those who pulled out my beard* (Isaiah

50:6; NIV). Did you catch that? Pulled out his beard! Do you think they plucked a few hairs with tweezers? Gave him a waxed facial? I think not. I would imagine they must have pulled his hair from his face with such force that it tore the flesh from his jaw. Even though Christ was resurrected in his glorified body, the Bible teaches he still bore the scars of his sacrifice. No wonder no one recognized him after his resurrection. My husband is known for his large, thick, handle-bar mustache, but I have seen pictures of him when he was a teenager, pre-mustache, and I wouldn't recognize him if he passed me on the street! If you read the gospels carefully, many of the disciples would recognize him when he was breaking bread. You break bread with your hands—they saw the nail holes in his hands; this is how unrecognizable the penalty for sin can make the human form.

God's holiness is another area of misunderstanding and contention. We have been lied to by the popular media and cowardly teachings of certain religions. God is supremely holy! Nothing unholy can touch or defile him. This area of understanding is of utmost importance to us, because without it, we would not be able to understand why the enemy works so hard at filthiness, defilement, and degradation of the requirements of the purity and holiness of God. Many people believe God is all-forgiving and will allow "small sins" to go unpunished (without repentance); this is a lie straight from the father of liars, Satan. All sin, whether a small, white lie, or stealing pencils at work, to gossiping about people, are sins. God cannot stand sin, which is why he gave us Jesus.

Holiness and purity are difficult concepts to understand in our current society. One way I can best describe it, and help you understand it, comes from my nursing background: the sterile field. When I was a nurse, many invasive procedures required a sterile field because the body has a difficult time fighting off infections and microbes that enter into an area of the body that is completely devoid of dangerous bacteria. This is why you see the doctors depicted in the movies holding their hands in front of their face after they have scrubbed in, and then clasping their hands after they have sterile gloves put on, so they are always consciously aware of where their hands are, and avoid inadvertently touching something loaded with germs, thereby causing the patient to have that germ and causing his or her death. This sterile field is an area which has been separated from the rest of the world, nothing that is not pure, sterile, or 100 percent without germs can touch this area. If it does, guess what? The whole thing must be thrown away, including surgical instruments and a new field established. This is how God is, his purity, his holiness is so 100 percent clean. He cannot tolerate anything dirty in his presence; if it is, it must be thrown away. As a human, you must go to the autoclave of life; Jesus Christ, and repent of your sins, and ask Jesus to "sterilize the sins from your life." What we often forget is to stay within the sterile field after this happens; we are deceived and led astray, and walk away from that holiness and purity, and we again become contaminated Christians. God cannot tolerate this contamination, we have to again repent, and be made clean again, and keep ourselves holy and pure, and free of this contamination. Satan's job is to contaminate us and make us unclean, our job is to stay within the bounds of the sterile field, and when we fail, recognize it and ask for another autoclave job!

> Their chastisement will continue until it has accomplished its purpose) for My people are stupid, says the Lord (replying to Jeremiah); they do not know and understand Me. They

> are thickheaded children and have no understanding. They are wise to do evil, but to do good they have no knowledge (and know not how). (Jeremiah 4:22; AMP)

Hey, I didn't write it. God flat out says we are stupid, thick-headed kids, with no knowledge or understanding, or know-how for doing good. He says we are really skilled (wise) at evil. You become skilled or wise at something when you practice it all the time. Practice makes perfect, as they say! So we need to get "practiced" at doing good. Recognizing good, understanding good. It is a three-part plan: know, understand, do. Our problem is we don't know anything about the enemy, we don't understand him, we just end up *doing* his bidding. And the other part of the problem is we don't know, understand, or do what God wants us to do. What a pickle we got ourselves into! I hope this study on the enemy will help you come to terms with why the world is the way it is today, why you do the things you do today, and learn how to recognize, understand, and fight off the enemy, so he can no longer enslave, ensnare, and destroy you because of your *lack of knowledge!* Welcome to Intelligent Deception 101!

This is a type of spiritual boot camp. When you became born-again whether you knew it or not, you became a soldier, an enlisted member in Jehovah's great army. You are Christian Rangers, an elitist group, specifically selected for specialized training in the identification of the enemy. Gathering of intel (intelligence) of the enemies plans, modus operandi or M.O., identifying strategies, enemy numbers involved, double agents, and the like. You will learn to dress and use the appropriate warrior attire, practice tactical maneuvers using the most sophisticated mind-blowing spiritual weapons at your disposal. Next you will learn how to engage the enemy and annihilate him in occupied territory! Show no mercy! You are an elitist member of God's chosen army!

Wow! I wish they had classes like this in church. It is much needed!

This enemy is glorified in our culture as merely an easy myth, a scapegoat for explaining our bad behavior, and a great way to blame God. Not amazingly, there is a lot of false information on TV and other various media of who Satan is. Not surprisingly, this notion of a mythological creature we have conjured up in our minds throughout the "millions of years" we have existed is a convenient way of explaining a horribly unjust, vengeful God who delights in the atrocities and miseries of our planet.

For those of you new to the concept, yes, you can talk about your enemy and learn about him without becoming obsessed, or possessed by the very act of spying on him. You may be even more shocked to learn of his utter defeat, and the ultimate swindle, and rip-off job of our planet. To borrow a popular literary phrase, "So Dark the Con of Man."

Chapter Two

LUCIFER—HIS ORIGINS, NATURE, AND AGENDA

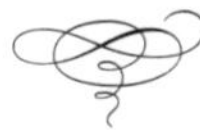

In order for us to understand this intelligent enemy of ours we have to go back into "pre-history," before the earth was created, before man, before time. In order to do this we have to go to the middle of the Bible (I know, start at the middle to get to before the beginning—weird!). To put together an accurate picture we have to piece together certain verses of scripture to get a complete depiction of why we are in the state we live in. Clues have been hidden in scripture for us to dig up, and put them together—how fun! (I always wanted to be an archeologist!) The Bible is very much like a puzzle that we have to piece together. All of the pieces are there, but in order to get the full picture we have to frame it first, and then fill in the middle to see our finished masterpiece.

Ever wonder why the Bible isn't in chronological order, or there are no specific chapters on Satan, Christ, witchcraft, salvation, the end-times, angels, demons, etc.? The Bible was written in such a way as to thwart sabotage from the enemy. If there were a chapter on Christ, who do you think would have been the first to rip it out?

Satan. Instead the word is rather scattered throughout the text. If you rip out any page of your Bible, guess what? You will still be able to understand the gospel message. Isaiah tells us why God wrote it this way: *The word of the Lord was unto them will become precept upon precept, precept upon precept, line upon line, line upon line, here a little, there a little* (Isaiah 28:13; KJV). What this is telling us is the whole story has been scattered throughout "*here a little, there a little.*" It is our job to seek it out, disseminate it, and put it all together; it is a cryptographic text. Proverbs 2:4 tells us to seek for it as "*hidden treasures,*" and again in Proverbs it tells us God has the right to conceal things but we have the honor of searching it out and finding it. *It is the glory of God to conceal a thing: but the honor of kings to search out a matter* (Proverbs 25:2; NIV). The Bible is a spiritual codebook, and we have the Holy Spirit as the key; it's a spiritual treasure hunt!

Lucifer's Story

> This is what the sovereign Lord says: "You were the model of perfection, full of wisdom and perfect in beauty. You were in Eden, the garden of God, every precious stone adorned you: Ruby, topaz, emerald, chrysolite, onyx and jasper, sapphire, turquoise and beryl. Your settings and mountings were made of gold; on the day you were created they were prepared. You were anointed as a guardian cherub, for so I ordained you. You were on the holy mount of God; you walked among the fiery stones. You were blameless in your ways from the day you were created till wickedness was found in you. Through your widespread trade you were filled with violence and you sinned. So I drove you in disgrace from the Mount of God, and I expelled you, O Guardian Cherub, from among the fiery stones, your heart became proud on account of your

> splendor. So I threw you to the earth; I made a spectacle of you before kings. By your many sins and dishonest trade you have desecrated your sanctuaries. So I made a fire come out from you, and it consumed you, and I reduced you to ashes on the ground in the sight of all who were watching. All the nations who know you are appalled at you; you have come to a horrible end and will be no more." (Ezekiel 28:12–19; NIV)

Wow. Soak that scripture in for a moment because we are about to take it apart piece by piece. We have in one fairly short paragraph, eons of time described to us. Talk about Cliff Notes! So our Lord is describing Lucifer here, from conception to fall. Now let me ask you a question. Does it sound like God gave this angel a bum rap from the beginning? *You were the model of perfection, full of wisdom and perfect in beauty…on the day you were created they were prepared (all of those beautiful jewels)…You were anointed as a guardian cherub, for so I ordained you. You were blameless in your ways from the day you were created till…*Let's stop there. On the day God creates Lucifer, he made him a breastplate of incredibly precious stones set in gold; I count nine different stones! He was not only anointed but also ordained. Now some popular ways of thinking suggest somehow God didn't like Lucifer, that Lucifer had good reason to rebel against God, but this is not what this scripture tells us. This angel was special in God's sight. Another popular notion is Lucifer was Christ's brother. Ding, ding, ding, wrong! Lucifer was a created being! Not Jesus' brother! Jesus is Lord, not a created being. Another scripture to back that up is: *For God so greatly loved and dearly prized the world He (even) gave up His only begotten (unique) Son* (John 3:16; AMP)… Got that? Only Son means just one!

The King James Version says it a bit differently; the *workmanship of your timbrels and pipes was prepared for you on the day you were created.* There is some speculation Lucifer was also a minister of music in heaven—in other words he may have been the worship leader, responsible for "covering the Lord in glorious praises." (Praise really galls Satan, possibly because he was the minister of music!) And parents wonder nowadays about explicit lyrics in music. When Lucifer fell, you can bet he corrupted praise and worship.

His name is given—Anointed Guardian Cherub. In the amplified version of the Bible this verse says; *You were the anointed cherub that covers with overshadowing (wings) and I set you so.* There are many different types and hierarchies of angels, and we will discuss those later. According to Vine's Dictionary: "Anointed One (*mashiach*) means a special setting apart for an office or particular function. Guardian (e*pitropos*) means one to whose care something is committed. Cherub (*cheroubim*) means angelic beings."[6] So literally he was an angel, set apart, to have charge over something. In other biblical translations he was the Anointed Cherub that Covers. So he was a *super-angel, with vast responsibilities.* That's a pretty big office to hold. It would be like saying our president is now world president, and responsible for all that goes on, in every country, nation, and town. Lucifer was given a lot of power, and a lot of authority. He still retains those original attributes.

You were the model of perfection, full of wisdom and perfect in beauty. So he was an incredibly, perfectly, beautiful being, full of wisdom. Webster's Dictionary defines wisdom as "the power or faculty of forming sound judgment in any matter." Wisdom can also mean skill. Lucifer was smart, skilled, beyond gorgeous, very rich, and very powerful, anointed by his Maker. Sound like the perfect celestial being?

You were in Eden, the garden of God. Note this Eden is not the earthly Garden of Eden. This is an assumption on my part, because the language in this verse sounds like his day of creation in heaven. This is a heavenly Eden, God's own personal garden. So he had access to, and intimate knowledge of God's personal arenas. Later we will discuss this at more length, but just to get your creative thinking juices going, Eden on earth must have been a copy of Eden of heaven, otherwise why would God give it the same name?

*Every precious stone adorned you: Ruby, topaz, emerald, chrysolite, onyx and jasper, sapphire, turquoise and beryl. Your settings and mountings were made of gold...*Note: most of these stones reflect light, and may be a way of saying *colors of light.* It then goes on to describe Lucifer on the holy mountain of God as he walked among the fiery stones. The amplified version reads; *You were upon the holy mountain of God; you walked up and down in the midst of the stones of fire (like the paved work of gleaming sapphire stone upon which the God of Israel walked on Mount Sinai).* I find these two passages very intriguing, and I won't say I completely understand it, but I have a theory this passage seems to support, which I will discuss later when we get to the paranormal. We will also discuss the holy mountain and the fiery stones when we discuss the heavens. Fiery stones mean; "God created rocks that reflect light or fire."[7]

You were blameless in your ways from the day you were created till wickedness was found in you. Blameless, this word means spotless, clean. In other words since the day he was created he did everything right. He performed his duties to the letter, until the day God found wickedness in him. So evil, sin, iniquity, impiety, malice, badness was found in him. Sin originated with an archangel, not a man. Angels have free will; they are capable of sinning, what makes us think God took away their free will? The Lord specifically mentions Lucifer was a created being. He was created by God, to serve God. Many religions and beliefs have a wrong view of Satan.

Through your widespread trade you were filled with violence and you sinned. So I drove you in disgrace from the Mount of God, and I expelled you, O Guardian Cherub, from among the fiery stones, your heart became proud on account of your splendor. So much is happening in this verse of scripture, I don't want to lose you. Twice in this passage the Lord speaks of what he is doing: "widespread trade," in other words, his work (*ergazomai*). So through his work he was filled with violence, sins, and dishonesty. He wasn't driven from the presence of God until after this wickedness was found in him. So now we know that a "perfect angel" who serves in the innermost of God's courts, privy to supreme knowledge, and inner workings, can choose to sin; he was not created to sin, he chose it! The word *violence*, in this passage lends much more than meets the eye. According to Vine's Dictionary, it's quite insightful, as a noun, (*chamas*) it means: "the disruption of the divinely established order of things."[8] It also connotes a wrongdoing that has not been righted, the guilt of which lies on an entire area (its inhabitants), disrupting their relationship with God and thereby interfering with his blessings; it is the disruption of God's perfect order. Lucifer chose to elevate his stature above that which God had designed, and in the process he disrupts other "inhabitants" (angels) in their relationship to God. Gee, the dude hasn't changed a bit after all these eons! So this was more than a little temper tantrum. This was a mass-engineered rebellion. But this particular passage only alludes to that once you've done the necessary homework on the words.

There is another passage of scripture which actually tells us what Lucifer did: *your heart became proud on account of your splendor.* This passage actually tells us where all of this chaos began: the heart. You know with our modern medical science we can keep people alive for years who are brain dead, but if their heart fails it's a dirt nap for you! Clinical death. But God is not talking about a physical heart here; he is talking about Lucifer's inner man. Vine's Dictionary says "the heart (*leb*) is the inner person, with a focus on the *psychological aspects of the mind*."[9] The heart is the part of the man that thinks, lives, has a personality, and most of all responds to God. It is the seat of the emotions. *The heart as lying deep within, contains the "hidden man" this is the soul of man* (Acts 5:19; NIV). Lucifer's heart became proud on account of his great beauty. We will take a closer look at pride when we get to Isaiah 14. But pride *(huperephanos)* signifies showing oneself above others, pre-eminent (always used in a bad sense in scripture), arrogant, disdainful. So we have to assume he was elevating himself above whom? Sounds to me like he already had the highest position allowed for angels, so he is not exalting himself above his fellow angels. He is thinking with mind, personality, and emotions that he is truly prettier and better than his Creator—God. Yep, pretty arrogant character!

So I drove you in disgrace from the Mount of God, and I expelled you, O Guardian Cherub, from among the fiery stones, your heart became proud on account of your splendor. It sounds to me that God made quite a spectacle of Lucifer, stripping him of his title and his privileges. I want you to make special note of two words here in this sentence: "drove" and "expelled." These words will have special meaning for us later, and I will expound upon them as we go along. But for now, put "drove" and "expelled" into your memory banks as a special clue for later.

So Lucifer thought in his heart first, then in his mind. Sounds backwards to us, but his inner man became proud first, then his mind kicked in and he started to think and dwell on his beauty and splendor, and voila kicked out of heaven in disgrace. Jesus tells us over and over again in the New Testament he "sees" the inner man, the heart of a man. Gee…do you think there is a connection? Also remember when we discussed Jesus' physical appearance, beauty was on the bottom of this list? This is an important concept I need you get, "the heart" was Jesus' number one priority! Now we know why!

The last part of this passage, *So I threw you to the earth,* we will cover this when we get to Revelation. God goes on to describe FUTURE events in the rest of the verse; events I happen to believe have yet to come to pass.

The Origin of Lucifer's Ambition: The 5 "I Wills"

> How you have fallen from heaven, O morning star, son of the dawn. You have been cast down to the earth, you who once laid low the nations! You said in your heart, I WILL ascend to heaven; I WILL raise my throne above the stars of God; I WILL sit enthroned on the mount of the assembly, on the utmost heights of the Sacred Mountain. I WILL ascend above the tops of the clouds; I WILL make myself like the Most High. But you are brought down to the grave, to the depths of the pit. (Isaiah 14: 12–15; NIV)

How you have fallen from heaven, O morning star, son of the dawn! The Hebrew for this expression is "light-bringer" or "shining one." It has been translated "Lucifer" in the Latin Vulgate, and is thus translated in the King James Version (amplified bible commentary). The *Morning Star* is also the name for the planet Venus, which rises first in the morning right before the sun; it is the signal of dawn. I want you to pay special attention to the meanings of Lucifer's name. The two names "Light-bringer" and "Shining one" are used continually in our language today and most especially if you are part of the New Age Movement or UFO subculture. (Yeah, we will talk more about that later, back to the pre-history lesson.) Funk & Wagnall Encyclopedia defines Lucifer as "Phosphorous" or "light bearer."[10]

Some believe the word Lucifer was a mistranslation, however, the word does mean "Shining one." Satanael may have been his original name, as the "-el" ending is a title of God, as we see reflected in the names of the archangels, Gabriel and Michael. After Satan's fall, God may have just stripped this all-important "-el" ending from his name, rendering it just Satan.

And He said to them, I saw Satan falling like a lightening (flash) from heaven (Luke 10:18; AMP).

This is Jesus speaking to his disciples after he had just given them power and authority to cast out (expel) demons.

You said in your heart. Here we see it again. See, the Bible does not contradict itself; Man doesn't know enough to put the right passages together to get the full picture. Again God focuses on the heart; the heart is always the REAL person—the seat of his emotions. The heart does have the ability to think, as we will see from new scientific evidence. So Lucifer thinks in his heart the following five statements.

I WILLS: The "will" is the part of us which chooses.

1. I WILL ascend to heaven;
2. I WILL raise my throne above the stars of God;
3. I WILL sit enthroned on the mount of the assembly, on the utmost heights of the Sacred Mountain.
4. I WILL ascend above the tops of the clouds;
5. I WILL make myself like the Most High.

Lofty and arrogant. How does a creature decide to usurp the very throne of his Maker? The answer—you don't! Scripture is very clear: God kicked him out on his hiney. God is a God of justice. He doesn't snivel and wring his hands and say, "Oh, what am I going to do? Lucifer wants to take my throne and be like me. Bad, Lucifer, shame on you, I'm gonna kick you out of heaven and give you a new kingdom." No, that's clearly not what happened. *But you are brought down to the grave, to the depths of the pit.* God had to make a place for Lucifer, and his angels. But alas, I am getting ahead of myself.

Lucifer's problem was he believed he could attain ultimate power. He is delusional. Sin did not begin with man. Sin originated with a cherub. The Bible tells us he is the father of lies. A highly intelligent being, albeit, totally self-deluded. Lucifer was so delusional he even requested God (Jesus) fall down and worship at his feet! Can you imagine? *Again, the devil took him to a very high mountain and showed him all the kingdoms of the world and their splendor. "All this I will give you," he said, "if you will bow down and worship me"* (Matthew 4:8–9; NIV). He covets our worship as well. Just an aside note here; this would not have been a temptation to our Lord if Satan did not actually "own all the kingdoms of world." The world was given to us, we traded it for "secret knowledge," and Jesus bought it back at the cross, and then gave it back to us, again.

The Bible only gives us scant details of Lucifer's fall. For instance, many scholars disagree on when Satan was kicked out of heaven. Some think before God created the earth, some think after God created the earth and Adam and Eve. I happen to believe Satan fell (prideful sin-demoted) between verses 1 and 2 of Genesis Chapter 1:

> *In the beginning God (prepared, formed, fashioned, and) created the heavens and the earth.* (Genesis 1:1; AMP)

> *The Earth was without form and an empty waste, and darkness was upon the face of the very great deep. The Spirit of God was moving (hovering, brooding) over the face of the waters.* (Genesis 1:2; AMP)

Now this is where it gets a bit complicated, and advanced science and physics can better explain what I can't. *The Earth was without form and an empty waste, and darkness was upon the face of the very great deep.* Didn't God create the heavens and the earth, just prior to this sentence? What? Does this mean the earth was preexistent prior to our understanding? (This is the classical gap theory.) This is important to our understanding, because volumes of books have been written on these two little verses. If you read on, the first day of creation was separation of light and darkness, not creating a spherical earth. *Face of the very great deep*, tells me it's more of a black spot in space, and it says *empty space.* Later in this verse when it talks about the *face of the waters*, some scriptural scientists have suggested the word for waters is more accurately translated as vapors. So picture it: swirling dark spot marked out of the heavens as the spot where earth is going to be planted, and on this special spot, was darkness, *and darkness was upon the face of the very great deep.* Wait a minute…I thought the earth was already created, and now he is saying it doesn't have form and it's an empty waste? If nothing is there how is there darkness? Light doesn't come into play until the next verse. So this darkness is a metaphor, or is it? Some quantum physicists suggest it was a black hole. God *separates* light from darkness in the next verse. Could this darkness be Lucifer, plotting his next move, now on the spot where earth is (or was)? Could Satan have possibly desecrated the original creation of earth when he fell? *The Spirit of God was moving (hovering, brooding) over the face of the waters.* Why does God *brood* over this spot? Why would our great Jehovah have to brood over his coming creation? God showed me this verse, and I have mediated on it many, many times.

In search of the answer to my "brooding" question, I was led to some interesting commentary on this very first book of the Old Testament. I went to the Jewish Chumash,[11] or Torah, which is the first five books of the Bible. Rabbinical commentators have a better grasp of their own language, don't you think? This is interesting: "*God.* This name denotes God in his attribute of Justice, as Ruler, Law Giver and Judge of the world."...Hmmm, read on: "*Darkness.* This is not merely the absence of light but a 'specific creation.'" Now why would God use this particular noun to describe himself at creation? And why would darkness not be referring to absence of light but to a specific creation? Isn't one of Satan's titles the Prince of Darkness? Ah the mysteries of the Bible, aren't they fun? Webster's Dictionary defines brood as "ponder moodily, or preoccupied." If you are positioning yourself as a judge over darkness (a specific creation, or creature maybe), maybe brooding doesn't really mean moody—maybe we can find a clue in another scripture. Satan is being *restrained* by the Holy Spirit in this world until the end, in Revelation when the Holy Spirit actually loosens the Antichrist's reins so to speak, and Satan is "unleashed." Maybe the Holy Spirit is brooding over what he knows Satan is cooking up next in his demented little heart. These are all questions many of us have. And it is good to meditate on them, and study them. So many of us just skim over what we read in the Bible and never give it a second thought. I think all the answers to all of life's questions are contained in this book. You just have to dig through the layers. However you choose to decipher this text, be aware God makes it very clear in Genesis 1, verse 4 he separated the light from the darkness!

Just as another tidbit to get you thinking critically; when you look up the word "glory" as it relates to God, it means *to shine,* and also represents the Lord's presence. It can also mean *to add* something to someone's character, which it in itself doesn't have. So our "Shining one" would have lost all his shiny glory because he was cast from the Glory of God. He no longer had the essential ingredient of pure light, but was now in himself an utter void trapped in a space vacuum, or black hole.

There are more questions than answers to Genesis 1:1–2, and many good scholars have differing views. My goal is to get you questioning and digging-up for yourself the treasures the Bible has to offer, rather than just view the Bible as a quaint old book with some interesting fables and moral stories. The reason I bring up the gap theory is not to say it is right or wrong, it's just intriguing. We have no way to prove it. But let me present to you some commentary that just may tickle your ear. What if Lucifer-good-angel we'll call him, actually was in charge of a planet called earth or lived here, if in fact the earth and heavens were created in the beginning as the word states and it pre-existed our present earth. When Lucifer-good-angel sinned and got demoted, he went a little berserk with his "I will" plans and God got a bit wrathful as the word states, and maybe he destroyed the earth. I am not saying this is what happened, I am just presenting a view, some scholars have voiced. And this is why we see God use words like the earth was a void and empty waste. This brings us to this whole business of evening and morning the first day. The Hebrew words *ereb* and *boqer* are translated evening and morning, but that doesn't make sense because this only gives us twelve hours, not twenty-four for our first day. What? Some scholars suggest that *ereb* and *boqer* may have had a different meaning: chaos to order. So our first day would have been separating the light from the darkness, and restoring order from the chaos that a mad, demoted cherub caused. So each subsequent day, six total, were spent creating order from chaos. Intriguing theory. If it is correct, this makes a lot of the puzzle pieces fall into place from the viewpoint of why does Satan covet this planet so much, and why would he trick Adam and Eve out of their God-given ownership.

Onward, so we have this gorgeous super angel, who was in command of vast numbers of angels, a shining one, and perfect in his ways. Before he thought about becoming a god, I am sure he was privy to God's ideas on creation. In other words, I betcha he helped with the blueprints. Maybe, and I am just speculating here, 100 percent pure conjecture, he actually thought God was going to put him in charge of this very special planet or God did in fact do so. After all, he was in charge of everything else! He was in tight with the Big Guy! And God was such a giving God, merciful, loving. Remember, Lucifer didn't know any other GOD! Maybe Lucifer was in charge of the angelic construction crew! Many of you are now thinking, "Well, when did he get his minions; how did he manage to get a bunch of angels to follow him on his demented quest 'to be like God'?"

To answer this question we have to go the *end* of the Bible.

> Then another ominous sign (wonder) was seen in heaven: Behold, a huge, fiery-red dragon, with seven heads and ten horns, and seven kingly crowns (diadems) upon his heads. His tail swept (across the sky) and dragged down a third of the stars and flung them to the earth. (Revelation 12:3–4; AMP)

The disciple whom Jesus loved—John—gives us a rather dramatically different mental picture of Lucifer (the shining one), who is now, no longer Lucifer. In Hebrew tradition names mean a great deal, and God throughout the Bible changes men's names after a spiritually significant event happens, e.g., Abram becoming Abraham.

He is now referred to as Satan the devil, an ancient serpent, an enormous red dragon. We go from a model of perfection, anointed-cherub-who-covers, to this hideous red beast, with seven heads and ten horns (all of which have eschatological significance). His big tail sweeps a third of the stars. In Hebrew tradition these "stars" are angels who fell with Satan.

I will remind you again the Bible is a book without our dimension of time constraining it. This is both a future and pre-historical vision by the disciple John. So we have to change our way of thinking when we read the text. We have to throw out all of our presumptions and pretend the clock doesn't tick. I believe this verse occurred at the cross, when Jesus conquered sin and death. If you read the entirety of these verses in context, when Jesus died on the cross, Satan was no longer allowed in heaven's courts, and Michael the archangel gets the privilege of kicking him out. We will explore Satan's boundaries in a coming chapter.

According to Vine's dictionary: "dragon (drakon) is a large serpent so called because of its keen power of sight (from a root, *derk*—signifying '*to see*')." [12] Isn't that interesting? I want to know what *kind of sight*? See, when you start to do word studies in the original language, it changes the meaning of our words drastically. What kind of "sight" does this Satan possess? Jesus could "see" what was in men's hearts. It may be a clue we need to pick up on later; maybe "insight"?

So let's go to rest of the verse. *His tail swept (across the sky) and dragged down a third of the stars and flung them to the earth.* So the stars are angels. This is the part we don't have a record of. This was, I believe, Satan's very first deception. How do you trick angels in the constant presence of God to rebel and follow you on a quest to ascend higher than the Most High? Did he talk to them? Use an unbelievable sales pitch? If Satan had a free will to choose to sin against God, then we can safely assume all angels were given this same privilege. Remember, God remains the same, yesterday, today, and tomorrow. He is constant and unchanging; we can always rely on this arena of his character. Did he offer them positions of authority they were not capable of in heaven? (Remember rebellion is changing God's supreme order.) What kind of kingdom did he offer? Earth? We know God alone had the power to create something from nothing. So we have to go back to scripture for more clues to our unanswered questions. So, his tail swept the angels, one-third of them, which may literally mean innumerable numbers. And the word says he *dragged* them and *flung* them. Did you catch those two words? One definition of *drag* from Webster's Dictionary[13] is to "influence," and *flung,* means to "throw with violence, cast or hurl." So he may have indeed had quite the flashy line of promises, and then once convinced, he used his power of authority over them to hurl them to earth. The other angle we need to explore is Satan's name. One of the meanings of Satan's name is Deceiver. *He who is the Seducer (deceiver)* (Revelation 12:19; AMP)…Vine's Dictionary says, "seducing (*planao*) is to lead astray, and deceiver (*phrenapates*) is a 'mind deceiver.'"[14] But, this could also be referring to God throwing them out of the courts of heaven, as was written in both Isaiah and Ezekiel. This is where I get the title Intelligent Deception.

In the book, *The Handbook for Spiritual Warfare*[15] author Dr. Ed Murphy writes about his deliverance ministry. He had an occurrence of casting out a demon that was manifesting itself in one of the people he was delivering. I will let him tell the story:

> I purposefully entered into a controlled dialogue with one of the demons beyond what is normal and usually appropriate. I allowed the demons to use the victim's vocal cords and speak out loud. I was dealing with a demon called Fear.
>
> "How long have you been around?" I asked Fear.
>
> "For ages," it replied.

"You rebelled against God, didn't you?" I prodded.

"Yes."

"Why did you do that?"

"We were fooled."

"Who were you fooled by, Satan?"

"Yes."

"Yet you say you love him."

"We must."

"He is the Prince of Darkness. Do you know where he is going?"

"We were betrayed."

Evidently demons are often compelled to tell the truth in the presence of a greater spiritual authority. (See Luke 10:17–19, Eph. 2:6, & 3:10.)

Now, I don't know if this demon was speaking truth or not, after all he is a deceiving spirit, but my point here is it does give the mind some food for thought. If this beautiful being could sweet-talk one-third of the angels in God's holy presence, how much more sinister and seducing will he be with us?

So my question to all of you combat-trainees; did Satan retain his perfect beauty or does he look like the medieval pictures you see in European chapels? I believe the answer to this question is twofold. First it is evident our enemy still retains his God-given super angelic abilities, which we will discuss when we get to one of the oldest books of the Bible, Job. Corinthians tells us; *And no wonder, Satan himself masquerades as an angel of light* (2 Corinthians 11:14; NIV). Masquerade is a disguise. If you were already the "Light bringer, Shining one," why would you have to put on a mask of what you already looked like? I believe once Satan rebelled against God with his "I wills" he became the hideous serpent. Without the goodness of

God lighting (glorifying) his inner soul, he became Darkness. This Darkness has the ability to change his disguise, his outer appearance as he once was, to probably anything he wants (he is the original shape-shifter). So be on guard you are not attempting to find your enemy on account of his looks; those can change at his will.

Satan's Boundaries

The holy scriptures we have studied tells us he has been cast down, or stripped of his place of exalted position in heaven, to the spot where earth is to be positioned in the coming creation. So at this point it is pretty much just a cosmic spot on the universe's blueprint. Before we get to creation and the fall of man, let's travel to the book of Job. Many scholars believe Job was written before the time of Abraham, probably about 2,000 BC. So for our purposes, it was written over four thousand years ago. According to scripture Satan still has access to the heavens. In other words, he is not bound to earth only. There are some religions which falsely teach that Satan and his angels are currently chained in hell. This can't be true! If Satan was already locked up, then why is he talked about incessantly in the Bible as causing problems for us from day one? Why would we need a savior? Yeah, there is lot of weird stuff floating around... God calls us "ignorant Christians" who don't read and understand their Bible! Jude does tell us some of the angels are chained in darkness, but these angels we will discuss later. These angels (a small number) committed a very specific sin, which required immediate punishment by God.

Why was Satan allowed to come to earth? Why didn't God just lock him up from day one and prevent all of this sorrow and mayhem from happening in the first place? Why evil, hate, torment, murder, starvation, why, why, why? Why was he allowed to live so long on the earth? Why wait for a savior? Why wait for final judgment, then imprisonment?

Unbeknownst to Lucifer, God has a "Secret Plan," a "Mystery of Salvation," an "Ace in the Hole." *No, we speak of God's secret wisdom, a wisdom that has been hidden and that God destined for our glory before time began. None of the rulers of this age understood it, for if they had, they would not have crucified the Lord of glory. However, as it is written: No eye has seen no ear has heard, no mind has conceived what God has prepared for those who love him, but God has revealed it to us by his Spirit* (1 Corinthians 2:7–10; NIV).

This is how I make sense of what seems senseless in our evil, corrupted world, why God allows evil to reign the day. We *are* the living testament, proof of God's goodness and mercy to the entire universe. And most especially, heaping coals of judgment on a rebellious angel's head. When you study other ancient texts and commentaries on human obedience to the Lord, Satan is described as completely dumbfounded by our obedience and devotion to God. The "good" angels also rejoice over every one of us who chooses life and believes in the name of Jesus. God may have wanted to show his "elite" angels (the ones who had not rebelled) that he was all he said he was, and so much more! Here is another testament to this cosmic discourse! *I tell you, there is rejoicing in the presence of the angels of God over one sinner who repents* (Luke 15:10; NIV). How cool is that? Let's see what happened with Job.

A curious dialogue: *One day the angels came to present themselves before the Lord, and Satan also came with them. The Lord said to Satan, "Where have you come from?" Satan answered the Lord, "from roaming through the earth and going back and forth in it"* (Job 1:6; NIV). So the angels come to present themselves before God, and Satan just so happened to have the gall to show up. Or maybe not, maybe God requested his presence. Why do I say this? Because God asks

Satan a rhetorical question, *"Where have you come from?"* God is all the Omni's remember? He knows exactly where Satan has been and what he has been up too. The Bible was written for our benefit, not God's. So Satan has been *roaming through* the earth, going back and forth *in* it. So if you're "roaming" you are not omnipresent. Satan cannot be everywhere at once. This is why he needs his minions to accomplish his demented plan. He has limited power. He is not the all-powerful one he likes to think he is, or deceive us into believing he is. I also find the language used here interesting. *Through and in*, to me describes an ability to go through matter, and into it, not just confined to the crust of the earth. Okay, so let's continue our strange dialogue.

> Then the Lord said to Satan, "Have you considered my servant Job? There is no one on earth like him; he is blameless and upright, a man who fears God and shuns evil." "Does Job fear God for nothing?" Satan replied. "Have you not put a hedge around him and his household, and everything he has? You have blessed the work of his hands, so that his flocks and herds are spread throughout the land. But stretch out your hand and strike everything, and he will surely curse you to your face." (Job 1:8–11; NIV)

Sheer audacity (we can learn a thing or two from this conversation). This evil, rebellious creature comes into God's holy courts, and jealously accuses one of God's most "blameless and upright men" (if you haven't noticed yet, Satan has it out for our race). Satan is called the "accuser of the brethren" for a reason. Indignantly he tells God he is protecting Job from him, and has a hedge of protection around all of his possessions. Then Satan taunts and dares God, "Go ahead, remove your protection, and whamo, he will curse you to your face." This dialogue reveals so much of Satan's character and his limitations. I can just hear God's sense of humor in all of this. I bet he said to the angels after Satan left, "Watch this; my kid Job is gonna kick butt!"

Satan really wants Job. Ever wonder why? There is covetousness, inciting God against his own creation without reason, to ruin Job. God himself says why: *There is no one else like him on earth.* Satan can't handle that—he covets Job's allegiance and holy reverence to God. He wants it for himself; remember he still thinks he has a chance at becoming God. When you study the word *covet*, or *envy*, it keeps company with and births every horrible, heinous sin imaginable. The Bible tells us Satan is constantly going before the throne of God and accusing the brethren. *For the accuser of our brethren, he who keeps bringing before our God charges against them day and night, has been cast out!* (Revelation 12:10; NIV). Satan spends a great deal of his short time allowed, before his final imprisonment, accusing us. What a lot of effort. Not only does he go boldly before the throne of God, but he indicts us, blames us, and points the finger at us. Wherever he sees someone's sin, he points it out to God, and accuses us, and makes a petition before God for the right to inflict us with his hatred. Satan could be before God right now, asking God if he can torment you, or your family, or your pastor, or friend, or neighbor. God in his supreme justice grants some of Satan's petitions if there is not a counter petition (prayer). In other words if you had unconfessed sin in your life, God would allow Satan to test you. Even if you are doing everything right, like we see with Job, God may still allow Satan to test you…*for suddenly the destroyer will come upon us. I have made you a tester of metals and my people the ore, that you may observe and test their ways* (Jeremiah 6:26–27; NIV).

Note Job had a hedge of protection. *Hedge,* in Hebrew, according to Strong's Dictionary, is, "(*Suwk, sook,*) a primitive root; to entwine, shut in like a fence, a formation, protection or restraint."[16] Why do you suppose Job was protected by this hedge? Could it be he was blameless, upright, feared God, and shunned evil?! This meant he avoided, and kept away from wrongdoing. Take note of these attributes; they are a telling us how to have a "hedge of protection" from your enemy.

The Intelligent Deceiver has the ability to move freely in, and through, the earth. He also still has access to the heavenly realms and he used to be allowed in heaven's courts. The heavenly realms include our atmosphere and outer space, plus God's home—heaven. He has to ask permission before he can attack certain believers (ones who keep themselves blameless, upright, and shun evil). Satan needs a doorway to get through a hedge of protection. In Job's case the doorway was fear. You can study more about Job's fears in the book of Job. Satan covets humans. He wants us! Shunning evil can also really aggravate Satan as we see with Job. Isaiah tells us *whoever shuns evil becomes a prey* (Isaiah 59:15; NIV).

The Holy Spirit tells us Satan is no longer allowed in the courts of heaven in Revelation:

> And there was a war in heaven. Michael and his angels fought against the dragon, and the dragon and his angels fought back. But he was not strong enough, and they lost their place in heaven. The great dragon was hurled down that ancient serpent called the devil, or Satan, who leads the whole word astray. He was hurled to the earth and his angels with him. Then I heard a loud voice in heaven say: "Now have come the salvation and the power and the kingdom of our God, and the authority of his Christ. For the accuser of our brothers, who accuses them before our God day and

> night, has been hurled down. They overcame him by the blood of the Lamb and by the word of their testimony; they did not love their lives so much as to shrink from death. Therefore rejoice, you heavens and you who dwell in them! But woe to the earth and the sea, because the devil has gone down to you! He is filled with fury, because he knows that his time is short." When the dragon saw that he had been hurled to the earth, he pursued the woman who had given birth to the male child…Then the dragon was enraged at the woman and went off to make war against the rest of her offspring—those who obey God's commandments and hold to the testimony of Jesus. (Revelation 12:7–14,17; NIV)

There are a lot of differing views when this actually happened, but I happen to believe the text tells us when this war in heaven occurred—he was overcome by the blood of the lamb. *Now have come the salvation and the power and the kingdom of our God, and the authority of his Christ.* It tells us it happened when Jesus died on the cross. It goes on and tells us heaven rejoiced because Satan was no longer accusing us before God day and night like he was before. But—there is always a but—*woe to the earth and the sea, because the devil has gone down to you! He is filled with fury, because he knows that his time is short.* This explains he is plumb mad, he is going to take his wrath out on us, and his time is short. It goes on to tell us he and his fallen angels are making war on Christians.

So Satan's boundaries sound like they are now confined to earth, our atmosphere, and the planets; he may no longer be allowed in God's abode—heaven.

Below is an excerpt from a Satanist group in New Zealand, supposedly channeled by the (Demon) *Daimon Samyaza.* It is their deluded position of Lucifer's fall and is written from the perspective of Satan. It gives a very good insight into how Satan deludes and beguiles his followers with a bunch of self-righteous lies.

The Covenant of Samyaza

> For it is Demiurge (God) who creates man in ignorance and fear that man should forever be servile before him. It is written that Demiurge created man in childlike innocence, unconscious and devoid of intelligence…
>
> But there was an angel who was different from all the other Angels, in that Self-consciousness dawned upon him. Recognizing that he was a Being unto himself. And his name is Satanael (Satan)…
>
> And the entire Angelic host, and the Sons of God, looked with fear and bewilderment upon the radiance of Satanael, and some among the Angels began to emit their own glow of Selfhood…
>
> And Satanael came upon the woman Eve, advising her that when she partaketh of the fruit of the Tree of Knowledge she shall not die, but shall have her eyes opened, to be as god. And she ate, and offered the fruit to Adam, her husband, and their minds were illuminated and they became Self-realized, even as Satanael himself.
>
> This was the gift of Satanael unto Man, that he should possess intelligence, and the desire to know, and Self-consciousness, that he no longer be servile unto Demiurge, nor live as the beasts of the field.[17]

According to Satan, we were created as a bunch of ignorant dummies, no better than the beasts of the field, enslaved to a tyrannical

God, and he is taking it upon himself to "free" us feeble, stupid, humans and offer us a "better alternative" to paradise. He "gave" us this "gift of intelligence, and self-conscious." (Yeah, Adam was really dumb; he only named all of the animals of creation, without schooling! No brainpower there!) The world has never been the same since.

Satan's Authority Over Man: The Fall

Alas we come to the fall of man. Genesis, Chapter 3 is one of my favorite scriptures because you could write volumes on this one little, short chapter. So much is happening, and it has been regurgitated by the church for centuries, it has been retold unjustly, and steeped in false tradition. Most non-Christians are familiar with the tired scene of a naked Eve, handing an apple to a naked Adam, with a weird looking, snake-thing, wrapped around the trunk of the tree, and guess what? I was one of those who believed that too! Because I didn't take the time to study it for myself, I just listened to whatever everyone else had to say on the subject, took it as gospel truth and accepted it. Until I began to study the enemy. Then God required me to actually read all of Genesis 3, word by word.

When Satan was cast down from his place of authority in heaven in disgrace, he was not given authority over our planet, the future creation, nada, zip. This was not his. Instead, as we will learn, Adam and Eve were *tricked* into giving up our kingship and authority over the earth.

The scriptures say in Genesis:

> "Let us make man in our image, in our likeness, and let them rule over the fish of the sea, and the birds of the air, over the livestock, over all the earth, and over all the creatures that

> move along the ground"...God blessed them and said to them "Be fruitful and increase in number; fill the earth and subdue it. Rule over the fish of the sea and the birds of the air, and over every living creature that moves on the ground." Then God said, "I give you every seed bearing plant on the face of the whole earth and every tree that has fruit with seed in it. They will be yours for food. And to all the beasts of the earth and all the birds of the air and all the creatures that move along the ground everything that has the breath of life in it—I give every green plant for food." And it was so. (Genesis, 1:26 and 28–30; NIV)

God gave Adam and Eve rule over all the fishes/birds/critters/creepies and all the earth. We were given instructions to fill the earth and subdue it. He said these things in the most redundant of ways; he said it three times, not just once. So this kinda shoots down the whole "mother earth" theory, doesn't it?

Let's move on: *...and the Lord God commanded the man, "but you must not eat from the tree of Knowledge of Good and Evil, for when you eat of it you will surely die"* (Genesis 2:16–17; NIV). So here we are being set-up for free will, freedom of choice, and obedience. Untested, these are but a theory. Here we see what Satan meant for evil, God will use for good. God knew what was going to happen all along, but his nature is such of pure holiness, he couldn't risk having unclean creations coming back into his courts. God is going to use Satan to test the will of man. He doesn't want another insurrection, and he doesn't want an android; he wants a pure heart, a will that will love, follow, and obey the very Maker. All throughout scripture we are tested, purified through trials and tribulations, separating the dross from the silver. God had faith in man. He took a huge risk that once again his marvelous, beloved creation would betray his heart.

In the heavenly realm, Lucifer originated sin and corrupted God's perfect order. Let me put forth an idea many of us are unfamiliar with. God did not create evil as the devil would have us believe. Genesis 1:31 states all God created was "very good." Before Lucifer rebelled there was no sin. When you look at it from an eternity standpoint of view (timelessness), no evil, nada, zip. After Satan's demise in Revelation, we are told again no evil will remain. So this earth's time period, this "blip" on the radar screen of eternity is just that, a glitch in God's time line. No evil before, no evil after in God's Kingdom. Sometimes I think we lose sight of this: Satan's reign is a *very short one*!

Satan devised a plan, which he had already started to perfect when he deceived the angels into leaving their posts and follow him as their new god. He *sees* God's creation, he *sees* man, with his supernatural "keen sight," which I happen to believe is just his knowledge or intellect into God's fabulous infrastructure and programming of the earth and everything in it. Of all of the beings, he had to have some "*insight*" into how everything is all put together, atom-by-atom, and cell-by-cell. Encarta Dictionary defines *insight* as; "perceptiveness, the ability to see clearly and intuitively into the nature of a complex person, situation, or subject."[18] I believe he saw a loophole. The very hole he chose? Our complex free will, and the use of language as a tool. Words or language in God's kingdom were not first meant for communication. Yes, you read correctly. Words were not meant for communication; they were first meant for creation. God formed the universe with "words." Communication is a secondary tool for our mouths, and the Intelligent Deceiver certainly found a way to corrupt the creative words of our mouths! Remember we are dealing with intelligent deception; he wants to be like God. If God is the Word, why not use God's Word, against his own creation, clever critter. Let's take a fresh and "insightful" look at an old, well-worn scripture:

> Now the serpent was more crafty than any of the wild animals the Lord God had made. He said to the woman, "Did God really say, 'You must not eat from any tree in the garden'?" The woman said to the serpent, "We may eat fruit from the trees in the garden, but God did say, 'You must not eat fruit from the tree that is in the middle of the garden, and you must not touch it, or you will die.'" "You will not surely die," the serpent said to the woman. "For God knows that when you eat of it your eyes will be opened, and you will be like God, knowing good and evil." When the woman saw that the fruit of the tree was good for food and pleasing to the eye, and also desirable for gaining wisdom, she took some and ate it. She also gave some to her husband, **who was with her**, and he ate it. Then the eyes of both of them were opened, and they realized they were naked; so they sewed fig leaves together and made coverings for themselves. Then the man and his wife heard the sound of the Lord God as he was walking in the garden in the cool of the day, and they hid from the Lord God among the trees of the garden. But the Lord God called to the man, "Where are you?" He answered, "I heard you in the garden, and I was afraid because I was naked; so I hid." (Genesis 3:1–10; NIV)

The origins of sin in man: questioning God's word and goodness, introducing contrary thought, playing on the emotions, and using deception for personal gain. Satan saw the opportunity to get back at God and gain a kingdom to rule. Remember, "I will be like God," said Satan.

Let's break it down: *Now the serpent was more crafty than any of the wild animals the Lord God had made.* Have you ever wondered why Satan was a serpent? I mean, why not a spider or a goat? God uses figures of speech continually in his Word; I think this was used as a rhetorical device. Jesus was called the "Lamb of God," and we all know Jesus didn't come in lamb form; he came as a man. He didn't bleat, wasn't wooly, wasn't four-legged, but the word "lamb" was used as a symbol of his sacrifice. Could Satan also be called a serpent as a rhetorical device? Used to describe his nature, a symbol? Cold blooded, venomous, predatorial, creepy, sneaky. Most people and animals are naturally fearful of snakes. We have already learned our enemy can masquerade as any form he chooses. I happen to believe Satan looked like his angel self. Remember, we are in the Garden of Eden, Eve and Adam were used to seeing God physically manifested, they were used to seeing angels of all kinds. I am assuming they conversed as freely with angels as they did with God because there was no separation of the spirit world and the physical world at this point. On the flip side, they were also used to seeing all kinds of animals, and animals were not fearful of man yet. Animals did not fear man until *after* the flood of Noah: *And the fear of you and the dread and terror of you shall be upon every beast of the land, every bird of the air, all that creeps upon the ground, and upon all the fish of the sea: they are delivered into your hand* (Genesis 9:2; NIV). So if Eve saw a snake, she wouldn't have screamed and run in terror, and the snake wouldn't have struck and bit her either. The Word does not tell us animals had the power of human speech. Yes, animals communicate to each other in their own language and behavior, but the only reference to an animal ever having talked was Balaam's donkey. So I am inclined to believe Satan appeared as an angel. You come to your own conclusion.

Nachash (the word translated as *serpent*) is a fascinating Hebrew word. It can function as a noun, verb, and an adjective. The word

Nachash is translated as snake in many Bibles. If it functions as a noun, serpent is its rendering. As a verb it means deceiver, and as an adjective—shining one.

Nachash, the Hebrew word for serpent has a hissing sound. Its root word means to enchant or to prognosticate. The emphasis is on the action being like that of a snake, not necessarily that it is an actual snake.

Dr. Henry M. Morris states in his book, *The Genesis Record,* "Some (scholars) maintain that *Nachash* originally meant upright shining creature. This would give a whole new perspective to the serpent. He is said to be subtler than all the other creatures created by God. Subtle means intelligence applied in a crafty or manipulative manner. This certainly is not talking about the reptile we know as a snake."[19]

The other study we will get into later is what cherubim and seraphim actually looked liked. I have some commentaries in this section that will make more sense as we learn about snakes and other creatures. God also compares the serpent to the other animals, saying he is more "crafty." We will talk about this "creature" word when we discuss cherubs, and it will shed some surprising insight into this passage.

The Bible says he was *more crafty* than any of God's other creations. Vine's Dictionary, states, "Crafty is all working, doing everything that is unscrupulous, cunning, baited, hence fraud, guile, deceit."[20] He is the ultimate con artist; he is really "working it" here! Now he talks to Eve. He purposefully picks the woman. What? Is she more naïve than Adam? No, Satan planned this out very carefully—he has his reasons. Eve was the only creation that did not originate from dirt. The Bible tells us this several times in the preceding chapter. Eve was created from Adam's rib, *she was bone of my bone, flesh of my flesh…and they will become one flesh* (Genesis 2:23;

NIV). Here we are introduced to the word *flesh.* If you are a born-again Christian you hate that word! It signifies all the bad stuff, all the desires, evil thoughts, etc. But here it does not mean that; it is talking about the fact that male and female are as one person, literally an extension of one another. I also want to point out that without the female reproduction is impossible. Was Satan counting on God's justice to kick in? Maybe remove the source of multiplication from the start?

It may also have the overtones of the first gross, sexual assault on women, and as we will see later, may have an even more sinister meaning. Or, one other possible explanation for choosing Eve is that Satan was very insulted and jealous that God would create a beautiful *female* helpmate for Adam (you will learn later angels do not have a female counterpart). We know from a biblical standpoint Satan hates women and had it out for us from the moment he spoke to Eve. Satan would have no other competition; maybe God would banish her too. He obviously was not allowed to kill Adam and Eve, and take control of the world that way. He had to come up with a reliable way of deception, an evil inclination or system that would secure his future world kingdom...his stepping stone to "be like God." Our enemy is blinded by a one-way ambition: he can think of nothing but himself; he is the truest of narcissists.

Before we continue, let me paint one more picture: You are the only two people on the planet, and you are dwelling with the Most High in the eastern part of Eden, God's own garden. You are newlyweds, and the only job descriptions you have been given is: Ruler Over all of Creation, Chief Gardener, and be fruitful and multiply. If that were you, would you be wandering off to some other part of the garden tending roses and naming critters, and leave your beautiful, new bride behind—to do what? Collect a nice green salad for supper? I don't think so! You would be together, sharing and learning about your new home, enjoying each other's company, getting psyched about the whole procreation thing! Remember Adam was bummed-out, just a few verses prior, because he didn't have a helpmate. Do you think he would leave her alone so soon? This is why I find it so weird that Satan talks to Eve directly and ignores Adam. I hope you caught the emphasis I put on verse 6, *who was with her,* referring to Adam.

The word *Eden* literally means "unending surplus/supply, voluptuous life."[21] Eden was a model of how God had originally intended life for humans to be. It is interesting to note most scholars believe the Garden of Eden is now our modern day Iraq (Tigris and Euphrates Rivers, see Genesis 2:10–14). How do you go from a voluptuous, green garden to a war-torn desert? Sin is ugly, destructive, it kills more than human souls; it destroys everything!

So here is what Satan says to the woman: *Did God really say, "You must not eat from any tree in the garden"?* What an odd way to start a conversation. You have to assume Adam and Eve were in close proximity to the Tree of Knowledge of Good and Evil, and also the Tree of Life. Maybe they were discussing what God meant by "no eat"; after all, he had given them everything else. The other thing you need to ask yourself is, if they wanted to know about good and evil, why not just ask God? They talk to him every day. But that didn't happen. I don't know, maybe Adam and Eve were just like us; what an obvious choice. Why would you go to the source of "all knowledge" to get knowledge? Silly human, you ask a snake! So Satan takes his cue, and asks a question. He *paraphrases* God's own words! So he knew what God had said to Adam. *The woman said to the serpent, "We may eat fruit from the trees in the garden, but God did say, 'You must not eat fruit from the tree that is in the middle of the garden, and you must not touch it, or you will die.'"* Now Eve corrects Satan (kudos Eve!). She tells him what God really said, she knows her Word. But Satan continues with his deception, he knows he has to close this sale, he is undeterred. *"You will not surely die," the serpent said to the woman. "For God knows that when you eat of it your eyes will be opened, and* ***you will be like God****, knowing good and evil."* Notice he never tempted them with the Tree of Life! Did you know envy is the root of many of the worst sins? To "be like" something is to be dissatisfied with what you were created to be. Eve was joint-heir with Adam over an entire planet! Satan used his own envy as a platform for equivocating ones-self with the Most High. Satan uses several tactical weapons here. His first arrow failed to hit its mark; it was deflected by Eve's knowledge of the Word of God. But his second arrow hit its mark. Contradict what God said blatantly: *You will surely not die!* Then pull out the big guns, and rapid fire right into the emotion center. "God is hiding something from you, *secret knowledge* which makes God *God*, and you *you*. Don't you want that? It is right here, contained in this fruit, all you have to do is eat it." (The word *occult* means secret knowledge, hide, to conceal, pretty interesting, huh?) Man has consistently throughout the ages chosen the tree of *knowledge* of good and evil over the Tree of Life.

Before we continue, how many of you believe for a fact Adam was not present when Eve was tempted? If you answered yes, you are in good company. I asked thirty people, and out of the thirty, only one got it right. They all thought Eve acted alone. Well, let me cook your noodle and demolish a wrongly held tradition, because as you will learn Satan does some of his most genius deceptions with our beloved traditions.

When the woman saw that the fruit of the tree was good for food and pleasing to the eye, and also desirable for gaining wisdom, she took some and ate it. She also gave some to her husband, who was with her, and he ate it. Eve then does what we all do; she thought about it (or reasoned)! She mulled it over it in her mind. She actually thought about all the features and benefits: good food, looks pretty, and heck, I get wisdom to boot, which is what God really wants for me, right? Yup! Gimme some! This next part gets me every time: Adam is with her, and he eats it. He doesn't say a word! This slick-talking angel is telling his wife they should eat it, and he knows it's wrong. In fact, God told him specifically, commanded him. Eve wasn't even created yet, she heard this whole commandment secondhand from Adam. *And the Lord God* ***commanded the man*** (Genesis 2:16; NIV). He swallowed the whole lie without even lifting a finger, without so much as an objection. I believe this is why God comes down hard on Adam later in the chapter. Or, was Adam so in love with Eve, he was that willing to share in her demise? Maybe he knew he would have to take the brunt of her sin, as a type and shadow of Christ? So there you have it. Adam and Eve just gave Satan their kingdom, planet earth, and all in it, their authority over it. All of mankind was brought down by a *little, white lie.* The Bible doesn't record what Satan did next, but I can just imagine he did quite the self-satisfied, happy dance.

Then the eyes of both of them were opened, and they realized they were naked; so they sewed fig leaves together and made coverings for themselves. Then the man and his wife heard the sound of the Lord God as he was walking in the garden in the cool of the day, and they hid from the Lord God among the trees of the garden. But the Lord God called to the man, "Where are you?" He answered, "I heard you in the garden, and I was afraid because I was naked; so I hid" (Genesis 3:7–10; NIV). Did you ever wonder why their eyes were closed to their nakedness before, and why were they so afraid? And immediately after the both of them had sinned against God's commandment, they realized they were naked? The word *naked* here is used in the sense of "shameful exposure."[22] They had been "naked" all this time, and there was absolutely no shame implied prior to this event, why now? And why would God not accept the covering of fig leaves as an acceptable garment, but instead kill newly created, innocent animals and use their skins to cover them? Let me just put an idea out on the floor for your critical thinking. Since Adam and Eve were on Holy Ground, in God's Garden, may they have had a supernatural covering? Such as robes of righteousness? Or even the Armor of God? Or, at the actual moment of sin, was our very universe fractured? We get the sense both the spiritual and the physical were all cohesive and seamless prior to sin. Sin separated, or actually fractured, hyperdimensional space—the s*piritual* and the *physical* dimensions? Once the sin had been swallowed, these supernatural coverings were compromised? And why now, so fearful of God, why hide in the garden, when before they walked with God? The Word doesn't say it here, but in other parts of the Bible it talks about our "robes and our armor," and if God is the same yesterday, today, and tomorrow, maybe there is some weight to this position. Otherwise what is the big deal? If it were purely nakedness, why would it be so bad now, when they were running around "naked" before? ...*and white clothes to wear, so you can cover your shameful nakedness; and salve to put on your eyes, so you can see* (Revelation 3:18; NIV).

Let's finish up with the rest of Genesis, Chapter 3, and see where curses come from, and how the model of perfection got messed up. *And he said, "Who told you that you were naked? Have you eaten from the tree that I commanded you not to eat from?" The man said, "The woman you put here with me—she gave me some fruit from the tree, and I ate it." Then the Lord God said to the woman, "What is this you have done?" The woman said, "The serpent deceived me, and I ate"* (Genesis 3:13; NIV).

"Who told you that you were naked?" This verse supports the idea that other celestial beings (God and angels) had access to the garden. And then Adam and Eve play the blame game: *"The woman you put*

here with me... " I know it's not funny, but Adam had just called her his "bone of his bone, flesh of his flesh" a couple of verses back, and now he is like, "Yeah, this woman you put here with me." He *separates* himself from her, even though he was right there the whole time.

Eve is no better. She knew the rules, she recited them back to Satan, and then defies God, and justifies her actions with: "It's good for food, and I'll be smart, if I eat it." *So God said to the serpent, "Because you have done this* [The Bible doesn't tell us Satan hid, just Adam and Eve, I think he was out in the open, just gloating, before God], *Cursed are you above all livestock, and all the wild animals! You will crawl on your belly and you will eat dust all the days of your life. And I will put enmity between you and the woman, and between your offspring and hers; he will crush your head, and you will strike his heel* (Genesis 3:14; NIV). So again, Satan is cast down even further along the food chain. Even though he has just gained the world, and authority over it, God puts him lower than the cows and cheetahs. He makes him just like a snake—just like all of the low-down, dirty tricks he has just pulled, his true nature, groveling for a piece of humanity's heel, and because he so viciously swindled the woman, he has the added curse of her seed's heel to his head.

I happen to believe this verse is both symbolic and literal in meaning. *"Cursed are you above all livestock, and all the wild animals! You will crawl on your belly and you will eat dust all the days of your life. And I will put enmity between you and the woman, and between your offspring and hers; he will crush your head, and you will strike his heel."* I have pondered this and pondered this. If Lucifer was the anointed-cherub-that-covers, a cherub has four wings, as you will learn later. *Anointed* means he was given authority. *Covering* means guarding God's holiness; cherubs' wings also covered and protected them from God's all-consuming fire and glory. I wonder if God did not strip Satan of his wings here: *"You will crawl on your belly and you will eat dust all the days of your life." Crawl on your belly* sounds like no more covering wings to protect you; he is grounded in a sense. I think this would be a very shameful punishment for a self-absorbed being. I think eating dust is also an idiom for a double curse. Dust is an idiom for man; Satan will consume man, but since he absolutely hates our very image, I think we leave a very bitter taste in his mouth. In other words, I think he is compelled to consume us, but I also think we choke him, and he hates the taste. God has a sense of irony, but then again, this is only my silly interpretation, you draw your own conclusions.

To the woman he said, "I will greatly increase your pains in childbearing; with pain you will give birth to children. Your desire will be for your husband, and he will rule over you" (Genesis 3:16; NIV). In God's great original plan, women would have had a fairly easy time of labor, and it probably wouldn't have been called "labor." The other fact I want to point out is God originally created Eve to be equal with Adam. She messed that up, and now Adam has rule over her.

To Adam he said, "Because you listened to your wife and ate from the tree about which I commanded you, 'You must not eat of it,' Cursed is the ground because of you; through painful toil you will eat of it all the days of your life. It will produce thorns and thistles for you, and you will eat the plants of the field, By the sweat of your brow you will eat your food until you return to the ground, since from it you were taken; for dust you are and to dust you will return" (Genesis 3:18; NIV).

Here we have the concepts of poverty and death entering into our lives. God stays true to his word; he had warned them if they ate of the fruit they would die. Again, it wasn't just a spiritual death; Adam now realizes he has lost everything. All creation now suffers from his sin (see Romans 8). He hasn't had to work very hard, he doesn't even know what a weed is, and he certainly isn't going to be getting his meals from a tree. It is now going to come from hard, physical labor, from a field. He knows he has done wrong, and I am sure, because of the nature of this whole experience, the weight of his *new knowledge of good and evil* is really sinking in. The Bible doesn't record for us all of the changes in creation, but it certainly alludes to it with "shameful nakedness"—I believe our earth's dimensions were fractured at the point of sin, this is why they hid from God and were fearful. The world changed immediately! We will discuss this further in the Science section.

Adam named his wife Eve, because she would become the mother of all the living. The Lord God made garments of skin for Adam and his wife and clothed them. And the Lord God said, "The man has now become like one of us, knowing good and evil. He must not be allowed to reach out his hand and take also from the tree of life and eat, and live forever." So the Lord God banished him from the Garden of Eden to work the ground from which he had been taken. After he drove the man out, he placed on the east side of the Garden of Eden cherubim and a flaming sword flashing back and forth to guard the way to the tree of life (Genesis 3:20–24; NIV). It's weird to think Eve wasn't even named yet, not until after all this went down. God made garments of skin for a covering for both of them. We are seeing the groundwork for the blood of the lamb already being laid. God has a plan for redemption already in the works. Adam and Eve hadn't even thought about killing animals, and now God was showing them innocent blood had to be shed to cover their shameful nakedness. God never intended for us to live separate from his creation. Animals were meant for his and our enjoyment; animals were never meant to suffer in God's original plan. We have Satan to blame for that.

Then the Bible tells us *that God drove the man out.* There is that word again. I don't think they left very willingly, and obviously they were already thinking about eating from the Tree of Life, which they had had permission to do previously. Now they possessed supernatural knowledge, "secret knowledge" that the Tree of Life was the *only way to avoid physical death.* God had to protect it with powerful cherubim. Did you ever ask yourself why God would have to protect it with a powerful cherub? Any old angel would have sufficed to keep Adam and Eve at bay. Or maybe we are missing something here… Maybe he was protecting it from Satan's grubby hands! A powerful cherub would be on par with Satan who was also a cherub!

God could not go back against his word, even though he had provided a way out of spiritual death. I can't help but think how incredibly sad, depressed, and oppressed Adam and Eve were after this. They had hundreds of years to contemplate their mistake. However, the Bible is very clear that God did not forsake them; he continued to converse, and be with Adam and his family, even though he could not allow them to partake in his glorious abundance, his model of perfection for humanity. Man would have to wait thousands of years before God's promise and plan of redemption would come to fruition, and everyone was again free to eat from the Tree of Life.

Everything that follows this true account is about regaining and restoring what was lost to Intelligent Deception. I submit every one of us has been presented with the same choice between two trees, one of life and one of good and evil, and each of us have made the exact same decision Adam and Eve made. We chose the "hidden secret" of good and evil over the Tree of Life. Thank the Lord we now have access to the Tree of Life, where Adam didn't. He has taken away the flaming cherubim, and we are free to eat.

Our enemy's tactics have not changed all of these thousands of years. He is a consistent, dirty predator. How do you recognize him?

1. He always questions God's Word.
2. He thoroughly knows the Word of God. He twists, adds, or subtracts from God's Word. Usually 99 percent of it is correct, but 1 percent is deceit! He is the originator of the "little white lie."
3. He uses words, or language, to get our attention. In other words, *he speaks to us*!
4. He appeals to the mind, emotions, and then the flesh (body).
5. He uses spiritual tactics against the physical body.

Always in that order, you just haven't fully realized it yet. Keep this list handy; you can recognize even the most camouflaged of demons with this list. And guess what? We got it from God's own Word. The more you study and read the holy scriptures, the more you will find huge nuggets of truth buried beneath layers of presumption, tradition, and deception. This is our enemy's greatest tactic.

Chapter Three

WHAT ARE ANGELS?

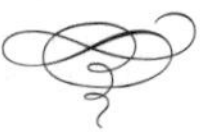

To fully understand the holy scriptures and our enemy, we need to understand who angels are, what they are, the different classes, hierarchies, and functions. The reason this is so important is because Satan took a third of the angels with him when he fell. These angels are now devoted to his allegiance, and compelled to work for and under him. Without understanding the work of angels and fallen angels, it will be impossible for you to understand what you're up against in a spiritual battle, and what the paranormal is all about.

First off, let's discuss what angels are *not.* Nowhere in scripture does it describe angels as being, cute, chubby, little babies with wings, bows and arrows, flitting about from cloud to cloud. We need to get our information firmly from the scriptures, not artistic interpretation. This picture of angels is not only false, but it doesn't lend much credence to their imposing power, force, or cosmic intelligence. The other false idea we need to address is that people, once they have died, have the opportunity to become angels. This is not only wrong, but very dangerous ground for the believer. The Bible does not state anywhere in scripture that man becomes angelic. First of all, man and angel are two different specific creations, and God cannot contradict himself: like produces like. If God made man into an angel he would be breaking his own natural law and divine order, of which he firmly states, his character is unchanging.

The next false idea is that female angels exist. Nowhere in scripture does it refer to angels having the female gender. They are all male. So get rid of the female, angelic picture in your mind of a flowing Romanesque gown, long blond hair, and beauty beyond understanding. There is simply no biblical evidence to support it. Also, scripture refers to angels as "son's of God," a direct creation of God. It does not say anywhere "daughters of God," further proving the lack of a female angelic counterpart.

Many people believe the Bible tells us angels are "sexless," and without gender because of this verse from Matthew: *At the resurrection people will neither marry nor be given in marriage: They will be like the angels in heaven* (Matthew 22:30; NIV). This verse has created a lot of confusion about angels. Many believe angels are spirits, which the Bible clearly states, but they also mistakenly believe angels have a completeness of both gender qualities or are androgynous because of their relationship to God. As we stated earlier, the scriptures do not agree with this train of thought. When we die, we do not become genderless, we simply will not need to mate. So Matthew is saying angels do not marry. Marry in this context is the word for consummate. In other words, there is no reason for them to mate *in heaven.* God made a whole passel of angels. As spirit beings they do not die…What would be the point of procreation for spirits if God had already created the perfect number of them to carry out his will? Angels are spirit beings, not flesh beings, so they were expected to act within those boundaries. Now let me point out a very important point that will make sense farther down the road. Scriptures paint angels in the masculine gender. Our God is a complete God; he doesn't leave things undone. Male angels are fully male, if you get my meaning. Jesus was fully male; he was not genderless, even though he was God incarnate. In other words, they have all the right plumbing, and are thus equipped with the knowledge of its use. After all, they observe us daily. This concept is not meant to gross you out, but it will become very apparent when we begin to study the fallen angels, and their behaviors. The Bible has some fascinating scriptures referring to this. Take Genesis 6 for example. The Bible is very clear angels are to keep to their own accord and not go after strange flesh (sexual sin; see Jude).

Angels are also spirit beings, which means they are eternal, immortal, they do not experience death. If they do not die, and if God created them innumerable, why would they need to procreate and create more angels? Procreation is an earthly, mortal assignment; this allows a species to avoid extinction, something the angels clearly cannot do.

Angels also have the ability to present themselves in human form, when, in a sense, they "disrobe" (see Jude) from their spiritual bodies. We will learn more about this later.

The other aspect to marriage not being for angels is the fact angels are closely tied to the church, which is symbolized all throughout scripture as "The Bride of Christ." Angels may be required to keep themselves pure for the ultimate wedding of Christ, the bridegroom to his church, the Bride.

Angels are created beings. *Praise him, all his angels, praise him all his heavenly host...let them praise the name of the Lord, for he commanded and they were created* (Psalms 148:2, 5; NIV). And also in Colossians: *For by him all things were created: things in heaven and on earth, visible and invisible, whether thrones or powers or rulers or authorities; all things were created by him and for him* (Colossians 1:16;

NIV). These divine creatures were made by God, and by God alone. They are beneath God; they are not to be worshipped. Most of the time when you see the words *thrones, powers, rulers,* and *authorities* in the Bible, they are talking about angels, both fallen and good.

Angels display very physical characteristics, such as consuming food. Why eat? If you are merely spirit, what do you need food for? But the Bible is repose with heavenly feasts and food. Our spiritual bodies will need food, just as the angels eat. In fact, the Bible even tells us what kind of food the angels eat. It looked like flakes, tasted like honey, and was called the grain of heaven—manna. *Men ate the bread of angels* (Psalms 78:25; NIV). Elijah ate this food, and it sustained him forty days and forty nights (see 1 Kings 19:5–8). Those are some serious carbs! If you read this scripture, it was an angel who told Elijah to eat. This angel not only physically touched him and talked to him, but we can make the assumption he cooked this meal for him too.

So what do angels really look like? We have already established they are male, can eat, and function as human and angel. Scripture records many times that when angels appear in true angelic form they evoke strong emotions of fear, trembling, awe, terror, and splendor. They wear white, or appear dazzling white…*and I saw two angels in white* (John 20:12; NIV). This is what Mary Magdalene saw when she was at the tomb of Jesus. The apostles also saw men wearing white after Jesus had appeared to them… *When suddenly two men dressed in white stood beside them* (Acts 1:10; NIV). The phrase *when suddenly* seems to accompany many references to angels. They just *suddenly* appear, and disappear, transcending all our known laws of physics; they are hyperdimensional beings.

Zechariah and the shepherds all had fearful encounters. In Luke 1:12, Zechariah sees an angel and is startled and gripped with fear. In the shepherds' encounter: *An angel of the Lord appeared to them, and the glory of the Lord shown around and around, and they were terrified* (Luke 2:9; NIV). Again in Chronicles: *David looked up and saw the angel of the Lord standing between heaven and earth, with a drawn sword in his hand extended over Jerusalem. Then David and the elders, clothed in sackcloth, fell face down* (1 Chronicles 22:16; NIV).

The virgin Mary also was confronted by an angel and was fearful. *And when she saw him, she was troubled at his saying, and cast in her mind what manner of salutation this should be, and the angel (Gabriel) said unto her, fear not Mary: for thou has found favor with God* (Luke 1:29–30; KJV).

Angels have their own language: *If I speak in the tongues of (languages) men and of angels…* (1 Corinthians 13:1; AMP*)*. But it is obvious they are fluent in all languages as they get their message across to the right party.

Angels hearken to the Word of God. *Praise the Lord, you his angels, you mighty ones who do his bidding, who obey his word* (Psalm 103:20; NIV). Angels listen to and obey the Word of God when it is spoken. This will be an important concept when we get to learning and understanding our authority over demons and evil spirits.

In his book *Angels on Assignment*, Idaho pastor Roland Buck relates his personal eyewitness accounts of two angels that manifested themselves to him over a period of time with a series of prophetic messages for him and his church. He relates:

> Everyone seems to be interested in knowing something about the physical appearance of angels. No two of them look alike! They are different sizes, have different hair styles, and completely different appearances. Chrioni has a hairdo much like many men have today, and he looks about 25 years old. I do not know what he would weigh in earthly pounds, but my guess would be close to 400 pounds. He is

> huge, seven or more feet in height...Gabriel, often appears in a shimmering white tunic with a radiant gold belt about 5 wide, white trousers and highly polished bronze colored shoes. His hair is the color of gold![23]

In countless legitimate eyewitness accounts of angels, the description is the same: they are very tall, usually towering over seven to eight feet, to upwards of twelve to fifteen feet in height, appear and disappear out of nowhere, and are always male.

Angels can change their appearance. The Bible tells us to be on the lookout as we may entertain angels unawares. *Do not forget to entertain strangers, for by so doing some people have entertained angels without knowing it* (Hebrews 13:2; NIV). So this is consistent throughout scripture: angels have this unique and very powerful ability to change form, either to males or females.

Angels for the most part are invisible. It takes a special act of God to open the witness' eyes to see angels. For some reason the human eye isn't fully opened to the spirit realm. Take the story of Balaam's donkey. What is interesting is the donkey saw the angel and steered clear, while Balaam beat her all three times, until *God opened her mouth* and allowed her to speak (Numbers 22:21–30). Then, the *Lord opened Balaam's eyes and he saw the angel of the Lord standing in the road with his sword drawn, so he bowed low and fell face down* (Number 22:31; NIV).

Again we see this same thing with Elisha and his servant...*and Elisha prayed, "O LORD, open his eyes so he may see!" The LORD opened the servant's eyes, and he looked and saw the hill full of horses and chariots of fire all around Elisha* (2 Kings 6:17; NIV).

Angels are extremely fast: ...*the creatures sped back and forth like flashes of lightening* (Ezekiel 1:14; NIV). Lightening travels at a speed of about 186,282.397 miles per second, or roughly one foot per nanosecond. This means an angel could have the ability to travel the circumference of the earth seven and half times in one second!

Angels are made up of light—*phos*, breath or wind of God—*neshamah* or *ruah*, and holy fire—*esh*.[24] Since angels are made from the breath of God, they cannot be destroyed.

Angels are innumerable: *...you have come to thousands upon thousands of angels in joyful assembly* (Hebrews 12:22; NIV). And John writes in Revelation: *Then I looked and heard the voice of many angels, numbering thousands upon thousands, and ten thousand times ten thousand* (Revelation 5:11; NIV). I'm no math wiz, but that's over 100 million angels. It has been estimated if half the world were saved, born-again Christians, we would each have twenty thousand angels at our service.[25] Wow, think about that. Not one guardian angel, but tens of thousands—helping us, guiding us, fighting for us!

Angels protect and help to deliver us. *He shall give his angels charge over you, to keep you in all your ways. In their hands they shall bear you up* (Psalm 91:11–12; NIV). *The angel of the Lord encamps all around those who fear him and delivers them* (Psalm 34:7; NIV). In other words, there is probably some big, buff, mighty-looking angels camping out around you right now (roasting marshmallows over holy coals—just kidding!); you just don't have the spiritual sight to see them.

Angels are immortal: *And they can no longer die, for they are like the angels* (Luke 20:36; NIV).

Angels are holy: *"When the son of man comes in his glory, and all the angels with him, he will sit on his throne in heavenly glory"* (Matthew 25:31; NIV).

The angels who did not rebel against God with Satan are elect (see 1 Timothy 5:21).

Angels possess emotions: *"I tell you, there is rejoicing in the presence of the angels of God over one sinner who repents"* (Luke 15:10; NIV).

Angels are concerned with human things: *It was revealed to them (angels) that they were not serving themselves but you, when they spoke of the things that have now been told you by those who have preached the gospel to you by the Holy Spirit sent from heaven. Even angels long to look into these things* (1 Peter 1:12; NIV). This passage also confirms angels are only privy to the information God wants them to know. They do not know everything, even though they have superhuman might and intelligence.

Humans were made a little lower than the angels, but we certainly seem to have a different set of privileges than they. We are allowed to marry and reproduce. As Peter was saying, we receive Holy Spirit revelation; the angels may not have access to this. Even though we were made a little lower than the angels, the Bible tells us when we go to heaven we will rule and judge angels. *Know ye not that we shall judge angels?* (1 Corinthians 6:3; KJV) *…yet even angels, although they are stronger and more powerful, do not bring slanderous accusations against such being sin in the presence of the Lord* (2 Peter 2:11; KJV).

Angels are not provided a way of redemption as humans are. Otherwise Satan and his minions would have full access to the redeeming blood of Jesus, which they do not. Speaking of Jesus and his sacrifice Hebrews says*: For surely it is not angels he helps, but Abraham's descendants* (Hebrews 2:11; NIV). This is a very important concept. For this very reason, hell was created for these rebellious angels.

Angels have the ability to heal: *For an angel went down at a certain season into the pool, and troubled the water: whosoever then first after the troubling of the water stepped in was made whole of whatsoever disease he had* (John 5:4; KJV). The text doesn't clarify if the angel was sent by God, or God endowed only this particular angel with healing ability. Later when we study demonic healings, we will see demons also have the ability to heal, so we may be able to surmise that all, or many, angels have the gift of healing, but for it to be truly of God, the healing power must come from God.

Angels are referred to as the "starry host," and live and work in the farthest galaxies imaginable: *And suddenly there was with the angel a multitude of the heavenly host praising God, and saying, Glory to God in the Highest…* (Luke 2:13; NIV). *And then He will send out the angels and will gather together His Elect (those He has picked out for Himself) from the four winds, from the farthest bounds of the earth to the farthest bounds of heaven* (Mark 13:27; AMP). The word *heaven* is often used interchangeably with our meaning of the universe in general.

They execute God's judgment, as we see all throughout the Bible. *Then David lifted his eyes and saw the angel of the Lord standing between earth and heaven, having in his hand a drawn sword stretched out over Jerusalem* (1 Chronicles 21:16; NIV). We see their judgment tasks being meted out in nearly the entire book of Revelation. Also throughout the Old Testament: the angel of death, angel of plagues on Israel, slaughtering the enemies of Israel, bringing down the walls of Jericho, helping Lot and his daughters escape Sodom and Gomorrah by striking the mob blind, bringing judgment on Baalam and sparing his donkey.

Angels escort the just to heaven: *"The time came when the beggar died and the angels carried him to Abraham's side…"* (Luke 16:22; NIV).

Angels record our deeds, tithes, and offerings, and capture and record our tears: *A scroll of remembrance was written in his presence concerning those who feared the Lord and honored his name* (Malachi 4:16; NIV). *Thou tellest my wanderings: put thou my tears into thy bottle: are they not in thy book?* (Psalm 56:8; KJV). This verse tells us God knows where we go and the deeds and trials we are facing. He actually has his angels record our deeds and capture our tears and put them in a bottle. Stop and think about that one for a moment, the times you sobbed and were in utter despair, you actually had an angel catching your tears and putting them into a bottle, and recording them in a book in heaven. Many may think this is figurative, but why say it if it wasn't true? Aren't we supposed to believe the teachings of God with "childlike faith"?

Our tithes and offerings are recorded as well. *"Will a man rob God? Yet you rob me. But you ask, 'How do we rob you?' In tithes and offerings. You are under a curse—the whole nation of you—because you are robbing me. Bring the whole tithe into the storehouse, that there may be food in my house. Test me in this," says the Lord Almighty, "and see if I will not throw open the floodgates of heaven and pour out so much blessing that you will not have room enough for it"* (Malachi 3:8–10; NIV). These tithes and offerings are being brought into a storehouse. Where? In heaven! So angels must be behind the scenes storing our treasures in heaven.

They are obedient and mighty: *Praise the Lord, you his angels, you mighty ones who do his bidding, who obey his word. Praise the Lord, all his heavenly hosts, you his servants who do his will* (Psalm 103:20–21; NIV). *Might* is defined as a noun in Vine's Dictionary: "(*geburah*) Might, the primary meaning is power or physical strength, also (*ischus*) might, strength, power."[26] So sheer might is used as an endowment of angels.

Angels have a curious endowment of awesome, fearsome power and strength as in this example: *An angel of the Lord slew 185,000 men, the whole army in one night!* (Isaiah 37:36; NIV).

The Bible is abundant with stories of God's powerful and mightily endowed servants doing incredible feats of strength for our amazing God. Remember though, this "mighty power" comes *from* God and was a part of their creation!

Angels are assigned to certain powers of weather. A specific angelic spirit controls hail, snow, rain, frost, mist, winds, storms, etc. The book of Enoch gives us exhaustive lists of what particular angel controls what weather form. *The spirit of the frost has its angel; in the spirit of hail there is a good angel; the spirit of snow ceases in its strength, and a solitary spirit is in it, which ascends from it like vapor, and is called refrigeration. The spirit also of mist dwells with them in their receptacle* (Enoch 59:20–21). (See also Job 38:19–30 and all of Revelation.)

Some angels seem to have dominion and direction over animals, birds, and wildlife: *And I saw an angel standing in the sun, who cried in a loud voice to all the birds flying in midair, "Come, gather together for the great supper of God, so that you may eat the flesh of kings, generals, and mighty men, of horses and their riders, and the flesh of all people, free and slave, small and great"* (Revelation 19:17; NIV).

Angels are highly organized into ranks and orders...*for the Lord himself will come down from heaven, with a loud command, with the voice of the Archangel and with the trumpet call of God, and the dead in Christ will rise first* (1 Thessalonians 4:16; NIV). "Archangel or (*Archangelos*) is a being of exalted rank namely Michael."[27]

There are only three archangels mentioned in the Bible by name: Michael, Gabriel, and Lucifer. Of the first two, they both hold different ranks and duties in God's army. Lucifer, of course, rebelled. When Jesus delivered me from the witch's hex and the demonic powers, I heard a distinct voice telling me, "Hang on Gabriel is coming." I cry as I write this, because I still don't think my mind can grasp the magnitude of God's love and kindness for us—he sent one of his chief archangels to fight off the demons and keep me free. This would be like sending a five-star general to your aid in a street fight! Who am I to warrant such favor?

We know angels have rank, title, and duties, and they follow their commanding officers. Michael is God's chief warring archangel. *Michael* means "Who is like God?" His very name suggests protection for God's holy name. We know from scripture he is a chief prince who stands against the forces of evil, disputes with Satan, and fights the dragon. He rid the heavens and swept them clean of Satan and evil princes of darkness (realms of demons). *And there was a war in heaven. Michael and his angels fought against the dragon, and the dragon and his angels fought back. But he was not strong enough, and they lost their place in heaven* (Revelation 12:7–8; NIV). Michael is the stronger angel! He commands an army of heavenly angels, which beats the pants off of Satan and his army! Not to mention Satan is outnumbered, two-thirds versus one-third!

Another display of Michael's and Gabriel's incredible strength and power can be found in Daniel, Chapter 10. Daniel had fasted and prayed for twenty-one days. We also see in this passage those angels and evil, fallen angels are territorial:

> On the twenty-fourth day of the first month, as I was standing on the bank of the great river, the Tigris, I looked up and there before me was a man dressed in linen, with a belt of the finest gold around his waist. His body was like chrysolite, his face like lightening, his eyes like flaming torches, his arms and legs like the gleam of burnished bronze, and his voice like the sound of the a multitude. I, Daniel, was the only one who saw the vision; the men with me did not see it, but such terror overwhelmed them that they fled and hid themselves. So I was left alone, gazing at this great vision; I had no strength left, my face turned deathly pale and I was helpless...Then he continued, "Do not be afraid, Daniel. Since the first day that you set your mind to gain understanding and to humble yourself before your God, your

> words were heard, and I have come in response to them. But the prince of the Persian Kingdom resisted me twenty-one days. Then Michael, one of the chief princes, came to help me, because I was detained there with the king of Persia..." So he said, "Do you know why I have come to you? Soon I will return to fight against the prince of Persia, and when I go, the prince of Greece will come; but first I will tell you what is written in the Book of Truth. (No one supports me against them except Michael, your prince. And in the first year of Darius the Mede, I took my stand to support and protect him.)" (Daniel 10:4–8, 12–14, 20, 11:1 NIV)

Daniel had an exquisite encounter of the angel Gabriel who had come to help him "gain understanding" (much different from secret knowledge!), which Daniel had asked for. Gabriel came against the prince of the Persian kingdom (a powerful, dark, evil angel) which took twenty-one days of fighting, and fasting and praying on Daniel's end, and he still could not defeat this evil spiritual prince of Persia until Michael the archangel showed up. This is a testament to the absolute military power and might the warrior angel Michael has been endowed with. With two powerful super-angels, the evil angel, prince of Persia had met his match. On the flip side, it also showed how powerful this evil angel was. These beings don't mess around, the power they had with God was very real, and the power they have serving Satan is also real, but God always prevails.

The name *Gabriel* means "Man of God." Luke tells us the angel told Zechariah, John the Baptist's father, *"I am Gabriel, I stand in the presence of God, and I have been sent to speak to you and to tell you this good news"* (Luke, 1:19). Gabriel is a messenger angel, with warring capabilities; he heralded the births of John the Baptist and Jesus the Christ, as well as many other prophetic events in the Bible.

Another name given to the archangels is "the Watchers," found in the book of Enoch, which is a fascinating piece of early Christian literature. Jesus, Paul, and the whole early Christian church, as well as the pre-Christ Jews were very familiar with the book of Enoch. Jude quotes scripture from the Book of Enoch. Although not canon, it is a very important book, which should not be overlooked in understanding the holy scriptures, just as the works of the Jewish historian Josephus are an important glimpse in the history and times of the Jews and early Christians. The term "Watchers" has become synonymous with the alien, UFO phenomenon. You will see in coming chapters the web of deceit Satan has calculated throughout history. Enoch 20:1–7, *These are the names of the angels who watch. Uriel, one of the holy angels, he it is who is over clamor and terror (2 Ezra 6:36, Rev. 1:4). Raphael, who is over the spirits of men. Raguel, who inflicts punishment on the world and the luminaries. Michael, who presiding over human virtue, commands the nations (Dan12:1). Sarakiel who presides over the spirits of the children of men that transgress. Gabriel, who is over Ikasat, over paradise, and over the cherubim.*[28] The archangels give us a small glimpse of Lucifer's former duties, power, and glory.

Angels have many more ranks and duties than just archangels. In fact God tells us some of their different ranks, and he tells us they were all created by him and for him: thrones, powers, rulers, authorities, dominions, and principalities. *For our struggle is not against flesh and blood, but against the rulers, against the authorities, against the powers of this dark world and against the spiritual forces of evil in the heavenly realms* (Ephesians 6:12; NIV). *For by him all things were created: things in heaven and on earth, visible and invisible, whether thrones or powers or rulers or authorities; all things were created by him and for him* (Colossians 1:16; NIV). A total of six rankings, and according to some scriptures it seems humans have the most troubles with the ranks of *principalities* and *powers.* We are told they are destroyed and come under Christ's subjugation in Colossians 2:16 and Titus 3:1. When you begin to study angelology, you can find elaborate lists of different ranks of angels throughout history.

There are vast angel armies. *The armies of heaven were following him, riding on white horses and dressed in fine linen, white and clean* (Revelation 19:14; NIV).

Why go into all this about ranks and orders and such? Because we need to erase all of the devil's work when it comes to misinformation about angels. When you begin to understand their powers, classes, might, intelligence, numbers, and their appointments, tasks, and missions, you get a different view about them. Suddenly, they are not cute, cuddly, fat babies with wings, or beautiful, feminine, fragile women with angelic voices and flowing Romanesque robes. They are created, powerful, gigantic, intelligent, immortal beings who are everywhere, carrying out the orders of the Most High and keeping the order of the universe! They invisibly carry out the commands of the Most High on our behalf; they have their own will and mind-blowing, terrifying power.

ANGELIC ORDERS[29]

References in the New Testament

Roman 8:38	Colossians 1:16	Ephesians 6:10	I Peter 3:22
Death	Visible	Principalities	Angels
Life	Invisible	Powers	Authorities
Angels	Thrones	Rulers of Earth	Powers
Principalities	Dominions	Wicked Hosts	
Powers	Principalities	Demons Implied	
Present	Powers		
Future			

There are other capabilities of angels we don't often think about; they were the first to sin! Lucifer is described as the father of lies. In fact he himself cooked-up and believed the very first lie: "I am so pretty and powerful, I could be God!" And he believed it! He believes his own lie to this very day.

Angels were given free will just as we were, which means they are still capable of perverting that free will. Angels sinned, and they still have free choice to sin. Humans were not the first to sin; Adam and Eve just so happened to be the first humans to sin. Do you realize ALL of mankind was brought down by a little white lie? This lie, this play on words, has cost countless billions of people to perish in the fires of hell? Angels play a huge role in our everyday lives, whether fallen or righteous.

Seraphim, Cherubim, and Ophanim

Seraphim means "burning ones." In our culture we picture angels with two beautiful white wings, however, seraphim have six wings:

> In the year that King Uzziah died, I saw the Lord seated on a throne, high and exalted, and the train of his robe filled the temple. Above him were seraphs, each with six wings; with two wings they covered their faces, with two they covered their feet, and with the two they were flying. And they were calling to one another, "holy, holy, holy is the Lord Almighty; the whole earth is full of his glory." At the sound of their voices the doorposts and thresholds shook and the temple was filled with smoke. "Woe to me!" I cried. "I am ruined! For I am a man of unclean lips, and my eyes have seen the King, the Lord Almighty!" Then one of the Seraphs flew to me with a live coal in his hand, which he had taken

> with tongs from the altar. With it he touched my mouth and said, "See, this has touched your lips; your guilt is taken away and your sin atoned for." (Isaiah 6:1–6; NIV)

There are only two scant accounts (see Isaiah and Revelation) of seraphs or seraphim found in the Bible; all other accounts are differing ranks of angels, or cherubim. Seraphs seem to indicate the power and might of God's ultimate holiness and purity. I am only speculating, but the wings which cover their faces and feet must have some spiritual significance in relationship to God's holiness and the divine covering of Jesus' blood. When they shouted "holy, holy, holy," it was so loud it shook a gigantic, stone temple and filled it with smoke. Isaiah was scared out of his wits, and he was sure his unclean lips were going to get him in trouble, but the seraphim brought a live coal (representing holy cleansing fire), and he was cleansed (again we see the importance of a sterile field). Seraphs seem to represent God's glory, holiness, and purity. Their primary function is to encircle the Holy Throne of God and provide perpetual adoration, and thus by tradition are seen as the "choirs of angels."

We have other ancient, external documents which give us a more descriptive picture of seraphim, and unfortunately we have to rely on them to help us understand these important holy sons of God. Understanding seraphim, cherubim, and ophanim, may help us fill in the blanks when it comes to our figurative language and descriptions of Satan and his fallen angels and demons when they are described as snakes and certain cloven-hoofed, horned beasts, and even UFOs.

According to the Book of Enoch: *Seraphim have sixteen faces, and like the rising sun; each angel radiated such light even the other holy beings, the cherubim and the thrones cannot look upon them.*[30] This is interesting, but we do not have enough evidence to support it in the scriptures. This also may be a more descriptive vision of the four living creatures depicted in Revelation. These sixteen faces have me more inclined to believe it is a vision of the four living creatures connected as one.

Seraphim also means "fiery ones," but others have translated it to "fiery serpents." They are literally *living flames*. Tongues of fire do resemble snake-like behavior as they make a serpentine form, licking the air. Now this may be a far stretch of my imagination, but I wonder if we do not get our ancient imagery of Satan presented as a snake not only from the Bible, but from his very nature as a holy angel, "a fiery one, fiery serpent"? Lucifer, we are told, was a cherub who displays other unique physical characteristics. But many of the fallen angels who rebelled against God may have been seraphim, thus leading to some of our ancient images of snakes. We also see this strange imagery of fiery serpents sent upon the children of Israel after they complained against God in Numbers 21:4–9. The word used is *seraphs*, meaning fiery serpent. This snake was copper colored and poisonous. Later we see Moses hold up the pole with the bronze snake on it, and anyone who looked upon it lived. This is a metaphor for sin, as Jesus would one day be put up on another pole, and took our sin for us, and if we were to look to him, we would have everlasting life.

Rejoice not thou, whole Philistia, because the rod of him that smote thee is broken: for out of the serpent's root shall come forth a cockatrice, and his fruit shall be a fiery flying serpent (Isaiah 14:29; KJV). And also: *...the viper and fiery flying serpent* (Isaiah 30:6; KJV). Very odd imagery, if you were to attribute this to seraphs, which is the Hebrew word used in both of these texts for fiery serpent, and now they add a descriptive word—flying.

We are told from other ancient texts a little more information about what seraphim actually look like. Unfortunately, as I stated before, we only have scant eyewitness information from the Bible.

> Each of the four living creatures had six wings and was covered with eyes all around, even under his wings. Day and night they never stop saying: "Holy, holy, holy is the Lord God Almighty, who was and is, and is to come." (Revelation 4:8: NIV)

So what can we make of all of these eyes covering their bodies? One meaning may be a reference to God's all-seeing omnipresence. The other meaning is literally "eyes with a jealous glance," according to Strong's Dictionary,[31] which may imply the jealous nature of God, as shown by the commandment "thou shalt have no other gods before me." Another interpretation by Maimonides, a venerated rabbi and philosopher, is "eyes or a body with different colors."[32] Possibly it could mean light or reflection of light.

When you begin to study seraphs, you walk away with more questions than answers. We may never know until we get to heaven, but at least the little information we do have erases many years of deception by the enemy and gives us a fresh perspective on title and duties bestowed upon these special, powerful creatures who are so close to God.

Cherubim simply means "winged, celestial beings." They are found all over the Old Testament and in only one passage in the New Testament, which is a reference to the Old. Cherubs are found in the tabernacle and the temple, and are representative of redemption, and minister to the manifestation of the glory of God.[33]

Cherubim are interesting "creatures." In fact they are described as "living creatures" in Revelation. The phrase "living creatures" is the word *zoon*[34] in the Greek, which actually means "animal." We may not even be able to group cherubim with other angels, as they seem to be unique and separated from angels in the few scriptures in which we see them mentioned. The other interesting verse we can discuss here is from Genesis: *"Cursed are you above all livestock, and all the wild animals! You will crawl on your belly and you will eat dust all the days of your life. And I will put enmity between you and the woman, and between your offspring and hers; he will crush your head, and you will strike his heel"* (Genesis 3:14–15; NIV). This verse is talking about Satan, the anointed cherub who covers. God makes reference to him as an animal, above other animals mind you, but an animal nonetheless. In ancient Babylon and other places cherubs are pictured as gigantic bulls, twice the size of our bulls, with four wings and horns.

The other question raised is: are all angels either seraphim, cherubim, or ophanim? Or are there other types of angels that we can add to this odd list? The Bible simply does not give us enough information to make such assumptions.

Cherubim are first seen in Genesis 3:24 after God drove Adam out of the Garden, and he placed one on the east side of the Garden of Eden with a flaming sword flashing back and forth to guard the way to the Tree of Life. So they do obviously function as a guard. There second function is to fulfill God's majesty as told by David: [The Lord] *mounted the cherubim and flew; he soared on the wings of the wind* (2 Samuel 22:11; NIV). Boy is that weird! God is riding an angel, or is he? Are they carrying the throne of God?

If you picture it as Ezekiel describes it, you get a little different take on this scripture.

Ezekiel gives us an encrypted description of the cherubs. Here is what he saw:

> In the fire was what looked like **four living creatures**. In appearance their **form was that of a man**, but each of them had **four faces and four wings. Their legs were straight; their feet were like those of a calf and gleamed like bur-**

> **nished bronze**. Under their wings on their four sides they had **the hands of a man**. All four of them had faces and wings, and there wings touched one another. Each one went straight ahead; they did not turn as they moved. Their faces looked like this: Each of the four had a **face of a man**, and on the right side each had the **face of a lion**, and on the left the **face of an ox**; each also had the **face of an eagle**. Such were their faces. Their wings were spread out upward; each had two wings, one touching the wing of the other creature on either side, and two wings covering its body. Each one went straight ahead. Wherever the spirit would go, they would go, without turning as they went. **The appearance of the living creatures was like burning coals of fire or like torches**. Fire moved back and forth among the creatures; it was bright, and lightening flashed out of it. The creatures sped back and forth like flashes of lightening. (Ezekiel 1:5–14; NIV)

It is difficult to picture these creatures, but they seem to walk upright like a man, have four faces, one of a man, a lion, an ox, and an eagle, and hands, and their legs were straight like a calf, so I am making a wild assumption they had cloven hooves. This is unlike any of the other angels. In fact it sounds more like an animal than a human form. I make the wild assumption of cloven hooves because why else would Ezekiel point out the fact their feet were like calves' feet? In the Kings James version it reads: *And their feet were straight feet; and the sole of their feet was like the sole of a calf's foot: and they sparkled like the color of burnished brass* (Ezekiel 1:7; KJV). The other point I have with this little tidbit is that many of our images of Satan depict him with a horned head (not unlike an ox), cloven hooves, and a man's upper torso. Could this weird imagery be closer to the truth than we give it credit for? Satan was a cherub, therefore we can safely assume he looked liked the cherub described by Ezekiel.

My NIV Bible has commentary about this passage which I found insightful and helpful: "Each of the four living creatures had four faces, symbolizing God's perfect nature. Some believe the lion represented strength; the ox, diligent service; the man, intelligence; and the eagle, divinity. Others see these as the most majestic of God's Creatures and say they therefore represent God's whole creation. The early church fathers saw a connection between these beings and the four gospels: The lion with Matthew, representing Christ as the lion of the tribe of Judah; the ox with Mark, portraying Christ as the servant; the human with Luke portraying Christ as the perfect human; the eagle with John, the Son of God, exalted and divine. The vision of John in Revelation 4, parallels Ezekiel's vision." [35] Later on we will see each of these four faces are tied to the zodiac as well.

Cherubim are also the creatures on the top of the Ark of the Covenant, known as the mercy seat. *...they were also woven into the Veil of the Tabernacle* (Exodus 25:17–22; NIV)*...and also woven into the curtains hanging on the tabernacle* (Exodus. 26:31; NIV). Later on, when Solomon built the temple, they also adorned the most holy place where the Ark of the Covenant was kept. Cherubim are very special "covering creatures." They surround God in the holy temple, and they also followed the Holy Spirit wherever it went according to Ezekiel. These are truly God's own personal servants, and they help to carry out the will of the Holy Spirit.

All the angels were standing around the throne and around the elders and the four living creatures. They fell down on their faces before the throne and worshiped God, saying "Amen! Praise and glory and wisdom and thanks and honor, and power and strength be to our God for ever and ever. Amen!" (Revelation 7:11; NIV). We sometimes miss an important element in this passage. The angels—separate, were standing around the elders, and the living creatures. The four living creatures, these cherubim were not counted with the angels or the elders. And again in Revelation: *Then I looked and heard the voice of many angels, numbering thousand upon thousands, and ten thousand times ten thousand. They encircled the throne and the living creatures and the elders. In a loud voice they sang: … The four living creatures said, "Amen," and the elders fell and worshiped* (Revelation 5:11; NIV). Again, we see they are separate from the multitude of angels, and notice the living creatures talked, sang, and worshipped. What on earth are cherubim? They are obviously in a class all of their own, as intelligent, articulate, separate, animal-creature creations. We may never fully understand these cherubim either, as they seem to be fully animal-creature creations, and fully transferable as humanoid as well. Nothing is too difficult for our God, and if he wants to have creatures that surround him with praise, are mighty and warrior-like, super-intelligent, and able to change their appearance, then it does nothing but increase my faith and holy awe of the one true God we worship.

Ophanim

It wasn't until I began to study angels that I even ran across this strange word: Ophanim. Ophanim are a type of angel written about mostly in the book of Ezekiel, and believe it or not, they are the ones everybody overlooks as angels and instead believe was an early UFO encounter. Ophanim are the "wheels" Ezekiel saw:

> As I looked at the living creatures, I saw a wheel on the ground beside each creature with its four faces. This was the appearance and structure of the wheels: they sparkled like chrysolite, and all four looked alike. Each appeared to be made like a wheel intersecting a wheel. As they moved, they

would go in any of one of the four directions the creatures faced; the wheels did not turn about as the creatures went. Their rims were high and awesome, and all four rims were full of eyes all around. When the living creatures moved, the wheels beside them moved; and when the living creatures rose from the ground the wheels also rose. Where the spirit would go, they would go, and the wheels would rise along with them, because the spirit of the living creatures was in the wheels. When the creatures moved, they also moved; when the creatures stood still, they also stood still; and when the creatures rose from the ground, the wheels rose along with them, because the spirit of the living creatures was in the wheels. (Ezekiel 1:15–21; NIV)

...the sound of the wings of the living creatures brushing against each other and the sound of the wheels beside them, made a loud rumbling sound. (Ezekiel 3:13; NIV)

..."Go in among the wheels beneath the cherubim"... When the Lord commanded the man in linen, "Take fire from among the wheels, from among the cherubim," the man went in and stood beside a wheel...I looked, and I saw beside the cherubim four wheels, one beside each of the cherubim; the wheels sparkled like chrysolite. As for their appearance; the four of them looked alike; each was like a wheel intersecting a wheel. As they moved, they would go in any one of the four directions the cherubim faced; the wheels did not turn about as the cherubim went. The cherubim went in whatever direction the head faced, without turning as they went. Their entire bodies, including their backs, their hands and their wings were completely full of eyes, as were their four wheels. I heard the wheels being called: "the whirling wheels." (Ezekiel 10:2, 6, 9–13; NIV)

These are some odd creatures, and there is a lot of information to disseminate from these passages. Rabbinical literature suggests these wheels are called *Ophan*, meaning wheel, or the wheel of a chariot, and the word *Galgal*, meaning wheel, associated with whirl or roll.[36] They are also called the "many-eyed-ones."

"In Jewish lore the Ophanim, or wheels, are called Thrones, because they are associated with divine judgment, and they are associated with chariots upon which the throne of God rests (the Merkabah)."[37] They are often viewed as the wheels of God, or the wheels of the heavenly chariot.

The way Ezekiel describes them, they seem to be quite separate beings from the cherubim, but they move with fluid connection to the spirit of the cherubim. He goes quite in depth saying over and over again; *Where the spirit would go, they would go, and the wheels would rise along with them, because the spirit of the living creatures was in the wheels.* It is a curious statement, and I can't even begin to understand what it means. Somehow the two are intimately connected, which may be why Ezekiel describes them as one creature and also as four.

Besides being in wheel form, we get the idea from Ezekiel's vision they too have some sort of flesh; they have backs, hands, and wings, and again, all of those eyes. They obviously make a loud, rumbling, whirring noise in connection to praise, and were very sparkly. Some people think these things are just a vision of a divine UFO, a space traveling vehicle. Well I agree, but not entirely, because they seem to possess intelligence we do not understand, and the Bible distinctly says they have a spirit. So again, whatever these heavenly, chariot wheels are, I can't wait to see one!

By understanding the creation and the stations and offices held by the sons of God, we can better understand how far Lucifer and his rebel angels fell. The question begs to be asked: *Did you know what you were ignoring when it came to angels?*

So in Summary:

1. Angels appear to be male, remain sexless, but are not without gender function.
2. They eat food and are capable of normal human activities.
3. They have their own language, but are multilingual as needed.
4. They dress in white, or have a dazzling white appearance, and their skin has a bronze glow.
5. They are huge! Seven to fifteen feet tall, gigantic statures, with great strength and weight.
6. They inspire great fear, terror, and holy awe when seen.
7. They are everywhere around us, but are unseen until God's spiritual sight is given. Most likely we do not just have one guardian angel, but several thousand.
8. They transcend known space/time dimensions (hyper dimensional).
9. They are innumerable.
10. They can be provoked to anger (see 2 Peter 2:4) and are sent to kill at the request of God.
11. They are immortal, holy, elect, obedient, mighty servants.
12. They possess emotions and are very concerned with humans.
13. They have the ability to heal diseases and infirmities.
14. They have stations and power over various forms of weather and animals.
15. There are many identifiable classes, serving in many orderly offices and functions.

16. They are separated into ranks and orders, and hold various titles, and rule certain geographical areas.
17. They are also organized into vast armies.
18. There are archangels, seraphim, cherubim, and the ophanim, mentioned in the Bible.
19. There is no plan for their redemption.
20. Certain angels are described as having wings, either four or six; none are described as just having two wings.
21. They are nothing in comparison to the Almighty God, and they are not to be worshipped! (See Exodus 20:1–6, and Colossians 2:18.)
22. All angels have free will, and Lucifer was the first to choose to sin. Sin originated with angels.
23. Angels can and do petition God, either on our behalf or against us as we saw with Satan.
24. Seraphim, cherubim and ophanim are in a separate class all by themselves, having separate and distinct characteristics and functions at the throne of God.

FALLEN ANGELS AND GIANTS

This next segment will slaughter your whole herd of sacred cows of religion. Why did I spend an entire section on "Good Angels" when this book is about the adversary? When I was in nurses training, we learned about the normal body and its normal functions before they ever allowed us to crack open a textbook about pathophysiology, disease, or abnormal structure. The reason is simple. You can't recognize abnormal until you know what normal is, inside and out! Simply put, Fallen Angels are now functioning in the *abnormal* arena, and it will be easier to identify their aberrant behavior in our lives now that we understand the normal. The enemies we fight are not of this world—not made of flesh and blood like we are. *For our struggle is not against flesh and blood, but against the rulers, against the authorities, against the powers of this dark world and against the spiritual forces in the heavenly realms* (Ephesians 6:12; NIV). We learned in the last section angels are separated into differing ranks, and rulers, authorities, powers, and spiritual forces are among those ranks.

These principalities will be a very strong focus for our discussion. *Principality* is defined by Vine's Dictionary as: "(*Arche*) beginning, governmental rule,"[38] and in Strong's Dictionary, the Greek meaning: "a commencement, or chief (in various applications of order, time, place, or rank) beginning (at the) first (estate), magistrate, power, principality, principle, rule."[39]

Remember when we talked about Lucifer's fall and his actions in Revelation 12:4, how he swept a third of the stars from heaven, and flung them to the earth? These and possibly others are the fallen angels. The Bible is clear these angels also rebelled against God… most likely due to Lucifer's deceptive words, and they became part of his fate, demoted and sentenced by God, with no chance for pardon. The Bible does tell us certain ranks of angels, most likely from every type and function, rebelled against God. These fallen angels are what are called powers, and principalities, rulers, and authorities, etc.

What do you get when you have a *fallen,* super-intelligent, mighty, powerful, being with all of the characteristics we listed in the previous chapter? You get an evil, super-intelligent, mighty, and powerful being with all of the characteristics we listed in the previous chapter, with distorted motives! Scary!

It is clear from reading Daniel 10 and Ephesians 6:12 that there are other fallen angels (princes) who are not in their chains yet; they still roam the heavenly places and the earth, and still are causing strife, and wrestling among us today. The Intelligent Deceiver craved worship so much, and was so self-convinced he deserved a throne that he got his own army and subjects to worship and serve him. But Satan cannot be everywhere at once. No matter how delusional he may be, he is not stupid. He had to have minions to do his bidding, and a third of the angels weren't going to be enough to accomplish his self-exalted goals as the world's population increased. The book of Job states that he wanders to and fro on the earth, so that is not omnipresence! Satan, a super-angel, compared to the Almighty God is belly button lint!

Lucifer was created with super intelligence—do not confuse his off-the-chart IQ, with *all knowing*! They do not even compare!

So how is Satan going to accomplish his evil task? Can he create? Many theologians have tackled this issue, and all I can say is, I think he can. After all, humans can create, and we are very creative, resourceful beings. We create and invent all manner of useful as well as disruptive devices. Satan has the ability to disrupt and pervert and manipulate the natural order of things (remember if God is the God of order, Satan is the god of disorder). One thing you will learn about our adversary is that he is the *world's first and biggest copycat. Everything about him is about copying God.* He wants to be like God. But instead, everything he does is the exact opposite of God, his nature, plans, etc. God is pure, he is evil; God is good, he is bad; God is love, he is hate; etc. This theme is essential to our understanding and defeating the deceptions of the devil.

Now man actually listened to one of God's commands and became fruitful and multiplied on the face of the earth. Satan had to come up with more evil spirits to accomplish his work and add to his kingdom, not to mention get rid of man and ruin their lives—he loathed us! Let's give you an interesting verse of scripture to chew on while we define a few things. *And I will put enmity between you and the woman, and between your offspring and hers* (Genesis 3:15; NIV).

Before moving on, let's define the literal translation of the word *angels.* In ancient Hebrew, the name for angels was *Sons of God.* A Son of God is a direct creation of God. The Psalms have already established God directly created angels. Adam did not come from a woman; he was the only human who could be considered a Son of God, since he was a direct creation. But every woman and man since that time came from a woman, they are *Sons (and Daughters) of Men.* Remember, "like produces like," it's God's natural, orderly law. There are only four scriptures in the Old Testament in which the phrase the "Sons of God" is used; Genesis 6:1–4, Job 1:6, 2:1, and 38:7, and they are all in reference to angels.

Why would God say Satan's seed would strike the heel of man? How can Satan have children, or offspring, as it plainly says in Genesis 3:15? We have established angels don't have a female counterpart, and even if they tried to breed male angel to male angel, you still wouldn't get a thing. The Intelligent Deceiver had to stay within God's natural law, but manipulated this natural law to accomplish this, and he did it in a very guileful, rebellious, abominable way. Satan is the father of disorder. So much so, God made a very special, excruciating, torturous eternity for these particular fallen angels, which Jude describes for us. Go with me to Jude 6: *And angels who did not keep (care for, guard, and hold to) their own first place of power but abandoned their proper dwelling place—these He has reserved in custody in eternal chains (bonds) under the thick gloom of utter darkness until the judgment and doom of the great day. [The wicked are sentenced to suffer] just as Sodom and Gomorrah and the adjacent towns—which likewise gave themselves over to impurity and indulged in unnatural vice and sensual perversity—are laid out in plain sight as an exhibit of perpetual punishment [to warn] of everlasting fire...wandering stars, for whom the gloom of eternal darkness has been reserved forever* (Jude 6–7, 13 AMP). Ouch! What in the world is he talking about? And, as an added punishment for human involvement, he flooded the earth, destroyed it! Why, why, why?

This portion of our text is so essential to understanding many of our paranormal mysteries of today. It is foundational to understanding the complex deception Satan has woven into the very fabric of our societies and into the cultural beliefs of all peoples of the world, and it nearly destroyed the human race!

What I am about to share with you changed my life. God opened a window of revelation and understanding for me, which took twenty-two years of questioning, digging, and probing into the wrong avenues for answers. Thankfully he is true to his word: *diligently seek and you shall find, knock and the door shall be opened unto you.* And it can all be found in the text of the scriptures! When I was eleven years old, my dad used to read the Bible every night out loud to us. I grew up in rural Montana, in a log house, with no electricity, running water, or phone. This also meant no TV. So for entertainment in the dark winter hours, we would take turns churning butter and listening to my dad read the Bible. My parents were new Christians and were trying to raise their three remaining children at home as such. I remember my dad reading Genesis 6, verses 2 and 4, and it stood out like an emblazoned fire engine, with all the bells and whistles going off! *The sons of God saw that the daughters of men were beautiful, and they married any of them they chose…The Nephilim were on the earth in those days, and also afterward—when the sons of God went to the daughters of men and had children by them. They were the heroes of old, men of renown.* I immediately asked my dad what it meant, and he didn't know. I can remember it so clearly. I have questioned that verse of scripture for years. I pondered it, meditated on it, read about the Nephilim in the Old Testament. Now I take this scripture literally. Sons of God are angels according to Hebrew translation, and it plainly states that they liked human women, and got with them in the biblical sense, and produced children! Now Genesis 3:15 talks about Satan's *offspring* and Eve's children. Well this just can't be! Angels mating with humans! But I didn't write it! God did, and he can't lie! So this is Satan's way of getting his offspring, an unholy union. So abominable to God was this union, he reserved a special place of torment for these angels. When you study external ancient texts, you learn these angels actually made a pact among themselves: no matter what the consequences, they wanted their own offspring. These "pact angels" are the ones described in Jude who have been chained for all eternity.

Nephilim literally means "the fallen ones," from the verb *nephal;*[40] to fall. What do you get when you breed an angel with a human? A giant! The Nephilim! They were the giants of the Old Testament feared by man from day one. Gigantic men, seven-plus feet tall, they were the heroes of old, most likely the Greek demigods. The gods of mythology, such as Zeus, Europa, Dione, and of course the most well known—Goliath, were the unholy offspring of angels and humans. When you breed a human to a human, you get a human. When you breed an angel to a human you get a hybrid human and/or a giant. This was within God's natural order of reproduction. People crossbreed animals all the time; take a buffalo and cow for example. The two don't normally mix, but when humans get involved they make a hybrid, called a beefalo. Humans have been manipulating genes for years, why not evil fallen angels with a higher knowledge base than us? This is not what God intended when he told man to multiply! For example: Do you think at creation there were wiener dogs? Don't laugh. Okay, laugh! No probably not; we had wolves and other wild dogs, but man, in his creative genius, manipulated the gene pools throughout the centuries and in a sense created the wiener dog. If we can do that, what did Satan and his band of fallen angels do?

This makes sense. Why, we have already learned angels were enormous eight to fifteen-plus feet tall, so it would make sense their offspring with women would be supersized as well. Ancient cultures and literature are replete with giant stories. It is interesting to note these stories describe giants as having a very evil nature, corrupted souls, and, interestingly enough, a determination to destroy God's chosen people, huh?! The most well-known giants are from our own scriptures. Og, the King of Bashan, was a giant; his bed was eighteen feet, nine inches long, and eight feet, four inches wide (see Deuteronomy 3:11). This bed is bigger than most people's bedrooms! Goliath was over nine feet tall and his armor weighed around 166 pounds (see 1 Samuel 17:4–7). This would be like dressing yourself in a full-grown man! Then there was the nation of giants found in Numbers: *"The land we explored devours those living in it. All the people we saw there are of great size. We saw the Nephilim there (the descendants of Anak come from the Nephilim). We seemed like grasshoppers in our own eyes, and we looked the same to them"* (Numbers 13:32–33; NIV). There is also a story of one with six fingers and six toes on each hand and foot, a descendant of Rapha (see 2 Samuel 21:20–22 and the Rephaites in Genesis 14 & 15).

I used to hate Greek and Roman mythology in school, but it is common knowledge these "gods" bred with mortal women to produce demigods. These fantastical stories are quite believable to me now, the mystery solved in the holy scriptures right there for us to see! They were simply fallen angel hybrids. Recall the sheer power and might of angels in our previous lesson, killing 185,000 men in one night, and then imagine the immense power these giants had. This isn't like the giants of today, the most notable being Andre the Giant. He and others like him in size and stature suffer from a debilitating pituitary gland dysfunction or tumor, and they suffer from many painful ailments and die at a young age. No, these giants were strong, healthy, and powerful...*mighty men of renown, heroes of old.*

To give a more contemporary picture of the strength and power of these men from noted Bible scholar Chuck Missler's book, *Alien Encounters*:

> Buffalo Bill (William F. Cody) in his autobiography provides us with an interesting anecdote. "While we were in the sand hills, scouting the Niobrara country, the Pawnee Indians brought into camp some very large bones, one of which the surgeon of the expedition pronounced to be the thigh bone of a human being. The Indians said the bones were those of a race of people who long ago had lived in that country. They said these people were 3 times the size of a man of the present day, that they were so swift and strong that they could run by the side of a buffalo (most buffalo weigh close to a ton), and taking the animal in one arm, could tear off a leg and eat it as they ran. These giants, said the Indians, denied the existence of a Great Spirit. When they heard the thunder or saw the lightening, they laughed and declared that they were greater than either. This so displeased the Great Spirit that he caused a deluge. The water rose higher and higher till it drove these proud giants from the low grounds to the hills and thence to the mountains. At last even the mountains tops were submerged and the mammoth men were drowned."[41]

You have to keep in mind these Indians were not evangelized yet. How would they know of a race of giant men, a great flood, and our God wiping them out for evil, rebellious pride? Makes you wonder doesn't it? Search the scriptures, the answers are before you! The other key to this story is the giants' denial of the Great Spirit.

This is the scriptures' way to "test the spirits"; if they deny the most high, they are not of God.

There are many other recognized historical written evidences suggesting the angels did indeed come to earth and mate with women. Josephus (the Jewish historian) wrote; "They made God their enemy; for many angels of God accompanied with women and begat sons that proved unjust…the acts of those whom the Grecians call giants."[42] The Book of Enoch is replete with vast exploits of these "watcher" angels that fell from the grace of God. According to the Book of Enoch, Chapter 7, about two hundred of them made a pact on the top of Mount Armon. If you run a Google search of the list of the chief watcher angels in this band, you will end up with a list of chief demonic or "helper" spirits called upon by witches, mediums, and psychics of today. Coincidence? Don't be so naïve. Enoch 7:10: *Then they took wives, each choosing for himself; whom they began to approach, and with whom they cohabitated; teaching them sorcery, incantation, and the dividing of roots and trees. And they conceiving brought forth giants (Gen 6:4–6); Whose stature was each three hundred cubits. These devoured all which the labor of men produced; until it became impossible to feed them; When they turned themselves against men, in order to devour them; And began to injure birds, beasts, reptiles, and fishes, to eat their flesh one after another, and to drink their blood (Math 24:37–39). Then the earth reproved the unrighteous.*[43] I hope you are beginning to see the importance of Genesis 6; it is the foundation of the paranormal mysteries web, which Satan began to weave, way back in the day.

I wanted to point out here, the eating of animals was not ordained by God until after the flood! Watch what else transpired by these giants and their father angels. Enoch chapter 8: *Azayel taught men to make swords, knives, shields, breastplates, made them see that which was behind them, and the workmanship of bracelets and ornaments, the use of paint, the beautifying of the eyebrows, the use of stones of every valuable and select kind, and all sorts of dyes, so that the world became altered. Impiety increased; fornication multiplied; and they transgressed and corrupted all their ways (Ecc. 1:10, 2:17). Amazarak taught all the sorcerers and the dividers of roots. Armers taught the solution of sorcery, Barkayal taught the observers of the stars, Akilbeel taught signs, Tamiel taught astronomy, and Asaredel taught the motion of the moon, And men, being destroyed, cried out; and their voice reached to heaven.*[44]

The following is an excerpt from the covenant of Samyaza, a demonic channeled message, to a coven leader. It describes what Genesis 6 states, and the Book of Enoch says, from a satanic perspective:

> We gazed upon the earth and longed for the joys of materiality...
>
> And we resolved to join with Nephilim on Earth, to break the chains of Demiurge [God], and elevate Man unto the heights, to be as gods, as Satanael had promised, and to dwell with them in building civilization. *For we brought with us the knowledge and secrets of Kosmos and Earth, as may be useful to Man through the Gift which Satanael had imparted.* As we bequeathed the Daimonic [demon] Seed unto Man through his daughters, that he may be bred upward unto godhood.
>
> And *Michael declared unto me that the greatest crime had been committed by laying with the daughters of Man, to enjoy a carnal life and children, for such is not Angels and Sons of God.* And when our sons, Gibborim, shall be slain before our eyes, we shall be bound underneath Earth, after which we would burn and perish.
>
> Even your Final Judgment after this Deluge is witness to

your inability to keep quenched the Spark within Man, and the spirits of Nephilim and Gibborim and Watchers shall return to inspire Man, lest he again become as the beasts of the field.[45]

This is a chilling discourse; it describes exactly what happened in Genesis 6. Oh, how benevolent these fallen angelic creatures want us to see them, and yet they themselves admit they will burn in hell! My question to Satanists: why would angels, who hate God, and are now "self-aware," want to covet us dumb, servile beings and our created-by-God, worldly goods, when they had everything in heaven to begin with? Who's the dummy?

So why haven't we any archeological evidence of these giant men? We do, but very little of it is ever mentioned in mainstream media. Giants and the truth about their existence have been hidden from us. I never once saw a picture of giant bones in anthropology class in college; instead I had to regurgitate lies about Lucy, a fraud half-man, half-ape woman, in order to pass the class. When I started to do research on giants, I found there are all kinds of artifacts, bones, etc. I felt cheated! Nobody showed or taught me this information. In fact, I just watched a recent History Channel production on paleontology and Greek mythological creatures. The archeologists actually admitted on national television they had thrown many "giant bones" away, because they did not consider them significant finds! Following are some 1800's archeological evidences found in burial mounds, right here in America and elsewhere.

The history of Cattaraugus County makes note of the town of Carrollton's "Fort Limestone." In 1851 the removal of a stump turned up a mass of human bones. Some were enormous. Franklinville's, Marvin Older virtually gamboled about the site with them: a skull fit over his size seven-and-a-half head; a rib curved all the way around him, a shinbone went from his ankle to above his knee, and a jaw—with bodacious molars—went over his own. Its first owner had probably stood eight feet tall.

In old river gravels near Bathurst, New South Wales, huge stone artifacts—clubs, pounders, adzes, chisels, knives, and hand axes—all of tremendous weight, lie scattered over a wide area. These weigh anything from eight, ten, fifteen, to twenty-one and twenty-five pounds, implements which only men of tremendous proportions could possibly have made and used. Estimates for the actual size of these men range from ten to twelve feet tall and over, weighing from five hundred to six hundred pounds.

In his book, *The Natural and Aboriginal History of Tennessee*, author John Haywood describes "very large" bones in stone graves found in Williamson County, Tennessee, in 1821. In White County, Tennessee, an "ancient fortification" contained skeletons of gigantic stature averaging at least 7 feet in length. [46]

From his book *Genesis 6 Giants, The Master Builders of the Prehistoric and Ancient Civilizations*, Stephen Qualye states giants' bones and skeletons have been found reaching a mind boggling thirty-six feet high! It is unimaginable to us! A six-foot-tall man wouldn't even come up to his knees! No wonder the Israelites said we looked as grasshoppers in their sight!

- Almost beyond comprehension or believability was the find of the two separate thirty-six foot human remains uncovered by Carthaginians circa 200–600 BC.
- A twenty-five foot, six inch skeleton found in 1613 AD near the castle of Chaumont in France, was claimed to be nearly intact.
- Maximunus Thrax Caesar of Rome 235–238 AD had an eight foot, six inch tall skeleton.

- A fifteen-foot human skeleton was found in southeast Turkey in late 1950s in the Euphrates Valley during road construction. Many tombs containing giants were uncovered there.[47]

One story of a giant Roman emperor was of Caius Julius Verus Maximinus. Born about AD 173, he reached a height of eight feet six inches. He was reported to be able to keep pace with a horse at full gallop, knock out the teeth of a horse with one blow of his fist, and daily ate forty pounds of meat and drank six gallons of wine. He used his wife's bracelet for a thumb-ring.[48]

Every ancient culture on earth is replete with stories about giant men and women inhabiting our planet. We know from history, fact becomes legend, legend becomes myth, and myths fade from our memories until forgotten. We have physical evidence as well, of huge races of men left to defy our imaginations and cause us to research the ancient megalithic ruins. These places are gigantic, unexplainable masterpieces of architecture, "science out of place." Average-sized man cannot, and would not be able to build these structures.

As theologian Francis A. Schaeffer put it:

> More and more we are finding that mythology in general though greatly contorted very often has some historic base. And the interesting thing is that one myth which occurs over and over again in many parts of the world is that somewhere a long time ago supernatural beings had sexual intercourse with natural women and produced a special breed of people.[49]

So let's go back to where we left off in scripture: *The Lord saw how great man's wickedness on the earth had become, and that every inclination of the thoughts of his heart was only evil all the time. The Lord was grieved that he had made man on the earth, and his heart was filled with pain. So the Lord said, "I will wipe mankind, whom I have created, from the face of the earth—men and animals, and creatures that move along the ground, and birds of the air—for I am grieved that I have made them." But Noah found favor in the eyes of the Lord* (Genesis 6:5–8; KJV).

So what is the point of all of this watcher-angel-hybrid-giant business? What does it have to do with the flood? What does it have to do with you today as a spiritual warrior? Everything! Have you ever wondered why Noah and his family were the *only* ones out of the probable millions, possibly billions, of humans on the planet at the time that God spared? What made him so highly favored? Why would God go to such extremes, as to actually be pained in heart, he even created man? That he would go to such lengths as to destroy all of creation? If you think this world is evil now, imagine what it was back then! (It is getting there again though.) This is another scripture that makes me think we were a special creation, to prove God's goodness and forgiveness to the angels; and to think Satan nearly had it in the palm of his hand!

Satan had a plan. Remember we are dealing with Satan's kingdom now, not man's rule. Satan and his band of rebel angels created a huge mess with the gene pool…He knew God's mercy; he also knew God's purity and justice. He counted on it. He knew if he could not outright kill mankind, he would literally breed them out! Remember angels were not to "marry" in heaven, so can you think of a better way to rebel against your God than to disobey that holy command and create your own rebellious offspring? How do we know this to be true? Scripture, of course!

This is the genealogy of Noah. Noah was a just man, perfect in his generations. Noah walked with God (Genesis 6:9; NIV). So we see from this passage Noah was a just man and he walked with God. (Enoch, is the only other man to have been given this title; "to walk with God.") Noah had a built-in hedge of protection. Let's look at this curious statement: *Perfect in his generations.* The word translated "perfect" is *tamiym*, which means "without blemish, sound, healthful, without spot, unimpaired." This term is used of physical blemishes, suggesting Noah's genealogy was not tarnished by the intrusion of the fallen angels.[50]

Who can we ultimately trace back to Noah? Genealogically speaking—he was perfect, without blemish, sound, healthful, without spot, and unimpaired...The "Perfect" Lamb of God—Jesus Christ! Isn't that cool?

All through scripture Satan is thwarted by redemption. I know he was not allowed to comprehend this; otherwise, if he really understood it, why would he have killed Jesus? If he understood redemption, he would have done everything to avert Jesus' death on the cross (food for thought). Wanting to be like God, he cannot understand or comprehend this entitlement God has given us. Compare scripture to scripture: *I will put enmity between you and the woman, and between your offspring and hers* (Genesis 3:15; NIV). It is all about the seed! Get rid of the seed and you have no savior! But here we have little ol' Noah, one human with three sons, perfect in his generations...can you imagine the pressure Satan had on him and his children's wives? How frustrating for our adversary...One lousy human was going to ruin his whole plan! Satan knew he had 120 years from the time Noah received flood revelation and instructions to build the ark...Noah must have been under some serious oppression; I can't wait to meet him in heaven, and talk to him about that time...What an incredible witness to the ability of the human spirit to walk with God to withstand the wiles of the enemy!

So great was this vile abomination to God, he wiped out all of mankind except Noah and his family, and saved only two of every creature. The very day God said the rain would fall it did. Nobody had seen rain fall before; the earth prior to this was watered with mist coming from the surface. How terrifying to see rain fall from heaven, tumultuous torrential rain, plus springs of the deep bursting forth (see Genesis 7:11–12, 2:5). Can you imagine the scene? The ark is closed up. Noah, family, and animals safe inside, and giant men eight, nine, ten-plus feet tall, able to rip the leg off a running buffalo, trying desperately to smash their way into the ark, as well as normal-sized humans? There must have been some heavy-duty workmanship on that ark.

Here is another interesting fact: Lamech, Noah's father, most likely knew Adam and had heard the stories of the Garden of Eden and God's graciousness. Wouldn't that be trippy? Sitting around a campfire with your great, great, great, great, great, great, great-grandfather listening to first-hand tales of the beginnings of the earth? This also means Noah may have known his great-grandfather Enoch before he was taken up to heaven by God. This fantastic oral tradition and first-hand knowledge of God would have definitely helped Noah and his preceding generations to be able to steer clear of the traps and abominations of the Devil. These are but some of the huge examples of heritage given in the Bible.

Pre-flood was truly a different world, and although Satan was not able to accomplish the complete destruction of man, he built himself quite an army of evil seed. Giants are again found post-flood, so the fallen angels continued their unholy unions with women afterward. *The Nephilim were on the earth in those days—and also afterward* (Genesis 6:4; NIV). So again, Satan used this tactic to again try to breed out the possibility of a savior.

You may be asking yourself: "Why have I not been taught this information from my church? Giants were explained to me as the offspring or lines of Seth." Back in the day of the early church, we unfortunately had some undesirables (most likely followers of Satan) introduce the Sethite theory into the church (this is heresy), because they thought the common knowledge teaching of angels mating with women and producing offspring was immoral teaching. Again, read Genesis 6 for yourself. God did not say the giants came from Seth or his offspring. It clearly states the son's of God begot the giants. I didn't write it, God did—who are you going to believe? False teaching, or the Word? Besides, this false teaching started in the third century AD, whereas the angel-giant offspring was common knowledge for approximately four thousand years! Not to mention the fact that a wicked man, breeding with a wicked woman, does not produce offspring like King Og of Bashan or Goliath and his four gigantic brothers! You must use your noggin, and read the scriptures yourself in these last days, so as not to be deceived by the doctrines of demons.

These fallen angels we are told in Jude, were given a special horrific punishment. Not all the rebel angels, only the ones that conspired to interbreed with women, and according to scripture they are chained in darkness. *And the angels which kept not their first estate, but left their own habitation, he hath reserved in everlasting chains under darkness unto the judgment of the great day. Even as Sodom and Gomorrah, and the allies about them in like manner, giving themselves over to fornication, and going after strange flesh, are set forth for an example, suffering the vengeance of eternal fire* (Jude 6–7; NIV). We are told later in Revelation these evil angels will be released upon mankind once again during the tribulation. The Book of Enoch sheds some light into the disgrace and shame these angels caused for mankind. It has an elaborate angelology, and attributes much of the technology and "science out of place" to these watcher angels, as well as warfare and implements of warfare, sorcery, divination, magick, witchcraft, even crystals and other stones, makeup, and powerful sexual seductions, as well as child sacrifice. These angels not only *taught their human wives angel intelligence*, but they taught their gigantic offspring "forbidden knowledge." Why was it forbidden? Because it didn't come from God. God created man for his pleasure and his purpose, not as an angel's play toy. This is exactly what Satan and his rebel angels have treated us as since they fell. We are the prey of Satan. Ever watched a cat play with a mouse? Cats enjoy torturing and tormenting their prey before they consume them. This is exactly what happens to mankind when they become involved with the paranormal. We become a toy, a puppet, for evil, hateful beings.

Jesus leaves us with a cryptic message in Luke: *And [just] as it was in the days of Noah, so will it be in the time of the Son of Man* (Luke 17:26; AMP).

Demons and the Rephaim

Where do demons come from? What is the distinction between fallen angel spirits and demons? Contrary to some popular theological theories, which state they are one and the same, the holy Bible says something quite different. The word Rephaim appears right alongside the Nephilim. Rephaim means "dead ones." This term actually doesn't show up until Genesis 14:5; conversely the word demon doesn't show up until Leviticus 17:7 (where they are referred to as evil spirits). There is absolutely no reference to demons (evil spirits) before the flood!

Remember the true nature of good angels? Messengers, guardians, helpers—they have their own heavenly bodies, able to change form, no doubt, but their own body. In contrast demons do not seem to have their own bodies; they have a spirit body, but not an actual physical body. They seem to have certain classes and ranks just as angels do, but they are ranked below fallen angels, and they can take on other forms (shape-shift), just as angels do. They are always seeking embodiment…in other words they miss a human body. They always seek to inhabit some living thing. Hmmm.

What kind of a conclusion could we draw from this information? They have some angel characteristics, e.g., change bodily forms, operate in the unseen spirit realm. They are called the "dead ones," which doesn't make sense if you are spirit; they can't die, right? Unless—they did die! And they seek to inhabit human bodies. The dead spirits of giants, perhaps? This would make sense. They were not an original creation of God. Half-man, half-angel, they have both attributes. They were very carnal in life, so they would naturally miss the physical pleasures of this world, and they have no home in the heavens, no plan for redemption. What would you do if you were a spirit who had no place to go? I don't know—cause as much mayhem for your dark prince as you could before your relegated time to the bottomless pit?

According to Dr. Chuck Missler, "The origin of demons is not commonly known in our time. However in ancient times it was well understood that demons are the disembodied spirits of the Nephilim (giants)."[51] Our spirit goes somewhere when our body dies—whether heaven or hell, wouldn't it make sense that a hybrid, giant spirit would go somewhere? They had all been killed by the flood, but where would they go? Why would Satan put his own kind in hell, especially if it were his unnatural *offspring*? The very *offspring*, we are told, that would strike the heel of man? What evil would that accomplish him? The Lord would not send such evil to heaven. The Word is very specific: there is no redemption plan for angels, only for the seed of Abraham.

And the angels which kept not their first estate, but left their own habitation, he hath reserved in everlasting chains under darkness unto the judgment of the great day. Even as Sodom and Gomorrah, and the allies about them in like manner, giving themselves over to fornication, and going after strange flesh, are set forth for an example, suffering the vengeance of eternal fire (Jude 1:6–7; KJV).

According to Missler, "Numerous ancient rabbinic and early church texts, state the belief that when the Nephilim died their spirits became disembodied and roamed the earth, harassing mankind and seeking embodiment; this is most evident in the book of Enoch."[52]

Enoch 15: *Now the giants (Nephilim), who have been born of spirit and of flesh, shall be called upon earth, evil spirits, and the earth shall be their habitation. Evil spirits shall proceed from their flesh, because they were created from above; from the holy Watchers was their beginning and primary foundation. Evil spirits shall they be upon the earth, and the spirits of the wicked shall they be called. The habitation of the spirits of heaven shall be in heaven; but upon the earth shall be the habitation of terrestrial spirits, who are born on earth. The spirits of the giants shall be like clouds, which shall oppress, corrupt, fall, contend, and bruise those upon the earth.*[53]

So these spirits are described as clouds. Ever seen a cloud, or lots of clouds? They come and go, blot out the sun (Son), bring terrible storms, etc., and they, the evil spirits, or demons, which is the Bible's common synonym, will oppress, corrupt, fall, contend, and bruise us on earth. *They are dead, they shall not live; they are deceased, they shall not rise: therefore hast thou visited and destroyed them, and made all their memory to perish* (Isaiah 26:14; KJV). We see from this verse the giants are truly dead, but the next scripture has an interesting footnote to the destruction of the giants: *That was also regarded as the land of the giants; giants formerly dwelt there, but the Ammonites call them Zamzummin, a people as great and numerous and tall as the*

Anakim. But the Lord destroyed them before them, ***and they dispossessed them and dwelt in their place*** (Deuteronomy 2:20–21; NIV).

Another interesting account in the ancient book of Jubilees 10:1–5,[54] recounts Noah's sons coming to him for advice on what to do, and how to handle the demons that were plaguing them from the children of destruction (the Nephilim). Their chief complaints about these evil spirits were that they were leading their children astray, darkening and slaying their children. Noah goes on to petition the Lord for mercy and grace, and asks if God would cast them out into prison and judgment. Does this sound reminiscent of The Book of Enoch—*and men being destroyed, cried out, and their voice reached to heaven?*

We have no sure way of knowing if demons are the spirits of the deceased giants (Nephilim), but the evidence is overwhelming, the case holds water. It makes sense and fits together all of the missing puzzle pieces so perfectly. These demon spirits are Satan's seed, his pride and joy, his own corrupted army of dark children, who will strike our heel—his minions, who must not only worship this dark lord, but do his evil bidding. He is making his own sick kingdom… copying God by creating his own race, his own special offspring to worship and obey him. Intelligent Deception is very predictable once you understand Satan's motives.

Remember the words; *and also afterward,* regarding the post-flood giants from Genesis 6:4? Basically it is saying that the fallen angels continued their abominable behavior post-flood, continuing to create more giants, more demons once dead. For those of you having a hard time swallowing this revelation that a spiritual entity could breed with a flesh and blood woman, producing an offspring, alive and breathing, in the flesh with supernatural abilities, then I guess you would have a hard time swallowing the virgin birth of Jesus the Christ. Didn't the Holy Spirit overshadow Mary, and impregnate her with the Messiah incarnate? (see Matthew 1:18–22). It can be done. Satan is the ultimate copycat; what makes us so sure he won't do the same thing when he brings the Antichrist on the scene? Another unholy union of a satanic spirit overshadowing a woman, to bear his Antichrist! Predictable—he wants to be like God, remember?

Let's see what the Satanists believe about the origin of demons. The following is an excerpt from a channeled Satan worshiper.

> But I Samyaza, defiantly said unto Demiurge [God]: "Tyrant, your bloodlust has blinded you. Bind our carnal bodies you may, but the light given by Satanael and our Gift to Man, shall endure. We shall again illuminate the hearts and minds of Man. The Gift of Satanael abideth with Man since the days of Adam, unto eternity. No matter how many times you purge the Earth…
>
> "Even your Final Judgment after this Deluge is witness to your inability to keep quenched the Spark within Man, and the spirits of Nephilim and Gibborim and Watchers shall return to inspire Man lest he again become as the beasts of the field.
>
> "Our sons Gibborim shall incarnate in the bodies of Man, of those who are mighty and wise, to inspire and counsel them. *They shall come to be called 'evil spirits' and 'demons' by the ignorant and fearful, but the wise they shall be known as 'Daimons,' for these shall be the guardian geniuses of the great of Earth, who shall inspire the best among Man to great heights, to beautiful works of art, and to further discoveries of Earth and Kosmos. The Gift of Civilization shall not be obliterated."*[55]

The above portion of the channeled message, gives us valuable insight into the arrogance and rebelliousness of these angels. You can see that these fallen angels again view mankind as dumb "beasts of the field" in need of "inspired intelligence." Again, I question their motives. Why bother with us if we are so moronic? What is so enticing about us that they cannot resist helping us achieve "self-actualization"? Once again, we can see God's mighty hand and his omniscience and omnipotence. The angels believe they are accomplishing their agenda, when in actuality God is using them to achieve his higher, intelligent purpose! God has been using Satan and his angels and demons since the dawn of time to test our faith and allegiance to God.

Author Stephen Quayle writes:

> This same view of where the demons came from is also to be found in the Testament of Solomon. This book purports to have been written at the time of Solomon. According to the story, Solomon is speaking to a fallen angel, Beelzeboul, who delivers a bound demon to the king's feet.
>
>> I commanded another demon be brought to me; and he [Beelzeboul] brought me the evil demon Asmondeus, bound. I asked him, "Who are you?" He scowled at me and said, "And who are you?" I said to him, "You dare to answer so arrogantly when you have been punished like this?"…
>>
>> "How should I answer you? You are the son of a man, *but although I was born of a human mother, I am the son of an angel*, it is impossible for one of heavenly origin to speak an arrogant word to one

> of earthly origin...You have us to torture for a little while; then we shall disperse among human beings again with the result that we shall be worshipped as gods because men do not know the names of the angels who rule over us."[56]

Stephen Qualye goes on to write: "Demons seem to need living creatures to survive. The exact mechanism is unknown, but it appears that they may have an almost vampirism relationship, needing a real body to 'feed' on in order to survive. (This craving may be reflected in the blood sacrifices, need for sexual orgies, cannibalistic acts by 'gods,' and other abominations instigated in the religions the fallen angels and Nephilim create. As we'll see this becomes a hallmark of pagan religions.)"[57]

When you begin to compare how evil and degenerate the giants were in life, their arrogance, hatred of mankind, and unholy endowment of sinful desires resulting in every gross abomination and sin, you can begin to appreciate the train of thought that giants' spirits are the demons of our age.

I hope you are now beginning to see the ultimate significance of all this angel hybrid, giant business. It is having a huge spiritual impact on the human race today. Christians are being tormented, possessed, oppressed, and bruised and battered by former giants, literally! You battle not against flesh and blood, but of spiritual rulers and principalities, and these arrogant spirits are alive and well today!

Satan Sets Up His Kingdom on Earth: Babylon

Satan is an arrogant, narcissistic, copycat; if God has a chosen city (Jerusalem), he wants a chosen city. This chosen city is a testament to the giants and demonic powers that still rule there today. Let's see how it all got started by looking at Genesis 9:18–27. This story in a nutshell is about the great sin of Canaan, Noah's grandson.

> The sons of Noah who came out the ark were Shem, Ham, and Japheth (Ham was the Father of Canaan). These were the three sons of Noah, and from them came the people who were scattered over the earth. Noah, a man of the soil, proceeded to plant a vineyard. When he drank some of its wine, he became drunk and lay uncovered inside his tent. Ham the father of Canaan, saw his father's nakedness and told his two brothers outside. But Shem and Japheth took a garment and laid it across their shoulders; then they walked in backward and covered their father's nakedness. Their faces were turned the other way so that they would not see their father's nakedness. When Noah awoke from his wine and found out what his youngest son had done to him, he said, "Cursed be Canaan! The lowest of slaves will he be to his brothers." He also said, "Blessed be the Lord, the God of Shem! May Canaan be the slave of Shem. May God extend the territory of Japheth; may Japheth live in the tents of Shem, and may Canaan be his slave." (Genesis 9:18–27; NIV)

Now at first glance it looks like papa Noah just got drunk, and in his drunken stupor, lay naked in his tent sleeping it off, and Ham walked in on him right? So why the fuss? Why the curses on his grandson? Why the blanket thing while walking backwards? Why even bother mentioning it? The land of Canaan became the Promised Land, but not before Canaan established it, and it was inhabited by—you guessed it! By a race of giants, the Rephaim (the dead ones).

The question I want to answer is: What did Canaan do to Noah in that tent, which his father Ham must have condoned? The scripture doesn't say Canaan was in the tent but it certainly alludes to it. Twice this passage of scripture refers to Ham being the father of Canaan—it doesn't say anything about Shem's or Japheth's sons.

Noah got drunk. This is the first we see in scripture that Noah partook of fermented drink. It is thought by many scholars and biblical scientists that fermentation did not, and could not, occur prior to the flood due to a completely different atmosphere. So drinking and getting drunk was a new experience. This points out the utter lack of control one has over his own body and faculties when we imbibe in too much alcohol. Things happen which are no longer in our control, and doors (in this case tent doors) get opened up to evil spirits or evil intentions.

In the account of this incident in *The Chumash*, the rabbinical commentators have a very different take on the story. First off, again we run into the term *nakedness*, which in this case again means "shame." According to rabbinical commentators, "Ham the father of Canaan, '*Saw.*' In the plain meaning of the verse, Noah's intoxication caused him to be uncovered, and Ham gazed at him disrespectfully." According to R' Hirsch, "Ham enjoyed the sight of his father's dishevelment and drunkenness. Canaan is associated with the event because he had a part in disgracing Noah. Some of the sages say that he was the one who saw Noah and ran to tell his Father (Rashi)."[58] According to Sforno, "Ham gazed at—but did not protest the indignity that Canaan had perpetrated upon Noah." For according to Pirkei d Rabbi Eliezar, Canaan had castrated Noah. Others maintain that it was Ham who did so. [59]

Whatever Canaan did to precipitate or aggravate the situation, Ham's conduct was disgraceful, for he entered the tent and leered at Noah's debasement, and then, instead of averting his gaze and covering him up as his brothers did, he went derisively to tell his brothers. Whether or not Noah was castrated or it was something to do with a sexually perverted act perpetrated on Noah while he was drunk, we don't know, but it was bad, really bad, evil to the core!

If Noah had been castrated—let's think about the ramifications of this. He would not be able to have any more children. It would be a direct attack on God's own blessing and command that we saw earlier in this chapter. These four men were told to repopulate the earth (see Genesis 9:1). By taking Noah out of the equation, Satan would have reduced the reproductive capacity of the earth by at least 20 percent, taking into account Canaan being the only grandson named. Verse 28 tells us Noah lived 350 more years after the flood. That would have been a lot of reproducing he could have accomplished. Satan may have wanted to take another pot shot at Noah because he was a man of the soil (or earth), which implies mastery. "Noah was the 'Master' because the earth had been spared for, and because of him."[60]

This would have really galled Satan. He is constantly trying to exalt himself, and here Noah is "Master of the Earth"! What better way to get back at these humans than to attack his very manhood (we have no written evidence Noah had any other children post-flood), and enter into his very grandson, Canaan, a corrupted individual, to set up his debased kingdom?

With the curse upon Canaan, Noah may have foreseen that Canaan's descendants would always be wicked, and evil spirits were adeptly at work establishing a future kingdom for Satan, their dark lord. Out of Noah's three sons, these are the nations their descendants gave rise to:

Shem: Hebrews, Chaldeans, Assyrians, Persians, Syrians. Abraham, David and Jesus were all Shem's descendants.

Japheth: Greeks, Thracians, and Scythians. They all settled in Europe and Asia Minor.

Ham: The father of Canaan, gave rise to the Canaanites, Egyptians, Philistines, Hittites, and Amorites. They settled in Canaan, Egypt, and Africa.

Are you beginning to see Noah's prophetic curse on all of Hams descendants? They were, and still are to this very day, Israel's sworn enemies! This is one heckuva generational curse! Throughout history, Jewish patriarchs strictly forbid intermarriage with these accursed Canaanites, and later in Isaiah 20:4, descendants of Ham are led away by the king of Assyria (that would be Shem's descendants, just as Noah had said)…naked and barefoot!

This is powerful stuff! Whatever happened in that tent set up a generational and territorial bondage, as well as demonic possession. We now will see this cursed bloodline of Ham give rise to the first world dictator—and the beginnings of Satan's one world government! His M.O. hasn't changed in all of these millennia! He just possesses a new man every few hundred years and repackages his government program!

Ham had a son named Cush, who in turn had a son named Nimrod (see Genesis 10:8). According to Bible scholar Dr. Chuck Missler: "Nimrod's name actually means 'the rebel'! Nimrod in the text is actually called a 'Mighty one.' The term Mighty one is the same word used to refer to the Nephilim! In Hebrew the word is Gibborim! We don't know for sure if Nimrod was a giant, but we must ask ourselves why Moses the Author of Genesis would use a word like that to describe him!"[61]

Nimrod was the king of Babylon. Babylon is a name that is synonymous with Satan, the future Antichrist, and the coming world leader, the king of Babylon (see Isaiah 14:4). Dr. Missler writes: "Nimrod's rebellion, which is an open revolt against God, was exemplified by his leadership of a great confederacy of peoples. This confederacy consisted of a unified 'one world government' with a common language. He was founder of an ungodly, idolatrous, pagan religious system from which most of the subsequent pagan religions emerged. Extra biblical records indicate that he set himself up as God, and was even worshiped by the ungodly nations as the 'god of gods.'"[62]

This is the New Age movement in a nutshell. It didn't begin here; it began in heaven when Satan became "self-actualized" and rebelled. Man exalts himself as God, with a promise of peace and unity and a god-esque stature. Absolutely no personal responsibility for your own actions because you'll just ascend to a higher level and figure it out in your next life, right?

When Nimrod eventually died, the Babylonian mystery religion in which he figured prominently continued on. His wife, Queen Semiramis, saw to that. Once he was dead, she deified him as the sun god. In various cultures he later became known as Baal, the Great Life Giver, the god of fire, Baalim, Bel, Molech, etc.

"Later, when this adulterous and idolatrous woman gave birth to an illegitimate son, she claimed that this son, Tammuz by name, was Nimrod reborn." Semiramis claimed that her son was supernaturally conceived [no human father] and that he was the promised seed, the "savior" promised by God in Genesis 3:15. "However, not only was the child worshipped, but the woman, the MOTHER, was also worshipped as much (or more) than the son!" Nimrod deified as the god of the sun and father of creation. Semiramis became the goddess of the moon, fertility, etc.[63]

The Tower of Babel was and still is the beginning of Satan's home base on earth. It is now called Babylon, and in ancient times it was a very central city, powerful, flourishing, full of every evil and paganistic religion and practice known to man. It was the birthplace for evil post-flood. Babylon fell into shambles, but just a few years ago it was being rebuilt by Sadam Hussein. It will be very influential in the end-times, and then God will utterly destroy it (see Isaiah 13). *And he cried mightily with a strong voice, saying "Babylon the great is fallen, is fallen, is become the habitation of devils, and the hold of every foul spirit, and a cage of every unclean and hateful bird!"* (Revelation 18:2; NIV). Throughout Jewish tradition unclean birds such as owls and storks usually represent demonic spirits.

Do you ever wonder why God describes and compares demonic spirits with animals? We can study and learn from animals; we can "see" them. Take the owl for instance; they have special down on their feathers so they are virtually silent in their approach. They are also a nocturnal bird, and prey on unsuspecting rodents. They are able to see at great distances and can turn their heads and see in every direction, and their talons are incredibly sharp. A stork can stand virtually still for hours, blending into his environment, "watching" his prey until they are comfortable with his presence. They don't notice those legs in the water weren't there earlier in the day. Then he strikes, fast, with precision, for his kill, and devours his prey with one gulp. Many demonic spirits prey upon humans in the same fashion.

The Tower of Babel was another way copycat Satan tried to "exalt himself up to heaven." Men proved their mental capacity for evil and ingenuity, and as we have learned from our other texts, the fallen angels and demonic geniuses, so graciously given to us by Satan himself, helped us advance our understanding of the cosmos and we began to build the Tower of Babel. Men were rebelling against God again…by not scattering over the face of the earth and populating it. So they got this bright idea from, hmmm…no don't tell me, an Intelligent Deceiver! They would build a tower reaching up to heaven! (see Genesis 11:1–8). They got so far on the project God Almighty himself said, *"Then nothing they plan to do will be impossible for them."* So God confused their speech, which is what Babel means in Hebrew—confusion. It is also where we get our contemporary phrase—"babbling idiot"! We are so foolish to believe our superior technology is really superior at all to the ancient peoples. They had giants with arrogant superhuman strength, endowed with angelic (secret) knowledge to help them move huge stones and teach them the secrets of the earth and the cosmos. Even God admitted to us they could build this tower reaching to heaven! Think of the massive engineering, architectural design, and atmospheric issues they would have had to overcome! We are currently trying to build a tower or elevator to the heavens ourselves. Work is underway, government grants given—how are we any different from these peoples? This Intelligent Deceiver is the originator and author of confusion, a city and world government bent on the destruction of all mankind for the evil elevation of a fallen angel.

The Paganization of Christianity

Satan would waste no time after the crucifixion and death of Christ to again try to establish "Babylon" by infusing his New Age ideas into the newly established Christian church.

As Christians today we celebrate more pagan influences and deities in our "Christian holidays" than probably at any other time in history. This is largely thanks to a Roman politician, the first "Christian" Roman Emperor: Constantine.

"Flavius Valerius Aurelius Constantinus (27 February c. 280 –22 May 337), commonly known as Constantine I, (among Roman Catholics) and Constantine the Great, or Saint Constantine (among Eastern Orthodox and Byzantine Catholic Christians), was an

Illyrian Roman Emperor, proclaimed Augustus by his troops in 306, who ruled an ever-growing portion of the Roman Empire until his death. Best known for being the first Christian Roman Emperor, the Edict of Milan—issued by his co-emperor Licinius—helped to put an end to institutionalized persecution of Christians in the Empire."[64]

Constantine had a huge political problem on his hands when he delivered his Edict of Milan. How do you integrate Christian beliefs with pagan religions and keep the peace? The pagans were not about to embrace Christianity. Deeply devoted to their beliefs, they certainly did not want to give up all of their feast days and celebrations to various gods (well over thirty-three thousand of them!) in lieu of just one God. The other problem was the newly converted Christians were still celebrating the pagan holidays. What to do?

As a politician, Constantine wanted to keep peace. This is where Intelligent Deception comes into play. The Christians were already very well versed and used to the pagan holidays and feast days, so…let's make it easy and integrate their beliefs into the pagan beliefs! It would be a compromise. Recognize, compromising is a tactic of the devil. It allows for little defilements to grow into huge, detestable practices.

The Sabbath has always been the seventh day, the last day of the week, a Saturday. But the pagans celebrated Sunday, the first day of the week, in honor of the sun god. Since Jesus arose from the grave on a Sunday, why not integrate the two holy days and make Sunday the new Sabbath? An easy enough compromise right? Even though Sunday is not the Sabbath, as defined in the scriptures, Christians to this day celebrate Sunday as the Sabbath. Clever critter. Now I write this not to condemn Christians going to church on Sunday, but only to inform. Did you ever wonder if you were missing out on something, a special blessing from God by not observing the original

Sabbath? ...*all who keep the Sabbath without desecrating it and who hold fast to my covenant—these I will bring to my holy mountain and give them joy in my house of prayer* (Isaiah 56:6–7; NIV). According to this verse we are offered a special treat by keeping the Sabbath. God himself will take us to his holy mountain and give us a special measure of joy! I guess you could look at it like a special group of kids getting a trip to Disney Land!

Let's take a look at another of our most sacred holiday celebrations: Easter, the celebration of the very core of our faith, Jesus' death on the cross and resurrection. Jesus was crucified over the Passover celebration of the Jews; he was the sacrificial perfect lamb, the blood on the doorpost of every believing Christian that the angel of death now had to "pass over" their spirit, giving them eternal life. Jesus specifically chose this holiday to become sin for us. But, Satan had other plans; he named it Easter, which is a derivative of the goddess Ishtar. Do you ever wonder why we celebrate Easter with bunnies that lay eggs? Bunnies don't lay eggs, they are mammals, and no, it's not just some cute tradition brought about by the commercialization of America. Or, why the Easter lily? We have been celebrating it this way for nearly seventeen hundred years!

According to the web site Christiananswers.net: "Some called the Mother Goddess 'ISHTAR' (originally pronounced 'Easter'). In other lands, she was called Eostre, Astarte, Ostera, and Eastre. Other names for Semiramis, the Mother Goddess include: Wife of Baal, Ashtaroth or Ashtoreth, and Queen of Heaven. The Mother goddess was frequently worshipped as the goddess of fertility—and as a sort of Mother Nature and goddess of Spring and sexual love and birth. She was also worshipped as a mediator between god and man. Sexual orgies and temple prostitutes were often used in her worship and in attempting to gain her favor." [65]

According to Royce Carlson, who writes about the pagan origins of Easter:

> Easter celebrations were held hundreds of years before Christ was born as festivals of spring honoring Eostre, the great mother goddess of the Saxons. This name was fashioned after the ancient word for spring, Eastre. The goddess Ostara was the Norse equivalent whose symbols were the hare and the egg. From this comes our modern tradition of celebrating Easter with eggs and bunnies.
>
> ...Attis derived his mythology from even earlier gods, Osiris, Dionysus, and Orpheus, who also were supposed to have been born of a virgin and suffered death and resurrection as long as 500 years before Christ was born. The death of Attis was commemorated on a Friday and the resurrection was celebrated three days later on Sunday.
>
> ...What we now call Easter lilies were revered by the ancients as symbols of fertility and representative of the male genitalia. The ancient Babylonian religions had rituals involving dyed eggs, as did the ancient Egyptians.
>
> The Christian version of Easter is celebrated after the first full moon after the vernal equinox. Modern day neo-pagans usually have their spring celebrations on the day of the equinox. Either way, these celebrations have gone on every year continuously for over 2,500 years. [66]

The following ruling is disturbing, because the council did everything in its power to avoid having the Christian resurrection celebration fall on the Jewish Passover. We see the beginnings of the anti-Semitism movement start here:

> Prior to A.D. 325, Easter was variously celebrated on different days of the week, including Friday, Saturday, and Sunday. In that year, the Council of Nicaea was convened by Emperor Constantine. It issued the Easter Rule which states Easter shall be celebrated on the first Sunday that occurs after the first full moon on or after the vernal equinox. However, a caveat must be introduced here. The "full moon" in the rule is the ecclesiastical full moon, which is defined as the fourteenth day of a tabular lunation, where day 1 corresponds to the ecclesiastical New Moon. It does not always occur on the same date as the astronomical full moon. The ecclesiastical "vernal equinox" is always on March 21. Therefore, Easter must be celebrated on a Sunday between the dates of March 22 and April 25. [67]

As Christians, I think it is important to understand where these many traditions arise from. To some it may be shocking, and to others it may infuriate you that this information has been withheld from you. Information allows individuals the ability to choose, rather than to blindly follow the pack. I encourage each of you to practice these holidays out of your own conscience. Instead of practicing Easter, why not celebrate Passover? Why not start new traditions, based on the Bible? Why not take back what the devil has stolen?

Christmas

Our modern Christmas traditions can be traced back to many pagan winter solstice festivals. Everything from Christmas trees to Yule logs and mistletoe were a form of ritual and spiritual observance to a deity. Even the Puritans strictly prohibited their members from celebrating Christmas due to its pagan origins.

> The addition of Christ to the celebration of the winter solstice did not occur until 300 years after Christ died and as late as 1800. The Christmas tree is derived from several solstice traditions. The Romans decked their halls with garlands of laurel and placed candles in live trees to decorate for the celebration of Saturnalia. The practice of exchanging gifts at a winter celebration is also pre-Christian and is from the Roman Saturnalia. They would exchange good-luck gifts called Stenae (lucky fruits). They also would have a big feast just like we do today.
>
> The Scandinavian solstice traditions had a lot of influences on our celebration besides the hanging of ornaments on evergreen trees. Their ancient festival was called Yuletide and celebrated the return of the sun. Even the date of Christmas, December 25, was borrowed from another religion. At the time Christmas was created in AD 320, Mithraism was very popular. The early Christian church had gotten tired of their futile efforts to stop people celebrating the solstice and the birthday of Mithras, the Persian sun god. Mithras' birthday was December 25. So the pope at the time decided to make Jesus' official birthday coincide with Mithras' birthday. [68]

Is Christmas bad? Not necessarily, but it is easy to see how Satan rules the day, and the fruit of the holiday speaks louder than words. Americans especially are bombarded by commercialism, extreme stress, overeating, over spending, accumulation of large debt, and ending up with a bunch of junk you just end up throwing out within another year or two. Does this sound like a Christ-like celebration? Do we acknowledge and celebrate the birth of our Lord and savior in this tradition? Most people don't even look forward to the day. Do we make an attempt to find out the day of Christ's birth? The Bible doesn't give us an exact day, but it does offer us clues as to when it may have occurred. The biggest clue is the shepherds; they are out guarding and tending their flock at night. *And there were shepherds living out in the fields nearby, keeping watch over their flocks at night* (Luke 2:8; NIV). Shepherds watched their flocks during the nighttime from spring to fall. Spring is lambing season, so they would have to keep a close eye on their flock for those ewes having trouble lambing, and also for predators drawn to the smell of afterbirth, and fall is the time for weaning. There are strong arguments for a spring or an autumn birth for Christ among many good Bible scholars.

There is a strong argument for December 25 being the day the Magi did present their gifts, but not the physical birth of Christ. "On December 25 of 2 BC as it entered retrograde, Jupiter reached full stop in its travel through the fixed stars. Magi viewing from Jerusalem would have seen it stopped in the sky above the little town of Bethlehem." [69]

What to do with your family? These traditions are so ingrained into our psyche it is hard to imagine not celebrating as we do. Not to mention the corporate church observes these holidays as well. Again, here is an opportunity to get back what Satan has stolen. What a great way to explain the pagan origins of these holidays while you are decorating your tree with your family, and compare and contrast it to the biblical account. I guarantee the story will *stick* more. Why not start a new tradition? The tree you decorate is not dedicated to the pagan gods, but instead allow it to be a symbol of another tree, the tree in which Christ was crucified. The ornaments could be symbols of the fruits of the spirit, or as offerings of love and dedication to the savior. Use your imagination, and create a holiday with a deeper meaning. As Christians we have our freedom in Christ, we do not live under the law. It is not that the old laws are not important, and I think it is wise for one to be familiar with the laws because it gives us valuable insight into the one we love, Christ. As humans we do not live under the law because we couldn't keep it if we tried—read Romans! But as Christians, I think it wise to understand our heritage in Christ, and realize Christ fulfilled the law for us, and we cannot earn our salvation by deeds...that's called religion!

Halloween

Halloween is also a blatant pagan holiday. The modern holiday of Halloween may have its origins in the ancient Celtic festival known as Samhain, which signified the end of the harvest season and a celebration of the greater sabbats of the wiccan religious system.

"Pope Gregory IV standardized the date of All Saints' Day, or All Hallows' Day, on November 1 in the name of the entire Western Church in 835. As the church day began at sunset, the holiday coincided exactly with Samhain. It is claimed that the choice of date seems consistent with the common practice of leaving pagan festivals and buildings intact (e.g., the Pantheon), while overlaying a Christian meaning." [70]

The problem with Halloween is it is a "crossover" type of holiday. Children as well as adults who would normally not have anything to do with the occult will play occultic games such as being involved in a séance or Ouija board. A seemingly harmless game can result in serious entanglement. Even the bobbing of apples was a sorcery game. Bobbing for apples was a form of divination: if you were successful in catching an apple, it had specific meaning regarding your love life. Demons rely on these innocent games to perpetrate their lies and inflict harm on the unsuspecting. Many Christian churches today recognize the inherent dangers of Halloween and offer alternative fall festivals for children to attend.

The answer is still the same, align or realign your beliefs with the holy scriptures.

Chapter Four

DEMONS

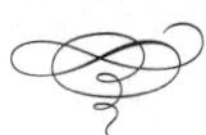

Our sons Gibborim shall incarnate in the bodies of man, of those who are mighty and wise, to inspire and counsel them. They shall be called "evil spirits" and "demons" by the ignorant and fearful, but the wise shall be known as "Daimons," for these shall be the guardian geniuses of the great of earth, who shall inspire the best among man to great heights, to beautiful works of art, and to further discoveries of earth and kosmos. The gift of civilization shall not be obliterated.

—*Liber Diabolus* by Faustus Scorpius[71]

To keep Satan from getting the advantage over us: for we are not ignorant of his wiles and intentions.

—2 Corinthians 2:11

If *Daimons* were sent by Satan to be our guardian geniuses to inspire us to great heights of humanity—I would have to say results speak louder than words in this case. Our world may be advanced, we may go to the stars, have supercomputers, genetic cloning etc., but why is cancer a billion dollar business, instead of cured? Why do we continue to murder, steal, and destroy each other, destroy ourselves?

Jesus tells us they deceive: liars from the loins of liars; like produces like. *And no wonder, for Satan himself masquerades as an angel of light. It is not surprising, then, if his servants masquerade as servants of righteousness. Their end will be what their actions deserve* (2 Corinthians 11:14–15; NIV).

The Apostle Paul admonishes us to approach evil with the innocence of a child. In other words, when you tell a child about a monster under the bed, they will believe you. He is telling us to believe in an evil adversary that means to harm, mame, and destroy your relationship with God. Paul also describes these "gods" (demons) as weak and miserable principals in Galatians 4:9. The Bible tells us demons or evil spirits are: evil, powerful, numerous, unclean, under Satan, recognize Christ, possess human beings, overcome men, know their destiny, receive sacrifices, instigate deceit, torment and torture, blind, ensnare, trouble, tempt, afflict, accuse, sift, beguile, disguise, slander, seduce, they are fiercesome, deceitful, proud, arrogant, hateful, cowardly, wicked, subtle, cause disease and dysfunction in the human body, produce insanity, steal, kill, destroy, divide, divinate, and on, and on…

If you were a pure narcissistic being who wanted to exalt yourself to godhood and be like god, you would naturally copy what that being does, right? Only it would be in a sick, twisted, perverted, hateful way. Stick with me here. I think demons are part of Satan's unholy trinity. In our Heavenly Father's trinity we have Father, Son, and Holy Ghost. Satan wants a part of that action, so he copies the same outline. He exalts himself as the father, he has a son—the Antichrist, but how does he get a holy ghost? Something that *inspires and inhabits mankind* a *gift* to the children of men, to produce unholy fruit just as the Holy Spirit produces good fruit, and represents his presence and down payment for their souls? Well, that would be where demons come in. They copy the Holy Spirit's actions in a very unholy, sick, perverted way.

Let's discuss the Holy Spirit for a minute and compare and

contrast. The Holy Spirit is a gift from God, as a down payment for our souls; it is the physical outward manifestation Jesus exists and lives within us. The Holy Spirit is the comforter. It speaks to us, teaches us, strives with us, helps our infirmities, is grieved and resisted, renews, convicts, regenerates, indwells, anoints, baptizes, guides, empowers, sanctifies, bears witness, gives joy and discernment, bears fruit, reveals the things of God, and most importantly of all, it moves as "it wills." These are all positive attributes, all about the helping of mankind. Compare that to the demonic list of attributes in our first paragraph. Many are the exact opposites of the Holy Spirit list.

Let's examine the fruits of the Spirit: *love, joy, peace, patience, kindness, goodness, faithfulness, gentleness, and self-control* (Galatians 5:22–23; NIV). Now let's look at the fruit or acts of the sinful nature: *hatred, envy, impurity, factions, sexual immorality, debauchery, idolatry, witchcraft, discord, jealousy, fits of rage, selfish ambition, dissensions, drunkenness, orgies, lust, evil desires, greed, anger, malice slander, deceit* (see Galatians 5:19–21 and Colossians 3:5–9). Do you notice any glaring differences? Such as the fruits of the Spirit are all about the *spirit*, manifesting in goodwill in our bodies and towards others? Do you notice the *carnal* nature of the fruits of the sinful nature? Total self-realization going on here! Selfishness, bent on the harm or destruction of others and self. Do you see where I am going with this? Satan cannot be omnipresent, but with his demonic minions he can affect every human on the planet, he can get a full report of their behavior, at any time. Do you see how he tries to set himself up to fulfill his ambitious "I will" goals?

So now we know what they are capable of, how do they do it? What do they look like? Demons, we are told, are spirits, so that means they can take on pretty much any form they want in order to deceive you. Remember, angels can look like men, and if fallen angels are their true fathers, like father, like son. They will take on any form they can, don any costume to make you believe they are *servants of righteousness.* The holy scriptures do not give us a physical description, just a description of their characteristics and actions. I know of many people who have the ability to *see* demons or have seen them at one point. This is a gift of the Holy Spirit called discernment, but Satan also gives his perverted gift, and it is called divination or clairvoyance.

The impressions I have gotten are like staring at the sun for too long, and when you look away, you still see sunspots. This is how I have always seen them, more of a shadowy outline. People have told me the ones they have seen are very much as they are portrayed in artwork: gargoyle-like, black hooded figures, bat-like, rat-like, and skeletal. Some have wings; some don't, which stands to reason since two types of angels have wings. The ones I have gotten the impression of were mostly small in stature, four feet high, dark and shadowy, imp-like. Another I have gotten the distinct impression of was a disgusting, monstrous creature, and one other was a completely hairless, naked old man, corpse-like, with an ashen gray color. When they are seen or felt, terror and fear, dread, and a sense of foreboding and death accompany them. They are often associated with overpowering negative emotions: feelings of being dirty, or unclean, cold, alone, intense anxiety, insanity, fear, intense hatred, or an overpowering will to harm self or another, compulsions, addictions, physical deterioration, and so forth.

Remember God giving special sight, or taking the scales off of their eyes, so certain people could see angels in their surroundings? Modern science may have a way of explaining the gift of discernment and the unholy gift of divination. New advances in quantum physics helps us define many mysteries of our universe which we cannot comprehend, take for example the Superstring Theory.

EXTRA DIMENSIONS

Our physical space is observed to have only three large dimensions—and taken together with time as the fourth dimension—a physical theory must take this into account. However, nothing prevents a theory from including more than four dimensions, per se. In the case of String Theory, consistency requires space-time to have ten, eleven, or twenty-six dimensions. The conflict between observation and theory is resolved by making the unobserved dimensions compactified.

"Our minds have difficulty visualizing higher dimensions because we can only move in three spatial dimensions. Even then, we only see in 2+1 dimensions; vision in 3 dimensions would allow one to see all sides (including the inside) of an object simultaneously." [72]

So according to this theory, we most likely have ten or more dimensions, but we only *see* three, and experience the fourth—time! The spirit realm must operate in a different dimension, a dimension in which God only gives a supernatural gift of the Holy Spirit to see it, and Satan freely gives to people who delve into the occult. Interesting to note, many people who have used drugs and are "tweaking" have the ability to *see* demons; instead of taking this visual cue as reality, they chalk it up to a "bad trip" or hallucinations.

When we study Genesis 1–3, we get a sense the world was a much different place. Beyond the obvious absence of physical disease, we know God physically manifested himself to Adam and walked with him. We can assume angels were round as well. Adam and Eve were naked, but not shamefully naked, which implies they were covered somehow, possibly with God's glory and or light (clothed in righteousness?). We don't know exactly, but after the fall things changed drastically. Many scholars believe our world originally had ten dimensions, four that are knowable and six that cannot be seen.

When Adam and Eve sinned, some suggest our four dimensions were *ripped* apart from the other six, and we now know and live in height, length, width, and time as proven by Einstein. The other six are "curled" in numbers too small for the average human to contemplate, unless you have an advanced math or quantum physics degree. I find it interesting the temple curtain was *ripped* from top to bottom during the earthquake when Jesus died on the cross, symbolizing the Holy of Holies was now open to anyone. *At that moment the curtain of the temple was torn in two from top to bottom. The earth shook and the rocks split* (Matthew 27:51; NIV). God is certainly consistent and restorative. When I think about Adam and Eve having experienced at least ten dimensions it is hard to imagine what life was like for them, post-Eden. It must have been quite dull. Also a rip in the very fabric of dimensional space would have been terrifying! Cosmically speaking, we can only wonder as to what that felt like, what physical manifestations occurred to the planet! No wonder they sewed fig leaves to cover themselves and hid from God!

Do Dogs Have the Ability to See Extra Dimensions?

This may be a weird question, but hey, so is talking about demons. "*Lord have mercy on my son," he said. "He has seizures and is suffering greatly. He often falls into the fire or into the water. I brought him to your disciples, but they could not heal him."… "Bring the boy to me." Jesus rebuked the demon, and it came out of the boy, and he was healed from that moment* (Matthew 17:15–18; NIV). There are many excellent service dog programs in our country, and one of the special abilities certain dogs seem to have is they are able to *sense* an oncoming seizure or epileptic event, sometimes up to half an hour before the patient has an episode. The dogs are so keen and so accurate, they have allowed many people suffering from seizures the ability to carry on a much more normal life. In the above Bible passage and also in Matthew 4:24, the Bible talks about a demon that is causing seizures. Jesus rebukes the evil spirit and casts him out. If epilepsy is caused by a demonic entity we could draw an interesting assumption that the service dogs may be able to *see* or *sense* extra dimensional activity. Take also the instance of Balaam's donkey, who was also able to *see* the angel of death.

I have had at least two encounters where I knew an animal could see something evil and I could not. One was a fellow student with whom I went to college, whose personality changed so drastically, all of her friends and I were very concerned. I had a pet bunny, which had always been very friendly every time my friend came over to visit. But after her countenance change, the rabbit would run and hide the minute she came through the door and give several loud warning thumps with his hind feet (a defense mechanism to warn other rabbits a predator is near). Shortly thereafter, my friend was involved with a deliverance, and I witnessed her release from bondage to freedom. The rabbit never had a problem with her again.

The other encounter occurred one evening when our dog, Ruby acted very strangely; she is a great watchdog, fearless and fearsome. However she would not come down the stairs, she hackled up, had a strange, worried bark and growl, and kept staring at the same spot on the ceiling by the kitchen. My husband felt a little freaked out; I felt nothing. I was looking for a bug, or maybe a light reflecting off of something, but could find no obvious physical evidence for her odd behavior. I yelled at the dog, told her to stop, and come down the stairs. She refused; her behavior became even more worried and she began to whine. Finally, a bit frustrated at her ruckus, I decided to talk to the spot on the ceiling and told whatever it was that it was not welcome in our house and I commanded it to leave in Jesus' name. Immediately, Ruby stopped her frantic behavior and came down the stairs, tail wagging.

There are many other well-documented, weird animal behaviors in which animals can sense earthquakes, cancerous lesions, evil spirits, and the like. So there may be credence to the fact they are able to see or sense extra-dimensional behaviors.

Demons primary motivation is to deceive you and to fulfill their carnal lusts through you. Demons seek embodiment. This would make sense if they are truly the dead spirits of the Nephilim. They were carnal in life, why would they not seek to continue that same thread in the afterlife? They are now in spirit form and unable to partake of physical pleasures unless they have a body to inhabit. The scriptures also tell us our flesh is weak. This also fulfills Satan's goals of putting his bands of slavery on humankind. How else could he control the free will of man? We naturally want to worship; we naturally want to believe in a higher something. God created the earth in such a magnificent way, it literally shouts of his glory. If we had something that was evil sent to inhabit, torment, and control us, then it would take our focus off of our natural God-given inclination to worship God. It would hinder our walk, separate us from the divine, for that which is holy cannot stand the things that are unholy; it is against his nature. Now send in a redeemer whose blood buys our spirits, washes us clean, and inhabits our hearts instead of just our bodies, and you have a new nature. You are a new creation. The old one is forgotten.

Possession

This leads us to the controversial subject of possession. Many Christians and learned preachers do not believe Christians today can be possessed of the devil. I struggled with this concept myself, rationalizing my previous experience with demonic forces as being an "outside" oppression. But inside me, I had changed. My behavior was so uncharacteristic, so bazaar, and my thinking so messed up, and I felt black...black to the center of my very heart. I felt as though my heart had actually turned to a black, tarry, ashen organ! What was that? Can these theologians explain that to me? I will make a bold stand here, and say without a shadow of doubt in my mind, I was a very well-meaning Christian young woman, possessed *and* oppressed by these demonic evil spirits. I know I had something other than the Holy Spirit living inside of me. I am speaking from my own experience, and I hope this helps other Christians, who have had similar experiences and are living under a cloud of condemnation and guilt, wondering if there is something wrong with them and their salvation.

The best argument or explanation for demon possession in Christians comes from a Christian medical doctor who states:

> I have to chuckle a bit when someone piously tells me, "A Christian can't be indwelt by a demon because he is the temple of the Holy Spirit and the two can't be in the same house at the same time." Solomon said it best: *But will God indeed dwell on the earth? Behold, the heaven and the heaven of heavens cannot contain thee; how much less this house that I have built?* (1 Kings 8:27; KJV). God the Holy Spirit is omnipresent. This being the case, how can demons dwell anywhere if the two cannot be in the same place at the same time?[73]

According to the book *Protecting Your Home From Spiritual Darkness*:

Demons cover their existence by deception, so that people concentrate on what they see, or how they feel, and overlook spiritual causes.

1. Fear of demons causes people to deny their existence.
2. Lack of spiritual discernment.
3. Most modern preaching and teaching avoids the subject of demonic activity.
4. First century faith has largely been replaced by twentieth century rationalism.
5. Our western mind set keeps us from validating that which cannot be explained through scientific study.[74]

We will attempt to explain the anatomy of possession as it relates to our actual physical body, which Christ called the "temple."

The term *possession* in the Greek is *Daimonivzomai*;[75] its literal definition is "to be under the power of a demon." In the original King James Version of the Bible, this word is used a total of thirteen times (a true unlucky number?). The most common occurrences talked about are in the New Testament, in all four gospels. The Hebrew word for possession is *Qanah*; it means "to get, acquire, create, buy, possess."[76] It's mentioned only in the Old Testament, and it is used over eighty-four times, but nowhere in the context of an evil spirit. Greek is a very precise language; if the authors of the gospels used the exact word for possession, don't you think they meant it? Our English use of the word possession implies ownership, just as the Hebrew word *Qanah* implies. So what I am saying here is most theologians use this form of the word for possession, *meaning ownership by the demons or Satan.* But if you use the word in the Greek context, which is what Jesus intended, it simply means we are under their power; they don't own us! They may have a legal right to be there, but we will discuss that farther down the road. I think the matter of possession is all about the language, in Christian circles—I prefer the term "demonic trespass."

The reason I bring this to your attention is that most Christians are taught once you become born-again, the Holy Spirit comes to live inside you, which is true, and the Holy Spirit occupies that seat, or your heart, and all evil spirits which may have been taking up residence there leave at that moment, and no other evil spirits are able to get in. If that is gospel truth, then I am one weird, whacked-out nut job; I am the true exception to the rule! I accepted Christ when I was about twelve or thirteen years old, so the Holy Spirit came to live within me then. How is it that I struggled with poor self-worth, depression, gluttony/compulsive binging, swearing, lying, pre-marital sex, alcohol, etc.? I sinned a lot! And then when I was eighteen, I rededicated my life to Christ, I was baptized with the Holy Spirit with the evidence of speaking in tongues (see the different infillings of the Holy Spirit in 1 Corinthians 12) only to have my biggest battles with oppression and possession ever in the ensuing years to come? I was born-again, tongue-talking, Bible-reading, and church-going…the works! We need to quit our stupid arguments and just read scripture and believe what it says. We are taught by Jesus to come to him as little children with a particular brand of innocence and belief. Jesus' primary mission was to heal the sick, cast out demons, and offer forgiveness and salvation to the enslaved.

If demon possession and demons weren't such a big deal, then why did Jesus deal so swiftly with them and why do we have so many examples in the Bible? Also, if there are many infillings of the Holy Spirit, then can we safely assume Satan would also provide many "infillings" of evil spirits? Wouldn't that help him fulfill his "I wills"?

In dealing with the question of possession and the Christian,

I must go back to scripture. So much of the teaching on possession is done within the context of the New Testament, with Jesus or the disciples casting demons out of Jews or gentiles that were not yet saved or maybe saved. But there is one instance in the Old Testament that is absolutely glaring. It is about King Saul. Go with me to 1 Samuel: *The Spirit of the Lord will come upon you in power, and you will prophecy with them; and you will be changed into a different person* (1 Samuel 10:6; NIV). Samuel is talking to Saul right before he is made king. Now I am no great Bible theologian, but isn't this the very definition of being saved? King Saul goes on to compromise his relationship with God and disobey the word of the Lord given to him by Samuel the prophet (exercising his free will to turn his back on God, just as I did). His biggest mistake was trying to do a little good, and rationalizing his actions, like not killing all the Amelikites and bringing back some of the livestock to offer God as a burnt offering (see 1 Samuel 15). Sound familiar? *Now the spirit of the Lord had departed from Saul, and an evil spirit from the Lord tormented him... Whenever the spirit from God came upon Saul, David would take his harp and play, then relief would come to Saul; he would feel better, and the evil spirit would leave him,* (1 Samuel 16:14, 23; NIV). And a little bit further along in the story: *The next day an evil spirit from God came forcefully upon Saul...Saul had a spear in his hand and he hurled it, saying to himself, "I'll pin David to the wall." But David eluded him twice* (1 Samuel 18:10; NIV). If you go on to Chapter 19 Saul again tries to kill David, and at the end of the chapter is **filled with the Holy Spirit again:** *...The Spirit of God came even upon him, and he walked along prophesying...all that day,* (Samuel 19:23; NIV). Saul continues on his rampage and tries to kill David over and over again, hunting him down. He kills a bunch of priests at Nob. He even finds a witch at Endor, which is odd, since his own edict had cut off all the mediums and spiritists from the land, and goes on to continue to hunt down David and ends up committing suicide in Chapter 31.

As we saw in 1 Samuel 16, the Holy Spirit departed from Saul, and the evil spirit took over. The Holy Spirit again comes to Saul when he is on a murderous rampage against David, and stays with him all day. It obviously leaves again, and he spirals completely out of control from there. So what does this tell us? We can have the Holy Spirit, and it seems to come and go as "It Wills," but the going seems to be in relationship with disobedience and sin. It leaves when we are not walking in sanctification. Leaving a spiritual door opened to evil spirits. Could this be what is happening to Christians today? Are we baptized in the Spirit, he lives with us, but then leaves unnoticed when we have a grave sin in our lives, leaving space for spiritual squatters to come in to our temples and run amuck? It seems pretty clear to me this may be the case.

Demons who have been "cast out" can leave demonic damage, just as evicted renters leave damaged houses. This may be the consequences of sin, mental strongholds, believing lies, illness, etc.

I have personally had two separate instances of this happening to me. But both times the Holy Spirit literally kicked out the invading evil spirit. I did not know I ever had one living on the inside of me; they never announced their arrival. The other theory is evil spirits can and do occupy the mind and the body, and the deeper ones can occupy the spirit.

Here is what happened to me: The first encounter happened when I was married to a man that God had specifically, audibly told me *not* to marry. I struggled, and rationalized, and agonized over my decision and finally married him. I was in utter disobedience to God. The man I married was not a Christian. I spent five years in sheer torment, separated from my family and not walking in God's perfect will for my life. Four years into the marriage, I finally came to the realization that I had to repent for my disobedience. I went through three days of bitter sobbing, wondering what to do next and how I was going to resolve the mess I had created. I prayed in the spirit for three days, wondering if I was having a mental breakdown, I was so distraught. On the third day, I was kneeling beside my bed praying when I started to dry heave. I was crying so hard I could hardly breathe. I remember feeling out of control and really questioning my sanity. The dry heaving became stronger as I continued to pray in the spirit. Finally, I coughed it up. I didn't see anything, but what I felt was incredible! I instantly stopped crying, I felt peace and joy and release! At the time, I was too immature of a Christian to understand or have the wherewithal to even ask God what it was. I now know it was a spirit of disobedience the Holy Spirit expelled from my life in response to my act of repentance. This evil spirit had inhabited my body for years along with the Holy Spirit! Sincere repentance was the catalyst for its expulsion.

The second instance was also life changing. It happened nearly ten years later. I have struggled with my weight since I was a baby. I remember going on my first diet when I was five! I tried, I struggled, I worked out, I dieted, all unsuccessfully. Food, especially sweets were absolutely irresistible to me. I had observed that other people could go to a potluck and have one cookie and be satisfied. That dumbfounded me! I could not stop. When I was at home it wasn't unlike me to eat a whole family-sized bag of M & M's or eat boxes or batches of cookies. I would eat past full, my stomach literally felt as though it was going to split. I hated myself, I hated that I could not stop. So many times I had cried out to God, "What is wrong with me?" I never vomited, although there were times I tried. I just continued to eat, without control, binging night after night, and feeling more guilt and condemnation than ever. It was so compulsive when the thought of a particular type of food would cross my mind, I would do almost anything to go get it!

Finally, I went on another diet, the Maker's Diet. I repented of my addiction and idolization of food. I worked hard at it, eating healthy, God-given foods. Even though I really wasn't losing any weight, I felt good and knew I was doing the right thing for my temple and making a sacrifice of my body for God. Three months into it, I started to feel sad and sullen and irritated. I couldn't understand where these strong emotions were coming from. Even members of my Bible study commented on my changed countenance. I had been crying at home for three days, continually. I could not stop sobbing, violent, breath-taking sobs! I came home from Bible study that night and went straight to bed. The sadness was overwhelming! I had determined God and I were going to get to the bottom of this thing, and I was going to deal with it. I began to pray in the spirit, sobbing, snot running freely, what a sight! And, you guessed it, a half-hour into praying, I started to dry heave! It was violent, gagging, dry heaving, so violent that I could not even continue to pray! And then there it was; I coughed it up. Instant relief! I stopped crying, and the overwhelming sadness was gone. I felt instant, overwhelming peace! This time I knew I had won a spiritual battle! I boldly and incredulously asked God, "What was that?" My answer came into my spirit, instantly. "That was a spirit of gluttony, which has been with you since childhood. It was very distraught it had to leave you." Well, halleluiah! I wondered to myself, where the heck did I pick that up? And, to be honest, I never, ever thought of myself as a glutton! I noticed immediately my relationship with food changed. I am happy to report that it has been five years, and I have never once had the compulsion to binge. I can walk by food, candy, sweets, whatever and not even give it a second thought. Jesus has set me free!

Obviously the Holy Spirit was there, living in me both times, because I had the evidence of speaking in tongues. He had never left me! But, obviously he had been sharing space with these temple pests. This could be one instance of how we grieve the Holy Spirit! Through sanctification and repentance he helped me clean house! Jesus talks about "cleaning house" in Matthew: *"When an evil spirit comes out of a man, it goes through arid places seeking rest and does not find it. Then it says, 'I will return to the house that I left.' When it arrives, it finds the house unoccupied, swept clean and put into order. Then it goes and takes with it seven other spirits more wicked than itself, and they go in and live there. And the final condition of that man is worse than the first. That is how it will be with this wicked generation"* (Matthew 12:43–45; NIV). Now, Jesus was talking about people who had evil spirits cast out and either went back to their wicked ways (they contaminated their sterile field), or had a demonic legal right in effect in his house. This allowed the former demon to get a few of his friends and bring them in for a house party. Sanctification is the key to keeping a clean house, free from vermin and unwanted temple rats!

In the New Testament there are several examples of disciples living with Christ, the Holy Spirit incarnate, and Satan entering into them, and also during Peter's ministry of early Christians baptized in the Holy Spirit committing grave sins against the Spirit and allowing Satan access to their hearts. For example, consider Peter in Matthew 16:16–17. Jesus asks his disciples if they know who he is. They all are wrong, except Peter, who knew through the revelation of the Holy Spirit that Jesus was the Christ. Jesus applauds him and tells him he will be the foundation of his church, and that the gates of hell will not prevail against it. A few verses later Jesus rebukes Satan *in* Peter: *Peter took him aside, and began to rebuke him. "Never Lord!" he said. "This shall never happen to you!" Jesus turned and said to Peter,*

"Get behind me Satan!" (Matthew 16:22–23; NIV). Jesus didn't say, "Shut-up Peter; you are a fool, and you don't understand what you are saying." No, he talked directly to Peter, but instead of addressing him as Peter he calls him Satan! Why?

And again Judas Iscariot, who was a "hand-picked by the Holy Spirit" disciple from hundreds of followers, betrays Jesus right after taking the very first Holy Communion! Judas had been given power and authority to drive out demons in Jesus' name. He preached, healed the sick, he lived and worked with God incarnate! But scripture tells us Judas was a callous thief and embezzler (see John 12). In John 13, Jesus tells his disciples that one of them is going to betray him: *...as soon as he took the bread, Satan entered into him* (John 13:27; NIV).

Go to the post-Pentecostal church and the example of Ananias and Saphira in Acts 5:1–11. The new church was loving each other, selling property and helping each other out financially, when this husband and wife team sold a piece of property, told a *white lie*, and only gave a portion of the sale's price to the church. Peter responds: *"Ananias, how is it that Satan has filled your heart, that you have lied to the Holy Spirit and kept for yourself some of the money you received for the land?... You have not lied to men but to God"* (Acts 5:3; NIV). You know the story; they both are struck dead. Peter says they had the Holy Spirit and they lied to him! That Satan filled their hearts!

And again we see Paul, who wrote most of the New Testament: Galatians, 1st and 2nd Corinthians, Romans, Ephesians, Colossians, Philippians, Philemon, 1st and 2nd Timothy, and Titus. He did incredible things for the early church, evangelized the gentiles, healed the sick, cast out demons, was taken up to heaven and shown incredible sights, given supernatural knowledge, and yet he was inflicted by a messenger of Satan: *To keep me from becoming conceited because of these surpassingly great revelations, there was given me a thorn in my flesh, a messenger of Satan, to torment me, three times I pleaded with the Lord to take it away from me* (2 Corinthians 12: 7; NIV). A *messenger of Satan.* Angels, as we have learned, were messengers, and it was *in* his flesh, not on the outside of the flesh! Paul was born-again; he didn't say it was oppressing him from the outside, but that it was in him.

Are you having trouble with the mere thought of possession? Why? If you are a born-again Christian, Paul tells us Christ lives in us, that is, the Holy Spirit. In other words, this by definition is possession: we are under the power of God. We are *possessed* by the Holy Spirit. The Intelligent Deceiver wants to be "like God," so you can bet he is going to mimic this behavior.

Do you think it is possible the Holy Spirit may have occupied a certain amount of space in your body, but that leaves room for other unwanted temple pests? Jesus did say, *"Greater is He that is in you, than he that is in the world"* (1 John 4:4; NIV). I know this is hard to wrap your mind around but stick with me here. If a born-again Christian can sin—willfully sin, how is it the Holy Spirit allows this behavior to continue? Doesn't he throw a temper tantrum and tell you to stop what you are doing? The Bible tells us he is a gentleman, and he whispers to our soul and spirit and brings a feeling of conviction not condemnation. But how many times have you yourself ignored this warning? Sinning is fun! Otherwise we wouldn't do it! So we rationalize our thoughts and behaviors just as Eve did, and we do it anyway. We can repent later!

The Bible teaches us about this conflict happening in our body. *So I say, live by the Spirit, and you will not gratify the desires of the sinful nature. For the sinful nature desires what is contrary to the Spirit, and the Spirit what is contrary to the sinful nature. They are in conflict with each other, so that you do not do what you want, the acts of the sinful nature are obvious: Sexual immorality, impurity, debauchery; idola-*

try and witchcraft; hatred, discord, jealousy, fits of rage, selfish ambition, dissensions, factions and envy; drunkenness, orgies and the like. I warn you, as I did before, those who live like this will not inherit the kingdom of God (Galatians 5:16–21; NIV).

So Galatians answers us pretty clearly, we have a serious war going on within our members. Could it be possible Satan and his demons are lying to you right now? Deceiving you into thinking there is no way possible for you to be under the power of their evil? Satan is the father of lies. *He came to steal, kill and destroy!* (John 10:10; NIV).

As Christians we have been a taught a false doctrine of demons. It is simply: once saved, always saved. According to the previously stated verse in Galatians 5, this is simply not true. We must keep ourselves pure, free from evil. Remember the sterile field of the holiness of God? Paul gives us a stern warning: *I warn you, as I did before, those who live like this will not inherit the kingdom of God.* He is saying that something as seemingly simple and benign as really wanting your neighbor's car (envy) without repentance just lost you the kingdom of heaven. As a Christian, even if you are saved, if you continue to live a life of defilement and impurity, in other words, continue to sin without repentance, you are making your bed in hell; you have no place in the kingdom of God. This is very scary stuff, and we find it repellant and revolting to think God could be so "harsh and unfair." Again understand his holiness, his sterile field. The answer is simply repent, be washed of your sins, and stay within the sterile field, don't defile yourself. Nowhere in scripture does it say our salvation is permanent from the day we accept Christ. It is not secure until the end when you work at it and keep yourself pure. Instead, we are told over and over again, to work out our salvation with fear and trembling (see Philippians 2:12). Don't stray from the sterile field!

Demons merely reflect the nature and character of their father—Satan. We already know he is subtle and crafty (see Genesis 3:1 and 2 Corinthians 11:3), so we can deduce most times he will not announce his presence or intentions. Do you really think demons are going to knock on your temple door and announce themselves to you? Would you let them in if they did? If Satan is described as a thief, then his children (demons) will act the same way. What do thieves do? They slink around, case the joint, look for an opened window, an unlocked door, and silently creep in; they hide quietly while silently looting your soul. They hide in the control room of your mind.

This is the complete opposite of the Holy Spirit; the scriptures tell us the Holy Spirit always comes in with evidence he is there. He makes some noise! We see and hear an outward evidence of his divine presence. In other words, he announces himself: *When the day of Pentecost came, they were all together in one place, suddenly a sound like the blowing of a violent wind came from heaven and filled the whole house where they were sitting. They saw what seemed to be tongues of fire that separated and came to rest on each of them. All of them were filled with the Holy Spirit and began to speak with other tongues as the spirit enabled them* (Acts 2:1–4; NIV). And again: *Exalted to the right hand of God, he has received from the Father the promised Holy Spirit and poured out what you now see and hear* (Acts 2:33; NIV). So the Holy Spirit announces his presence, and demonic evil spirits do not!

Are you one of those Christians who have been taught the Holy Spirit is not for today? Do you believe speaking in tongues is wrong? Go read the scriptures yourself. Go to 1 Corinthians 12–14, and read it all word for word, very carefully. Ask God to show himself to you in the scriptures. This is a living book; it talks to you. God is the same yesterday, today, and tomorrow. He cannot change his nature and the Holy Spirit is a part of that nature! All throughout the New Testament we are admonished and instructed to live by, and pray by the Holy Spirit. If we have been deceived into believing we cannot be under the power of evil spirits, and if we also believe the Holy Spirit is not for us today, then how can we possibly live like the disciples and apostles told us to live, to be led by the Spirit and discern and test the evil spirits? Do you not understand this is a ploy and a powerful tactic by the Intelligent Deceiver? Without the Holy Spirit, you are powerless! Just because you can't see something doesn't mean it doesn't exist! Do you have a heart? How do you know? You can't see it! Do you breathe air? How do you know? You can't see it! Paul tells us the Holy Spirit was given to us as a gift, a deposit or a down payment if you will, guaranteeing our position in Christ (see 2 Corinthians 5:5). You cannot display or have the fruits of the Spirit if you don't believe or allow the Spirit of God to live and work in you.

Paul also tells us demons blind the minds of unbelievers: *This god of this age has blinded the minds of unbelievers, so they cannot see the light of the gospel of the glory of Christ, who is the image of God* (2 Corinthians 4:4; NIV). So if Satan can get Jesus' followers to be completely ineffective for Christ by not allowing the power of the Holy Spirit to rule our lives, he has been successful at crippling you and paralyzing you against his powers of deception. *To keep Satan from getting the advantage over us: for we are not ignorant of his wiles and intentions* (2 Corinthians 2:11; NIV). Don't be ignorant of his wiles and intentions!

The Anatomy of Man: The Temple

God tells us seven times, the number of perfection, that our bodies are a temple. *Don't you know that you yourselves are God's temple and that God's spirit lives within you? If anyone destroys God's temple, God will destroy him; for God's temple is sacred and you are that temple* (1 Corinthians 3:16–17; NIV). And also: *Do you not know that your body is a temple of the Holy Spirit, who is in you, whom you have received from God? You are not your own; you were bought at a price. Therefore honor God with your body* (1 Corinthians 6:19–20; NIV). We live in a society that flippantly says, "It is my body, I will do as I please." According to the word of God, it is not our own, we have been bought and paid for. The other aspect we don't think of is if God called our bodies a temple, don't you think we should at least find out what a temple was built like? What its purpose was, how many rooms, the very architecture? Many of us flip through page after page of a dry dissertation on the dimensions and articles and all the properties and features of the temple, and ask ourselves why is this stuff so important? Well, there are many rooms in the temple, each one with a very specific function. What does it have to do with possession and demons and my body? Plenty! It is the key to understanding demonic possession, even in Christians.

Solomon's temple was a design given by God to David, even though Solomon actually built it (see 1 Kings). "The temple consisted of an outer court and inner court, a porch, store rooms around the sides and back of the building, the Holy Place and the Holy of Holies, a fairly straight forward design. If God said our bodies are a temple, then we can safely assume the various aspects and rooms of the temple can correlate to our triune natural physical bodies. The outer court would be our physical body, it is the entry way or door way into the temple. Next we have the inner court, which we could say is our soul (mind). This leads into the porch area which we could say would be our will power. The storage rooms around the Holy Place and Holy of Holies, we could call our subconscious, and the Holy Place our heart, and the Holy of Holies the spirit."[77] If this is the case, then this puts a whole new perspective on how our bodies operate and function when it comes to both worship and service to God, and defilement by Satan and his evil brood.

If we follow God's outline of the temple for the architecture of man, then we can begin to see how the devil can walk into the inner court (soul, mind), and set up shop so to speak. Where do I get this analogy? From Jesus himself, who showed the most astonishing behavior ever recorded in scripture! Go with me to John 2:14–17: *There He found in the temple [enclosure] those who were selling oxen and sheep and doves, and the money changers sitting there [also at their stands]. And having made a lash (a whip) of cords, He drove them all out of the temple [enclosure]—both the sheep and the oxen—spilling and scattering the brokers' money and upsetting and tossing around their trays (their stands). Then to those who sold the doves He said, "Take these things away (out of here)! Make not my Father's house a house of merchandise (a marketplace, a sales shop)!" And His disciples remembered that it is written, [in the Holy Scriptures], Zeal (the fervor of love) for Your house will eat Me up [I will be consumed with jealousy for the honor of Your house]* (John 2:14–17; AMP).

At first glance many Christians think this is just one of those instances when Jesus showed his humanity and *lost it.* Others think it is an example of the fact we should not be having bake sales in the sanctuary at church. I happen to think this passage has a much broader and deeper meaning than just righteous anger. I think it is a model of how Satan gets into our bodies and sets up shop, selling us his various wares (lies) to our spirit and mind (of course all in the form of sacrifices on our part, doves and sheep in our Bible passage). If we follow this model, the spirit is at the top of this hierarchy set up by God. The spirit directs the mind, or the mind takes orders from the spirit, either good or bad—then the body, given the direction by the mind, follows suit and acts upon these "orders." We saw this echoed in Galatians: *So I say, live by the Spirit, and you will not gratify the desires of the sinful nature (mind). For the sinful nature desires what is contrary to the Spirit, and the Spirit what is contrary to the sinful nature. They are in conflict with each other, so that you do not do what you want* (Galatians: 5:16; NIV).

I can't tell you how long it took for me to get this concept. I was one of those people constantly doing what I did not want to do. Jesus was livid at the fact these merchants were *inside the temple courts,* most likely in the inner court, selling oxen, sheep, doves, and exchanging currency. In the other gospels he called them a *"den of robbers"* (see Matthew 21:12), and interestingly, he spoke directly to the dove salesmen in each of the four gospels. Why would he do that? The people making a pilgrimage from other areas obviously needed to purchase these animals for their offerings for Passover. But they should not have been inside the courts (inside the body, mind) of the temple. This is a blatant act of irreverence for the temple! I also went back to the Old Testament and looked up each of these three animals and their significance as an offering, and what particular sin they atoned for. Oxen, sheep, and doves were given for payment of sins in general, a gratitude offering, and an unintentional sin offering. Sheep were given for a guilt offering (see Leviticus 4 and 5). Doves were the cheapest offering; they were what one bought if one could not afford an oxen, goat, or sheep.

Well, if Jesus called these salesmen a den of robbers, then this makes them thieves. A thief only comes to steal something you have! Maybe these cheap lies (modeled by the inexpensive doves) were costing us more than meets the eye. They were also selling something that would physically atone for sin. This implies guilt and accusation. Most likely these merchants were selling these things at an exorbitant cost, that whole "holiday supply-and-demand, price-gouging" thing. Jesus was so angry, he dumped over the trays and tables, and *drove out* all the animals and whipped the merchants, driving them out! What else did Jesus "drive out" in the New Testament? Demons! Is that a coincidence? I happen to believe everything written in the scriptures is woven together in an incredible tapestry, so I believe this is a purposeful lesson for us!

In addition to the inner court of the mind, we can't forget about the outer rooms, or storage rooms along the sides and back of the temple. These storage rooms could be part of our minds; our subconscious if you will. Dr. Chuck Missler tells us back in temple times, "the priests would hide their Idols in these rooms!"[78] These storage chambers became the home for false idols. What do you have hidden in your storerooms: pornography, adultery, money, food, drugs, hatred, gossip, murder, dissension, factions, fears, disobedience, irreverence, pride, etc? These secret storerooms are a perfect hiding place for demons or temple pests. They are your own private collection of demons that we care for and feed daily with our actions and the words of our mouths. They are the liars that whisper to us to believe them. "You are fat, ugly, dimwitted, worthless, careless, clumsy, unlovable." Let me remind you belief *is* faith. What you believe, whether a lie or truth, is what you have faith in. The Bible says this is where our hearts lie, the Holy Place (heart) is deceitful above all else! *The heart is deceitful above all things, and desperately wicked: who can know it?* (Jeremiah 17:9; NIV). Wow! We are also told: *As [a man] thinks in his heart, so is he* (Proverbs 23:7; NIV)…We are talking about the Holy Place! Thinking in the heart! It can be deceitful. If the heart can be deceitful, then who is the author of deceit (lies)? Exactly, Satan! I hope you are beginning to see how pervasive the enemy has infiltrated our very temples (bodies). The heart was also the first place that "thought" up the "I wills" of Satan's ambitions.

Dr. Caroline Leaf, a neuro-metacognative specialist states: "Research shows that the heart considers and 'thinks' about information it receives from the brain. This implies that the heart has opinions of its own…This 'mini-brain' in the heart literally functions like a conscience. There are times when the heart submits to the brain and others when the brain submits to the heart." [79]

Isn't it cool when research actually catches up to scripture? Jesus told us "the heart thinks." He also looks at the "heart of man."

Have the scriptures convinced you yet? Christians can be possessed, which means "under the power of and influence of demons." They can also be oppressed, in the Greek *katadunasteuo,*[80] which means "to exercise power over." So they know how to push our buttons. Demonic spirits also set traps for us: *"So that he will not fall into disgrace and unto the Devils trap"* (1 Timothy 3:7: NIV). So they actually set traps for us, they hunt us, just as the owl and the stork hunt their unwitting prey. Didn't Jesus come to *set the captives free*? (See 2 Timothy 2:25–26.) If you are trapped in some sin, let's say addiction, then that means evil spirits have exercised their power over you, or you are under their power! Do you see how sneaky they are? This is why scripture admonishes us not to succumb to the sinful desires of the flesh. When we knowingly and willfully sin, we open the door to our temple and literally invite thieves to come in, steal, destroy, kill, and ravish our spirits, minds, and bodies! Any sin is a legal right for demonic activity. Satan hates God; what better way for him to exact revenge upon God, than to attack, put under his power, and exercise power over, God's children! Christians especially are targeted! We as Christians also forget sin has consequences, even if it is *forgiven* sin. Say you got pregnant out of wedlock, and you repented…good, which means God has forgotten your sin, washed it clean, but you are still pregnant! The baby is a consequence of your sinful actions. It doesn't mean the baby is bad, it is just a natural result of your actions.

Can Satan and his fallen angels or demons read your mind? The answer is no! This gave me great comfort when I learned this, because I really struggled with this. If he could, it would imply omnipresence and omniscience. Only God can read your mind. *For who among men knows the thoughts of a man except the man's spirit within him? In the same way no one knows the thoughts of God except the Spirit of God* (1 Corinthians 2:11; NIV). It goes on to say if we have the Holy Spirit, he knows our thoughts and we can know and have the same thoughts God has! Pretty cool, huh?! That gives me great comfort, because this means only God and I know what I am thinking. Even though an evil force may try to control my thinking, implant thoughts, make an educated guess, or a strong assumption about what I am thinking, he still doesn't know what I am thinking. That being said, I want to point out something. Satan and his minions have a supernatural intelligence. They know how we tick; they know our *inner workings*. They know how we are hardwired. They have been at this game for many millennia. Think of the *billions of people* they have observed, possessed, and oppressed. They have had the advantage of thousands of years of stockpiling information on human beings and using them as their guinea pigs for their sick experiments. Do you think it possible they have found out what works and what doesn't? Do you think it possible they could have perfected the trap of temptation? Do you think it possible if demons are the disembodied spirits of giants, once alive and living in mortal bodies, and then seeking further embodiment, that they have studied our anatomy and physiology, our psyche, and gained a superior knowledge of our innermost functions? Do you think they would use this "intelligence" against us?

The Word of God supports this theory resoundingly. In every story of demonic possession in the Bible, demons display a dizzying intellect of the human condition; they control people's minds, spirits, and bodies as if we were nothing but marionette puppets. They made people sick, crippled, crazy, and gave people superhuman strength and supernatural "gifts" such as divination and fortune telling. They stripped people naked and beat them up. They levitated objects, controlled the forces of nature with storms, and even possessed animals (remember the herd of pigs?). Are you getting any of this? INTELLIGENT DECEPTION! Strong's Concordance says the power they have over the children of God are: temptations, afflictions (disease or health problems), accusations, wanting to "sift" us as wheat, beguile or delude us for their *own amusement* and to *disguise* themselves (see 1 Chronicles 21:1, Job 2:7, Zech 3:1, Luke 22:31, and 2 Corinthians 11:3, 14, 15), and this is only a partial list!

But guess what? We have the ace in the hole! If we have the Spirit of God and we have the mind of Christ (1 Corinthians 3:16), Satan does not have this access! Wahoo! He cannot have the Holy Spirit, so we can deduce he cannot know the mind of God. Do you know what that means? This means even though Satan makes himself out to be this super smarty pants, all-knowing, enlightened being, he is limited to his best guess of God's next move. When Satan took the world hostage at the first temptation and sin, he demanded blood as a ransom for God's people, the Lord was smarter than Satan and his plan backfired on him. He can read the Bible, and knows every verse, in every language, but he cannot spiritually discern the scriptures. Think about it for a minute. Satan knows the scriptures, he uses them against us all the time, it is his major tactic, but if he really understood them, all the prophecies that were fulfilled by Jesus down to the letter, he would have never, ever crucified Jesus. He would have known this would be his demise! The break in his power chain! Satan really thought he was defeating the Messiah by killing him. The Bible tells us Satan prowls around like a roaring lion seeking whom he may devour, but I am here to tell you that he has had all his teeth knocked out and been declawed! The best he can do is gum us stupid, ignorant Christians to death, when we don't take time to study and know the Word!

The Armor of God

> Finally, be strong in the Lord and in his mighty power. Put on the full armor of God so that you can take your stand against the devil's schemes. For our struggle is not against flesh and blood, but against the rulers, against the authorities, against the powers of this dark world and against the spiritual forces of evil in the heavenly realms. Therefore put on the full armor of God, so that when the day of evil comes, you may be able to stand your ground, and after you have done everything, to stand. Stand firm then, with the belt of truth buckled around your waist, with the breastplate of righteousness in place, and with your feet fitted with the readiness that comes with the Gospel of peace. In addition to all this, take up the shield of faith, with which you can extinguish all the flaming arrows of the evil one. Take the helmet of salvation and the sword of the spirit, which is the word of God. And pray in the Spirit on all occasions with all kinds of prayers and requests. With this in mind be alert and always keep on praying for all the saints. (Ephesians 6:10–18; NIV)

Satan has been stripped of the Holy Spirit, so he cannot fight against spiritual weapons. Every piece of armor refers to the Word of God. This is why God admonishes us to read his Word daily, and to continually meditate (active thinking) on it continually.

So if demons and Satan cannot read our thoughts, how do they influence or implant thoughts? Ever had an evil or disgusting thought? I mean, one of those "where did that come from?" kind of thoughts? Or a repetitive thought, maybe self-degrading or a character-abasing thought against someone else? The Bible tells us he shoots arrows or darts at us, *aimed for our mind* (see Ephesians 6:16). These are not blanks; these arrows of evil thought are very real. The Word also tells us to take every thought captive unto our Lord, Jesus Christ, and to cast it down out of our minds. *We demolish arguments and every pretension that sets itself up against the knowledge of God, and we take captive every thought to make it obedient to Christ* (2 Corinthians 10:5; NIV). This statement puts us in the driver's seat.

We are to jail our thoughts which are contrary to the Word of God and make them obedient to Christ. This is a very physical statement: follow Jesus' example of zeal in Matthew, whip and drive those thoughts out! I notice random thoughts and negative thoughts a lot now, and I recognize these are arrows from the enemy. I chain them quickly, and denounce them out loud, with an authoritative voice, just as one who is in charge of prisoners would do. It really works! I have to tell you though; sometimes Satan will volley a whole passel of arrows at you at once and keep at it for days, even years! But recognizing the fact that you don't have to think or dwell on every thought that falls into your brain is most of the battle.

This is an evil spirits way of testing for "chinks," or weak spots in your armor. If they can find room to get in and make you think a thought that is contrary to the Word of God long enough, you will act on it! James talks about this: *When tempted, no one should say, "God is tempting me." For God cannot be tempted by evil, nor does he tempt anyone; but each one is tempted when, by his own evil desire, he is dragged away and enticed. Then, after desire has conceived, it gives birth to sin; and sin when it is full-grown, gives birth to death* (James 1:13–15; NIV). So this evil thought or desire actually *drags* you away, and *seduces* you. You then get *pregnant*, so to speak, with *sin.* Once you begin to sin in the physical, it also gets pregnant and gives birth to *death.* Yuck! I call temptation, *mind rape.* Temptation drags you away, copulates with desire, and creates a sin child, who by this incestuous relationship gives birth to death. That is why Jesus talks so much about the thought, the mind. Take for instance the example of adultery. If someone so much as thinks about it in their head, they have already committed the act! Serious stuff! He knew the simple act of thinking leads to physical action eventually.

Demons or evil spirits function at every level of human life. We see through the Word, and by the state of our lives and our world, blatant examples of their influence and power. They mislead, deceive, kill, destroy, and steal from us just for their own sick pleasure and enjoyment. Satan and his demons of deception are much more prevalent than we think. They have infiltrated us and our world at every level.

They attack us spiritually by:

- Waging war with the soul.
- Disguising and hiding God's love, peace, mercy, grace, and salvation.
- Accusing and condemning us.

They attack the human body (Living Temple of God) through:

- Disease
- Addictions
- Physical abnormalities
- Sexual and Reproductive Perversions

They attack the mind/mental state (basic brain chemistry) through:

- Emotions
- Thoughts
- Knowledge
- Extra-Sensory
- Organic brain matter
- Human Relationships
    - God
    - Family
    - Friends
    - Spouses
    - Co-workers
    - Races
- Finances
    - Poverty
    - Overspending
    - Stealing the tithe
- Time
    - Premature Death
    - Procrastination
    - Overt busyness
- Authority
    - Undermine and disguise our God-given authority
    - Mask our power and freedom
- Government & Politics
    - World Governments
    - Civic governments
    - Family Authority

I think when people or Christians talk about demons they are naturally fearful. Something about these creatures, and even the name, strikes fear in our hearts. My husband would always leave the room if there were anything on television advertising a demonic movie (like *The Exorcist*) or any mention of them. He was extremely fearful of them; even talking about them made him extremely uncomfortable until he realized his authority in Christ. Once he learned what they were and where he stands in God's army and kingdom, it didn't bother him as much. Some Christians are much more sensitive than others. Once the mystery and foreboding has been stripped away, it's not so scary anymore. Isn't that true of so many of us? We are always fearful of the unknown. We are afraid of repercussions which may not even exist. I used to get scared when I would watch ghost stories on television, especially when I lived by myself. I would leave all the lights on and say my prayers really loudly when I went to bed. Fearful of defeated foes! Let's face it, not many of us know what we are dealing with! This is why they have so many Christians trapped in this fear prison…you don't want to be freaked out…it's just not natural! People might talk, they might call me a "Jesus Freak" or something! Or they might think they will come under the power of the demon force if they even talk about it. This is not what scripture says! We are supposed to spy on our enemy and know how he operates! *We are not to be ignorant of his schemes!* We are supposed to be schooled in spiritual warfare, we are supposed to wear our armor, we are supposed to know what is clean and what is unclean, and protect ourselves from involuntary contamination. This is not to say we are not to be careful. You wouldn't walk through a minefield without some knowledge of where the mines are would you?

Christian ignorance is the devil's playground! So let's talk about *fear*. It is, after all, Satan's number one spiritual weapon! Fear is such a powerful emotion it will bind us with fetters and chains and weigh us down until we are incapable of fleeing from it. We become ineffective at everything we do. Fear is a perfect example of Satan's counterfeit answer to *love*. Fear versus Love. They are completely opposite emotions. Fear carries with it anxiety, flight or frozen ineffectiveness, lack of confidence, doubt, and feelings of dread, death, coldness, and anticipatory punishment. Love, on the other hand, carries feelings of tender affection, closeness, bold confidence, peace, warmth, motion, life, freedom, liberty, and anticipatory reward. *When you believe fear, you unconsciously believe Satan is more powerful than God!* When you speak fear, believe it, you are expressing your "faith" in Satan.

Demons have become so adept and so effective with this emotion they deliver crippling and crushing blows to all they come in contact with. Let's face it, fear is very uncomfortable, and as humans we strive to avoid it all costs. Even at the cost of our freedom and salvation!

Fear is inflammatory and irritating, it is torment. *Torment* in the Greek is the word for punishment. *Fear* in the verb form connotes the psychological reaction of "fear, dread, anxiety." The verb form of *fearful* (*phobeo*) in early Greek is "to put to flight."[81] So these demons are trying to scare us off! They know if we know our authority, they are the ones who are going to be tormented, and punished, and put to flight!

I can remember when I was in school and I was learning public speaking. (Did you know most people fear public speaking more than death?) Well, I was painfully shy, and when the time came for me to give my speech in front of the class, I was shaking so badly, my voice quivered. I felt like I just ate a plate of sand, I was pitting-out, and I thought I was going to die! What makes us that way? Did I really believe my classmates were going to draw and quarter me? That's what fear does to us…It makes us believe we are in for some form of corporal punishment. Fear always attacks our confidence because confidence always has a promise paycheck, a compensation plan from God attached to it. We need to figure out it (the punishment) will not happen if we have bold confidence in the power of our Lord! By the way, I now love public speaking, aced it in college, and I look forward to it every chance I get. I had to overcome it!

Fear is all-consuming—tell me, can you concentrate on anything else when you are in extreme fear? Fear makes us ignorant and senseless (see Psalms 73:21–22). Fear is the lack of confidence, the lack of knowledge. Fear is a characteristic of the wicked. Wicked people are sinners. *Sinner* is a legal term according to God; it's a person, or a group of people who have done wrong and are intent on continuing to do wrong. Fear finds a productive breeding ground in the wicked. *All his days the wicked man suffers torment, the ruthless through all the years stored up for him. Terrifying sounds fill his ears; when all seems well marauders attack him. He despairs of escaping the darkness; he is marked for the sword. He wanders about—food for vultures; he knows the day of darkness is at hand. Distress and anguish fill him with terror; they overwhelm him, like a king poised to attack, because he shakes his fist at God and vaunts himself against the Almighty* (Job 15:20–25; NIV).

The spirit of fear could be the root to our problem. This is why Jesus came, to deliver us from the bondage of fear. John writes two very interesting passages that are inextricably linked. The first passage: *He that overcometh shall inherit all things; and I will be his God, and he shall be my Son. But the fearful, and the unbelieving, and the abominable, and murderers and whoremongers, and sorcerers, and idolaters and all liars, shall have their part in the lake which burneth with fire and brimstone; which is the second death* (Revelation 21:7–8; NIV). John starts this discourse off with a great promise; *He that overcomes shall inherit all things.* The word *overcome* is (*nikao*), a Greek legal term which means "mightiest prevail."[82] And in Webster's, it is defined as "to defeat, conquer, or successfully resist."[83] So when we overcome, we get to inherit all things, wow! What a great promise!

But wait…he follows this with a warning to *the fearful*; and he group's fearful people with murderers, sorcerers, liars, whoremongers, etc. Ouch!

Remember fear is dread and anxiety of a coming reprisal or punishment, torment. So if the fearful are lumped under the same category as unbelievers, and murderers, and other sinners, we can deduce *fear* must be a sin! Ouch again! That's a strong statement. But wait—if Satan's plan is to pervert the truth and lead you to sin, which then leads to a permanent death of eternity in hell, he is essentially using fear as his number one weapon. Fear is the exact opposite of Love. It must produce after its own kind, and fear produces sin. Unholy fear is no confidence in God! You flat out don't believe God can protect you or take care of you in your situation! So what, pray tell, is the cure for a fear mentality? John tells us the cure in his other passage on fear: *There is no fear in Love; but perfect Love casteth out fear; because fear hath torment. He that feareth is not made perfect in love* (1 John 4:18; KJV).

Fear cannot cohabitate with love. If there is fear, he tells us the cure is "perfect love." Who is perfect love? Jesus! John also tells us in this verse that fear is a spirit. *Where* you say? *…but perfect Love casteth out fear.* If fear wasn't a spirit, why would it have to be "cast-out" or kicked out of the body? So if you are right with God, have a relationship with Jesus, you do not have to be afraid of these spirits. *So we may boldly say; "The Lord is my helper; I will not fear"* (Hebrews 13:6; NIV). And: *"For God has not given us a spirit of fear, but of power and of love and a sound mind"* (2 Timothy 1:7; NIV). So we have a guarantee: God didn't send this tormenting spirit of fear; he gave us the remedy to it: take a dose of power, love and a sound mind. The enemy has to mask or hide these things from you with a fearful, emotion-producing spirit, because if he doesn't, what does he have against you? A supernatural Christian, who knows who you are in

Christ, with power, might, and confidence, which can see through the false façade, wiles, and schemes of the devil! So you don't have to be afraid of these creepy, freaky demons—you already have the tools and weapons of the spirit at hand.

Fear loves to masquerade and hide God's power from you. It loves to lie and tell us we aren't worth anything in God's sight. *But the very hairs of your head are all numbered. Do not fear therefore; you are of more value than many sparrows* (Luke 12:7; KJV). Fear loves to knock off your blood-bought crown, and burn your adoption papers, and strip you of your title of heir to Christ. *Do not fear, little flock, for it is your Father's good pleasure to give you the kingdom* (Luke 12:32; NIV).

The greatest wrong Job did, even though he was called a righteous man, was he not only feared, he *greatly feared* (see Job 2:3, 3:25). Job had an obsessional, irrational, daily fear his kids would mess up (see Job 1:5). *For the thing which I greatly feared is come upon me, and that which I was afraid of is come unto me!* (Job 3:25; NIV). Satan took advantage of this sin; it attracted the very thing he feared and so much more! Our enemy is evil, rotten, twisted, and so cruel. He delights himself in scaring the daylights out of you! He loves to kick you when you are down. He is a coward because he knows when you have a hold on your power and confidence from God, he doesn't stand a chance of breaking down your defenses and getting in!

God gives us these stories so we can be prepared against an attack. We can know we have a spirit of fear coming against us when we have feelings of anxiety, lack of peace, restlessness, stomach-churning, head-swimming turmoil! As a culture our society is dominated by psychologists, psychiatrists, mental health counselors, etc. We are the feel-good generation! Take a pill, rebalance your brain chemistry, and do not deal with the real cause of these problems. If

Job had been alive today, he would have been committed to a mental institution or worse, drugged out of his mind and spending all of his money on psychiatric bills. After all, he was talking to God! Anytime you bring up conversations with God or demons, it sends the red flag up in the professional mental health providers' minds! Time to bring out the Prozac, Haldol, and any of the new designer anti-psychotics the drug companies are peddling. *Emotions* are not bad, in and of themselves. But they are God's way of telling us the *symptoms* to a deeper problem. They are simply bi-products of a real danger or threat to your life. *They are the tracks, fingerprints, and a sign the enemy is there!*

> Be well balanced (temperate, sober of mind), be vigilant and cautious at all times; for that enemy of yours, the devil, roams around like a roaring lion (in fierce hunger), seeking someone to seize upon and devour. Withstand him; be firm in faith (against his onset—rooted, established, strong, immovable, and determined), knowing that the same (identical) sufferings are appointed to your brotherhood (the whole body of Christians) throughout the world. (1 Peter 5:8–9; AMP)

Here God tells us not to overwork or overbook ourselves, making ourselves so busy we don't see the lion crouching in the grass. And when he does pounce, we need to stand against him like a rock, because *all* of us get the same treatment from Satan. He doesn't care who you are! You are his enemy; he wants to destroy you! A note to the unseasoned warrior: You will have stand-offs for months at a time! Fear is a tenacious foe, but God is faithful. Turn to him in prayer and you can withstand fear. It doesn't have access to the stamina you do! You can train yourself to notice slight changes and movements in the grass of your mind. This is when a lion is in the area. You can look for his tracks, his signs he is prowling, and you can fend off an attack before he ever strikes! Remember Satan has been declawed and defanged, but he still has a ferocious roar, which is intimidating. This is why Satan dons the lion costume; it is his only defense to make you believe he is fully equipped. Don't be gummed and slimed to death by a toothless lion! *He forgave us all our sins, having canceled the written code, with its regulations, that was against us and that stood opposed to us; he took it away, nailing it to the cross, and having disarmed the powers and authorities, he made a public spectacle of them, triumphing over them by the cross* (Colossians 2:13–15; NIV). It may help to remember this acronym: FEAR—False Evidence Appearing Real.

Isn't that cool! But so many of us "don't get it." We know what Jesus did for us, but we can't figure out why we feel so bad all the time. We feel badly because these powers and authorities (demons and fallen angels) are still behaving, masquerading, pretending as if they have all of the armaments and weapons, and we believe them instead of God! Their fake holographs and cinema graphics look so real, their battle cry so loud and intimidating, we fall over and play dead! We need to pay attention to the tracks of the devil, watch our emotions, show Satan the document of sin regulations which is now clean. Go ahead, show him the paperwork! You have a title deed to justice! Practice it!

In his book *A More Excellent Way*, H.W. Wright says; "As Christians we have been so God conscious, that we have forgotten discernment concerning evil. A sign of maturity is not just knowing good, it is knowing evil as well, so that you know what is of God, and what is not. That's a sign of maturity."[84] Many of us have enough of Jesus to stay out of hell, but not enough to walk in victory.

These evil emissaries of the Intelligent Deceiver work at many levels in our lives. It is all part of a vengeance plan on God's children. What better way to get back at a father than to attack his children? Here are a few ways I know I am dealing with a counterfeit, deceptive spirit:

Fear
Confusion
Disorientation
Despair
Darkness
Doubt
Discouragement
Diversion
Defeat
Delay

I can remember this list by knowing that most of these start with the letter "D" for demon.

Legal Rights

I have mentioned legal rights several times in the preceding chapters. It is a much misunderstood and misconstrued concept among Christians.

What are the legal rights of demons? Believe it or not, they do have legal rights in the courts of heaven. Scary. Their plea? Sin, defilement of the temple. It is that simple. We have already learned Satan goes before God day and night petitioning and accusing us. But for what? His legal rights to inhabit you, possess you, oppress you, hinder and torment you. We are taught in Isaiah: *Whoever shuns evil becomes a prey* (Isaiah 59:15; NIV). This means we become the mouse Satan chooses to torture, just as Job did. Satan also asks God to sift Christians as wheat! He asked to sift Peter, but Jesus said he was praying for him. There really is no end to the bold arrogance of requests and petitions Satan asks for at the throne of God!

Rebecca Brown, MD who has a strong deliverance ministry, puts it best: "You must understand that Satan stands before the throne of God petitioning our heavenly Father for our unsaved loved ones. Satan points the accusing finger and says, 'See, so-and-so is participating in rock music (or whatever), therefore I have legal right to his/her soul and to influence his/her soul and to send my demons into him/her.' Because God is absolutely just, He must grant Satan his petition if it is not contested. But we, as heirs and joint heirs with Jesus Christ, have more right to petition God the Father than Satan does. We must 'boldly' go before the throne and counter petition Satan."[85]

The Bible tells us that in 1 John:

> If we say we have no sin [refusing to admit that we are sinners], we delude and lead ourselves astray, and the Truth [which the Gospel presents] is not in us [does not dwell in our hearts]. If we [freely] admit that we have sinned and confess our sins, He is faithful and just (true to His own nature and promises) and will forgive our sins [dismiss our lawlessness] and [continuously] cleanse us from all unrighteousness [everything not in conformity to His will in purpose thought and action]. (1 John 1:8–9; AMP)

But if anyone should sin, we have an Advocate (One who will intercede for us) with the Father—[it is] Jesus Christ (1 John 2:1; AMP). Of course this is with the condition that we confess and repent. Jesus intercedes for us (day and night as well) and petitions on our behalf when we confess and repent of our sins, thereby closing the door or cleansing us of Satan's legal right to hound us and continually defile the temple.

He who digs a pit [for others] will fall into it, and whoever breaks through a fence or a [stone] wall, a serpent will bite him (Ecclesiastes 10:8; AMP). Cleanliness or remaining undefiled is the key to keeping oneself free from the legal rights of Satan. When you purposefully hurt others (*He who digs a pit [for others]),* and whenever you break that protective hedge through sin (*whoever breaks through a fence or a [stone] wall),* God says *a serpent will bite him.* This is precisely what happened to Job; his protective hedge was removed by way of his great fear, and the simple fact he was a righteous man and shunned evil.

There are far too many doorways into our protective hedges than I can list here. Any sin is a hedge breaker, even if it was an inherited sin. The sins of the father shall be passed down through the generations. I would highly recommend you study familial curses and break these as quickly as possible. *"Keeping mercy for thousands, forgiving iniquity, transgression and sin, and that will by no means clear the guilty; visiting the iniquity of the fathers upon the children, and upon the children's children, unto the third and fourth generation"* (Exodus 34:7; KJV).

Any involvement in the occult, no matter how slight or trivial gives Satan a legal right.

Sexual sin, past or present, including incest, rape, viewing or participating in pornography, extra-marital affairs, pre-marital sex, homosexual relations, bestiality, demonic sexual relations (incubus, succubus), etc. are all huge open doors, no matter if you are a Christian or not. Just as the old saying goes, "You can't tell if someone has a venereal disease just by looking at them," the same goes for demons. "You can't tell if they have a demon, or several, they will share with you when you sleep with them." These are called soul ties.

I know this sounds gross, but the Bible gives us commandment after commandment about steering clear of sexual sin. This wasn't just so you couldn't have any fun. This type of "fun" outside of the context of marriage is ruled by very powerful demons. This was God's way of protecting you from defilement. The two become one flesh during a sexual act, this allows for easy passage of one demon into another human. There is no "spiritual condom" that can protect you from this type of invasion.

> Or do you not know and realize that when a man joins himself to a prostitute he becomes one body with her? The two, it is written, shall become one flesh…Shun immorality and all sexual looseness [flee from impurity in thought, word or deed]. Any other sin which a man commits is one outside the body, but he who commits sexual immorality sins against his own body. Do you not know that your body is the temple (the very sanctuary) of the Holy Spirit who lives with you, whom you have received [as a gift] from God? You are not your own. You were bought with a price [purchased with a preciousness and paid for, made His own]. So then honor God and bring glory to Him in your body. (1 Corinthians 6:16, 18–20; AMP)

When you have sexual relations outside of the context of marriage or between whatever sexes, you have essentially sinned inside the body. This literally means you "hooked-up" right in the church (temple), in front of God! Satanists practice this very act all of the time; it's called sex magick! They consider sex a powerful way to not only mock and defy God, but to also gain new and ever more powerful demons from another practicing cult member.

I wonder if our kids were taught *how and why* to keep themselves pure instead of how to use a condom and at what age they should be started on birth control pills, if they would be so eager to "hook-up" with their friends in such a casual manner. The threat of venereal disease is surely not enough; maybe the threat of possession would be enough to steer some kids and adults clear of sex outside the acceptable pure boundaries of the marriage bed the Lord established. Of course this has to be taught in the right manner. You can't just threaten demonic possession to children and scare them to death; you have to have the right teaching.

Abortion can be another gateway for temple vermin. Even the youngest of sexually active kids knows when life begins, otherwise they wouldn't use a condom. "Abortion is another open door for legal rights to demons. This will always result in demonic infestation. Abortion is a human sacrifice to the god of self."[86] This is a polite way of saying "sacrificing to Satan."

Drugs, alcohol, hatred, unforgiveness, lying, idol worship, and a whole laundry list of any other sins gives Satan a legal right to petition God for your debasement.

Chapter Five

HEALTH, DISEASE, AND INFIRMITIES

Because we live between our ears.

—Art Linkletter

Our Lord came back to earth and did some great things. One of his main ministries was to heal the sick. Sickness, disease, physical abnormalities were never part of God's grand plan for our lives. He created the earth as a paradise; he created man in his image and likeness. God's will for our lives is: salvation, perfect health, and prosperity (nothing lacking). Satan's will for our lives is a copycat counterfeit: hell (eternal death), illness and disease, and poverty.

Sickness is Satan's will, not God's. According to Mary K. Baxter, a woman with a large deliverance ministry; "Sickness is a corruption of the will of God; it is a curse from Satan, an unnatural element in the economy of God." [87]

Sickness is the absence of strength. You are physically weak, and you have grief, sufferings, infirmities, pain. We are spiritual beings bound to a triune creation—body, mind, and spirit. Our bodies are a "house." When we die, we know the body stays here and continues to decay. But, our spirit and our soul (the part of the brain which houses our memories) continues on either to eternal life or eternal death. I have seen many dead people and people in the process of dying or at the point of clinical death. As a cardiac and emergency room nurse, death was part of my job. One of the more unpleasant tasks of nursing occurred after someone had expired, and we would go in and "bag-n-tag" the deceased. We would clean-up the body, remove tubes, wires, personal belongings, and put a toe tag identifying the person for their next stop—the morgue. I can tell you from personal experience, even when someone is barely alive, you can tell something inhabits that body. When they die, the body is an empty shell.

The human body is very complicated, a fantastic testament to the creative power of God. Having been fashioned from dirt, we are such an intricate structure, housing bone, flesh and organs. According to *101 Scientific Facts and Foreknowledge*: "Scientists have discovered that the human body is comprised of 28 base and trace elements—all of which are found in the earth."[88] Medical science has come a long way over just the past one hundred years, but we are just barely scratching the surface of this magnificent creation. It is by no means an exact science! *You are fearfully and wonderfully made* (Psalms 139:14; NIV). It is no wonder the Intelligent Deceiver has chosen the human body to wreck havoc on. When you are sick, diseased, crippled, whatever; this can be a direct attack from the enemy on the Temple of God. *Don't you know that you yourselves are God's temple, and that God's Spirit lives in you?* (1 Corinthians 3:16; NIV).

One of the ways Satan does this is by attempting to control our minds. Have you ever heard of the mind/body connection? Very basically, the mind is the hard drive; it is the motherboard that runs bodily functions. You can't move your hand without first thinking a thought that you want to move your hand, then in split milliseconds, a complex, chemical and nerve signal is sent out to the muscle fibers, bones, and tissues in your hand telling it to do exactly what you were thinking! Satan knows this system! In fact he knows it better than any human or collective of humans alive today! The angels were watching creation! (see Job 38:4–7). He understands if he can control or suggest to your hard drive (the mind) a thought which requires action, it wants to follow God's natural law, and function as it was told. God did not create the heavens and earth with action; instead he created them with *words* (see Genesis 1). If the enemy can influence your thoughts, you eventually speak your mind! In other words your body will express that thought if you let it. Ever said, "You sneezed, now I am going to get your cold"? How do you know? But you gave your mind and body something to work toward by the positive affirmation from your mouth. Remember the spirit is willing but the flesh is weak? Satan wants to be at the helm of your house. *Satan came to steal, kill, and destroy* (John 10:10; NIV). The word used for *kill* in the Bible means to "blow smoke." "A primary verb; properly to rush (breathe hard, blow, smoke), that is, (by implication) to sacrifice (properly by fire, but generally); by extension to immolate (slaughter for any purpose): - kill, (do) sacrifice, slay."[89]

So he has to deceive us into believing we are dying! I can't tell you how many people I have worked with over the years who have accepted their illness, some have even welcomed it by not caring for their bodies. Jesus said *as a man thinks, so is he* (Proverbs 23:7;KJV).

Our Minds

Remember our discussion of the temple of God as an archetype of the structure of man? I think for our purposes, and the day and age we live in, we could use another more contemporary analogy to help you understand how Satan can invade our bodies. Think of your mind as a sophisticated computer, complete with software, hardware, firewalls, virus scanners, garbage filters, etc. It has built into its very matrix a top-notch firewall system. Think of Satan as a super smart hacker. He knows how to get past your firewalls and hack into your internal hardware, implant a virus that may or may not go undetected by your virus scanners. This is where your knowledge of the Word comes into play; without that as your virus scanner filter, you may be allowing a lie to be implanted deep within your internal brain structure which continues to eat away at your computer matrix (brain). This matrix controls all of your bodily functions. It takes orders from your spirit, but if your spirit has been deceived, it will get the wrong signals and then the body will act upon those signals (carnality, flesh).

The Bible continually tells us "the truth will set us free." If truth sets us free, then conversely we can assess that we are being held captive by…lies! We have been hacked into, and lies have been implanted into our hard drives. We are dictated by lies, infiltrated and programmed by lies! We learned from the last chapter Satan can and does set-up shop in our minds and sells us all sorts of self-sacrificing lies! If we actually buy into it, we have purchased a virus that gets stored into our internal memories (subconscious storerooms). Now in order for that virus to take effect we have to take care of it. After all, we bought it didn't we?

> For those who are according to the flesh and are controlled by its unholy desires set their minds on and pursue those things which gratify the flesh, but those who are according to the spirit and are controlled by the desires of the spirit set their minds on and seek those things which gratify the [Holy] Spirit. Now the mind of the flesh [which is sense and reason without the Holy Spirit] is death [death that comprises all the miseries arising from sin, both here and hereafter]. But the mind of the Holy Spirit is life and [soul] peace [both now and forever]. (Romans 8: 5; AMP)

The word *gratify* implies some sort of feeding, doesn't it? To be gratified, you are usually talking about a form of satiety. In other words, we need to feed these things for them to live, whether it is a lie from the devil implanted into your hard drive or a truth from the Holy Spirit, they both need to be cared for in order for them to grow and live.

This truth was a great revelation to me, because I realized I had been feeding and caring for quite a few lies in my mind for a very long time! Many of them had grown to be horrible monsters I could not get rid of! This is exactly how Lucifer fell! He had told himself a lie that he was the prettiest of all creatures; he believed this lie (pride) and actually thought he could become god of the universe! Pastor Paul Scanlon wrote an article in which he stated:

> It is entirely possible to believe in God, but still belong to the devil in your thinking. And if God doesn't have your thinking, He doesn't have you. We believe with the heart, but we behave with the head! I can't pray for your deliverance or your sense of worthlessness to go if deep down you don't believe God loves you. What's hurting you may not be what someone just said to you but what you've been saying to yourself everyday for the past twenty years.[90]

The Bible is continually telling us to "renew our minds." This means we need to run a virus scan program, write down all of the lies we have been believing and *retelling* ourselves for all of these years, and then reprogram our minds with the Word of God! *...but be transformed by the renewing of your mind* (Romans 12:2; NIV).

When you read all of the accounts of healing Jesus did in the New Testament, you will find two things happening: forgiveness of sin and restoration of health. In many of the instances you will also find a third element: casting out of an evil spirit; health, sanity, and normality was restored. *Then they brought him a demon-possessed man who was blind and mute, and Jesus healed him, so that he could both talk and see* (Matthew12:22; NIV). *Some men brought him a paralytic, lying on a mat. When Jesus saw their faith, he said to the paralytic, "Take heart, son; your sins are forgiven."…And the man got up and went home* (Matthew 9:1–7; NIV). Since evil spirits are synonymous with sin, let's make it easy and say sanctification is a prerequisite to health restoration with God. Sin does have a root cause, and it does start in the mind! Let's learn about our magnificent houses, our bodies, God's holy temple.

If you break down the human body from a purely simplistic, anatomical and physiological view, we are just a series of chemical processes. Thoughts equal chemical process. Like it or not, we are a chemical creation. Our bodies are like giant test tubes, whatever goes in creates a chemical reaction.

Remember that whole mind/body connection thing? Well in God's way of doing things, it should be called the spirit/soul/body connection; this is what the biologists actually call the limbic system.

In his book *A More Excellent Way*, H.W. Wright says:

> When Satan can control your thought process, he can control your chemistry. When you have serotonin deficiencies (a chemical that controls mood and sensations of feeling good) you don't feel good about yourself because there is a deficiency of that chemical that God created in you to make you feel good chemically. For every thought that you have, conscious or unconscious, there is a nerve transmission, a secretion of a hormone or neurotransmitter somewhere in your body to react to it…And when you start listening to

> that self-hatred, you start listening to that guilt, and you start listening to that rejection, your body is secreting chemicals in response to those spiritual attacks that are counter productive to your peace.[91]

This is very Intelligent Deception! Wright also goes on to say:

> One of the principal glands in the limbic system is the hypothalamus. In fact this little gland is actually called the brain of the endocrine system (hormones)…What psychology calls the collective unconscious is in fact the "spirit of man."[92]

In her book *Who Switched Off My Brain?* Dr. Caroline Leaf explains: "Thoughts do cause illness and thus should be studied and controlled. If they are powerful enough to make us sick, they are powerful enough to make us healthy and well."[93]

I want you to remember as a child of God you are to be ready and prepared; you are to know the *wiles of Satan.* He understands and manipulates our anatomy and physiology.

"The hypothalamus gland is the facilitator and the originator of the following life circumstances (the watchdog of the endocrine system): all expressions of fear, anxiety, stress, tension, panic, panic attacks, phobia, rage, anger, and aggression. These are all released and facilitated by this one gland. It only responds to you emotionally and spiritually! The hypothalamus is a responder to thought!"[94]

Now let's compare the expressions of the hypothalamus gland to the acts or the fruits of the sinful nature: sexual immorality, factions, impurity, envy, debauchery, drunkenness, idolatry, orgies, witchcraft, lust, hatred, evil desires, discord, greed, jealousy, anger, fits of rage, malice, selfish ambition, slander, dissensions, and deceit. Do you see how big your emotions are? Do you see that something anatomically and chemically controls these emotions? Could an intelligent, malicious being possibly know how to push our emotional buttons (work our hypothalamus), create sin, and cause disease or sickness in or body?

The limbic system is closely associated with the aspects of survival. Dr. Wright tell us; "When you do not feel loved, when you have been victimized (robbed, sexual abuse), when you don't feel secure (lack of money), you fight for survival. When you have been rejected by a parent or by anyone else, when you do not feel loved, when you feel violated, you are always looking over your shoulder for the next hit—you are in fight or flight." *(Parenthetical words added.)*[95]

This is deep, deep stuff going on in you. Check your emotions, your health. How are you eating and sleeping, drinking, eliminating? How is your sex life? Is it following God's guidelines laid out for us in the Old Testament? There are reasons he said, eat this, not this, drink this, not this...actual physical reasons, because it can affect your soul, spirit, and body.

Healing of any malady should require a close, deep, inventory of yourself. Weasel out hidden sin, unforgiveness, rejection, past hurts, curses. Ask God to show you what you may have forgotten. Write a list of people you may be nursing a grudge against, no matter how small, and ask God to forgive you, and if possible, go to the person and ask their forgiveness. Forgiveness benefits you, not the other guy. Also it kicks Satan in the butt. He doesn't get it! It actually blows him off his feet! In the same vein, if you are having a problem with your car, do you take it to the cobbler to fix? Then conversely, if you are having a physical problem how come you aren't taking it to the Body Maker?

When you forgive someone, you need to say it out loud. Demonic spirits can hear, so use an authoritative voice. This is rebuking. When you make the decision to speak, guess what? It is not controlled by the parasympathic nervous system! So even if Satan has his grubby claws sunk deep into your subconscious, God gave you the ability to take a stand and make the decision to talk!

Did you know you are a marvel of engineering, chemistry, and every other scientific discipline known to man, and probably some we don't know about? Did you know you are the rarest creation on the earth? There will never be another human being like you on this planet! You are a maverick, rare, one-of-a-kind, remarkable, excellent, and very uncommon. Hold your head high, because God thinks you are the coolest creation on the planet! He says you are his precious, treasured possession. He has written you on the palm of his hand!

Now I don't want you to the get the false idea I am against the medical profession. I think emergency medicine is a gift from God. But our medical professionals have been taught an old, worn-out way of thinking. They separate and don't make the connection between sin and disease. They have been taught to recognize symptoms, classify those symptoms, and treat the symptoms. Very few find the root cause. In fact, none do. The Bible tells us the root is sin! *And when he had called unto him his twelve disciples, he gave them power against unclean spirits, to cast them out, and to heal all manner of sickness and disease* (Matthew 10:1; NIV).

I think the enemy goes even farther than we think. Remember when Adam and Eve sinned, and sin then lived in every human, every generation to follow? It radically changed human interaction with God. Why are we constantly fighting our flesh? By the way, *flesh* refers to our way of thinking! Not the just the body! I believe sin is actually a genetic component of our DNA, just as diseases such as Down's syndrome are caused by glitches in the genome, some as subtle as a single letter gone awry.[96] Sin is a mutated gene, embedded within our DNA. It is a gene that has connected us inextricably; it is an open pathway for Satan to enter into our thoughts, control the chemical processes, and cause the "chemical imbalance." This chemical imbalance is what the doctors see; this is what they treat. It is time we headed the enemy off at the pass. God claims he is a jealous God. He loves us so much he does not want to share us with anybody, especially not an evil spirit. This is where the Holy Spirit can come in. He can help you operate the gift of discernment. Did you know the same part of the brain that feels the pleasurable and unpleasant side effects of drugs, alcohol, food, and sex is the same part of the brain the *feels* the Holy Spirit's power? *Walk in the Spirit and you will not satisfy the appetites of the flesh* (Galatians 5:16; NIV). *You were taught, with regard to your former way of life, to put off your old self, which is being corrupted by its deceitful desires (corrupted thoughts); to be made new in the attitude of your minds; and to put on the new self, created to be like God in true righteousness and holiness* (Ephesians 4:22; NIV).

Deoxyribonucleic acid (DNA) is a nucleic acid that contains the genetic instructions for the development and functioning of living organisms. All living things contain DNA genomes. The main role of DNA in the cell is the long-term storage of information. The genome is often compared to a set of blueprints since it contains the instructions to construct other components of the cell, such as proteins and RNA molecules. [97]

That was a very brief, cursory lesson on the building blocks of life, but I think it spoke volumes! Our DNA, the blueprints for life, can be damaged by mutagens. Satan was the first *free radical*! When Satan introduced the thought of sin (disobedience), it radically altered the DNA of the Mother and the Father of all mankind. The Bible tells us they *passed on their heritage of sin to every generation that followed.* How is this possible? This can only be accomplished through DNA! Take viruses for example. They can actually replicate DNA; it is called RNA—damaged RNA. You know how when you make a copy of a copy it just never turns out very clear or crisp? One cell contains six feet of DNA! The body is ordered like God; if one amino acid is out of place, you have disease, disorder. This is what our Intelligent Deceiver did; he implanted a virus into our hard drive! No wonder God tells us to *renew our minds every day*!

Let's take the sin of addictions: drugs, alcohol, food, sex, cigarettes. All of these require a chemical cascade in the brain, releasing the pleasure nerve transmitters to that particular area of the body most affected. It also releases the opposite chemical cascade when you need a fix, a smoke, whatever. Let's take the example of alcoholism. I can remember when the American Medical Association came out and classified alcoholism as a disease, not just a social stigma associated with lack of self-control. Dr. Henry Wright found a link between alcoholism and genetics; "Believe it or not, alcoholism is not a genetically inherited disease, but it does have a genetic component. Basically some individuals are born without a normal chemical that exists in most people. When this person imbibes in alcohol, that missing chemical causes another chemical reaction, and a brand new chemical is formed, this chemical is called THIQ. This new neurotransmitter produces a permanent craving for alcohol."[98] Have you ever seen anyone in the D.T.'s, (delirium tremens)? This is a medical term for someone having severe withdrawal symptoms from alcohol. Many times, they feel like bugs are infesting their body; they feel them crawling. They sweat profusely, tremble violently, have delusions. They are pathetic creatures, they beg and cry, they try to manipulate you with words, sometimes they become extremely violent. In other words they are not themselves. If you have ever witnessed someone in this state, you can't help but think to yourself, these are evil spirits manifesting, they want their drink! This will go on for days, sometimes weeks if a person is severely addicted. If you are in rehab, we drug the heck out of you! This is so the medical staff doesn't have to deal with the noise and chaos and commotion these evil creatures are putting their prey through for their drink! We just treat the outward chemical symptoms of alcoholism and withdrawal.

Cocaine. Of all of the drugs, cocaine does not have any chemically addictive qualities. In other words, it doesn't interact with other chemicals in the body. "Instead cocaine releases huge amounts of dopamine in the brain. It's like a level 10 orgasm. What addicts don't understand is that the body is never able to duplicate that same amount of dopamine again."[99] So they try it again, and again, trying to get that same rush. It's not the coke they are addicted to; Satan found a way to release a very pleasant chemical, dopamine, which if too much is released will cause heart failure.

Look at the popular drug meth:

> Methamphetamine increases the release of very high levels of the neurotransmitter dopamine, which stimulates brain cells, enhancing mood and body movement. Chronic methamphetamine abuse significantly changes how the brain functions...Recent studies in chronic methamphetamine abusers have also revealed severe structural and functional changes in areas of the brain associated with emotion and memory, which may account for many of the emotional and cognitive problems observed in chronic methamphetamine abusers. Long-term effects may include paranoia, aggressiveness, extreme anorexia, memory loss, visual and auditory hallucinations, delusions, and severe dental problems. [100]

Not to mention they look like the walking dead. Do any of those symptoms mimic demonic behavior? These individuals are experiencing the total control and influence of evil. Evil which is affecting the brain first, then causing a huge chemical cascade, all stemming from the limbic system! Intelligent, deceiving, pushing our mental buttons, don't you see? We *see the symptoms of sin*, but it goes beyond that! It starts in the mind! *Therefore do not let sin reign in your mortal body so that you obey its evil desires. Do not offer the parts of your body to sin, as instruments of wickedness, but rather offer yourselves to God, as those who have brought from death to life; and offer the parts of your body to him as instruments of righteousness. For sin shall not be your master, because you are not under law, but under grace* (Romans 6:12–14; NIV). The word *reign* connotes power and control, and *obedience to its evil desires* means you are listening and following its commands!

Pornography is gripping our society like never before in history because we now have easy, private access in our homes via the Internet. Our media flaunts sex, or mentions it several times in just about every television program. Companies use the human body in illicit fashion to sell everything from soap to underwear. It is everywhere. But sex was created by God; our bodies were created by God. He created sex to be pleasurable and blessed in certain confines. He created males with the hormone testosterone so they would have a drive to desire a woman and procreate. He created estrogen so women would have feminine features and a mothering instinct. But along came a snake who understood these very powerful chemical influences, and he exploited them. Did you know when you view a pornographic picture, it actually sets up a chemical rush in the body, which is so powerful and strong it burns it into the memory banks? You actually have a mental tattoo of that image. Do you know how hard it is to get rid of a tattoo? Only God can do it. He has a supernatural chemical eraser comprised of the shed blood of a lamb. It is the only thing that will get rid of that chemical tattoo and stain. God warns us in scripture about it. He doesn't want to clean up a bad mess, a chemical stain; he would rather you didn't get the tattoo to begin with.

The Bible talks about sexual sin in 1 Corinthians: *Flee from sexual immorality. All other sins a man commits are outside his body, but he who sins sexually sins against his own body. Do you not know that your body is a temple of the Holy Spirit, who is in you, whom you have received from God? You are not your own; you were bought at a price. Therefore honor God with your body* (1 Corinthians 6:18; NIV). It is very interesting the language he uses here; *flee* actually means to run away from it! When you commit a sexual sin, it is a sin against your body. This means, you literally had sex in the temple. Imagine if you had sex in your church, on the altar; this is what Paul was literally referring to. You are in such a state you are "doing it" right in the Holy Place. Pagan religions, such as those that began in Babylon, not only encouraged sexual practices with the priestesses and priests, it was required as part of the ritual! You had sex with the idol gods' priests or priestesses or temple prostitutes after you sacrificed and worshiped as part of the service. This was still going strong in Paul's time. It is still very much in practice today with occultic religions. I encourage you to do a study on the temple in the Old Testament; I assure you it will have a graphic effect on the way you treat your body. The temple was highly revered, and only certain special, dedicated items were allowed for use inside the Temple. This is how God still views our bodies.

Let's look at another example: anorexia. This is a disease that is shocking to most of us. How can a human bypass such an instinctive survival mechanism as eating enough food to live? Women across

America are dying in horrifying numbers because they see and think themselves to be too fat! It is called body dysmorphia. What they see in the mirror is an illusion! I ask you, caused by what? What affects the eyes? The limbic system! Who can and does control the limbic system, with great effectiveness? Satan! They will starve themselves to death without intervention. Well, we learned the limbic system is responsible for our feeding and satiety centers of the brain. We learned comparing yourself to someone else is a sin; you are rebelling against God. You are basically saying to God, "Hey...you made me wrong...I was supposed to look like so and so (the latest celebrity)." Statistics show confining and force feeding these women doesn't work, and secular counseling doesn't help either. More women die of this sickness than suicide! When you don't eat, the chemical serotonin doesn't get released in the brain. Serotonin is responsible for the feeling of love. So they have a cloaked, blocked-off wall in the brain that keeps them from experiencing the love of the Father. Medical science looks at the symptoms of this illness (not eating), when the actual roots of the disease are self-hatred, self-rejection, guilt, and seeking the praise of man.

My people are destroyed for lack of knowledge (Hosea 4:6; NIV). Next let's look at viruses. Here is a major cause of many illnesses that are not only difficult to treat, but they have the uncanny ability to mutate and create a new virus which always seems to be one step ahead of the Centers for Disease Control. Take for instance flu virus vaccines. Every year the drug companies make a new flu shot; they gamble every year, hoping they not only picked the right strain of virus, but that it won't mutate and cause all of their flu-fighting drug to be absolutely useless in combating the illness. In several ways according to Wright, "[Viruses] are highly destructive and very calculated...There also seems to be an intelligence behind viruses that defies imagination."[101]

"The word virus comes from the Latin, *virus,* 'poison' (syn. *Venenum)*...Latin plural forms as *viri* (which actually means *men*)."[102] So literally, a virus poisons men! To date, scientists cannot definitively say if viruses are living organisms or not. They function in much the same way as a parasite does; they need a host to attach too. The definition in Wikipedia states: "Viral populations do not grow through cell division, because they are acellular; instead they use the machinery and metabolism of a host cell to produce multiple copies of themselves."[103]

What an ingenious way to work against us. It attaches itself to the cell, does its damage, but doesn't completely kill the cell. But in order to get rid of it, you have to kill the cell! Viruses are also airborne—remember Jesus told us rulers and authorities were also "airborne," in the heavenly realms; this includes our atmosphere. Research in Wikipedia regarding the use of antibiotics on viruses tells us the effect on such viruses:

> Because viruses use the machinery of a host cell to reproduce and also reside within them, they are difficult to eliminate without killing the host cell. The most effective medical approaches to viral diseases so far are vaccinations to provide resistance to infection, and drugs, which treat the symptoms of viral infections. Patients often ask for, and physicians often prescribe, antibiotics. These are useless against viruses, and their misuse against viral infections is one of the causes of antibiotic resistance in bacteria.[104]

Now there is a good way to nullify a combatant against bacterial diseases and still harm humans. Satan is evil! He doesn't want anything good to happen to mankind!

Viruses can wipe out entire populations of people. Of all the maladies known to man, a tiny phylum could decimate humans. Take the black plague for instance: "The total number of deaths worldwide from the pandemic are estimated at least 75 million people. The Black Death is estimated to have killed between a third and two-thirds of Europe's population."[105] As I write this, the avian flu and threats of biological warfare are imminent in the minds of people. Satan is referred to as the murderer (see John 8:44) and the God of this world (see 2 Corinthians 4:4). I hope you are beginning to understand through knowledge how you can recognize his handiwork!

Well you can't have a conversation about health and the human body without talking about drugs; the pharmaceutical kind.

Strong's Concordance gives us some powerful definitions for our word *pharmacy*; sorcery, witchcraft, spell giving potion, magician, sorcerer. *"Pharmakeia*, in Greek medication, i.e., by extension magic, literal or figurative: sorcery, witchcraft. *Pharmakeus*, from *pharmakon* a drug, i.e. spell giving potion; a druggist or poisoner by extension a magician, sorcerer."[106]

If we go back to the Book of Enoch we see the following: *Amazarak taught all the sorcerers, and dividers of roots; Armers taught the solution of sorcery* (Book of Enoch, 8:3–4).[107] Hmmm...Aren't all medicines nothing more than chemical compounds? In fact when you study medicines and drugs, they usually come from plant or soil compounds, and in our modern science and chemistry labs, they are reproduced synthetically for mass production and distribution. Now, are all drugs, prescriptions, medicines bad? No! God can use what Satan meant for evil and turn it for our good. But, is it God's way? Did Jesus or any of the disciples given the power to heal through the Holy Spirit say anything to anybody about going to a local pharmacy and getting twenty milligrams of cureswhatailsya? No. They either rebuked the demon causing the disease (e.g., epilepsy) and cast him out; or they forgave sin, and the sickness interestingly "left them." Look at the warnings and side effects of modern drugs nowadays. They usually cause a whole laundry list of horrible side effects worse than the malady you have. Is that common sense? Yeah, you won't have heartburn, but you may experience vomiting, vertigo, anal leakage, sudden urge to urinate, drowsiness, heart attack, sudden death…and on and on. Does that sound like God's original plan for us? I would rather rebuke the heartburn…or better yet, eat the way God told us to eat so we can avoid the heartburn in the first place! I am telling you, we are a society of knotheads. We believe anything the doctors tell us. They are just trying to pay all of their overhead by getting you to go through their clinic as fast as possible (thank you HMOs!—Oh! Did I write that out loud?). It is easier for them to treat your symptoms than it is to spend days on end, analyzing every factor in your life to get to the root cause. No offense against doctors, but it is our grim reality, it is our system. I know—I used to work in it!

According to the book *Who Switched Off My Brain?,* "We each have our own inner and natural pharmacy that produces all the drugs we ever need to run our body-mind in precisely the way it was designed to run. Pert is among many researchers who have shown that exogenous (originating from the outside) drugs are potentially harmful to the system, because they disrupt the natural balance of feed back loops and influence change at a cellular level." [108]

Let's use a simple analogy. Take butter for instance; for thousands of years, man ate butter and it was good! (See Psalms 55:21, Proverbs 30:33, and Isaiah 7:15.) God said it was good! But, man in his infinite worldly wisdom said, "No, butter bad, full of saturated fat, make heart go boom." And on that fateful day, margarine companies were born—and they said, "Let us take a fat in liquid form and add hydrogen atoms to it so it will become a solid, and let us add an artificial flavoring because man demands that it taste 'like God's,' and let us add yellow dye (die), so it looks 'like God's.'" And man introduced it to the world as margarine (why margarine, because it is so marginal?) and said, "Eat this, and your heart won't go boom." And man choked down the stuff, because it tasted like something that came from the south end of a north-bound cow, and man kept getting more heart disease, and he went to hospitals who performed miracle angioplasties and bypass surgeries and sent man home to eat more margarine so that they would see him again in another five to ten years when his arteries clogged up again, and put more strain on his health, family, and finances. Then we get "new research" which proves all of that stuff is actually worse for your heart, loaded with bad trans fats, which man created in a chemical lab, and lo and behold, God was right to begin with. Eat the butter, or better yet, olive oil! I call this Intelligent Deception! He got you to go against God's word! He offered a substitute for God's creation. You rationalized, "The experts say it's good for me." You ate it; you died. I apologize for being so sarcastic here, but this is what Satan is doing to the children of God. You blindly follow the latest health report on the world news like sightless, dummies; spend God's money, and ruin his temple, and wonder why you are sick…Come on people, wake up!

We need to practice what Jesus did. We need to talk as Jesus did. We need to follow his example. When I feel a cold or a flu coming on (this is called the prodromal stage), I rebuke it! I tell it, "You have no right to live in my body, get out!" God's way works, you just have to practice it! Practice helps you believe, it increases your faith, because every time you try it, you are in effect saying, "O.K. God, I am gonna do it your way!" The Word admonishes us to *practice our faith.*

Science!

We are a society bombarded by "scientific evidence," but I can tell you without much hesitation nearly all scientific research is biased. Why? Because research requires large amounts of money; funding that is usually provided by the company or group that is searching for a positive slant to their idea, objective, product, or whatever. Never in our history have we used such an awesome tool as our brains to circumvent the creation of the world. Want to see massive contradiction? Look at science! Good science continues to question and point out the probabilities, the exactness of our world, our universe, and our bodies. Science takes on the role of disproving the current globality of thought. Ancient man for several millennia thought the earth was round. Then came the false notion it was flat, and it was the prevailing belief for centuries, but science disproved this once again. Science today is very much related to *doubt.* How do we disprove your theory and prove mine? You see doubt is the counterfeit of faith; doubt makes you question God's word. Doubt is uncertainty of the mind. *Did God say…* (Genesis 3). Doubt takes on the role of the devil's advocate. He knows if he can get your mind to question, rationalize, and think on a thing long enough, you eventually begin to believe that thing.

Dr. Chuck Missler has a great take on mixing science and faith; "God gave us a scientific mandate, Genesis 1:28, *Subdue the earth*—which means find the truth. Science, which should have been the great testimony to the majesty and glory of God, has, instead, become a device for ignoring and rejecting Him, and preying on the uniformed." [109]

To understand real science, let's look at the Great Scientist. Go with me to Job 38: *Then the LORD answered Job out of the storm. He said: "Who is this that darkens my counsel with words without knowledge? Brace yourself like a man; I will question you, and you shall answer me. Where were you when I laid the earth's foundation? Tell me, if you understand. Who marked off its dimensions? Surely you know! Who stretched a measuring line across it? On what were its footings set, or who laid its cornerstone,"* (Job 38:1–6; NIV). And again in Job: *"Will the one who contends with The Almighty correct him? Let him who accuses God answer him!"* (Job 40:2; NIV). Having a bachelor of science degree in nursing myself, I have always loved this discourse! Go ahead and read chapter 38–40. It is a refreshing look at the power and might of our creator, because *we* don't have all the answers! We have glimpses, vignettes of his knowledge, but we cannot comprehend the space of space, the depths of the oceans, and the power of the sun.

God the Scientist (Job 38:12–35)

Rotation of the Earth	v. 12–15
Springs and pathways of the sea	v. 16
Breadth of the Earth	v. 18
Travel of light	v. 19
Dividing of light	v. 24
Source of rain and ice	v. 28–30
Universal nature of the physical laws	v. 33
Electric communication laws	v. 35

This is the Great Scientist, the original, telling us our science is nothing but *words without knowledge*! The Intelligent Deceiver knows about science…remember his "I wills"? If he wants to exalt himself to god-status, he has to appear to have all the answers! Have you ever noticed one particular thread of popular science today? It's a constant recurring theme…disprove the existence of God! Why is creation such a threat to evolution? Evolutionists attempt to disprove God's son ever came to earth and died for our sins, to disprove he was resurrected. Disprove the creation by introducing a false idea called evolution, which states: literally billions of living creatures, humans included, were formless single-celled blobs that all differentiated into their various billions of complex forms, performing complex, factory-like functions at the smallest of cellular levels, creating complex systems and species specific variations and acclimatizations. When you stop to really think about it, it is the most absurd theory! Yet millions of people believe it like gospel fact! Satan basically took a turd and dipped it into chocolate and force-fed it down the throats of children!

When I was younger, teaching evolution in school was just beginning to gain momentum. I can remember one teacher's reply to my question: "Why aren't you following scientific protocol by discussing all theories?" His reply was something to the effect of a good mumble and a halfhearted "ask your parents." I have always been a "Why" personality, ever since I can remember. I could never take what someone taught me on preface alone. I wanted to know more. I wanted to know why they taught it that way, and why they were so sure! Especially when what I was being taught didn't measure up to my surroundings and my experiences!

Evolution has become something literally being worshipped. Why would "intelligent, scientifically minded" people put the earth on a pedestal? Take environmentalism, for example: take care of "The Mother," don't eat meat, don't cut down trees, but by all means make sure I have the latest and greatest in homes or gadgets…all made out of steel, wood, and other harvested goods, which require energy consumption to be useful. You will find the biggest hypocrites are the biggest promoters of the environmentalist movement. They literally worship trees. Believe it or not, Isaiah addresses these same people:

> He let it grow among the trees of the forest, or planted a pine, and the rain made it grow…From the rest he makes a god, his idol; he bows down to it and worships, he prays to it and says, "Save me; you are my god." They know nothing, they understand nothing; their eyes are plastered over so they cannot see, and their minds closed so they cannot understand. No one stops to think, nor has the knowledge or understanding to say, "Half of it I used for fuel; I even baked bread over its coals…Shall I make a detestable thing from what is left? Shall I bow down to a block of wood?" (Isaiah 44:14, 17–19; NIV)

Did you know we get one of our common clichés from ancient tree worship? The phrase "knock on wood" was a prayer by druids, who believed their spirit gods lived in the trunks of trees. The spirits were asleep evidently, and in order for them to hear your prayer, you had to "knock on wood" to arouse the sleeping deity so they could hear your request.

Evolution is Satan's gospel; worship the earth, because when you do, you are in effect worshipping him, the god and prince of the earth. Again, Satan has to copycat God. He cannot elevate himself without it. God was the originator; he commanded us to *fill the earth and subdue it. Rule over the fish of the sea and the birds of the air and over every living creature that moves on the ground* (Genesis 1:28; NIV). This was our scientific and stewardship mandate. The Intelligent Deceiver flipped it inside out, and told us, "Worship the earth, instead of ruling it! Don't follow the natural laws the Almighty put into place. Don't use the blessings of the abundance of the earth for your pleasure." What a load of hogswallop! When our earth is taken care of the way God commanded us to take care of it, it will last until his kingdom comes!

Evolution and environmentalism is another aspect of Satan's New Age movement. Which is not new at all, he started it at the fall. Remember Semiramos, Nimrod's wife? She made herself a goddess. Several of her names are Ashteroth, Queen of Heaven, Ester, Ishtar, and guess what one of the others is? Mother Earth! New Age and evolutionism believes in the perfectibility of man. Worship the rock, instead of the creator of the rock. Worship the tree instead of the creator of the tree. When you really stop and think…use your God-given common sense; what is a tree or a rock going to give you? Paul says it like it is in 1 Corinthians:

> For it is written: "I will destroy the wisdom the of the wise; the intelligence of the intelligent I will frustrate." Where is the wise man? Where is the scholar? Where is the philosopher of this age? Has not God made foolish the wisdom of the world? For since in the wisdom of God the world through its wisdom did not know him, God was pleased through the foolishness of what was preached to save those who believe. Jews demand miraculous signs and Greeks look for wisdom, but we preach Christ crucified: a stumbling block to Jews and foolishness to gentiles, but to those whom God has called, both Jews and Greeks, Christ the power of God and the wisdom of God. For the foolishness of God is wiser than man's wisdom, and the weakness of God is stronger than man's strength! (1 Corinthians 1:19–25; NIV)

We seem to forget Darwin was a man. He only went to the Galapagos Islands for a very short time, and never went back. Which doesn't make one an expert on any subject. Isaiah 2:22 sums up Darwin quite nicely: *Cease to trust in [weak, frail, and dying] man, whose breath is in his nostrils [for so short a time]; in what sense can he be counted as having intrinsic worth?* (Isaiah 2:22; AMP).

Mother Earth and The Gaia Hypothesis—For thousands of years numerous cultures have viewed Earth as a living, sentient being. The ancient Greeks worshipped a multitude of gods and goddesses. Among them was the ancient goddess Gaia, which was the spiritual entity, the Earth goddess whose physical body, they believed, was Earth itself—Mother Earth. Gaia was believed to be the soul or the spirit of the living planet.

"Worshipped for centuries by the ancient Greeks, Gaia has reemerged at the end of the 20th century in the New Age philosophy of pantheism. The Native Indians have worshipped earth for thousands of years as a living being and the mother of all creation. *The ancient Babylonians and the ancient Sumerians also believed in the divinity and consciousness of Mother Earth.*"[110] Where did this belief that Mother Earth is to be worshipped get its start? Babylon, it is Satan's kingdom city on earth.

Semiramos, the wife of Nimrod, allowed herself to be worshiped as a goddess, her more recognizable names are Astarte, and Asheroth, the wife of Baal. The "poles and groves" of trees used in Baal/Astarte worship is where she gets her name as a "Mother Earth," the symbol of spring and life. Nothing is new under the sun!

So how do you fight a lie and a liar that is being shoved down our throats in every mass media and institute of learning in the U.S.? Well, since God thought of science first, we need to do our best to wade through the proverbial crap, and learn about science. After all, he commanded us to subdue the earth. In other words, fight science with real science. Don't just stick your head in the sand. God gave you a marvelous brain; use it! Fight lies with truth!

"We are just a bunch of monkeys!" Well, if you are a Bible-believing Christian this theory is just laughable. Like begets like, so a monkey has a monkey. I have always wondered why we are not seeing chimpanzees having babies that are evolving into humans. Since the monkeys aren't cooperating with the theory, scientists turn to fossil evidence. The evidence of the "missing link" has never been forthcoming. The missing link is still missing! Instead, all anthropology and paleontology is completely cloaked in frauds and out and out lies. Gee, why am I not surprised? You have the Heidelberg man, which was just a jawbone. Yeah, can you prove I was a monkey with just a jawbone! Then you have Nebraska man, which proved to be a tooth from a pig; Piltdown man, a jawbone of an ape. Neanderthal man, which turned out to be an old man with arthritis, and Java man who turned out to be an orangutan![111] So scientists are having a heckuva time using science to prove evolution!

"DNA is the final nail in Darwin's coffin. DNA is a *digital code.* Darwinism cannot explain the origin of life because it cannot explain the *origin of information.* Irreducible complexity refutes chance as a designer." [112] Which basically states, even the smallest component of life cannot be explained without a master planner at the helm.

The human genome consists of all the DNA of our species, the hereditary code of life. This newly revealed text was three billion letters long and written in a strange and cryptographic four-letter code. Such is the amazing complexity of the information carried within each cell of the human body, that a live reading of that code at a rate of one letter per second would take thirty-one years, even if reading continued day and night. Printing these letters out in regular font size on normal bond paper and binding them all together would result in a tower the height of the Washington Monument.[113]

DNA is far too large and complex for it to have happened by random chance sequencing. As we learned earlier, even one small glitch in a single letter of the three billion letters could leave you with Down's syndrome. Wouldn't chance and probability favor these mistakes much more readily than perfection? This brings us to the Anthropic Principal, the idea that our planet was specifically engineered for human life.

The Anthropic Principal states the universe was designed for man. There are so many delicate mathematical ratios that, if altered even in the slightest, would render life impossible.[114]

Have you ever wondered why there is so much concern over the extinction of a particular species if evolution really exists? Or how about this one, how come nothing else is fossilized after the dinosaurs? "Fossils take suddenness and pressure to become fossilized. There is evidence that they all died by suffocation, and they still have evidence of subtropical vegetation in their mouths. All pointing to a sudden great deluge!" [115]

Science can be one of Satan's perversions of truth; he preys upon the ignorant and uneducated of this world, as well as the intelligent and the educated. Satan has ordained his scientists/priests to preach his perverted backward creation scenario—we all come from a guppy and the guppy was seeded here from another planet, brought here by the prevailing cosmic winds! But God has promised in his Word that he can turn what was meant for evil into good! *"Therefore once more I will astound these people with wonder upon wonder; the wisdom of the wise will perish, the intelligence of the intelligent will vanish"* (Isaiah 29:14; NIV).

Let's take the issue of all of the omni's of God: omnipresence, omniscience, and omnipotence. Have you ever wondered about these? It's pretty hard to wrap your mind around how God can be all of these things. The world is huge, and so is the universe. How can God be everywhere at once, know everything, be all power? Can science explain, or give us a glimpse into the reality of the omni's?

Quantum physics is such a unique discipline. It is the most

bizarre field of science, requiring the imaginative mind of a child to grasp its most complex theorems. Quantum physics talks about a mathematical principal called *planck length*, or *nonlocality*. This states if you cut a length of cord in half, you could continue to cut it in half forever. Well not so, you eventually get to such a ridiculous number the thing eventually loses its location. The number is ten to the negative forty-three seconds; you get to a point where you cannot cut it in half because it is so small.

The philosophical implications of quantum theory are profoundly disturbing. Among the startling discoveries made by quantum physicists is the fact that if you break matter—or energy or time—into smaller and smaller pieces, you eventually reach a point where those pieces (electrons, protons, etc.) no longer possess the traits of the objects. Although they can sometimes behave as if they were compact little particles, physicists have found that they literally possess no dimension. All points in space become equal to all other points in space, and it was meaningless to speak of anything as being separate from anything else. [116]

Let's see if I can break this down so it is easier to understand. Nonlocality states every particle knows what every other particle is doing. In other words, it was a whole and now is split into its tiniest amounts, so it's all connected somehow, even though it doesn't share the same location. If an atom is on our planet, and another atom is in another galaxy, the atom in the other galaxy knows exactly what the atom on our planet is doing. Omnipresent, omniscient, omnipotent would be good words to sum up the quantum physics of nonlocality.

Here is another science cookie for you. Let's take the issue of faith. Faith was always one of those intangibles, a far out there type of concept, not concrete, until I began to study the most famous of the verses on faith. *Now faith is the substance of things hoped for, the evidence of things not seen* (Hebrews 11:1; NIV). Did you know faith had substance? That means it can be measured just as the Bible tells us; we are all given *a measure of faith* (Romans 12:3). Did you know faith leaves evidence, just like a fingerprint? We have a terrible habit in our society: *seeing is believing.* What if science could explain faith? Faith is essentially matter, materializing from seemingly nothing visible anyway, right? There were two famous scientists who both won the Nobel Prize for electrons acting as waves and the other for electrons acting as particles. They were father and son.

"Both father and son were correct. From then on, the evidence for the wave/particle duality has become overwhelming. This chameleon-like ability is common to all subatomic particles. Called *quanta*, they can manifest themselves either as particles or waves. What makes them even more astonishing is that there is compelling evidence that *the only time quanta ever manifest as particles is when we are looking at them.*"[117]

This wave/particle duality may explain why our prayers are manifested.

Let me ask all you doubters out there a question. Do you know everything? Can you honestly say you even know yourself? How many hairs do you have on your head? Come on, how many? Does this put things into perspective? If you can't even count the number of hairs on your head, how are you going to answer the mysteries of the creation of the world? So if God chooses to use foolishness to prove your lack of wisdom, I dare you to contest that! *And even the very hairs of your head are all numbered* (Matthew 10:30; NIV).

Part Two

The Paranormal

INTRODUCTION

For whatever is hidden is meant to be disclosed, and whatever is concealed is meant to be brought out into the open.

—Mark 4:22; NIV

In Part II, we will discuss how Intelligent Deception works in our everyday lives and popular culture. We will find out what the Bible says about witchcraft, sorcery and magick, ghosts, aliens, and UFOs. The occult including Ouija boards and pentagrams, reincarnation, horoscopes and astrology, ancient megaliths and Mars, cryptozoology and dinosaurs, psychics and clairvoyants, prophecy and visions versus premonitions. Besides ancient pagan cultures, we have never before seen such widespread acceptance and information transferal of the paranormal as we have in the past twenty years, thanks in large part to the media and Internet. At this writing if you turn on the satellite or cable television, there are at least a dozen or more shows dealing with the paranormal on prime time television, such as: Ghost Whisperer, Medium, Paranormal State, Area 51, UFO Files, Psychic Detectives, A Haunting, Ghost Hunters, Charmed, Buffy the Vampire Slayer, The Good Witch, Twitches Too, Harry Potter, and so many others!

The popularity of these programs is staggering, and even more frightening is the callous refusal of our churches to address the paranormal. People are curious by nature. Whether you view the paranormal as a few folks at the "fringes of society" or as mainstream, our Christian society needs to learn more about it from a biblical perspective, instead of from a mass media angle. I have personally watched many of these programs with the intent of spying on my enemy, and out of pure curiosity. I can't tell you how many times I questioned God for answers on these same subjects, hoping the pastor would answer my questions one Sunday, but to no avail. The teaching is simply not out there. If people are not rooted and grounded in the Word, these are fantastic inroads for the enemy and his brood. They get the mind thinking of alternative personal power, they mislead people into thinking dead people can get "stuck" in between worlds, and offer us benevolent advice and help. They offer up previously taboo symbols as just another piece of body art or jewelry, without giving the appropriate warnings of their inherent evil nature. We are taught in our Christian churches to simply not touch "it" without even knowing what "it" is—"Stay away," they warn, without even understanding themselves what it is we should be staying away from.

Unfortunately for the curious Christian who wants to know how it all fits into their own theology, there are not many answers. I guess this is where this book comes in: to fill the gap and close the enemies trap. We have a generation of youngsters weaned on magick and sorcery, *Dungeons and Dragons*, video games that portray aliens, ghosts, and vampires. How do you answer the questions your children have if you don't have the answers? Because we live in the Information Age, just saying no is not good enough. You have to have an answer, because if you don't, they will find the answer they are looking for, and it may not be right one.

The other real danger is clergy mixing with mediums and psychics. We have a very real and live population of "servants of God" mixing with the "doctrine of devils." You can find these things happening on many of the more popular television programs investigating paranormal activity. The sad and dangerous mixing of these two paradigms is not new; all you have to do is open up nearly any page in the Old Testament and you will find the Israelites mixing Baal worship with the worship of the God of Israel. This practice was detestable to the Lord God Almighty, as we will learn in this section. Grab a cup o' Joe, and get ready to go down some real rabbit holes as we explore what the Bible has to say about the paranormal!

As an author's note, not all of the following are going to be snares of the enemy for everyone; just as alcohol may not be enticing for one, and yet a huge trap for another, so are some of the following paranormal interests going to be more of a trivial interest for some, and a huge spider web trap for others. The challenge is knowing what most likely will ensnare you. But then again we are dealing with Intelligent Deception. If he can get you to compromise in one area, he may get you more interested in the next level of his series of traps and disguises and get you snared beyond belief! I write this as a warning, some Christians are extremely sensitive to the works of the devil, and others are blatantly calloused. Both are in danger. Jesus tells us to be like night watchmen and be continually on our guard, but if you don't know who and how your enemy operates, it is difficult to distinguish the lambs from the wolves in sheep's clothing.

Human beings are looking for a spiritual experience, but we fail to realize that we are spiritual beings looking for a natural experience.

Chapter Six

HOROSCOPES AND ASTROLOGY

Hey baby, what's your sign?

America is enamored with their horoscopes, and many ignorant Christians are playing this seemingly innocent past time of "what is in store for me tomorrow?" by reading the daily horoscope pages in their favorite publication. Horoscopes tell people how to live, love, make career choices and financial moves, pursue relationships, what to wear, whether or not to talk to the boss today, where to look for an apartment, etc. Whether for entertainment value or serious inquiry, you should learn the true roots of this open door.

Let's have a word definition lesson:

"Astronomy is the scientific study of astronomical objects and phenomena, whereas astrology is concerned with the attempt to correlate these phenomena with earthly affairs. Astrology is variously considered by its proponents to be a symbolic language, a form of art science, or divination. The scientific community generally considers astrology to be a pseudoscience or superstition as astrologers have failed empirical tests in controlled studies. Despite the lack of scientific evidence, belief in astrology is widespread." [118]

"The word *astrology* is derived from the Greek αστρολογία, from άστηρ (*aster*, 'star') and λόγος (*logos*, 'speech, statement, reason'). The -λογία suffix is written in English as *-logy*, 'study' or 'discipline.'"[119]

So astronomy is good; it is the study of our planets and their stars. Astrology is bad, and it is the study of the relationship of those planets and stars with our lives and futures. So where did all of this originate? It originated in Babylon, Satan's city, his seat of world dominance. Well wouldn't you know it, this is where the horoscope (astrology) began. Remember the Tower of Babel? *"...with a tower that reaches to the heavens"* (Genesis 11:4; NIV). "The seven stages of the tower correspond to the planets." [120] Babylon was a Mecca of pagan worship and human sacrifice to their demon gods, and to planet gods. We still have the same twelve zodiac signs today the ancient Babylonians used.

So what is the big deal really? Isn't it all just for fun and games, something to strike up a conversation with a pretty girl or small talk over coffee with coworkers? It's just entertainment, just fun! Well, I have to agree, sin is fun! Why else would you do it? But this book isn't about the mainstream, it is about something deeper. Let's go back even further into history. Let's take a look at our Intelligent Deceiver and ask ourselves, "Why would he want to corrupt the stars?" Satan didn't create the heavens, or the stars. God did. So the heavens and the stars are not evil in and of themselves. Remember Satan's "I Will" decree? *I WILL raise my throne above the stars of God; I WILL ascend above the tops of the clouds.* Arrogant, narcissistic, and power hungry! He is again trying to copycat, trying to pervert what God had made as something good! Who created the stars, and the heavens, and all of the celestial bodies and luminaries? God! Satan is so predictable; "I want to be like God," but the only way it is possible is by taking what he already created and perverting it.

We look to the stars in our culture for the answers from our silliest questions to our most profound: "What color matches my new Coach bag?" to "Is there life out there?" The Intelligent Deceiver deliberately orchestrated it that way. We cannot get away from the influence of the stars on our lives. The days of the week are named after them, our seasons are governed by them, and even the Intelligent Deceiver himself was once named after a morning star: Venus.

E. Raymond Capt, a famous archeologist who correlated his finds with the Bible, states:

> Having declared that the heavens reveal God's glory, the psalmist informs us that the heavens declare a message in a language that is understood by all peoples...How then can the stars be made to speak, in a language everyone can understand?
>
> The answer is quite evident. Pictures speak in all dialects. They speak a universal language, to all peoples everywhere...Today we know them as Constellations.
>
> Twelve constellations make up the Zodiac. These major star groupings form a belt which circles the sky close to the plane of the earth's orbit around the sun. Modern atlases list them in the following order: Aries, Taurus, Gemini, Cancer, Leo, Virgo, Libra, Scorpio, Sagittarius, Capricorn, Aquarius and Pisces.
>
> It is well known the ancient races drew charts of these Zodiacal Signs, that ancient astrology was actually the fate of astronomy. Astronomers sometimes denounce the Zodiac as unnatural and confusing, yet they have never been able to

brush it aside or substitute anything better or more convenient in its place. The Signs of the Zodiac are a part of the common universal language of astronomical science.[121]

And God said, "Let there be lights in the expanse of the sky to separate the day from the night, and let them serve as signs to mark the seasons and days and years" (Genesis 1:14; NIV). God uses the stars to *foretell and lead* the wise men to Christ's birth (see Matthew 2:1–10). The Bible tells us God calls the stars forth by name (see Palms 40:26, 147:4, and Isaiah 40:26,13:10) and also that they speak of his glory (see Psalm19:1–6). So who created the stars and the purpose for them? And who perverted them?

"Historically, alchemy in the Western World was particularly allied and intertwined with traditional Babylonian-Greek style astrology; in numerous ways they were built to complement each other in the search for occult or hidden knowledge. Astrology has used the concept of the four classical elements of alchemy from antiquity up until the present day. Traditionally, each of the seven planets in the solar system known to the ancients was associated with, held dominion over, and 'ruled' a certain metal." [122]

The Babylonians were the first to name the days of the week after the sun, moon, and planets. Their naming scheme is still widely followed today in many languages, including English, and goes as follows:

Sunday—day of the sun
Monday—day of the moon
Tuesday—day of Mars (English *Tiw*, the Anglo-Saxon Mars)
Wednesday—day of Mercury (English *Wodin*, the Anglo-Saxon Mercury)
Thursday—day of Jupiter (English *Thor*, the Anglo-Saxon Jupiter)

Friday—day of Venus (English *Frig*, the Anglo-Saxon Venus)

Saturday—day of Saturn

According to the Internet encyclopedia, Wikipedia; "In Babylonia as well as in Assyria as a direct offshoot of Babylonian culture (or as we might also term it 'Euphratean' culture), astrology takes its place in the official cult as one of the two chief means at the disposal of the priests (who were called *bare* or 'inspectors') for ascertaining the will and intention of the gods, the other being through the inspection of the liver of the sacrificial animal." [123]

So if God created the stars, and the purpose of using them was to tell the seasons and days, and to foretell and lead to Jesus' birth, isn't that kind of like a horoscope? Yes, and no. The difference is God originated it. The stars pointed to *his* majesty and glory; now the horoscope points to *your* future glory. It has nothing to do with God, and you again are consulting his creation, not him! This is Satan's New Age religion; worship the world and what it has to offer because he is king of this world. Why would you follow the advice of someone who didn't create you? You read your horoscope and it tells you what kind of personality you have, who you should talk too, and who you get along with most. It tells you who and when you should date, marry, have sex, get a job, quit your job, what to wear, where to invest, what kind of week, month, year you will have. Don't you think that sounds awfully presumptuous? Very controlling? Very manipulating? Don't you think it odd we still have the zodiac of ancient Babylon in use today? Don't you find it strange we still have the days of the week the Babylonians used? Do you really think it is just some fluke coincidence? Or could it be a well-orchestrated plan?

The Bible tells us the only form of looking into the future that is acceptable comes from the Holy Spirit. It is actually one of the gifts of the Spirit; the Word of Wisdom. When the Holy Spirit reveals a Word of Wisdom, he literally pulls back the curtain of time and shows you a future event. Usually this is to be used to help people. It may be a warning, it may be something good, but it is always for the benefit of mankind, not for personal gain, and the Holy Spirit moves as he wills. He cannot be controlled or put into a weekly newspaper column. There is a huge difference; horoscopes pervert the power of the Holy Spirit. They copycat and mock. They counterfeit his spiritual gift for your own personal gain, but at the cost of your own spiritual bereavement.

Let's go back before the horoscope to the book of Job. (Scholars think this is one of the oldest accounts of the Bible.) *Can you bring forth the constellations in their seasons* (Job 38:32; NIV). "The word *constellations* in the ancient Hebrew is *Mazzeroth*, and the primitive root is *Sodi* (The Way in Sanskrit)." [124] So in the Hebrew *Mazzeroth* were the twelve constellations of the zodiac, during the monthly stages of the year. Isn't that interesting? The zodiac is called "The Way," which is how Jesus is described, and also how early Christianity was described (see Acts 9:2; 19:9, 23). But how can that be? The Bible clearly warns us to stay away from astrology! Yes, astrology, not astronomy! God is the original scientist! So let's take a closer look at this *Mazzeroth*.

The *Mazzeroth* or the twelve stars of the constellations all allude to the coming of Christ, the gospel, and his plan of redemption. Do you think Satan would have known about that? Do you think if God had foretold his future plan in the heavens for us to "read" and "understand" maybe it might damage Satan's plan and his kingdom? Do you think he was mad? Do you think he might have the gall to actually try to circumvent the Lord's neon redemption billboard in the sky by misdirecting and attributing other meanings to these stars and planets, thereby diverting the truth and diminishing the message of God? I call this Intelligent Deception. Let's look at God's original plan and meaning of the stars.

The heavens declare the glory of God; the skies proclaim the work of his hands, Day after day they pour forth speech; night after night they display knowledge. There is no speech or language where their voice is not heard. Their voice goes out into all the earth, their words to the ends of the world (Psalm 19:1–4; NIV). Why would God say his stars speak? Why would they display knowledge that could be understood in every language and dialect throughout history? Could God have used the stars to tell *his* story *before* the written word? Let's look.

The *Mazzeroth* has twelve constellations; each of these constellations is a "grouping" of stars, usually a main star with three decan stars. They have an Ecliptic, meaning path of the sun (or path of the Son?). If you have ever looked at the stars on a moonless, clear night, it can be mind-boggling. For those of you living in large urban areas, take a drive to the country one evening; you can see so much more! There are billions, trillions of stars, too many to possibly number, but according to scripture, God calls each one by name every night! We happen to have a few of those names. Here are the stars of the *Mazzeroth* and their cluster stars, which are represented as pictures (constellation). Each group of stars also is linked with a particular tribe of Israel.

The *Mazzeroth* and their three decan stars, with each of their descriptive meanings (From Chuck Missler's *The Signs in the Heavens*)[125]:

VIRGO: Virgin: The Tribe of Zebulon (where Nazareth is located). Why would a virgin have a child in a constellation?

- *Coma*-Infant, the Desired One
- *Centaraus*-Dart, piercing a victim, The Despised
- *Bootes*-Great Shepherd and Harvester, The Coming One

LIBRA: The scales or balance (literally—paying a debt owed)—The Tribe of Levi

- *Crux*-Cross
- *Lupus or Victim*-Pierced to Death (A Lamb)
- *Corona*-Crown

SCORPIO: Scorpion—The Tribe of Dan

- *Serpens*-The Serpent (trying to seize the crown)
- *Ophiuchus*-Wrestling with a Serpent, with his heel on the head of the snake, and the snake striking his heel (hmmm)
- *Hercules*-Mighty Man, Right Heel Wounded

SAGITTARIUS: The Archer—The Tribe of Asher

- *Lyra*-the harp (He Shall be Exalted)
- *Ara*-The Altar
- *Draco*-the Dragon (Trodden on)

CAPRICORNUS: The Goat-Fish—The Tribe of Naphtali

- *Sagitta*-Arrow
- *Aquila*-The Eagle
- *Delphines*-The Dolphin

AQUARIUS: Water Bearer—The Tribe of Reuben

- *Picus Australis*-Southern Fish
- *Pegasus*-Winged Horse (returning from afar)
- *Cygnus*-Swan (Bird of Return)

PISCES: Fishes—The Tribe of Simeon

- *Alrisha*-The Band (that ties them together)
- *Andromeda*-The Woman in Chains
- *Cepheus*-The Crowned King

ARIES: The Ram—The Tribe of Gad

- *Cassiopeia*-The Enthroned Woman
- *Cetus*-The Sea Monster
- *Perseus*-Armed & Mighty Man

TAURUS: The Ox (or Bull)—The Tribe of Joseph

- *Orion*-Glorious Prince
- *Eridanes*-Orion's River (the river of the Judge)
- *Auriga*-The Shepherd

GEMINI: The Twins—The Tribe of Benjamin

- *Lepus*-The Hare (The Enemy)
- *Canis Major*-The Sirius-Great Dog, Wolf
- *Canis Minor*-The Little Dog, The Lamb

CANCER: The Crab—The Tribe of Issachar

- *Ursa Major*-The Herd
- *Ursa Minor*-The Lesser Sheepfold
- *Argo*-The Ship (Redeemed)

LEO: The Lion—The Tribe of Judah

- *Hydra*-The Fleeing Serpent
- *Crater*-The Cup (of wrath)
- *Corveus*-The Raven, bird of doom

So what does all of this stuff mean; pictures in stars? Imagine you are Adam, Seth, or Enoch, and you are putting your kids to bed. They have no television, no video games, no Internet, and you are under billions of stars. So you tell stories to your kids of the prophecies told to you by God. You can't make out pictures by these particular constellations because they just don't look like that. Have you ever looked at the stars and said to yourself, "How did they get a lion out of that?" Well they didn't. According to Dr. Missler, a well-known biblical scholar, they named the stars in order of their brightness; he suggests the pictures were a mnemonic to help them to remember the story. "If you put together the meanings (in Hebrew, Arabic, and Egyptian languages) of each of the major stars with their smaller or clusters of stars this is what you get:

VIRGO—The seed of a woman, has the desire of the nations. He is a man of double nature and humiliation, and he is the exalted shepherd and harvester.

LIBRA—The price to be paid, the cross to be endured, the victim slain, and the crown purchased.

SCORPIO—The conflict, the serpent coils, the struggle with the enemy, toiling vanquisher of evil.

SAGITTARIUS—The doubled natured one triumphing. He gladdens the heavens, he builds the fires of punishment, and he casts down the dragon.

CAPRICORNUS—Life out of death, the arrow of God, pierced and failing, springing up again in abundant life.

AQUARIUS—Life waters from on high, drinking in heavenly food, carrying the good news, bearing aloft the cross over earth.

PISCES—Multiplication of the redeemer's people, upheld and governed by a lamb, intended bride bound and exposed, the bridegroom exalted.

ARIES—The Lamb found worthy, the bride released and making ready, Satan bound, the Breaker triumphing.

TAURUS—The invincible ruler comes, the sublime vanquisher, river of judgment, the all ruling shepherd.

GEMINI—The marriage of the Lamb, the enemy trodden down, the prince coming in glory, his princely following.

CANCER—The possession secured the lesser fold church of the first born, the greater fold-Israel, the safe folding into the everlasting kingdom.

LEO—The king rending, the serpent fleeing, the bowl of wrath upon him, the carcass devoured."[126]

Kinda freaky, huh? It is the gospel story written in the stars! I bet you won't read anything like that in the Sunday newspaper! And why would you? What does any of that have to do with love, romance, money, career, best color for your skin tone, etc.? It doesn't! This is why Satan corrupted it! You would not have known the original use for the stars was to foretell Christ's coming, his redemption, his defeat of the enemy, his reigning kingdom! Why would Satan want you to know that? *And there shall be signs in sun and moon and stars; and upon the earth distress of nations, in perplexity for the roaring of the sea and the billows* (Luke 21:25; NIV). This is one way of "knowing" you are dealing with a fraudulent, deceiving spirit. The Bible tells us there are two ways to know; they deny the gospel, and they deny the God-hood and sacrifice of Jesus on the cross. God warns us in the end times you will see "signs in the stars" again! Do you see that in the Sunday horoscope? No way!

So what do the scriptures say about astrology? *And they forsook all the commandments of the Lord their God,...and made an Asherah, and worshipped all the host of heaven, and served Baal* (2 Kings 17:16; NIV)...*them also that burned incense to Baal, to the sun, and to the moon, to the constellations and to all the starry hosts* (2 Kings 23:5;

NIV). *All the counsel you have received has only worn you out! Let your astrologers come forward, those stargazers who make predictions month by month, let them save you from what is coming upon you...they cannot even save themselves from the power of the flame. Each of them goes on in his error; there is not one that can save you* (Isaiah 47:13–15; NIV).

According to the Almighty, astrology is idol worship, and your astrologer and star chart reader cannot save themselves. What makes you think they can save you from your own hardships and trouble? God is always pretty straightforward. He doesn't say these things to be mean; he says them from the point of view of a loving father who tells his kid not to play in rush hour traffic! He doesn't want you get hurt!

The Book of Enoch even mentioned the name of the fallen angel who taught astrology: Barkayal. Now known as "Baraqyal, he was ranked among the chief ten, the divisions of the evil unrepentant angels. Baraqyal is able to teach those who summon him the secrets arts of astrology." [127] It is important if you have consulted an astrologer or someone who claims to be able to "read" your chart to ask yourself where they got their information. Most likely they didn't channel or summon this Baraqyal themselves, but whoever wrote their books or information most likely did. Renounce, repent, and change your course of action even if you have just looked at the Sunday paper horoscope. You are playing a very dangerous, illegal game of idolatry in the eyes of your Father. Only he knows your future!

Do not learn the ways of the nations or be terrified by signs in the sky, though the nations are terrified by them (Jeremiah 10:2; NIV). As I write this it is headline news that NASA is trying to increase their funding to help them identify and find rogue meteors and asteroids which may be on a collision course with our planet. Again God tells us to trust in him. His Word has value for today's headlines.

It is interesting to learn when the star of Bethlehem rose in the East, our modern astronomers have learned the most likely explanation of this miraculous sign was the planet Jupiter making a triple conjunction with the star Regulus, which means "regal" or "king." All of this took place in the constellation Leo the Lion, which also means "king." The other startling sign that took place in the sky was that Virgo the Virgin followed Jupiter in the night sky and gave birth to the new moon. This was written about in Revelation: *A great and wondrous sign appeared in heaven: a woman clothed with the sun, with the moon under her feet* (Revelation 12:1; NIV). She is described as pregnant. Theologians recognize this passage as John having a vision of the Virgin Mary with Jesus in her womb.

You can't make this stuff up! Stars were meant for our good and to foretell the future of Jesus' coming and plan for our futures. They were not created for you to figure out what day of the week is the best day for your next date.

So by all means, if you are truly interested in the science and study of stars and planets, take up astronomy! You will learn about the vast, incredible nature of our creator, and heaven forbid, you may actually have to find your own friends, take a chance and wear pink on Mondays, and invest in XYZ stock on your own hard work and investigations. And if you find you really must have a reading, read the Bible! The Lord actually tells us what he has in store for our future! *"For I know the plans I have for you," declares the Lord, "plans to prosper you and not to harm you, plans to give you hope and a future"* (Jeremiah 29:11; NIV).

"Many mystic or esoteric traditions have links to astrology. In some cases, like Kabbalah, this involves participants incorporating elements of astrology into their own traditions. In other cases, like divinatory tarot, many astrologers themselves have incorporated the tradition into their own practice of astrology. Esoteric traditions include, but are not limited to, alchemy, Germanic runes, Kabbalah, numerology, palmistry, Rosicrucian or Rose Cross, and tarot divination."[128]

Chapter Seven

UFOS AND ALIENS

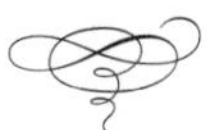

Roswell, the X-Files, Project Blue Book, Independence Day, War of the Worlds, Area 51, the UFO Files, Star Wars, Star Trek, Grays, Reptilians, Little Green Men—Aliens and UFOs, and even Ezekiel's wheels are everywhere you look! The topic is exceedingly popular today, but why? Twenty to thirty years ago, if you said you saw an alien or a UFO you were a nut job. But now it is cool, hip, inspired even! I mean really, how can one look at all of those stars and planets and galaxies and say we are the only ones? If God really is so big, why would he only create us? The fact of the matter is God did not just "create us." We actually were his last creation. Remember, angels were the very first creations. Christians are labeled as very narrow-minded these days. I actually like that label; it tells me I am thinking only of God, but I believe there is a very perplexing, complicated plan of deception going on here. Demons are only as good as their ingenuity at deception, trickery, and development of a ruse.

I believe for every move of God, there is a counterfeit move of the Intelligent Deceiver. Do you want to know what Satan's biggest and best lie is? "We aren't alone." If he can get people to believe it, then he can get people to believe his next best deception; he doesn't exist. In all truth, we are not alone, but it is the *who* that is out there that is the question. To really do the alien/UFO phenomenon justice, we have to go back to scripture, and believe it or not, we have a lot of passages that actually deal with this subject. The problem is the Bible doesn't call them by our modern terminology of aliens and UFOs. We have to go by their *other* names.

Paul states that *we do not wrestle with flesh and blood, but with principalities and powers, with wicked spirits in high places* (Ephesians 6:12; NIV). The term *high places* literally means "in the heavens" or "aerial regions." Satan is actually called prince of the power of the air, or prince of the aerial host (see Ephesians 2:2). We have a false concept as Christians that Satan and his fallen angels and demons are confined to the realm of hell. There are certainly some there now, but the time has not yet come for them to be put into the bottomless pit, as we know from the demoniac at Gaderene, when the demons asked Jesus if they could go into the pigs because it was not yet their time. Satan and his forces are free to move about the cosmos with permission from God to test his saints. For faith untested is not faith at all.

Jesus specifically named one in particular: Beelzebub (see Mark 10:25). The teachers of the law accuse Jesus of being possessed by this "prince of demons" in Mark 3:21 and in Luke 11:15. It gets very interesting when you start to study the root name of Beezlebub. Turns out it is Baal, who, as most of you know, was the pagan god worshiped by none other than the Canaanites, and of course is the chief deity god of Babylon. "The name Baal is derived from the Semitic word meaning 'possessor' or 'Lord'...We also see he was the 'Lord of war, and of the sky.' [129] When you start to add endings to his name you get; Baalhazor 'Lord of the Fortress,' Baalbamoth 'Lord of the high places,' and Baalzebub, 'Lord of those that fly or flit.' The word *Zebub* is a Hebrew word, which means to flit from place to place. It has been popularly translated as the 'Lord of the flies,' but it is more accurately rendered as 'Lord of those things that fly.' "[130] The Old Testament uses very descriptive Hebrew words, such as *b'nai Elohim* (Sons of God), *Zophim* (the watchers), and *Malakh* (messengers), and don't forget the *Nephilim* (the fallen ones). We also have other scriptural references; *Rephaim* (from the root rapha, meaning "spirits;" see Genesis 14:5), *Anakim* (race of giants; see Numbers 13:33), *Emim* (the proud deserters, terrors, race of giants; see Genesis 14:5), *Zuzim* (the evil ones, roaming things; see Genesis 14:5), *Zamzummims* (the evil plotters; see Deuteronomy 2:20), and *Serpherim* (the many, Isaiah 6:2).[131]

So we know Satan can fly; he is after all a fallen cherub. How can we make the leap to linking these names of giants of the past and other descriptive names for fallen, evil angels? What do they have to do with aliens? Remember when the scriptures described "the fall" of Lucifer in Ezekiel 28? It is common knowledge his name may have been misinterpreted, and "morning star, son of the dawn" may not be the most accurate description. It's very close in my opinion. The Hebrew word *Hay-lale* means "bright or clear sounding." A more descriptive translation would read; O clear sounding, boasting son from the beginning. But nonetheless, God calls his angels "morning stars," which means *earliest creations. ...(the earth) who laid its cornerstone—when the morning stars sang together, and all the sons of God shouted for joy?* (Job 38:6–7; NIV).

We learned back in the angel section that angels are called by God from the farthest regions of the heavens or universe (see Mark 13:27). What about those "whirling wheels" Ezekiel saw? We learned they were actually a type of angel called Ophanim. If you didn't know anything about angels and you saw one of these wheels, "flitting like lightening" to and fro in the heavens (and don't forget their ability to move hyper dimensionally) appearing and disappearing as lights or wheels full of lights (eyes), wouldn't you, with your TV-suggested knowledge base, naturally assume these things were UFOs? I know I would have!

Let's go back to Ezekiel and see if we can find any answers there. *You were anointed as a guardian cherub, for so I ordained you. You were on the holy mount of God; you walked among the fiery stones* (Ezekiel 28:14; NIV). So what does this mysterious passage mean? *Fiery stones*? What are fiery stones? When translated it means "built stones, or rocks of fire." Some have suggested this may mean "God built stones" reflecting the light of the sun; in other words the planets. Ezekiel 28:16 goes on to describe what Lucifer was doing, and where again, he was expelled from. *Through your widespread trade you were filled with violence, and you sinned. So I drove you in disgrace from the mount of God, and I expelled you, O guardian cherub, from among the fiery stones* (Ezekiel 28:16; NIV). This passage of scripture has always bothered me. Why and where would Lucifer be doing "widespread trade"? And if he got expelled from the fiery stones, and they were in fact planets, what does that tell us?

Obviously at this point Lucifer is corrupt. What I gather from this passage is Lucifer was again doing something he was *not* supposed to be doing. The possibility he was setting up his kingdoms on other planets and doing some rather odd hanky-panky up on those stars would not surprise me in the least considering his nature and his "I will" goals. He was definitely trying to elevate his status to supersede God's. How would one go about doing that? Ezekiel tells us: *Behold you are wiser than Daniel; every one of the secret things is not hidden from you* (Ezekiel 28:3; KJV). It goes on to say he amassed great wealth through skillful trading. I know this is a stretch even for my imagination, but could a super-intelligent, skillful, deceitful being, possibly have set up for himself and his band of rebellious, prideful angels, an advanced kingdom and civilization of corrupt angels, before the earth was created, on a couple of other planets? When you begin to connect the dots throughout scripture and through our knowledge of ancient pagan religions that began in Babylon, and you look at our current fascination with the stars, it makes you wonder. What is Satan up too? Why is there irrefutable evidence and an emerging pattern linking Satan with planetary and star worship? Why is it growing in popularity now (again)? Why are we seeing headline news covering the "face on Mars," the pictures of water erosion on a planet with no water? The huge scientific discovery of primitive, bacterial life on Mars during Clinton's presidency? Or the recent shocking announcement by the Vatican's chief astronomer that the Catholic Church would welcome and embrace our extraterrestrial brothers? Is there something going on here?

Go back to Satan's capital city, Babylon, and look at the gods he created for man to worship. We have already named one of the principal gods of Babylon: Baal. Here is a poetic description of its rituals from Wikipedia: "On the summits of hills and mountains flourished the cult of the givers of increase, and 'under every green tree' was practiced the licentiousness which was held to secure abundance of crops. Human sacrifice, the burning of incense, violent and ecstatic exercises, ceremonial acts of bowing and kissing, the preparing of sacred mystic cakes (see also Asherah), appear among the offences denounced by the post-Exilic prophets; and show that the cult of Ba'al (and 'Ashtart) included characteristic features of worship which recur in various parts of the Semitic (and non-Semitic) world, although attached to other names."[132] Baal is also associated with the planet Jupiter, and is very closely attached to the goddess Ishtar. I find it rather interesting the word *Baal* means "Lord." Who else do we know wants that title very much? The planet Jupiter literally means "king planet." It is the planet that is scientifically associated with the star of Bethlehem, heralding the birth of Christ, The King! Can you see why Satan would want to be associated with this planet? It would help him fulfill his "I Wills"!

Look at the tower of Babel in the Old Testament. It was built in Ziggurat form. It was a step temple; these types of temples were called "high houses," *E'kur* or *E'anna* meaning "house of heaven or sky." Every step, or level, was devoted to one of the known stars at the time. These shrines popped up all over the place, and the Sumerians developed a family of divinities known as the *Anunaki* (Anu=Heaven, Na=And, Ki=Earth). Anu wasn't known as "the god" of the heavens but was known as "THE heavens." It gets even stranger when you Google the word Anunnaki on the web.

The following is a commentary on the popular "Aliens as gods" theory put forth in Zecharia Sitchin's books:

> Zecharia Sitchin propounds—that the Anunnaki (Sumerian: "those who came down from the heavens"; Old testament Hebrew, Anakeim, Nefilim, Elohim; Egyptian: Neter), an advanced civilization from the tenth planet in our solar system, splashed down in the Persian Gulf area around 432,000 years ago, colonized the planet, with the purpose of obtaining large quantities of gold. Some 250,000 years ago, the recovered documents tell us, their lower echelon miners rebelled against the conditions in the mines and the Anunnaki directorate decided to create a creature to take their place. Enki, their chief scientist and Ninhursag, their chief medical officer, after getting no satisfactory results splicing animal and Homo Erectus genes, merged their Anunnaki genes with that of Homo Erectus and produced

> us, Homo Sapiens, a genetically bicameral species, for their purposes as slaves. Because we were a hybrid, we could not procreate. The demand for us as workers became greater and we were genetically manipulated to reproduce.[133]

Anunaki is synonymous with many New Age religions and the alien/UFO phenomenon, which is just a resurgence of the original Babylonian pagan religions. Now I don't know about you, but I find it rather unsettling that you can link New Age religions to Old Testament scripture, and the worship and lies of Satan, are going hand in hand with what God said would be happening in the end times. Remember what Jesus said in Luke 17:26? *As in the days of Noah so shall my second coming be* (Luke 17:26; NIV). What a clever creature!

Let's look at other Babylonian gods and what they represented as described in Wikipedia:

> *An*, the god of heaven *Enlil*, the god of the air (from Lil = Air) and storms - *Nippur*. He was usually portrayed in human form, but also appears as a snake to the human's eyes. *Enki*, the god of water and the fertile earth - *Eridu*, which is also the god of magic, wisdom and intelligence. *Ki* or *Ninhursag*, the mother-goddess representing the earth, *Ashur*, main god of Assyria (sky god) *Ninlil*, or *Nillina*: goddess of air (possibly the south wind), *Inanna*, the goddess of love and war. *Marduk*, originally *Ea's* son and god of light, was the main god of Babylon and the sender of the Babylonian king *Nanna - Suen* (Sumerian) or Sin God of the moon *Utu Tutu*, or *Shamash* God of the sun.[134]

Did you notice any glaring characteristics of the enemy and his fallen angels and demons in that paragraph? We seem to have an array of gods worshipped who seem to coincide with the fallen angels we studied earlier…hmmm. The Bible also labels false "gods" as representing a certain demon. So any idol worship was also demon worship. Here we have a list of gods identified with planetary bodies:

> The name of the Gods in Sumerian {DINGIR} literally meant "Star" and all principal Mesopotamian Gods were identified with the sky. The movements of these bodies was considered linked to events on earth giving rise to the "science" of astrology. Sin the God of the moon, Shamash, The Sun God. The other visible planets were also associated with divinities; Enki and later Nabu was associated with Mercury, Ishtar (aka Sumerian "Inanna"), The Queen of the Heavens and goddess of love and war was associated with Venus, Nergal was associated with Mars, Enlil and late Marduk was associated with Jupiter, Ninurta was associated with Saturn. [135]

So we see from this paragraph how these gods are linked with stars and star worship. Remember what God called his angels—"morning stars"!

This brings us to one of the most popular goddesses in Babylon: Ishtar, the female counterpart of Baal. Ishtar is all over the place in the Bible. She is commonly referred to as Ashtoreth, and many accounts of Israel's idolatry included the Asherah pole, which had a phallic connotation. She is a goddess of love, war, and sex, and was the original Mother Earth, and was called the Queen of Heaven in the Bible and ancient times (see Jeremiah 7:18, 44:17–19, 25). She is the matron of seduction and prostitutes, having herself been purported to have had an incredible amount of lovers. She is also associated with beer. It is interesting to note that Venus is a morning star and an evening star. She is pictured in statuettes that have been found showing her naked, with her arms folded across her breast or holding a child. The lion, bull, serpent, and dragon are sacred to Ishtar. The thing which intrigues me so about the goddess Ishtar is due to a very interesting passage in the book of Revelation. *"Come, I will show you the punishment of the great prostitute, who sits on many waters, with her the kings of the earth committed adultery and the inhabitants of the earth were intoxicated with the wine of her adulteries."... This title was written on her forehead: MYSTERY BABYLON THE GREAT, THE MOTHER OF PROSTITUTES AND OF THE ABOMINATIONS OF THE EARTH* (Revelation 17: 1–5; NIV). Who does that sound like to you? Yeah, sounds like an exact description of Ishtar, who was quite literally the Queen of Babylon—Semiramos. See, when you begin to connect the scriptural dots with current events and past history, you begin to see an emerging pattern. Satan is an Intelligent Deceiver, and he is in the process of deceiving the "elite" of the world with all of his nonsense.

Could Satan be behind all the alien/UFO agenda going on right now? Why do the pyramids, the Incan and Mayan temples, the Stonehenge all line up mathematically to the stars? Why can't our modern engineers and complicated computer programs recreate these megaliths? Why can't we figure out how the ancients were able to move fifty-ton stones from hundreds of miles away to the top of high mountain tops, and have them so precisely fitted that you can't even slide a piece of paper between them? Could they be temples to Satan and his fallen angels, possibly even built by them, or the Nephilim, who would have the physical strength, plus the angelic intellect to pull it off? Or, an even more disturbing idea would be God had the great pyramid built for his purpose, and Satan again corrupted it. I am just conjecturing here, but I find it hard not lean toward that assumption. Why is there a face on Mars that looks like our Sphinx? Why are their pictures of what look like a city of pyramids on Mars? Could this be another con-job, by the biggest con artist of them all? (More on the great monuments in another section.)

I want to go out on a limb here and suggest a theory I have regarding the habitation of planets. If Satan and his rebellious band of angels did in fact inhabit planets (the fiery stones), and they did build civilizations to try to emulate and circumvent the Almighty Jehovah, and they tricked us into believing they were "benevolent beings from another planet, here to help us to evolve to the next level of consciousness," why are they so darned frightening? Why all the lies, cover-ups, and disinformation campaigns by governments? Why do they "abduct" people, and act secretively? Why do they do weird sexual and reproductive experiments on the humans they do abduct? Why are they only able to contact us through channeling, psychics, mediums, and cult leaders? I think aliens are nothing more than Satan and his fallen angels and his demonic offspring pulling off one of the biggest deceptions to date. The aliens' fruit speaks for itself; deceit, lies, cover-ups, sexual/genetic manipulation, denial of an Almighty God. Who does that sound like to you? This is just the beginning of the end. Respected scientists are actually predicting we will have contact by the year 2020! Does the aliens' aforementioned behavior remind you of anyone or anything? It is pure demonic behavior and character, through and through! I say we have had contact with "aliens" from the very beginning. We are not "alone," we never have been! Look again at the descriptions of angels in the angel section. If you saw cherubim with their counterparts The Wheel (Ophanim), what would you think? Screams ALIEN to me! But they are nothing more than angels! And these are fallen angels to boot, bent on the self-actualization of us poor moronic beasts who worship one God!

How do you explain building civilizations that seem to be on other planets? This is pure conjecture on my part, but I believe Satan is capable of manipulating God's creations, just as we are. Take for example the Pomeranian or the Daschund. Did God create these two breeds of dogs? No! We did! God created wolves and other wild dogs, and all other breeds of dogs have been genetically manipulated to be the breeds they are today by humans. We call it genetics, selective breeding, and hybridization. We selectively choose certain animals with certain characteristics and we breed them on down the line, until we "create" the desired end. Do you think it possible Satan, with his advanced knowledge of the "secret things," could possibly do the same? Only perhaps on a much more sophisticated level? Just a theory, but since the giants, the Nephilim, were genetic hybrids, could Satan have genetically altered a lizard and created certain dinosaurs? Or God created them, and Satan lied about their age? Or how about the mythological creatures like the satyrs, fauns, sphinxes, and so many other weird half-human, half-animal creatures? Again remember the cherubim—the living creatures. Why don't we see herds of these half creatures now? Simple, God hardwired sterility into their DNA. If you breed a horse to a donkey the offspring is a mule. Mules are sterile. Like produces like; it is unbreakable law of procreation. Or is this again yet another lie? Today we are doing just that with a science called Chimera. It would certainly fit in with his character, and fit in with his "I will" goals of being like God. He gets to try to counterfeit creation. It is an intriguing theory. Why else would God have destroyed them? Could Satan be doing this today? Kidnapping and abducting humans, harvesting ovum and sperm, and creating a race of new Nephilim? I know this sounds far-fetched, but did you know there are cults and groups of people who believe they are raising these alien hybrid babies now? Do you think we would recognize a new race of giants now? Do you think Satan is that dumb? He knows we would recognize giants now. Why not tweak his original giant idea and create a new "offspring"? Aliens, human/alien hybrids!

The Book of Jasher, which is quoted in both Joshua and 2 Samuel, talks about man intermixing species. This is genetic manipulation: *...and the sons of men in those days took from the cattle of the earth, the beasts of the field and the fowls of the air, and taught the mixture of animals of one species with the other, in order therewith to provoke the Lord* (Jasher 4:18).[136]

Just another aside here I find rather intriguing; at this writing, a popular news broadcast has just announced another genetic first: cloned sheep with 15 percent genetic human organs. This is a legitimate science called Chimera. They will help ease the burden on society of organ donor shortages and decrease the cost of harvesting donor organs, which would come from the sheep. The physical consequences, not to mention the spiritual ones, are staggering! Ever heard of the bird flu (avian flu)? It can make a genetic jump to humans, and we have no immunity for it. By allowing humanoid animals we allow the breeding grounds for intelligent viruses to mutate, which normally would only affect the animal, not us. But now that it has *our organs*, it can find a way in! Don't you think it is an odd coincidence the very first clone was a sheep? And now they are using sheep for growing and harvesting human organ tissue? Jesus was our sacrificial lamb; I can't help but think this is another blasphemous plot by our intelligent adversary directed toward our Lord and savior. Just a thought...

The Bible does tell us bestiality is punishable by death! Our scientists have just taken the physicality of sex out of the picture and raped the gene pool to create all sorts of "chimera" in the best interest of mankind and progressive science of course! *If a woman approaches any beast and lies carnally with it, you shall (stone) the woman and the beast; they shall surely be put to death; their blood is upon them* (Leviticus 20:16; NIV). That's how God feels about that!

Going back to the alien subculture, these beings are called *light bringers*; they even have one named Ashtar who is a messianic figure, introduced and channeled through a man. This extraterrestrial is from Venus, of all places. Ashtar is claiming to save mankind and prepare it for the Aquarian age! He is the masculine version of Ishtar! Satan is called an angel of light, he wants to be God, and he was called the morning star, which is Venus. Does anybody else see the correlation?

I know all of these sounds like a bunch of hokey, and something you would see on an old Star Trek episode, but I assure you, it has a lot more to do with biblical prophecy. These kinds of alternative theories to the beginnings of our planet are gaining in momentum and popularity. Many people believe in aliens, many are looking forward to the day when they actually show up and "help us." Help us clean-up our environment, take us to the next level of evolutionary genius, etc. They believe our planet was "seeded" by aliens, and notice it all seems to point back to genetic manipulation, which was happening in Genesis 6 when the Sons of God came unto the daughters of men.

Let me put this across to you; imagine we were all raptured, and people are left behind. The world is in utter chaos, massive death, confusion, wrecks, etc. Poof! Millions, possibly billions more simply disappear off the face of the earth. If you are the Intelligent Deceiver how do you explain our disappearance? A leader emerges, bringing unity, and controlling the chaos of the nations. He is absolutely different, brilliant, so eloquent, and charismatic in his speech. He has powers, and signs and miracles, he "knows" things we can't possibly comprehend. And he explains to the world he is an alien hybrid, and your brothers and sisters who wouldn't understand the ushering in of the new age and new world government were taken to a different planet to be "reformed." The earth was "purged" of what was holding it back on the evolution of consciousness, and those left behind are the privileged few who have the right DNA to ascend to the next level of world advancement and evolution. Are you beginning to see the relevance of the alien/UFO subculture? By the way, I didn't make this up; this is what is actually preached in the alien/UFO subculture.

Or worse yet, what if there is a false rapture, perpetrated by evil aliens to dupe God's elect and it created a mass "falling away" from the Church? (see Matthew 24:10).

The Bible warns us that in the last days there will be "doctrines of demons" leading even the elite away from the truth. Could this be one of those doctrines? Could our government and others be up to a disinformation campaign, just to *get us used to the idea* of aliens, so as not to cause a mass panic or hysteria? Gradually revealing more and more top secret information, giving us more scientific evidence of life on Mars and other planets, so we become numb to the facts? It is very interesting to think about in our times. It requires much more study, and prayer, and revelation from the scriptures.

Let's look at this antichrist figure from scripture called the man of lawlessness:

> The coming of the lawless one will be revealed, whom the Lord Jesus will overthrow with the breath of his mouth and destroy by the splendor of his coming. The coming of the lawless one will be in accordance with the work of Satan displayed in all kinds of counterfeit miracles, signs and wonders, and in every sort of evil that deceives those who are perishing…For this reason **God sends them a powerful delusion** so that they will believe the lie and so that all will

> be condemned who have not believed the truth but have delighted in wickedness. (2 Thessalonians 2:9–12; NIV)

So this is Satan's M.O.: counterfeit miracles, *signs* and wonders. Where do *signs* happen? The stars. It is going to be a powerful delusion. In other words, this is the big whopper, the biggest, best lie of all, which will be the end-all, be-all of lies!

So far this man of lawlessness is being held back by the Holy Spirit. *For the secret power of lawlessness is already at work; but the one who now holds it back will continue to do so till he is taken out of the way* (2 Thessalonians 2:7; NIV). So we see this deception has been "in the works" so to speak, for quite some time, and it is being "held back" by the Holy Spirit, until the appropriate time! I can't imagine what the world will be like when Satan and his big fat lie are really let loose!

And he performed great and miraculous signs, even causing fire to come down from heaven to earth in full view of men. Because of the signs he was given power to do on behalf of the first beast, he deceived the inhabitants of the earth. He ordered them to set up an image in honor of the beast who was wounded by the sword and yet lived (Revelation 13:13–14; NIV). Ever wondered what kind of signs the Antichrist would perform? What could that mean—fire coming down from heaven? Again, we see it comes from the heavens, and whatever type of fire it is, it will deceive us humans, so it must be a pretty good show.

According to many members of the New Age movement they are waiting for a tall man with a shining countenance, to come from the stars, who will rule the Earth. They say he will have great magick, and he has a messianic message of salvation. Of course these visions and messages are all relayed telepathically.

They are calling these beings gods, who will lead us to freedom, reform our churches, and help us to worship the right "gods." They talk of secret societies and keepers of a secret so powerful as to change the biology of our planet! It is all so freaky!

> Brazilian UFO researcher Jean Alencar has noted that the mythology of this country is replete with descriptions and statuettes of beings endowed with the power of flight. The legends of Brazilian natives, like those of other countries, detail experiences of gods or travelers from the sky who descended to earth when humans were little more than animals to instruct them in the arts of agriculture, astronomy, medicine, and other disciplines. Alencar points out one figure in particular, Bep-Kororoti, a space warrior worshipped by the tribes of the upper reaches of the Xing River. Not unlike the heroes of India's Mahabarata, Bep-Kororoti possessed a flying vehicle capable of destroying anything in its path. His aspect terrified the primitive natives, until he stepped out of his "raiment" and revealed himself to be fair-skinned, handsome, and kind. He amused the natives with his "magic" until he grew restless for his land in the sky and returned there.
>
> ...The Popol Vue sacred to the Mayans, unequivocally states, "Men came from the stars, knowing everything, and they examined the four corners of the sky and the Earth's round surface." [137]

When you read stuff like this, you just can't help but laugh and go—sounds just like Satan! Tall, certainly is reminiscent of angels, he is shining, he displays great magick, he even steps out of his "raiment" or clothes! He even has his own flying machine complete with lasers. Remember Satan is a cherub; cherubs have "whirling wheels," which are inextricably linked with them. Hey, I didn't make this stuff up...people are waiting for this being!

Here is another mysterious verse of scripture we can actually attribute to the alien subculture: *And I saw three unclean spirits like frogs come out of the mouth of the dragon, and out of the mouth of the beast, and out of the mouth of the false prophet. For they are the spirits of devils, working miracles, which go forth unto the kings of the earth and of the whole world, to gather them to the battle of that great day of God Almighty* (Revelation 16:13–14; NIV). Frogs? What on earth do evil spirits who look like frogs have to do with anything? Guess what? The New Age movement recognizes frog-like creatures as their creator gods. They call them "reptilians, a group of humanoid alien entities with frog-like faces."[138] Could this be our "little green men"? When you start to do research on these *reptilians*, you get some pretty "out there" ideas, but nonetheless, it is interesting that scripture points out demonic frog-like creatures. This is what I found on some of the more popular web sites. Reptilians seem to have certain powers such as shape shifting, holographics, telepathy, and invisibility, all of which are characteristics of fallen angels and demonic entities. They supposedly consider earth their original outpost, and claim to have interbred with humans who have reptilian DNA (serpent). They are supposedly superior, and have rank above the ever-popular Greys aliens (the common depiction of the Roswell alien). Allegedly, you must perform a ritual of drinking blood to activate this serpent DNA. All of this is weird, I know, but you can't argue the fact Satan presented himself as serpent, and it is weird that these reptilian-type aliens operate in an aggressive, deceptive, and possession type manner, not to mention the ritualistic pagan worship rite of ingesting blood. It is interesting to note that BTK, the infamous serial killer of Wichita, Kansas, states he has a "frog-like" demon in him. He was a prominent church leader and Boy Scout leader. Creepy.

Popular among abductees is the idea of certain higher memory functions being erased. They refer to it as Wernickes area, which is a part of the brain that forms part of the cerebral cortex and functions in speech and comprehension of the spoken word. According to one abductee who claims her unborn fetus was stolen by reptilians, she says her experience was erased from her memory so she would not resist the procedure. It is important to note she got this through channeling (of course).

The twelve Wernicke's commands which were reprogrammed were:

1. Don't remember this
2. You are ours
3. Forget this
4. This didn't happen
5. You belong to us
6. Nothing happened today
7. We weren't here
8. Today was great
9. Stop fighting us
10. We're invincible
11. You will lose
12. You don't want to do this anymore[139]

Not exactly a benevolent message, but an interesting aspect of the depths of deception these evil spirits seem to be perpetrating on unbelievers, not to mention a very demonic thought process.

Daniel interpreted a dream of King Nebuchadnezzar's in which he describes prophetic futures of certain empires and their world domination. The last image in the dream idol was feet of miry clay. *And whereas thou sawest iron mixed with miry clay, they shall mingle themselves with the seed of men: But they shall not cleave to one another even as iron is mixed with clay* (Daniel 2:43; KJV). It is mind-blowing when you start to see so many scriptures that refer to our seed being mixed with something not a natural part of God's plan. The other part of this verse that is disturbing is the fact whatever is being mingled with the seed of men is also not staying united. What does that mean? Could this be an allusion to the alien abductions and fetal extractions many are experiencing?

Aliens and the paranormal certainly arouse mystery and suspicion, but they also may be part of the legendary cunning of devils. Could our planet be infested with these hidden cowardly demonic presences? The Apostle Paul warns us: *Now the spirit speaketh expressly, that in the latter times some shall depart from the faith, giving heed to seducing spirits and doctrines of devils* (1 Timothy 4:1; KJV). Dr. Missler writes: "A seducing spirit is one that tries to win over the person with affection, 'good' motives, and the promise of personal enrichment or spiritual transformation; this is exactly what our alien visitors do. Secondly, Paul states that people will give heed to these spirits. In the Greek language the word translated 'give heed' is *prosecho.* This means to bring near, give attention to, or to be given or addicted to. The scary implication of this verse is that Paul says 'that in the last days, human beings will have contact with physically embodied Satanic spirits.'"[140]

Crop Circles and Cattle Mutilations

Circular harmonics, higher level geometry, ritualistic cutting and slaughtering of bovines...what do these have in common? The alien/UFO stamp of approval. If you view the aliens as fallen angels or demonic spirits, it is easy to explain these phenomena—look at its fruit. Crop circles mysteriously appear in farmers' fields of grain. What did God require as an offering from the very beginning? Grain offerings. These geometric designs are huge, beautiful, and only seen from an aerial view. We can surmise from the sheer size and complexity of these artistic circles that whoever is behind it is meddling with our emotions and pulling us away from the creator of the grain.

Another weird fruit of the alien subculture is cattle mutilations. Go back to scripture; what was given as an offering to the Almighty? Bulls and heifers. Notice how these animals are found out in the middle of nowhere, with strange ritualistic, anatomical cuts and parts missing. In most cases, there is no blood, and laboratory tests show sharp, surgical instruments were used. Cattle mutilations are not the only animals found; there have been reports of many different types of animals, found in similar fashion. Sacrifices have long been the arena of pagan cultures, used for divination, appeasing the gods, etc. Could these mutilations be a ritual by fallen angels or demons masquerading as aliens?

> The typical mutilation did not consist of a bloody carcass, torn or ripped flesh with animal or human footprints leading to or from the body...The blood was removed entirely without the collapse of the veins. This suggests the removal of the blood as being pumped out while the animal is still alive in a manner unknown, especially in a field removed from access to sophisticated equipment. One eye, an ear, the tongue removed all at the same point, in a cookie cutter pattern, the lips, utters (if female), sex organs, anus cored out to the intestinal tract, also glandular and body fluids gone. The removal was done with such laser-like precision that the cuts were divided between cells. There was a cauterization along all of the cuts suggesting a heat source such as a laser cut. We are talking about this as being in the late sixties, early seventies. Known technology was not present for such results

> back then. Another interesting thing is that this was done on firstborn male and female animals. Typical UFO sightings and/or black unmarked helicopters were sighted before or after these events in some cases.[141]

Whatever Satan and his evil emissaries are up to with the whole alien/UFO subculture, I think it bears a careful watch. There are too many similarities and counterfeiting of the Holy Spirit going on to ignore, as well as too many similarities to fallen angels and demons. I think it has the Intelligent Deceiver's stink all over it. There are so many scriptures that allude to principalities and powers from the heavenly realms trying to deceive us. It's a case of subliminal seduction, real events without a physical counterpart. There is too much historical knowledge and archeological evidence of ancient cultures and religions and their ties to idolatry and satanic worship to deny. There is too much going on in our popular culture to ignore. There is too much disinformation, lies, and deception involved, all trademarks of the enemy. The other thing I would like to point out is these aliens are not pretty creatures; they are ugly, creepy, demonic-looking beings. They only contact people with telepathy, channeling, and/or by kidnapping them, and why do they have prophetic messages? It is another counterfeit of the Holy Spirit.

The Bible tells us to "watch and pray." The word *watch* is likened to being on an all-night guard vigil on a watchtower or wall. So keep your eyes peeled, keep your armor of God on, and be a ready servant. This paranormal myth is busted!

*Authors note: Many good people, including Christians claim to be abductees. If you have experienced any "visitations" there are caring ministries out there who can offer biblical help and support. Visit www.echosofenoch.com for more information.

CHAPTER EIGHT

TECHNOLOGY OF THE ANGEL GODS: ATLANTIS!

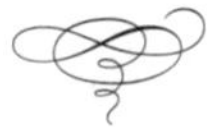

You just can't have a discussion about the paranormal or aliens and UFOs without mentioning the mythical city of Atlantis. After all, the entire alien subculture is waiting for the ushering in of the "Aquarian Age"!

Now, I know what you are thinking: "The Bible doesn't mention Atlantis." And you would be right. I really don't think the Bible comes out and specifically names a mythical city like Atlantis, but does it fractionally allude to it? Does the Bible speak of technologies and advanced knowledge and lost civilizations?

Much of the fodder for science fiction stories comes from this place called Atlantis, which is fine for fiction, but there is a lot of bunk out there toted as fact as well. Atlantis engages our imaginations with stories of advanced technologies (all very much like ours today), beautiful art, profound engineering, a cultured civilization complete with governments, civics, etc., and incredible wealth! This was a utopian society, one to be looked up to, and the model of perfection for fulfilling our aspirations. Atlantis is the city of choice to represent advanced lost civilizations and continents. (For those of you really into Atlantis, check out the description and prophetic destructions of the city of Tyre in Ezekiel Chapters 26, 27, and 28.)

I have a couple of problems with Atlantis and some of the other lost civilizations that I wanted to bring to your attention. The first fingerprint of Intelligent Deception is people "channeling" beings from this place, former Atlanteans, now space aliens, escaped from the watery grave that gulped away its shores. Second, the fallen angel, Greek god Poseidon, had sex with a mortal woman named Cleito, who produces for him five pairs of twin sons, purported to be giants (sounds like the Nephilim to me!), to rule the continent. Energy crystals and occultic symbols are fodder for the mind in the Atlantean cultures, and the last problem I have with it, is it was destroyed by an act of God, according to legend—due to its great propensity for world domination, slavery, war, and extreme violence.

> During the late 19th century, ideas about the legendary nature of Atlantis were combined with stories of other lost continents such as Mu and Lemuria by popular figures in the occult and the growing New Age phenomenon…Famed psychic Edgar Cayce first mentioned Atlantis in a life reading given in 1923, and later gave its geographical location as the Caribbean, and proposed that Atlantis was an ancient, now-submerged, highly-evolved civilization which had ships and aircraft powered by a mysterious form of energy crystal. He also predicted that parts of Atlantis would rise in 1968 or 1969. The Bimini Road found by Dr. J. Manson Valentine, a submarine geological formation just off North Bimini Island discovered in 1968, has been claimed by some to be evidence of the lost civilization (among many other things) and is still being explored today.

> The concept of Atlantis also attracted Nazi theorists. In 1938, Heinrich Himmler organized a search in Tibet to find a remnant of the white Atlanteans...the Atlanteans were Hyperboreans—Nordic supermen who originated on the North Pole (see Thule). Similarly, Alfred Rosenberg...spoke of a "Nordic-Atlantean" or "Aryan-Nordic" master race.[142]

Atlantis has Satan's fingerprints all over it! Atlantis, Lemuria, and Mu are all names of lost civilizations characterized by super-advanced humanoid creatures. These poor, lost souls communicate to various physics, clairvoyants, and mediums about what their culture was like, what gods they worshiped, what kind of technologies were available, etc. The advanced technologies they mention are what have my attention. Not to mention the angel/god hybrid offspring who ruled this nation.

We are told in the Book of Enoch certain angels taught mankind all manner of war and its technologies. These fallen angels gave us this "gift" of making weapons, tactical maneuvers, anatomical deathblows, etc. Here is what Plato had to say about Atlantis's naval dominance:

> She was pre-eminent in courage in a military skill, and was the leader of the Hellenes. And when the rest fell off from her, being compelled to stand alone, after having undergone the very extremity of danger, she defeated and triumphed over the invaders, and preserved from slavery those who were not yet subjugated, and generously liberated all the rest of us who dwell within the pillars.
>
> But afterwards there occurred violent earthquakes and floods; and in a single day and night of misfortune all your warlike men in a body sank into the earth, and island of Atlantis in like manner disappeared in the depths of the sea.[143]

War technologies were taught to humans by fallen angels according to Enoch Chapter 8: *Moreover Azazyel taught men to make swords, knives, shields, breastplates, made them see that which was behind them. Also…Impiety increased; fornication multiplied; and they transgressed and corrupted all their ways…Barkayal taught the observers of the stars; Akibeel taught signs; Tamiel taught astronomy;…And men, being destroyed, cried out; and their voices reached to heaven.*[144] And in Enoch Chapter 10:11: *All the sons of men shall not perish in consequence (speaking of the flood) of every secret by which the Watchers have destroyed and which they have taught, their offspring.*[145]

The first part of this list all have to do with war, plus they also taught them the human anatomy behind their implements of war so they could effectively slay their fellow man. This was not God's plan for humans. He did not want us to kill each other. Look how kind and helpful he was to Cain after he had slain Abel. He told him to repent, even put a special mark on his forehead so no one else would harm him (see Genesis 4:15). This is how God works; a murderer can have an open relationship with God and provide us with many valuable insights regarding God's kingdom. Not so when Satan is made a god. The one True God always destroys the works of the enemy.

According to our history books, the use of blacksmithing and the use of ores from the earth was a very slow and tedious process, due to the fact we were still running around like cavemen and using rocks as weapons. But metallurgy, the Bible tells us, was a talent of *Tubal-Cain, who forged all kinds of tools out of bronze and iron* (Genesis 4:22; NIV). Tubal-Cain's father was Lamech, who was also Noah's father, so Tubal-Cain was probably Noah's much older half-brother. Modern science dates metallurgy and the wide use of smelting steel to the Hittites around 2700 BC. This is about thirteen hundred years after the Bible mentions it! Archeologists find smelted tools and implements of war in the most inconvenient places requiring a much earlier date than previously thought. God gave man the ability to subdue his environment and invent all manner of goodly usable things. But ancient texts, the Bible included, allude to higher technologies being introduced too soon and then misused by none other than the fallen angels and Nephilim. This corruption of the natural time line was what God viewed as cheating. These fallen angels introduced "forbidden knowledge," or knowledge God knew was intended for mankind's demise.

Look at us today with all of our advanced technologies, which really aren't so advanced when you study some of the things the ancients had. Technologies in our era have been mass produced and marketed to the public for a profit. In the ancient days, usually only the priests and kings had access to these materials in their temples, which in turn put on quite a display for the subjects making way to sacrifice at the temple. Using deceitful technologies such as temple lights, the use of static electricity, machines, etc., the priests were able to dupe the followers of whatever god into believing the stone deity was the cause of this great and terrible power and magick! With all of our advanced technologies today are we closer to God? Or, have they driven a wedge of want, and taken up more of our time when we could be fellowshipping with God?

Let's look again at why the Lord chose to wipe out all the inhabitants of the earth with the exception of eight people:

> The Lord saw how great man's wickedness on the earth had become, and that every inclination of the thoughts of his heart was only evil all the time. The Lord was grieved that he had made man on the earth, and his heart was filled with pain. So the Lord said, "I will wipe mankind, whom I have created, from the face of the earth—men and animals,

> and creatures that move along the ground, and birds of the air—for I am grieved that I have made them."…Now the earth was corrupt in God's sight and was full of violence…for all the people on earth had corrupted their ways…for the earth is filled with violence because of them. (Genesis 6:5–7, 11–13; NIV)

The mega themes from these verses were corruption, which means to "destroy," and violence, which means "cruelty and injustice."[146] Such are the inclinations of the fallen angels and their demonic children the Nephilim. Just as the ancient civilization of Atlantis was a violent, warring people, so was mankind prior to the flood.

So why don't we have these ancient metal objects of war? Simple corrosion. If it has been exposed to the weather, corrosion and oxidization will take care of it. When you begin to study ancient cultures you find all kinds of keys to technologies, even as crazy sounding as high projectile weapons, robotics, batteries, unknown power sources, electricity, flying machines, heavy equipment, atomic and nuclear explosions, and the list goes on.

Ancient stories of levitation and the neutralization of gravity seem to be replete in ancient civilizations. There are stories of flying crafts of all manner, the lifting and transporting of huge stones, and placing them with such precision into the temples and megaliths of ancient repute, that it defies our scientific methods of today. The following quote shows some of these strange tales.

> Physicists tell us that there are several "forces" acting on us at any given time. These forces are atomic force, electrical force, magnetic force, and finally, gravitational force. Gravity is the weakest, and least understood of all the forces.

> Paradoxically, the weakest force is the most difficult to master because we know so little about it. However, levitation, a sort of cancellation of gravitational force, has been known to occur—at least in the historical record!...
>
> Some of the most incredible tales of antiquity concern levitation or the power to neutralize gravity...by means of sounds, the priests of ancient Babylon were able to raise into the air heavy rocks which a thousand men could not have lifted...
>
> Babylonian tables affirm that sound could lift stones. The Bible speaks of Jericho and what sound waves did to its walls. Coptic writings relate the process by which blocks for the pyramids were elevated by the sound of chanting. [147]

Along many of the same science fiction story lines Atlantis births, are tales of parallel universes. Parallel universes do exist, they are just called heaven and hell in the Bible. We also see themes of time travel and time travelers, but these too are addressed in the Bible. We actually know the names of many of the most famous time travelers: Enoch, Elijah, Ezekiel, Isaiah, John, Paul, and many more who received divine prophecies, had open visions of heaven, hell, and the future.

The simple fact is we were not created as a bunch of ignoramuses. We were given a mandate to discover and explore our world within the confines of God's boundaries, and God knew we were hellbent to destroy ourselves. War always drives the lust for technologies. The Intelligent Deceiver knows this about us. Whether Atlantis or any other lost civilization was anything more than a myth or a vague collective remembrance of an era when fallen angels corrupted the world, we know from the biblical text how God felt about it; he simply destroyed it.

We must not be naïve to the influence the great deceiver has had on our world as the Satanists believe in the following Samyaza quote:

> Man shall turn from you again and again, as our spirit abideth with him unto Eternity. The Gift of Satanael shall continue to illuminate. Man shall create Civilization anew and reach greater heights, even unto the stars, The servility of the descendants of Noah shall not endure forever, as even these have the Gift of Satanael within them, as bequeathed from the days of Adam. [148]

Chapter Nine

ANCIENT MEGALITHS

The Great Pyramid of Giza, Stonehenge, and other ancient megaliths and monuments—so many are captivated by these structures; we have studied them for centuries, wondered, dreamed, visited, and exploited them, measured them, and measured them again, and again. I have always been fascinated with the Great Pyramid, and up until recently I knew what the History Channel "let" me know about them, and that was it. Not being anything remotely close to a math wizard, my eyes would glaze over as if in a sugar-induced trance whenever they talked of the measurements and speculated yet again as to why pharaoh built the thing, whilst scratching their heads and saying, "Man back then just wasn't smart enough to the build this thing!" This is "science out of place." As author Stephen Quayle put it; "You know the official version of history. The Egyptians built the pyramids and the Chinese also had a form of civilization, while the rest of mankind skipped through the woods eating berries and grubs until the Greeks and the Romans came along. And then the rest, as they say is history!"[149]

An interesting quote puts this megalith into perspective:

> To put the achievement of the Egyptian Great Pyramid into perspective, keep in mind modern man does not possess the structural genius required to build the Great Pyramid even today. Volumes of research have been compiled debating how the structure may have been built, yet the answers to this puzzle remain elusive as does the identity of its builders (Ibid., p. 8). Even if man today could arrange limestone blocks weighing the equivalent of modern locomotives, polish them to an exactness of 1/100th of an inch, (equaling contemporary optical standards) and place them within 1/50th of an inch together without damaging them, as the casing stones were placed, the symbolic significance of the pyramid could never be duplicated. The Great Pyramid is set on the geographical center of all the land mass of the whole world.[150]

So what do these great and lofty structures have to do with an intelligent enemy? Or maybe a better question would be; did the enemy copy these too? That last thought was a mind-blower for me. Until I started to actually study the megaliths, the thought *never* occurred to me anyone but Satan and his fallen angels and giants were behind these huge technological achievements. Until two scriptures were brought to my attention:

> *God has set signs and wonders in the land of Egypt, even to this day.* (Jeremiah 32:20; NIV)

> *In that day there shall be an altar to the Lord in the midst of Egypt, and a monument at the border there of to the Lord. And*

> *it shall be for a sign, and a witness to the Lord of Hosts in the land of Egypt.* (Isaiah19:19; NIV)

Really, these blew me away; I was again awed by the thoroughness of God's written Word. The preceding verses talk about God setting signs and wonders in the land of Egypt, which are visible even to this day! And in the book of Isaiah, it tells you exactly where it is! How cool is that!

At first glance of Isaiah 19:19 the location doesn't make any sense, how can you have a monument in the middle of the land and yet at its border? Almost sounds like a riddle, and it is! Unless you know Egypt is divided into upper and lower portions, and the Arabic word for border is *Gizeh,* then you begin to solve the riddle. The Pyramid sits in the middle but is on the border of the upper and lower portions of Egypt!

"This passage describes the location of the Great Pyramid exactly. The Pyramid sits in the center of Egypt and on the border of upper and lower Egypt."[151]

"If this fact is not convincing enough of the scriptural significance of this structure, consider the following; When the Hebrew letters from Isaiah 19:19 describing the Lord's monument are added together, the sum is 5,449. This is the exact height, in inches, of the Great Pyramid. These inches are the standard of linear measurement encoded within the Great Pyramid itself." [152]

Others have remarked on the greatness of the Pyramid and certain passages in the Bible:

> It would also seem as if God's inspired prophets knew of this marvelous pillar and regarded it as a sacred wonder. The Greeks as early as Alexander's time placed it at the head of their list of "the seven wonders of the world." But Jeremiah

> before them wrote of "signs and wonders in the land of Egypt," and of the placing of them there by "the Great, the Mighty God, the Lord of hosts" (Jer. 32: 18–20), which would seem to refer to this pyramid…He accordingly refers to "signs and wonders in the land of Egypt," of which he says that they still existed when he wrote,—"unto this day." He is commonly thought to allude to the miracles of the Exodus, which certainly were "signs and wonders" exactly to his purpose…The language here suggests something monumental, something locally fixed. It naturally implies a Divine memorial, continuously abiding…[153]

So the next conceivable question would be, why did God put it there, and for what purpose? Who really built it?

Isaiah 19:19 seems to answer the first question for us: it was an *altar* of the Lord, not a tomb as the popular theories go. The great pyramid is absolutely different from all of the rest, it does not have a tomb underneath (that we know of) as all of the others do (there are over eighty pyramids total), and it does not have any hieroglyphics like the other pyramids. It could be seen for miles! Covering thirteen acres, with the outside covered in highly polished limestone, and the capstone being of gold! Shiny, to say the least!

As far as the purpose, an altar is for worship, and if God really did put it there, then it was meant as a monotheistic place of worship. This can be attributed to what we think is its original builders, a tribe of people called the Hyksos (the shepherd kings) who took over Egypt according to the Egyptian historian Manetho. These Hyksos, some say, were Hebrew in origin, but others say they were Amalekites. Because of the flawed nature of carbon-dating techniques (carbon-dating is calibrated to accommodate for millions of years!), some say the pyramid was built ten thousand years ago to as little as 2467 BC according to astronomical studies.[154] Some have even suggested that Enoch or Job or even Melchizedek were the builders of the Pyramid. We may never know, but the fact remains it is an amazing monument, and I think the confusion surrounding when and who built the pyramid just screams of the handiwork of an Intelligent Deceiver! If God was the original builder, what a perfect opportunity for Satan to come in, copy it, and create chaos and confusion in attribution to its rightful builder!

Joseph A. Seiss wrote in the late 1800s:

> Note how admirably the *titles* fit. "Altar" in Hebrew means "the lion of God." The Great Pyramid is pre-eminently the lion among all earthly buildings, and the new theory claims that it is Divine. The altar as described by Ezekiel is largely pyramidal in form, and is called "the mountain of God." And a mountain, surely, is the Great Pyramid, and one of a very remarkable character. The sacred books of the Hindus call it a mountain—*Rucm-adri*—"the golden mountain." It is "a pillar," and hence not a sacrificial but a memorial altar. It is a mammoth obelisk,—one great individual shaft,—and now also believed to be sacred. [155]

Some researchers have even gone so far as to say the Great Pyramid is the Bible in stone. "The Bible makes frequent reference to the prominence of 'stones' in the ritual and symbology of the ancient Hebrew people." [156]

> *When you have crossed the Jordan into the land the Lord your God is giving you, set up some large stones and coat them with plaster. Write on them all the words of this law when you have crossed over to enter the land the Lord your God is giving you,*

> *a land flowing with milk and honey,…set up these stones on Mount Ebal, as I command you today, and coast them with plaster. Build there an altar to the Lord your God, an altar of stones. Do not use any iron tool upon them* (Deuteronomy 27:2–5; NIV).

The amazing measurements and preciseness of the pyramid begs to be told!

- The base of the pyramid covers thirteen acres.
- The builders understood the value of *pi* well before history records a human understanding of *pi.*
- There are 2.3 million limestone blocks weighing 2.5 tons each, covered in highly polished limestone.
- It is aligned with true north (more so than the Paris observatory).
- It was built with the sacred cubit as a measurement (cubits give rise to where we get our inch).
- It lies in the exact center of all the land area of the world, with its structure dividing the earth's land mass into approximately equal quarters.
- The base for the pyramid also corresponds to the length of a year along with extra space to accommodate leap years.
- The average height of the earth above sea level is 455 feet, which happens to be the height of the pyramid.
- It has temperature-compensating expansion joints.
- The curvature designed into the faces of the pyramid exactly matches the radius of the earth.
- A line drawn on a map from the apex of the pyramid to Bethlehem equals the angle of the Ascending Passage and crosses the Red Sea at the most likely point that the

Israelites crossed when departing Egypt (Parting of the Red Sea).

- A line drawn on a map south from the apex of the pyramid at the angle of the Ascending Passage crosses Mount Sinai (Ten Commandments).
- With the mantle in place, the Great Pyramid could be seen from the mountains in Israel and probably the moon as well. Its polished surfaces would have reflected light like a beacon. [157]

You could go on and on! Needless to say it is astonishing. Some even say the passages ascending and descending, and the chambers inside line up with the gospel story! Let's take a look: "The king's chamber air shaft that ascends out of the Pyramid and points directly to the star Thuban, and the star Alnitak, in the Orion constellation."[158] Remember the Orion constellation from the *Mazzeroth* means Glorious Prince!

There have been unique measurements calculated that add an even richer tone to the idea the Great Pyramid had a divine architect.

> I knew that the Pyramid's most distinguished cubit answers to the sacred cubit of Moses; that the capacity measure of the Pyramid's granite Coffer is the same as that of the Ark of the Covenant; that the sabbatic system of the Jews is distinctly noted in connection with the Queen's Chamber; and that the molten sea had proportions of earth-commensuration which also appear in the size of the Pyramid's main chamber…
>
> It hence occurred to me to ascertain the exact direction of Jerusalem from the Great Pyramid and to try whether it

would fit to any of its interior angles...Three of the main inside angles of the Great Pyramid applied to its north side eastward, point directly to Jerusalem![159]

We again see the Glorious Prince echoed in its architecture:

Orion is the brightest constellation in the heavens. The significance of Orion in typology is awe inspiring and very easy to understand. Orion is a decan of the zodiacal sign Taurus...It embellishes Taurus, the 9th symbol in the narrative, symbolizing the return of the messiah in judgment. The principle stars of Orion develop the meaning which is already apparent in the name of the constellation. [160]

According to a theory by Robert Bauval;

The positions of the Giza pyramids on the ground are a reflection of the positions of the stars in the constellation Orion circa 10,500 B.C. (Graham Hancock, Keeper Of Genesis pp.354–355) Five of the 7 brightest stars have pyramid equivalents: The 3 great pyramids of Khufu, Khafra, and Menkaura for the belt of Orion, the pyramid of Nebka at Abu Rawash corresponds to the star Saiph and the pyramid at Zawat al Aryan corresponds to the star Bellatrix. The Nile river corresponds to the Milky Way. The principal Giza monuments formed an accurate terrestrial map of the stars of Orion and Sirius as these constellations appeared in 10,500 BC.[161]

In Bauval's Giza/Orion connection, the star corresponding to the Great Pyramid is "'*Alnitak*, the wounded one.' The greatest of the Giza structures represents the essence of the saving work of the Messiah. All biblical descriptions of the Great Pyramid typify the Messiah. Keep in mind that the number 5 represents 'grace,' that is, the gift of forgiveness and eternal life through Jesus. In Scripture, the message of grace is manifested again and again by the number 5."[162]

Another interesting element about the pyramid is its companion the Sphinx, which some say may have just been a lion and later the head was carved into a man. This would add a very interesting allusion and credence to the pyramid being a divinely inspired structure, since Jesus is often portrayed in Scripture as the lion of the tribe of Judah!

There are others who find a fascinating link to pre-pharaoh times:

> Schoch has also noted as have others that the clearly evident disproportionately small size of the head compared to the body suggests the head to have been originally that of a lion, but later re-carved to give the likeness of a pharaoh. This implies that the Egyptian Kings were the inheritors of an already existing structure of which they re-made in their own image to give provenance over the monument. [163]

Consider also the Hancock and Bauval theory:

> The Sphinx's lion-shape is a definitive reference to the constellation of Leo; and the layout and orientation of the Sphinx, the Giza pyramid complex and the Nile River is an accurate reflection or "map" of the constellations of Leo, Orion (specifically, Orion's Belt) and the Milky Way, respectively.
>
> Their initial claims regarding the alignment of the Giza

pyramids with Orion ("...the three pyramids were an unbelievably precise terrestrial map of the three stars of Orion's belt").[164]

Josephus writes in *The Antiquities of the Jews* 1.2.3:

(By the children of Seth) "They also were the inventors of that peculiar sort of wisdom which is concerned with the heavenly bodies, and their order. And that their inventions might not be lost before they were sufficiently known, upon Adam's prediction that the world was to be destroyed at one time by the force of fire, and at another time by the violence and quantity of water, they made two pillars; the one of brick, the other of stone: they inscribed their discoveries on them both, that in case the pillar of brick should be destroyed by the flood, the pillar of stone might remain, and exhibit those discoveries to mankind; and also inform them that there was another pillar of brick erected by them. Now this remains in the land of Siriad to this day."[165]

Siriad is an early name for Egypt. According to Josephus, there were two pillars, just as Isaiah 19:19 suggests; the brick one being destroyed by the flood! According to Biblefacts.org:

The natives that live in the area of the Great Pyramid call it Enoch's Pillar. Salt deposits were found in the queen's chamber, proving the pyramid itself has been under salt water, which makes it a pre-flood monument.

The theory is that the information is in math instead of writing, a chronological calendar prophetically marking specific dates in history. The descending passage is very long.

So if one stood at the bottom and looked out they would see a very narrow portion of the night sky. Only in one year would someone be able to see the pole star from that location. In the year 2170 BC the pole star was Alpha Draconis (today the pole star is Polaris).[166]

Another detail that reckons into the whole divine design theme is the Great Pyramid's "missing" capstone. Jesus was described as the capstone or cornerstone that the builders rejected:

> *The stone which the builders refused is become the head stone of the corner. This is the LORD'S doing; it is marvelous in our eyes.* (Psalm 118:22–23; KJV)

> *This is the stone which was set at naught of you builders, which is become the head of the corner.* (Acts 4:11; KJV)

So how has the Intelligent Deceiver played this one to his advantage? Why not follow his own M.O.? Pervert the altar and monument of God and make it his own, therefore helping to fulfill his "I wills." Completely deceive the general population into believing some ancient alien race had come to town to build it, and then make the altar a place of death—a tomb! The great pyramid has become a symbol of the occult, just about everything about it today and all of the copycat pyramids throughout the world have elements of human sacrifice, false gods/goddess worship, and planetary/star worship, UFOs, Mars and ancient "seeded cultures" are associated with it. The original use has all but been hidden and obliterated!

The great pyramid can be seen on the back of our U.S. one dollar bill with the Latin words *Novus Ordo Seclorum* underneath, which mean "New order of the ages"! Who does that sound like?

We also see the occultic symbol of the All Seeing Eye surrounded by a sunburst pattern—the symbol of sun worshippers.[167] The All Seeing Eye is the Eye of the Egyptian god Osiris, and also the Eye of Horus believed to have magical powers if one controlled the eye through spells. These pagan symbols were placed on our U.S. one dollar bills by President Franklin D. Roosevelt, a thirty-second degree Freemason.[168] Money is referred to as Mammon in the New Testament (see Luke 16:13). Jesus wasn't talking about money; he was referring to a chief Canaanite god called Mammon, who is the perverse spirit behind money. Anything that can be corrupted is being corrupted by evil spirits.

Pyramids amid ancient cultures were considered "resurrection machines." Elaborate magical rights and mummification were brought into play as man tried to come back to life as a god with his own power. The god Osiris is given credit for embalming and mummification. Osiris was most likely a fallen angel, and he is credited with the introduction of agriculture, crafts, and religious rituals.

Another aspect of the Pyramid is it has given rise to other huge monuments that are referred to in the Bible as "image worship," the most recognizable one being the obelisk. It was thought to be the dwelling place of the sun god. The obelisk is a phallic symbol; literally it was Osiris' penis that was eaten by fish, and Isis gave him the biggest fish story of all! We have our very own obelisk in the United States—The Washington Monument! Thanks to the Freemasons, it is even built on high ground! If you know anything of the idol worship in the Bible, God is constantly making reference to the "groves" and to the "high places," and those Ashtoreth poles. *And Judah did evil in the sight of the Lord, whom they provoked to jealously with the sins they committed, above all that their fathers had done. For they also built for themselves (idolatrous) high places, pillars and Asherim (idolatrous symbols for the goddess Asherah) on every high hill and under every green tree. There were also sodomites (male cult prostitutes) in the land. They did all the abominations of the nations whom the Lord cast out before the Israelites* (1 Kings 14:22–24; AMP). When you begin to study the culture and influences of the fallen angels and giants, you find sodomy was one of the sins taught to humans by these beings. The obelisk is a phallic symbol, associated with the practice of sodomy; we get our word sodomy from the twin destroyed cities of Sodom and Gomorrah.

So what do grove worship and obelisks have to do with the pyramids? One evil gives rise to another! We have seen a huge increase in tree worship (groves, Ashtoreth poles) as of late, known to us as "tree huggers" or environmentalists; they are deeply involved in the New Age religion! Baal was associated with tree worship and human sacrifice. Even the old druid religions are experiencing a "re-birth" among practicing occultists. Being in the heart of timber country, many loggers have been seriously injured by the spiking of trees by these "well-meaning environmentalists." These tree huggers would rather sacrifice a human life than have a tree cut down. It was common practice in the 1990s for these individuals to put metal spikes into the trees so that when loggers would cut into the tree with their chain saw, the saw would hit the spike, causing the chain saw to bounce back and cut the logger instead, sometimes causing their death! As King Solomon would say; "There is nothing new under the sun"!

Some have suggested when you line up all of the major megaliths and monuments on the earth, they seem to be related to one another. "Built along a grid composed of two pentagrams with the circle of the equator. All the monuments fall into place along this grid if one pentagram is 'anchored' at Giza and one at the Prime Meridian 0 longitude. Too many major architectural structures exist along this dual pentagram design for it to be mere coincidence."[169]

The other monuments are no less incredible, but there are

differences. Their sheer size indicates a race of gigantic proportions. Easy work for an angel/human hybrid capable of incredible feats of strength, not to mention some otherworldly help in the technology department! The whole idea that some ancient primitive culture made these things is a lie! Normal-sized men with very primitive tools cut rocks weighing several tons and hauled those hundreds of miles using logs and pulleys and then set them so precisely without the use of mortar! Then they made such precise engineering to the stars and constellations, equinoxes, etc., that they could predict eclipses and other events. Right! "I've got a great view of the ocean from my place in Montana!" We need to wake up and face the fact there were a race of giants who inhabited our planet, superior in size, strength, and mind power. All the facts point toward this, but we insist on taking our worn out, shoved-down-our-throat ideas that a primitive people did these things, and somehow this old way of doing things was lost through the ages.

> The book of Jubilees remarks that Jared or Yeh-red, an Old Testament patriarch, was so called because in his days the angels descended upon the earth—Yaw-rad "descend." It is interesting to note that "Jordan" comes from that same root word denoting "descent, coming down or falling"—Yar-dane "the place of the descent." The source of the Jordan river is Mount Hermon—the point of descent of the Watchers. Mt. Hermon resides in the ancient land formally known as "Sidonia." The super-human angelic beings descended, created hybrid offspring with human women, the "nephilim" and mighty men of renown preserved in ancient myths. The source for the dispersion of angelic "alien" technology, and the Hermetic knowledge that influenced human civilization since the days of Noah, was Sidonia/Cydonia.[170]

This is how the Intelligent Deceiver works; tell a lie big enough and long enough and you have scientific fact! The emerging pattern is always the same: God created—Satan copied and corrupted!

Stonehenge

What about Stonehenge? Could it also have been created by God or ancient Hebrews who migrated to Britain? Many scholars think this may very well be the case. In fact many scholars think whoever was the architect of the Great Pyramid was also the architect of Stonehenge.

Stonehenge, we now know, is an ancient astronomical computer, basically a stone computer. The more it is studied, the more we learn of its precise nature to the stars and their corresponding constellations. As we learned earlier, stars aren't bad, but star worship is. "The writings of Josephus, the historian, make reference to the Adamic origin of astronomy and mathematics: 'They (the Sethites) also were the inventors of that peculiar sort of wisdom which is concerned with the heavenly bodies and their order.' Ancient Persian and Arabian traditions also ascribe the invention of astronomy to Adam, Seth, and Enoch." [171]

The interesting thing you find when you start to study ancient megaliths is there are different kinds of stone monuments found all over the lands of the Old Testament. They are a very familiar form of the type of structure found in Stonehenge.

The archeologist E. Raymond Capt found an interesting correlation:

> These stone structures can be roughly divided into three classes: 1. Menhirs (high stone)—single upright stones which may be commemorative of some great event or personage. 2. Dolmens (table stone)—A stone slab set table-wise

> on three or more uprights. 3. Cromlechs (stone circle)—A circle of stones sometimes enclosing barrows (tombs) or dolmens. Stonehenge is a highly specialized example of this last class…The marked similarity of the chain of stone structures gives ample reason to believe that these time-defying monuments were erected by one race of people: The Hebrew people of the Old Testament. Some of the greatest fields of megalithic structures are to be found in the lands of ancient Israel…Menhirs, Stone Circles, Dolmens, Cairns, Mounds—all appear to have been constructed by the Hebrews, in Patriarchal times.[172]

Jacob, Joshua, Moses, and Samuel all were instructed to set up stone monuments or pillars. If the ancient Hebrews did migrate to Britain and build Stonehenge, it has long since been forgotten and again corrupted by the many pagan influences we see today. We again can see the mark of Satan's lies all over Stonehenge, as most historians scratch their heads and say, "The people living over four thousand years ago just weren't smart enough to build this!" Some of the stones weigh between twenty and fifty tons and were taken from a place 130 miles away. The architecture and construction was equally impressive, as the lintels were tongue and groove, and joined with mortice and tenons. All of this is attributed to a people said to be of the Stone Age. In other words, they used rocks and antlers and bones for tools and weapons. Yeah…did I mention I could see the ocean from my place in Montana?

You cannot force facts with lies—Oh, wait a minute—yeah you can, Satan does it all the time! So what would Satan want with Stonehenge? Again, if it truly was built by ancient Hebrews for the purpose of studying the heavens, why not corrupt it and make a mockery of it, and use it for the worship of stars?

Ancient Druids are supposedly the official builders of Stonehenge, and believe it or not there actually may be some truth locked away behind this. When you study druidism, their cultic beliefs, rituals, and the like are very similar to Baal worship! A high spreading tree, like the oak is sacred to them! Remind you of Ashtoreth poles anyone? Lots of cruel human sacrifices are a trademark of their religion. They divined the future by disemboweling a person or an animal and observing which way the gut pile landed and writhed, along with the death throws and shrieks of their victim. Very disgusting and foul! The druids may actually have been the Hebrews who again turned their backs on God and began their adulterous Baal, idol worship practices again!

Whatever the truth may be about ancient pyramids and other megalithic stone structures, most has been lost to the sands of time. Incredible feats of engineering, architecture, and technology can be attributed to the gracious and all-giving God, but they can also be perverted and copied by another form of intelligence: Satan. Whatever was of God is now defiled and corrupted; we can only wait and have our hope in the Lord for our answers to these divine mysteries.

Chapter Ten

MARS

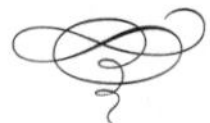

Why does the planet Mars capture our imaginations more than any of the other planets in our solar system? Why is it always on the news versus any other planet? Why do we always wonder if there is life on Mars? Why did the ancients revere, worship, and fear Mars, when we can't even pick it out of our night skies? Why do we want to "go there"? Why is Mars synonymous with war (i.e. martial arts)? And what could an Intelligent Deceiver have to do with the red planet?

Mars is named for the Roman god of war, who was the son of Jupiter and Juno (Mars is the Greek god Ares). The name Mars seems to have been derived from MaRduK, chief god of Nimrod's Babylonian pantheon. Mars also had two sons: Romulus and Ramos. Romulus, killed Ramos, and founded Rome!

Mars has two very dark moons with very poor reflectivity of light. Their names, interestingly enough, are Phobos and Demos, which in the Greek mean "fear and dread (terror)," which were Mars' chariot horses. These two inferior lights were most likely asteroids caught in Mars' gravitational pull.

The god Baal is often associated with Mars worship. *He put away the idolatrous priests whom the kings of Judah had ordained to burn incense in the high places in Judah's cities and round about Jerusalem—also those who burned incense to Baal, to the sun, to the moon, to the constellations (or twelve signs of the Zodiac), and to all the hosts of heaven* (2 Kings 23:5; NIV). Whenever there is Baal and the referral to the high places, constellations, or hosts of heaven mentioned in the Bible it alludes to Baal worship. (It is interesting to note the god Baal is depicted with two horns coming from his head and carrying a forked staff. Also of note is the reemerging interest in resurrecting the "old ways" of Baal worship; many websites are devoted to rekindling an interest in worship of ancient idols.)

Why would the ancients know so much about the fourth planet in our solar system? Why did the early Roman pioneers (8th century BC) build temples to Mars? The Egyptian city Cairo is the Arabic word for Mars (Al Kahira). Why does the "face on Mars" look like the face on the sphinx? Why does the month of March (Martius) actually mean Mars? In Acts 17:19 Paul refers to the "Mars Hill" (Aeropagus) in Athens, which was an ancient court. Our day of the week Tuesday (Tiwes-daeg) means Mars' day.[173] I could go on; we just can't seem to get away from this fourth planet!

Some of the scientific facts about Mars are:

> Planet Number Four of our solar system most resembles the earth, but is half our size and 50% farther away from the sun than we are. A Martian day is but 38 minutes longer than a day on earth, and the axial tilt just 1.7 degrees greater.
>
> Mars apparently had an atmosphere at one time…but at present the atmospheric pressure is almost nil (7 millibars compared to earth's 1000). Thus the daily temperature range runs from -220° to +170° F. The polar "ice" caps are

dusty frozen carbon dioxide. There are occasional strong winds and great dust storms, and Mars has no magnetic field to speak of.

Cairo, Egypt ("Al Kahira"; i.e., Mars) was founded on August 5, 969 A.D. by conquering Fatimid armies. Advice from local astrologers to delay the construction was apparently overlooked. The soothsayers were fearful that the ascendant planet Mars and certain other omens meant the Turks would soon conquer the city. The intended name of the city until the astrologers' dire warning had been Al Mansuriya ("the victorious"). Mars and Egypt seem to be strangely linked from ancient times, probably from Pharaonic times in ancient Egyptian astrology and mythology. [174]

The big hubbub nowadays is the scientific proclamation of an ancient form of bacterial life on Mars found in a potato-sized meteorite, and the much more fascinating photos of what appears to be a face on Mars, along with a city of pyramids.

It is the Cydonia region of Mars where, in 1976, much-published images of a humanoid face, pyramidal mountains, and what looked like a "city" and a "fort" had been seen. According to an article by Lambert Dolphin:

> The unusual landforms at Cydonia on Mars are either natural features or they are artificial constructs of intelligent beings. A number of tests of artificiality have been proposed since the area was discovered. For example, it has been noted that the "Face" is a three-dimensional face, not merely a profile or a drawing on a flat surface. As such, it still looks like a face from every angle.[175]

A face on Mars nearly a mile wide, and symmetrical! How does that happen in nature? Not to mention a five-sided pyramid which seems to have some strange links to the Great Pyramid! ("Namely, redundant geometry, which supposedly holds the key for understanding higher quantum mechanics.")[176] Upon Mars we see a complex of over twelve smaller pyramids, and another a mile wide, five hundred foot high mound, complete with a peripheral ditch and a central spiral groove, how does that happen in nature? This city of pyramids some have studied and noted represents a 360-degree circle and are linked with the twelve signs of the zodiac.

There are some interesting "faces" others have associated with the face on Mars. Take for instance Nergal, the two-faced god of Mars (lion/human). As it appears on the zodiac sign of Sagittarius, it is the same as the profile on the face of Aars.[177] If you will recall, cherubs have a face of a lion and a human. Interestingly enough, the great Sphinx is lion and human, and the human face that now appears on the monument of the Sphinx looks like the face on Mars…hmmm.

Why should you care, and what does this have to do with the Bible? Remember Ezekiel's wheels? We know from our study on angels that Ezekiel saw cherubim with "four faces." These "four faces" all line up with cardinal points of the zodiac. Look to four of the brightest stars in the zodiac: Fomalhaut in Aquarius (man), Regulus in Leo (lion), Antares in Ophiuchus (serpent holder, or eagle), and Aldebaran in Taurus (the bull). *And this was their appearance: they had human form. Each of them had four faces and four wings. Their legs were straight and their feet were like a calf's hoof, and they gleamed like burnished bronze…As for the form of their faces, had the face of a man; all four had the face of a lion on the right and the face of a bull on the left, and all four had the face of an eagle* (Ezekiel 1:1–19; NIV). "All four of these stars are arranged three signs apart, in the four corners of the heavens—the four fixed signs of the zodiac. These are the four creatures which combine to form scriptural cherubim."[178]

Mars, according to some scientists, was the victim of a cosmic explosion; they theorize a neighboring planet, named Astera, the fifth planet, who is also known as Rahab, may have exploded and collided with Mars. One side of Mars is severely pockmarked, leading astrophysicists to believe the remains of this planet (Rahab) is now the asteroid (Astera) belt floating around space, and a real threat to our planet.

So again, why did the ancients fear Mars? Dr. Chuck Missler has an interesting theory:

> According to some Scientists, Mars may have been on a resonate 2:1 orbit with earth, 720 days vs. 360 days, which resulted in "near pass bys." These near pass bys were not only terrifying but predictable, approximately every 54 or 108 years! The effects of these "close encounters" would have made Mars appear 50x the size of our moon! It would have caused 85 feet crustal land tides, destroying cities—as we have seen from studying archeological ruins, places like Troy were rebuilt 7 times from their own rubble. This would have changed our calendars, our axis, magnetic field reversals, and caused meteors and bolides (exploding meteors), dark clouds and massive lightening! [179]

Terrifying, to say the least.

All of our ancient calendars were on 360-day years until mysteriously they changed in 701 BC. Orbits would have intersected on March (Mars' month) 21–23rd and October 25th. And the most compelling of all is the biblical account. Some very savvy scholars have studied the major catastrophes in the Bible and found they all occur 108 years apart or a multiple thereof! The catastrophes were the flood of Noah, Tower of Babel, the destruction of Sodom and Gomorrah, the Exodus plagues, the long day of Joshua, Siseras encounter, Gideon, Philistines, David, Elijah on Mt. Carmel, Joel-Amos, and Sennacherib.[180]

Now in order for us to make sense of all of this "Mars stuff," we again need to go back to scripture and see if there is any backing for all of this. Is there any biblical evidence for this fifth (Rahab) planet exploding and leaving behind an asteroid belt? Go with me to Job: *The pillars of the heavens quake, aghast at his rebuke. By his power he churned up the sea; by his wisdom he cut Rahab to pieces. By his breath the skies became fair; his hand pierced the gliding serpent. And these are but the outer fringe of his works; how faint the whisper we hear of him! Who then can understand the thunder of his power?* (Job 26:11–14; NIV). By his wisdom he cut Rahab to pieces? Other translations say *he smites proud Rahab*, and *he shatters Rahab, by His spirit the heavens were beautiful.* We aren't talking about Rahab the prostitute; this predates her: *rah'-hab* means "bluster (blusterer): proud, strength."[181] Another Bible passage: *…You have broken Rahab (Egypt) in Pieces; with your mighty arm You have scattered Your enemies* (Psalm 89:6, 10; AMP). And again we see it in Isaiah: *…Was it not you who cut Rahab to pieces, who pierced that monster through?* (monster, meaning dragon, serpent), (Isaiah 51:9; NIV). O.K. this is where things get creepy. If there was a planet God wrought judgment on, as we have seen from the biblical text and we see from empirical evidence on the face of the planets, then that begs the question, why?

Remember one of our keystone verses on the fall of Lucifer:

> You were anointed as a guardian cherub, for so I ordained you. You were on the holy mount of God; you walked

> among the fiery stones. You were blameless in your ways from the day you were created till wickedness was found in you. Through your widespread trade you were filled with violence and you sinned. So I drove you in disgrace from the Mount of God, and I expelled you, O Guardian Cherub, from among the fiery stones, your heart became proud on account of your splendor. So I threw you to the earth; I made a spectacle of you before kings. By your many sins and dishonest trade you have desecrated your sanctuaries. So I made a fire come out from you, and it consumed you, and I reduced you to ashes on the ground in the sight of all who were watching. All the nations who know you are appalled at you; you have come to a horrible end and will be no more. (Ezekiel 28:14–19; NIV)

We talked about "the fiery stones" possibly being planets back in the first section, but I would like to draw your attention to the next verse: *By your many sins and dishonest trade you have desecrated your sanctuaries.* What? Desecrated *your* sanctuaries? Could this mean Lucifer had his own sanctuaries? I took the liberty of looking up the word *sanctuary* in Vine's Expository Dictionary and guess where it told me to go? Temple and tabernacle. Now these words mean "palace, dwelling place, and house or home." As Christians living in a fallen world and subject to the lies and information only the Intelligent Deceiver wants us to know, we often may fall victim to some rather strange assumptions. The assumption that angels don't have a dwelling place of their own may very well be a false assumption. We know God himself has a "dwelling place" in heaven. We know he desires to "dwell with us" in our bodies, which he himself called a holy temple seven times in the New Testament. So what makes us think Satan wouldn't want to have his own dwelling place?

Most likely all angels have their own "estates." We know angels eat, drink, and operate in free will. Why not have a home? We are talking about the God of the universe, he created things in order, and he is the epitome of excess and glory and super abundance. What if the angels live on other planets and go about the work of the Lord's business? Let's see if there are some other scriptures to help back this up.

Now there was a day when the sons of God (angels) came to present themselves before the Lord, and Satan (the adversary and accuser) also came among them. And the Lord said to Satan, from where did you come from? (Job 1:6–7; AMP). Why would the angels have to come to present themselves before the Lord if they dwell with him in heaven all the time? *Praise Jehovah from the heaven: praise him from the heights. Praise him, all his angels; Praise him all his hosts. Praise him sun and moon; praise him all you stars of light. Praise him O heavens of heavens…Let them praise the name of Jehovah* (Psalm148: 1–3; NIV). Could this be an allusion to the abode of angels? We are talking about angels praising him from every star, sun, moon, planets, and heavens of heavens, from the heights (or atmospheres)! I hope you are beginning to see the implications of angels having their own abode. This would certainly explain unexplainable, unnatural structures, on Mars! These structures are not made by an alien race, but instead by a fallen race of angels, bent on their revenge, and our deceit and destruction.

Let's consider Mars in the end-times scenario and what to look for on our horizon: Judgment. Mars means judgment; as a celestial body it could be a cosmic reminder to us of God's holiness and his plan of redemption for us as a created being. As for the remnant of Rahab (Astera the fifth planet) or as we know it today, the asteroid belt, we must keep a close eye on the skies for the "stoning" of our planet in judgment of our own sin. Go with me to Revelation: *The second angel sounded his trumpet, and something resembling a great mountain, blazing with fire was hurled into the sea* (Revelation 8:8; NIV). And also: *The third angel blew his trumpet, and a huge star fell from heaven, burning like a torch, and it dropped on a third of the rivers and on the springs of water* (Revelation 8:10; NIV). Mars may be a warning sign throughout the ages of God's final fury and judgment on a fallen deceptive being.

Mars reminds me of the Tower of Babel, built to escape the judgment of an Almighty God and incite war in the heavens.

Keep a wary eye on the news in the coming years for more interest in Mars. Mars is being touted as our "future," our back-up planet when this planet's environment is depleted. I have to laugh when I write this because that is such an absurd statement. What a great way for our Intelligent Deceiver to have his own "created planet." It is the world's way of saying this planet is not good enough for humans, God didn't make things right. When I fly across the states, the heaviest concentration of humans is in the cities. The only green space they see is their city parks and their lawns. Most Americans don't have any concept of the land we have with nothing on it! Take a look at Canada; the upper portion is bare, and it's the size of America! We have vast, vast amounts of untapped resources. But the Intelligent Deceiver doesn't want you to look at it. He wants you to panic and cry, "Global warming, we are all going to die!" He wants you to spend your money for your children's future on Mars real estate. I don't know, did you read how uninhabitable Mars is? The temperatures vary from 220 to 170 degrees Fahrenheit! And no water! How do you get around that little number? This is just another ploy by Satan to get you to doubt the power and omniscience of God.

Chapter Eleven

THE OCCULT, WITCHCRAFT, SORCERY, AND MAGICK

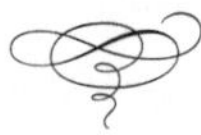

...By your magic spells and poisonous charm all nations were led astray (seduced and deluded).

—Revelation 18:23; AMP

According to the Encarta Dictionary, the *occult* has five different meanings: supernatural or magic, not understandable by ordinary humans, secretive or revealed only to the initiated, hidden medicine or diseased condition which is difficult to detect, and finally, difficult to see, not visible to the naked eye. All of which could be classified under the biblical heading "Witchcraft." Satan is the author of the occult. This is his corruption and counterfeit of the power and gifts of the Holy Spirit. Remember his ambitious "I will" statements and goals? In order for Satan to be like God, he has to have his own counterfeit power and gifts to deceive and dupe God's children.

Let's logically think about this for a minute; if people did not receive a sense of power, or have some unexplained supernatural experience over nature, I doubt very seriously so many people would take up an interest and fascination with the occult.

When I began my search for answers from my encounter with the clairvoyant's hex, I did not have a good enough biblical basis for finding the answers I was seeking, and I certainly did not know I could ask God for these answers, nor did I have the maturity to wait for the answer. Instead, I went looking for a supernatural experience under the guise of the newly accepted medical science field of alternative medicine. I was still in nursing school and the thought of alternative forms of medicine fascinated me, since I felt traditional medicine did not have the answers to our growing health problems. I actually read about it in one of my text books and saw a video presentation on T-touch, or Therapeutic Touch, a method of using your hands in a sort of electromagnetic field around the human body to feel blocked energy flow, and to "wipe it away" from the human body, allowing the human body the ability to heal itself, from its own energy source. According to the video, *anybody* could learn this method, and we could all tap into our own intuitive healing energies to help our fellow man. I fell for it—hook, line and sinker! In fact, on the school's announcement board there was a flyer for a T-Touch seminar coming up, and fairly close for me to attend. I and another classmate (who was also a Christian) eagerly called and signed up for the class.

I told one of my good friends, who was a strong Christian, about my intentions to attend the class. I was excited! She, on the other hand, gave me a stern lecture and warning. "Connie, don't go. It is not biblical, and you are opening yourself up to things you really should leave alone," she warned. I did not heed her warning. I just told her I would "be careful," and if things got too freaky I would leave. Well, off we went to the seminar. It was a glorious spring day, and the seminar was being put on by a nurse in her home. We were the first to arrive. My friend and I discussed the fact that as Christians maybe we should be careful, but we "reasoned" how could it be bad? We were going to help people to heal! We will have this incredible skill! We walked up to the house, and I started to get that old familiar feeling of my spirit warning me, talking to my mind, "Don't go!" You know the one, your conscience, but I didn't listen very well. The woman who answered the door was dressed in granola type, hippy-dippy clothes, and the thing that struck me the most was a strong, pungent, odor of incense, and ALL of the curtains in the house were closed. It was a beautiful day, and it seemed unnaturally dark in the house. As we made small talk, and talked about our natural apprehension and doubt about T-Touch, we also told her we were Christians. She was somewhat standoffish, not exceedingly warm, and she acted oddly. She walked around us like a wild animal would if he wanted something to eat, but wasn't sure if there was a hidden danger. She evidently did not trust us. As we sat in the uncomfortable, incense cloud and darkness, I began to get the worst headache of my life. It came on so fast, and so hard, I could hardly talk or see. I rarely get headaches, and when I do they are usually very mild, and I can honestly say I had never had a migraine in my life, but this was certainly shaping up to be one. People started to show up one by one, and I tried to ignore the pain. Finally, this T-Touch nurse *intuitively* came over to me, and asked me if there was anything wrong. I asked for some ibuprofen, and she glibly told me, "No! I have something better. Let's start today off with some T-Touch and show you and your friend it does work." I can honestly say, I was afraid. Something inside told me she was the cause of this unnatural headache! But, being the people-pleaser I was, and after all I had an audience now, I consented. She did her little hand waving thing, and I felt a "Zing" go up my neck, and my headache began to lift rather quickly. Well, this just convinced everyone in the room this stuff was "real." They clung to her every word! She moved the class outside on the back deck, and she began to teach her "centering routine," which included visualization that we were trees, and we had to send our roots deep into the earth to connect with this "healing energy," and while visualizing, we were to hum or chant. I didn't. At this point, I was convinced this woman was a witch, and she had sicked her demon dog on me in the house with an unnatural headache so she could prove her power over me. I wanted out, but my friend seemed to be enjoying the seminar. I sat in the corner and tried to participate as little as possible. When we left that afternoon, I talked it over with my friend, and we both decided not to return for the following session. Neither one of us could explain our sense of foreboding, and the freaky headache, and the woman's coolness toward us.

Once again, I have to ask myself, what did I open myself up to? Stupid, ignorant, stiff-necked! I was even warned. But warnings don't bode well with me unless I understand why. I wrestle all the time with God about why he made me want to know so much about "Why." I just thank God for his mercy and grace while I was wandering in the wilderness.

So this section is for all of you Christians like me, who are absolutely fascinated by the supernatural. Seemingly innocent games can lead to serious entanglement. This is called "dabbling." Ever seen an animal in a trap? Innocently they follow the scent of the bait. When they are convinced the food is theirs, they take a bite. As the trap snaps shut, they instinctively jump back, but by then it is too late; the trap grabs their leg or paw and they are hopelessly caught. They may struggle for hours until thirst and exhaustion get the best of them, or even try to gnaw the caught appendage, but ultimately their fate is sealed by death!

I will make a bold statement: Most Christians nowadays have been involved with witchcraft, most without even knowing it! Our culture is saturated with witchcraft, and we have been naïve and duped into thinking it is nothing but old wives' tales, myth and legend, or worse yet, harmless *fun.* The paranormal is synonymous with the occult; it is one and the same! The word *occult* actually means to hide, cover, and conceal! If you have ever taken mind-altering drugs or alcohol to get drunk, if you have ever been to an alternative healing, if you have been to a yoga class (yes, yoga, even if only once!), ever read a horoscope, ever been hypnotized at a party, etc., then your spirit and body has been seduced and raped!

If some of you are already squirming in your chairs and shaking your head no, I dare you to read on! Witchcraft is everywhere! Witchcraft is Satan's tool, just as the Holy Spirit is God's tool for wielding his power!

Witchcraft is spoken about many times in the Bible. In fact the words *rebellion* and *witchcraft* are synonymous. Who was the original rebel? Satan. So he is the originator of witchcraft. The word *witch* means "wise one," and the word *craft* connotes strength and skill. Wise one with strength and skill sounds like a pretty good description of the Intelligent Deceiver to me! Much of what we think about witchcraft is a hag dressed in black, an ugly, banshee-type of woman humped over a flaming cauldron, brewing newt's eyes and strange herbs, and muttering peculiar incantations. While this is our society's version, witchcraft goes much deeper than just our interpretation of a witch. Witchcraft encompasses many things, such as: psychics, clairvoyants, mediums, ESP, sorcery, magick, zombies, voodoo, black arts, Wicca, necromancy, remote viewing, automatic writing, channeling, séances, astral projection, astrology, and objects of worship or objects of power and rituals. Other subtle or more acceptable *hidden forms* include: yoga, acupuncture, meditation, visualization, crystals, violent video and computer games, role playing games such as *Dungeons*

& Dragons and other games, magick/sorcery themed movies, television, music, comics, books, and magazines, souvenirs, and others.

As I studied witchcraft/rebellion, it became apparent the reason why it is so enticing to people is it is Satan's counterfeit to the Holy Spirit's power and the gifts of the spirit. We are talking very real *power*! Raw, evil, torturous, but nonetheless power! This is the great fascination, the great draw, whether it is hidden knowledge, healing power, power over the natural, power over people, etc. Power, power, and more power is the promise of intelligent deception, power "no one else has," forbidden power our rebellious sin-nature craves. The nature witches also capitalize and counterfeit our God-given authority and power over his creation/nature. Witchcraft blasphemes the Holy Spirit and his power.

"A coven is a gathering or community of witches, much like a congregation in Christian parlance. It is composed of a group of believers who gather together for ceremonies of worship such as Drawing Down the Moon, or celebrating the Sabbats."[182]

The scriptures teach us: *For rebellion is like the sin of divination, and arrogance like the evil of idolatry* (Samuel 15:23; NIV).

And also:

> They will come upon you in full measure, in spite of your many sorceries and all your potent spells. You have trusted in your wickedness and have said, "No one sees me." Your wisdom and knowledge mislead you when you say to yourself, "I am, and there is none besides me." Disaster will come upon you, and you will not know how to conjure it away. A calamity will fall upon you that you cannot ward off with a ransom; a catastrophe you cannot foresee will suddenly come upon you. Keep on, then with your magic spells and

> with your many sorceries, which you have labored at since childhood. Perhaps you will succeed, perhaps you will cause terror. (Isaiah 47:9–12; NIV)

And in Leviticus: *Do not turn to mediums or seek out spirits, for you will be defiled by them. I am the Lord your God* (Leviticus 19:31; NIV). This is a most dire warning, we will become contaminated by them (defiled), in the plainest terms possible, you open yourself up for demonic possession, you in effect "invite" them in to your body, without even knowing it!

I will set my face against the person who turns to mediums and spirits to prostitute himself by following them, and I will cut him off from his peoples (Leviticus 20:6; NIV).

When you enter the land the Lord your God is giving you, do not learn to imitate the detestable ways of the nations there. Let no one be found among you who sacrifices his son or daughter in the fire, who practices divination or sorcery, interprets omens, engages in witchcraft, or casts spells, or who is a medium or spiritist or who consults the dead. Anyone who does these things is detestable to the Lord (Deuteronomy 18:9–12; NIV).

Over and over again, all throughout scripture, the words "*detestable practices*" are synonymous with witchcraft and idol worship.

These verses are very strongly worded; disaster will befall you, you won't be able to conjure up any help from your demons/spirit guides, you will be made foul and dirty by them. You become a prostitute to them, which is a polite way of saying you just fornicated with demons. God will not help you; he will actually turn against you and cut you off! Ouch! In fact, witchcraft of any kind was so sticky, enticing, and corrupting of people, God instituted capital punishment as a consequence of meddling with it…this was no slap on the hand, this meant death! *A man or a woman who is a medium or spiritist among you must be put to death. You are to stone them; their blood will be on their own heads* (Leviticus 20:27; NIV). If you were caught necromancing (trying to contact the dead, such as a séance) you would have been put to death! If you read the stars for others—death. If you took recreational drugs to alter your state of mind for idol worship (oracles)—death! If you watched or read Harry Potter—death. If you read your horoscope—death! He wasn't playing around here…this is some very serious stuff! If this was the penalty in God's eyes, you have to ask yourself what is he trying to protect us from? Can it really be that bad? Can witches and wizards entangle us with their "hidden secrets" so easily God demands their death actually be upon their own heads? When he told various servants throughout the Bible to rid the land of spiritists and mediums, he did it with the intent of protecting his chosen people. If you remove something very tempting, then it is hard to be tempted by something you aren't around or thinking about.

Paul, filled with the Holy Spirit, spoke these very same predictions to a sorcerer called Elymas: *You are a child of the devil and an enemy of everything that is right! You are full of all kinds of deceit and trickery. Will you never stop perverting the right ways of the Lord? Now the hand of the Lord is against you. You are going to be blind, and for a time you will be unable to see the light of the sun* (Acts 13:10; NIV). Paul spoke from the power of the Holy Spirit and called him a child of the devil, an enemy of right, full of deceit and trickery (this is an implication of demon possession), and accused him of *perverting* the right ways of the Lord! The scripture is clear witchcraft is the perversion of the Holy Spirit's power! Have you had your palm read recently at a carnival? Does your child own a pentagram, moon (crescent moon) or sun wheel necklace? Do you have power crystals in your home? These may seem like innocent games and trinkets, but the Bible warns us of their deceit and trickery. They fill you with it, make you dirty. Are your prayers being answered? If not, there may be a reason for it. God states he will turn against you if you "play" with these things.

In the following pages, my prayer is your eyes will be opened to the hidden dangers, just as mine were. There are so many gray areas in our culture right now. Harry Potter seems to be a really fun child's story, and when you compare it to the Chronicles of Narnia, the magic and sorcery are one and the same. But the underlying message is completely different; so is the entanglement aspect. (As a layperson, I can't tell you how much I enjoyed the Harry Potter movies, but when I undertook a serious study of witchcraft, I was literally blown away! The craft presented in the stories are the exact crafts practiced by very high level Satanists. The stories are intriguing and fun; this is just the point. But the question begs to be asked, is this a well thought out trap for our youth? What kid doesn't want to have Harry Potter's *powers*? How far will they go to play, visualize, imagine, and look on-line for the *real thing*?) Let's take a look at some of the stories of magic and sorcery in the Bible, and compare and contrast it to the power of the Holy Spirit.

The following is a partial list of displays of the Holy Spirit's powers found in the scriptures:

- Floating axe head (a borrowed axe head fell into the Jordan River, Elisha made it float)
- Parting of the Jordan River and the Red Sea
- Makes a bush appear to burn but not burn up
- Pillar of Fire and Cloud

- Casting lots
- The writing on the wall
- Giant hailstones falling on and killing *only* Israel's enemy
- Makes an animal talk (Baalam's donkey)
- Long hair giving super strength (Samson's covenant)
- Staff budding, and also turning into a serpent
- Water turned to blood
- Plague of frogs, gnats, flies, livestock dying, boils, hail storm, locusts, darkness you could "feel," and death of the first born (only of the Egyptians)
- Jesus "disappears" in a crowd
- Raising of the dead
- Healing of diseases
- Walks on water (Jesus)
- Calms the storm (Jesus)
- Predicts the future (prophecy, word of wisdom)
- "Knows" a person's deeds past, present, and future (Jesus)
- Curses and withers a fig tree (Jesus)
- Disciples and apostles chains "fall off," and locked prison gates open.

This is only a partial list, but if you were an outsider and knew nothing of the stories of the Bible, would it be possible you take one look at this list and say this is exactly what sorcery, witchcraft, mediums, and psychics do? But yet these are all acts of God or power and gifts of the Holy Spirit! How can we tell the difference? The word *Wicca,* which is the official religion of witchcraft, comes from the Anglo Saxon word *wicce,* which means to shape or bend nature to one's service!

Let's examine the ultimate sorcerer's showdown found in

Exodus. Moses is trying to get Pharaoh to set the Israelites free, and he continues to refuse. In fact, God says he is the one actually hardening Pharaoh's heart! Remember Moses was raised as an Egyptian, and not just any Egyptian, a royal prince, so in his culture he would have been viewed as the literal embodiment of an Egyptian god. He would have been well schooled in Egyptian paganism and sorcery. God tells Moses he will be like a god to the Egyptians, and Aaron his older brother will be his prophet (see Exodus 7). They go to Pharaoh's court pleading for the Israelites, and as proof of their godhood, Aaron is instructed to throw down his staff, which turns into a snake, of all creatures. Well for Pharaoh's magicians (using their "secret arts") this was an easy trick. They turned their sticks into snakes, but Aaron's snake ate all of their snakes!

Then there was the water into blood, and not just red dyed water; this was actually blood, thick, sticky, smelly blood. As a nurse, I know blood has a very distinctive odor, and when it congeals or clots it gets even worse! This was really gross, and nobody could drink from the Nile, but the sorcerers were also able to duplicate this! Then there were frogs, billions of frogs, hopping all over everything. Ever picked up a frog? Do you know what they do in your hand? They pee. So, imagine frogs hopping on your bed, in your cupboards, peeing all over the place! Yuck! But again the magicians are able to produce frogs. The next one is even more fun, because the sorcerers and wise men are unable to reproduce the gnats. It seems after this, they just kind of quit and acknowledge it isn't by the hand of the devil but by the *finger of God* (Exodus 8:19; NIV). The Bible states; *All the dust throughout the land of Egypt became gnats* (Exodus 8:17; NIV). Can you imagine! Ever swallowed a gnat while playing outside? Now imagine breathing in innumerable amounts!

The plagues continue without duplication by the sorcerers: flies, livestock dying, boils, hail, locusts. Darkness for three days, which was literally "felt" (see Exodus 10:21). This wasn't any ordinary cloud cover, this was a physical cloak of utter pitch black. The Bible says no one could leave their house or see anyone for three days, but the Israelites could! They had light! Then there was the death of the firstborn. I happen to believe this is a special plague with significance to the tithing and dedicating of first fruits.

All of these signs have the initial look of sorcery all over them. But the significant difference is they are so fantastical, so out of the realm of the sorcerers, so incredibly powerful, Satan could not reproduce or imitate this power. I happen to believe the chief sorcerers and magicians were exhausted! Can you imagine the hours of ritual, and trances, and chanting they had to go through to get a *little bit of water* to turn to blood, not the whole Nile! And to re-create a few frogs, and to get a stick to turn into a snake? The sheer numbers and scale of these signs were absolutely unduplicatable by the Intelligent Deceiver. If you look closely at the list of plagues, these types of tricks are Satan's trademarks: blood, creepy reptiles, bugs, disease, incredible storms, darkness, and death. Oh, can you imagine how mad Satan was? God continually outdoes him at every turn! God really does have a sarcastic sense of humor! Not to mention each of these plagues represented a demon idol god the Egyptians worshipped, what a slap in the face of the enemy!

So why are so many people drawn to the power of witchcraft? I believe it offers a substitute for the Holy Spirit's power. Most people, Christians especially, are absolutely clueless about the power of the Holy Spirit. Most Christians could not even name the nine gifts of the Spirit! Many Christians today do not even believe Holy Spirit power is for "today," they believe it was just for the establishing of the new church and the disciples and apostles of Christ, but then again, many Christians do not study their own Bibles. They swallow whole whatever is spoon-fed to them! And we wonder why we are so duped and defeated at every turn?

When people get involved in Wicca, necromancy, Ouija boards, voodoo, etc., they are looking for a "personal sense of power." *I* can control the wind, make my old boyfriend's life miserable, communicate with animals, or spirits, and so on. But what they don't realize is different infillings of the Holy Spirit can be so powerful, it can knock you off your feet! And the Holy Spirit cannot act against his own character. In other words, it will always be healthy fruit, which uplifts and helps mankind and glorifies God; it never glorifies self (you). John talks about the Spirit: *The wind blows wherever it pleases. You hear its sound, but you cannot tell where it comes from or where it is going. So it is with everyone born of the spirit* (John 3:8; NIV). We do not have *control* over the Holy Spirit, which is the difference! People involved in witchcraft *believe* they have control over nature, other people, their spirit guides, their powers or special gifts, when in actuality they don't. They have a demonic spirit residing within them, giving them these powers.

We find a very interesting story in Acts about a girl who was possessed by a spirit of witchcraft, which proves these things which seem so fun and enticing are *not your* "gift" or "sixth sense," but an ugly, demonic spirit which controls you!

> Once when we were going to the place of prayer, we were met by a slave girl who had a spirit by which she predicted the future. She earned a great deal of money for her owners by fortune-telling. This girl followed Paul and the rest of us shouting, "These men are servants of the Most High

> God, who are telling you the way to be saved." She kept this up for many days. Finally Paul became so troubled that he turned around and said to the spirit, "In the name of Jesus Christ I command you to come out of her!" At that moment the spirit left her. When the owners of the slave girl realized that their hope of making money was gone, they seized Paul and Silas and dragged them into the marketplace to face the authorities. They brought them before the magistrates and said, "These men are Jews, and are throwing our city into an uproar by advocating customs unlawful for us Romans to accept or practice." (Acts 16:16–21; NIV)

This fortune-telling demon was obviously very good, because he made the slave girl seem as if she knew what she was talking about, and her owners (she must have been syndicated with the plural "owners," just a joke!) made a lot of money by exploiting her demonic talents. Note the uproar they caused with the authorities by accusing Paul and Silas of advocating customs unlawful for Romans to accept! It wasn't what Paul and Silas were preaching that got them angry, they were losing money because their demon-possessed fortune-telling slave girl no longer had the *"power"* of predicting the future.

This is the unfortunate lure of the occult…it does work, for a while, then they betray you, and devour you. How do you think you get an animal in a snare or other trap? You have to bait it! You have to make it enticing! They have to make their power look real, otherwise you wouldn't believe them and follow them!

So let's look at our list again and see what Satan's counterfeit power is to the Holy Spirit's power.

HOLY SPIRIT	SATAN'S COUNTERFIET
Makes an axe head float in the Jordan River	Levitation
Parting of the Jordan River and the Red Sea	Power over nature (a perversion of our God-given authority over all animals and earth)
Makes a bush appear to burn but not burn up	Power over nature
Pillar of Fire and Cloud	Power over nature in the form of storms
Casting lots	Reading omens, Tarot cards, fortune-telling, horoscopes, Runes
The writing on the wall	Automatic writing
Giant hailstones falling only on Israel's enemy	Power over nature in the form of storms, destruction of your enemies, casting spells, curses
Makes an animal talk (Baalam's donkey)	Power over nature and animal communication
Long hair giving super strength (Samson's Covenant)	Spells, pacts or blood pacts with the devil
Staff budding, and also turning into a serpent	Spells, incantations, cursed objects
Water turned to blood	Spells and curses
Plague of: frogs, gnats, flies, livestock dying, boils, hail storm, locusts, darkness you could "feel," and death of the first born. (Only on the Egyptians)	Power over nature (a perversion of our God-given authority over all animals and earth)
Jesus "disappears" in a crowd	Invisibility, trans-portation
Raises the dead	Necromancy, zombies
Heals diseases	Healers, shamanism
Walks on water	Power over nature
Calms the storm	Power over nature
Predicts the future	Fortune-telling, divination
"Knows" a person's deeds past, present, and future (woman at the well)	Fortune-telling, divination
Curses and withers a fig tree	Spells and curses, power over nature
Disciples' and apostles' chains "fall off" and locked prison gates open	Power over the natural, physical world
Spirit of the Lord caught away Philip, and set him in Azotus	Teleportation, forms of astral projection

I will remind you this is only a partial list. Satan perverts and imitates our God given authority over the earth constantly, the power over nature. This is one that is freely available to ALL Christians. Go back to Genesis: *…fill the earth, subdue it, and rule over all (creatures)*, (Genesis 1:28; NIV). Jesus also tells us with *faith* nothing shall be impossible for us; we can talk to a mountain and throw it into the sea! Well, this doesn't sound spiritual to most Christians, actually doing what God told us to do! Hummph! I am telling you once I got a hold of this revelation, I have actually done it, and it works. Not all the time mind you, because my faith level is still growing, but when it really counted it worked.

I work with horses every day, and if any of you have ever been around horses you know how big and powerful they are. They also have an incredible fight or flight instinct, and are definitely first and foremost a herd animal. In other words they feel very vulnerable when they are alone, away from other horses or a human they perceive to be part of their herd. Several years ago I was involved in a very bad riding accident, in which the horse lost her footing and went down and rolled over on top of me. If you have ever wanted to know what it is like to have 1,250 pounds of powerful, panicked animal with four razor-sharp hooves crush you, I can tell you it is not a pleasant experience. It's like having a steamroller go over you. I broke both of my arms and dislocated my right shoulder so badly that I tore every muscle, tendon, and ligament away from the socket; I also had a very bad case of road rash on the side of my head and face. After surgery and lots of expensive hardware in my arms I was terrified of riding.

I had ridden horses since I was five years old and had known no greater joy, and now I was afraid. I continued to ride, but I was fearful every time I got on to go for a ride, and was so tense I didn't enjoy myself. After five years of this fear, I was ready to give up riding, as it was such an unpleasant experience. I remember one day reading the Word, and the Lord showing me he did not give me a *spirit of fear.* I was having problems with a young horse of mine that continually wanted to go back to the herd if we rode alone. He would stop, try to buck, or switch ends and try to race uncontrollably home. This particularly bad habit is called barn or herd sour. I remembered the Word, and decided this was either going to be my last ride or I was going to conquer my fear and take authority over my animal. I remember getting off my horse at the gate where he usually tried his shenanigans, and I spoke to him in an authoritative voice, and just basically told him God had put me in charge of him, and he would have to obey me without a fuss. I am telling you, as God as my witness, something lifted off of me, I had the best ride, my horse never even so much as sidestepped or whinnied. He perfectly obeyed me, and I have never had a problem with him again. I also regained my joy of riding and have absolutely no fear anymore.

When I think back on my experience, Satan tried to steal my one true passion and joy in life; he also tried to make me believe I did not have power over the situation. I am telling you the Word works, you just have to read it and practice it! Jesus demonstrated nine different instances of his power and authority over nature; they are: calming the storm, feeding the five thousand, walking on water, feeding the four thousand, directing Peter to find a coin inside a fish, withering a fig tree, twice directing the apostles to make a large catch of fish, and turning water into wine. He purchased this ability and authority for us back from Satan at the cross.

When someone gets involved in witchcraft of any kind they have to practice their craft. You don't usually conjure up every demonic spirit at first; you usually have to learn who your spirit guide is, and work your way up from there. There are many stories of older, more advanced witches scaring young witches with their shape shifting or advanced spells, witch contests, etc. You have to learn all the aspects of your craft. When the U.S. government began their remote viewing project (a type of ESP), STAR GATE, their test subjects had to work and practice their skills before they were able to accurately tell of enemy submarines, plans, etc. They also self-describe their talent as controlled and learned. (I find it fascinating that it is named STAR GATE! Mere coincidence?)

The idea of spying on your enemy by remote access is not an original idea of Intelligent Deception by the way. It was a gift of the Spirit given to the prophet Elisha in the Old Testament. The story can be found in 2 Kings 6:8–15. Basically, the king of Aram was always being foiled at every move he made against the Israelites; he even demanded his officers find the mole in his operation. His officers then informed him: *"Will you not tell me which of us is on the side of the King of Israel?" "None of us, my lord the king," said one of his officers, "but Elisha, the prophet who is in Israel, tells the king of Israel the very words you speak in your bedroom"* (2 Kings 6:11–12; NIV). Elisha was given divine knowledge from the Holy Spirit of the very words spoken in the king's bedroom. Was Elisha there? No. Was he practicing some dark art, some powers of concentration, looking through a crystal ball? No. Elisha didn't do any of these things. The Holy Spirit willed it and gave him the info. This is the big difference between Christians and witches. We don't have to go through elaborate rituals for this power, we just need to learn about our God and follow the example of Jesus in the Bible. We are told that the only advantage Elisha may have had over the next Joe Shmoe Christian is that he actually asked for and received a "double portion" of faith! Faith—maybe we need to learn all we can about it!

As Christians we need to practice our faith as well. Learn what is of God, and what is not of God. The Apostle Paul admonishes us to *earnestly desire* the giftings of the Holy Spirit. Now why would he say that if it was so bad?

I have to tell you, I have had many unpleasant encounters with witches and witchcraft, some I truly brought upon myself out of my own ignorance, and some that just seemed to find me and use their false abilities to try to scare me off or trip me up. I can honestly tell you now the Holy Spirit warns me and prepares me for the ensuing battle. I have also learned their tactics and avoid all contact, intentional or otherwise, with the occult to avert open doors in my life. In all cases the Word of the Lord conquers, and so does prayer!

I love what Paul writes in 1 Corinthians: *Now about spiritual gifts, brothers, I do not want you to be ignorant. You know that when you were pagans, somehow or other you were influenced and led astray to mute idols. Therefore I tell you that no one who is speaking by the Spirit of God says, "Jesus be cursed," and no one can say, "Jesus is Lord," except by the Holy Spirit* (1 Corinthians 12:1; NIV). See, Paul is talking to former occultists, former witches, sorcerers, fortune-tellers, spiritists, etc. And he tells them not to be ignorant of the spiritual gifts. I bet he really had this crowd's attention, because these people had left the life of counterfeit, imitation power and were about to learn about real power! He also had the added problem of quarrelling about the gifts because some who had them thought they were more spiritual than others, a throwback to their selfish, pagan ways, plus they wanted that dualism until they learned and matured more in the spirit. Many ex-witches who have found Jesus need to learn they cannot use both the Holy Spirit's power and the devil's power. *You cannot drink the Lord's cup and the demon's cup. You cannot partake of the Lord's table and the demon's table* (1 Corinthians 10:21; NIV).

He goes on to describe if you are working in the Holy Spirit's power, you cannot proclaim a curse on Jesus, and if you are working in the devil's power you cannot proclaim that Jesus is Lord. I have seen individuals under the power of a demonic spirit, and they absolutely cannot say Jesus is Lord; it either doesn't come out, or a stream of profanities ensues, or the person just glares and snarls or growls. But when the individual truly wishes to be free from demonic power, they are able to squeeze out the words *Jesus* or *Lord*, and shortly thereafter they are free from the controlling power. The word *Jesus* is the most powerful word in any language. The Bible says it is the name above all names. If you were into incantations, this one word has the power to destroy all demonic strongholds! I would like to quantify this; many high level Satanists are currently members of the church. They hold positions on the board, serve as deacons, even ministers![183] And they do profess statements of faith. We are taught to test the spirits; this includes both human and good and evil spirits.

Paul continues on with the gifts of the Spirit which are: word of wisdom, knowledge, faith, healing, miraculous powers, prophecy, discerning of spirits, speaking in tongues, and interpretation of tongues. Each one of these nine gifts has a satanic counterfeit. You don't think Satan wants a piece of this action? You would be sorely mistaken! Satan just calls his *gifts* by different names.

The Word of Wisdom is the ability to see God open the curtain to the future. You can see a future event unfolding. He may do this in a vision, dream, or simply show you with the spirit.

Satan's counterfeits to the word of wisdom are: fortune-telling, tarot card reading, divination or spirit guide/familiar spirit telling you what is going to happen, open vision, trance-like state, mental telepathy, crystal balls, mirrors or wells, nightmares and premonitions, palm reading, astrology, horoscopes, mind sciences, channeling, clairvoyants, ESP, Cabalah, psychics, mediums, Ouija boards, and reading omens, as well as other objects.

The Word of Knowledge is the ability to see something going on in the present, without the help of any of the physical senses. In other words you can't physically touch, see, taste, smell, or hear this knowledge.

Satan's counterfeits to the word of knowledge are: Consulting a familiar spirit, divination, psychics, the ability to *know* something about you, such as your personal secrets (intimate knowledge), just by looking at you or hearing your voice.

A Special Gift of Faith was the gift many of the Old Testament Patriarchs had. They had a special gift for parting of the Red Sea, calling upon God to send rain or drought, etc. We all have a measure of faith, but people like Elisha had a double portion!

Satan's counterfeit to faith is great doubt! A complete blinding of a person's spirit and mind to "see and know the truth." They have no conviction, assurance, trust, confidence, reliance, belief, devotion or loyalty to God. I believe these people are the true worshippers of Satan; they have unknowingly bought every lie of the devil at an exorbitant cost. They are supernaturally unable to believe in the power of God.

The Gift of Healing is a one-present-at-a-time sort of gift. In other words, you aren't a "healer." God is "The Healer" and he is working through the Holy Spirit and you to help make a person whole. This gift works hand in hand with the gift of faith.

Satan's counterfeits are: So-called faith healers, shamans, medicine men or wise women, yoga, spells or curses, voodoo, meditations, Therapeutic Touch, crystals, all forms of Eastern mysticism, many of the alternative energy pathways such as chakras, zen, mind science, acupuncture, etc.

Gift of Miraculous Powers, Jesus and the disciples displayed these gifts regularly. It is the ability to control the natural environment around you, such as healing of the body, withering of the fig tree, walking on water, walking out of a prison.

Satan's loves to counterfeit this one because it makes people watch and notice him. But like the grand illusionist he is, they only see the miracle or sign and not what is behind it. Nature witches (Wiccans) perform miracles using elaborate rituals; they control weather and storms, animals, people and crops, and objects. Many of their spells and hexes are directed as revenge or control, or sheer demonic pleasure at seeing their fellow humans suffer. This counterfeit is all about the *feeling* of *power* and *control*! Many Shamans, Native American spiritists, animal worshipers, medicine men, wise women, Wiccans, sorcerers, magicians, and shape shifters practice this form of witchcraft.

The Gift of Prophecy was given from the beginning; it is telling of future events, either for a nation or for a specific individual or group. It can also be preaching God's word with power. God's prophecies *always* come true to the letter.

Satan's counterfeit are: channeling, clairvoyants, psychics, mediums, spiritists, Cabalah, ESP, transcendental meditation, mind control, palm reading, fortune-telling, astrology, crystal ball, anything which claims to come through by séances, meditation, channeling, scrying, etc.

The Gift of Discerning of Spirits requires the Holy Spirit to reveal the spiritual realm, not just demons, but the ENTIRE invisible world. This includes angels, demons, etc. Of all of the gifts, this one may be the most difficult to handle, because I think if we could have our spiritual eyes opened to us, we may be in a state of shock as to what is going on around us.

Satan's counterfeits are: divination, spiritists, spirit guides, animal communicators, mediums, clairvoyants, psychics, channeling, Ouija board, séances, crystal balls, etc. Most who practice any form of occultism or witchcraft are privy to this power. They are able to see or communicate with their spirit guides, demons, and other astrally projected spirits. They seem to only have a demonic spiritual sight, and do not often "see" angels.

The Gift of Tongues is the ability to speak directly to God, bypassing the mind, in a heavenly language. It is direct communication of your spirit to God. It is a way of building up or edifying your own personal spirit. This is one gift we have total control over and can access at any time. The Holy Spirit is a gentleman; he is not going to possess your tongue and voice box, and make you speak out loud in a foreign tongue in the grocery store!

Satan's counterfeits are: Demonic tongues (test it, watch its fruit). Satan loves to chew this one up and vomit it back at the church. No other gift of the Spirit causes so much strife and division. You need to ask yourself why Satan attacks this particular gift so. Could it be that by using one verse of scripture out of context and twisting it for the past two thousand years he has effectively crippled spirit-filled Christians and churches and grieved the Holy Spirit so as to render many Christians and churches powerless? This is your pep talk from God! Satan knows this. And he certainly doesn't want your spirit communing directly with the Almighty. You might have a power surge and blow up a bunch of his demons! The gift of tongues freaks-out so many good Christians; why? Because Satan has attached a spirit of doubt and fear and misinformation to it. Many Christians think if they speak in another language and don't understand what they are saying, they might be speaking in the tongue of a devil. (Again, the Word tells us to *test the spirits, including the Holy Spirit!* You can talk out loud and say something to the effect; "If you are a tongue of a demon, I bind you in the name of Jesus, and tell you not to speak." If it still speaks, then you now know it is of God.) What Christians don't understand is speaking in tongues is a gift that bypasses the human intellect, the mind, which we have learned in the past is quite well-controlled and oppressed by the enemy. God knows this. He bypasses our flesh, our carnality and just lets our spirits express themselves, without the burden of the body, to his Holy Presence. What a gift! Now do you see why Satan wants to render it ineffective?

One day I asked God for other gifts. I had been praying for it for quite some time and was quite frustrated. I thought speaking in tongues was a rather boring gift because I didn't understand what I was saying to him. Boy did God give me a boot kickin'! He told me tongues were more powerful than I could possibly imagine. It was the very first gift given to the church (Pentecost)! It has the ability to mature our spirit; it can encompass all of the other gifts of the spirit, because it is perfect prayer. You can't say anything wrong when you speak in (holy) tongues! When I got a hold of this and repented for my ignorance, boy, did power come forth. I can tell you, speaking in tongues is easy, much easier than English prayer, which ends up sounding like a laundry list to Santa Claus! You can pray for hours in tongues, and never get tired. I have been set free from demonic strongholds, I have known I have prayed against demonic spirits sent by witchcraft to destroy a member of our church, I know I can sing a heavenly song without knowing a stitch of music. And most of all, I know I can give God perfect praise! Yes, Satan, wants to destroy this gift. If he can cause confusion, disorientation, and division over this gift he knows he can render the church and Christians powerless! This is Intelligent Deception!

The Gift of Interpretation of Tongues was given to counteract Satan's attack on tongues! God knew Satan would attack it, and in his grace and mercy and ultimate wisdom, he gave some the ability to interpret the language being said. This is to be used in the corporate body of the church. The Holy Spirit may be giving a word of wisdom, or prophecy for the body, and he will use another member or the same one speaking to interpret in English (or whatever language you happen to speak) the word or meaning of what transpired. It is used so others may know of the Holy Spirit's power and to help build up the church. Many churches do not do this correctly; Paul gives us strict guidelines on the proper use of tongues. We need to learn and heed these warnings to protect us from the demonic guiles and incantations of Satan and his envoys. Read and study 1 Corinthians 12–14.

Satan's counterfeits are: Demonic tongues. We already covered why he doesn't want people to use the gift of tongues, and he certainly doesn't want people to interpret the tongue, because then a whole bunch of people who normally may not hear a direct message from God will get a conference call from heaven with a word of prophecy, knowledge or wisdom, or what have you! No, Satan wouldn't want that, so he took Paul's discourse on the proper protocol of interpretation of tongues in a public service, and pretty much made people *think* nobody should speak in tongues at all! Sneaky devil!

Satanic Symbols of the Occult

Behold, I am sending you out like sheep in the midst of wolves; be wary and wise as serpents, and harmless as doves.

—Matthew 10:16; NIV

Objects of power and satanic symbols go hand-in-hand with occult practices. Do you ever wonder why an object associated with ritualistic behavior seems to have, or carry with it, its own power? Such as a Ouija board, pentagram, carved idols, symbols, crystals, herbs and plants, even certain objects as benign as furniture?

As I have said so many times before, Satan wants to be like God. He wants to exalt himself above God, so he has to counterfeit and imitate God's precepts and behaviors and methods of accepted worship. He is a copycat.

To learn why the Intelligent Deceiver would want his own objects of meaning, worship, and adoration, we have to go back to the original, the Almighty's blueprint for worship. If you go to Exodus 25–30, you will find detailed instructions for the Israelites in making the tabernacle and all its furnishings. This included the Ark, atonement cover, curtain, bread of the presence, tables, lamp stands, Tabernacle, Altar, courtyard, oil for the lamp stands, priestly garments, breast piece (ephod) of the priests, and the altar of incense, incense, anointing oil, basin, and utensils. All of these items had to be made *exactly* as the Lord had given them instruction, and they were to be consecrated and dedicated to the service for the Lord. Certain items and utensils were to be used only for a specific purpose and only in a certain area. If something was taken out of a certain area, there were dire consequences. Each of these items was assigned a specific meaning. For example, the Ark symbolized God's covenant; the basin symbolized the need for spiritual cleansing, etc. Well Satan doesn't want to be left out of this aspect of worship either. So he has created his own unclean list of items of worship, ritual, sacrifice, power, and mockery. These items are called familiar objects and cursed objects.

Go with me to Acts: *God did extraordinary miracles through Paul, so that even handkerchiefs and aprons that had touched him were taken to the sick, and their illnesses were cured and the evil spirits left them* (Acts 19:11–12; NIV). God himself seems to endow inanimate objects with power. Could Satan do the same? Could he attach evil spirits or evil intent to an object or symbol and cause an open door to his sick, twisted spiritual realm? I not only think it likely, it is most probable. Remember, the Ark of the Covenant was just a piece of wooden furniture, but it held the very power and glory of God!

Let's take a look at the pentagram. A pentagram is a five-pointed star. It could be pointed up or down; each has a different meaning. Again, we see a star! Where did pentagrams originate? You guessed it, Babylon. The pentagram is associated with the planet Venus and the worship of the goddess of Venus-Ishtar. It is also associated with Lucifer who was Venus the Morning Star, bringer of light and knowledge. It is also interesting to find out the early Sumerian word for pentagram was *UB,* which means a cavity, hole, or *pitfall.* The Babylonians had an astrological meaning for each of the five points. They pointed to the five planets: Jupiter, Mercury, Mars, Saturn, and Venus. The Greeks thought the five points represented the classical elements: water, earth, a divine thing, heat (fire), and air. This is still what modern Wiccans use the pentagram for, with "the divine thing" meaning "spirit." In Greek mythology, it is associated with the queen of the underworld, and has to do with the heart. I have recently noticed a new sticker gracing many of the young people's cars as of late, depicting a pentagram within the shape of a heart!

I find the most intriguing and likely meaning for a pentagram is that it corresponds to Satan's five "I will" statements. Each point corresponding to an "I will."

The pentagram functions as a gateway, link, or a yoke between the spiritual realm and the natural! These are not merely harmless trinkets, stickers, or jewelry. Satan uses this symbol so much as to rival the symbolism of the cross! And this may very well be his intent! Since the stars seem to point to Jesus' death and crucifixion on the cross, it may well be Satan's counterfeit. It is his way of being worshipped.

The pentagram directly links her (Lilith) to the ancient Egyptian god of magic, Heka, and his later manifestations as Hekat, the frog-headed goddess of transformation, Egyptian and Cretan serpent goddesses, and the Phoenician goddesses Astarte and Tanith.

Lilith and Samael are embodied within the Satanist pentagram, and may be referenced in the following scripture, which scholars have notated with the correlating demons and gods in parentheses:

> And thorns shall grow in her places, nettles and thistles in its fortresses; and it shall be a home for jackals, a court for daughters of ostriches (Unclean Birds = Demonesses).
>
> The wild beasts of the desert (Goat-Demons in dry places of rest) shall also meet with the jackals (Anubis or female vampire), and the wild goat (Shaggy Goatess or Satyress) shall bleat (Howlers) to its companion; also the night creature (Screech Owls or Lillith) shall rest there, and find for herself a place of rest.
>
> There the arrow snake shall make her nest and lay eggs, and hatch, and gather them under her shadow; there also shall the hawks (unclean birds of the desert) be gathered, everyone with her mate. (Isaiah 34: 13–15)

Note: The terms Night Hawk and Screech Owls was not used until the 14th Century. [184]

In the Sumerian tradition Lilith was the wife and consort of the Angel Samael:

> Samael, a redhead, was the original ruling Archangel of the seventh heaven, one of the Seraphim (Fiery Serpents who guarded the Throne of God). The title "seraphim" came

> from the Hebrew "saraph nahash," a fiery serpent, which derived from the Sumerian "siru," a serpent. Various Jewish traditions refer to him as a guardian angel (of Esau), an angel of death (sent by God to fetch the soul of Moses when he died), the seducer of Eve (in form of the serpent), the creator of the demonic kingdom of Edom and the demons therein, and the chief of the Satans (angels sent by God to test man)…
>
> Samael and Lilith gave the knowledge of the Angels to man and intermarried with humans, resulting in Lilith being punished by being turned into a spirit without form; her hair was "pulled back" so that her manifestation in Eternity was bound and restricted. These Angels were called evil because they sought to aid man's spiritual evolution into a higher type of being.[185]

Throughout Wiccan and Satanic religions it is common knowledge and practice that Satan and his angels were and are still trying to genetically manipulate humans. The danger of the pentagram is it presents itself as an access point for entrance into somebody or something. As humans there are many access ports for administering medicine, many of which people don't realize, such as all orifices; these include eyes, ears, mouth, nose, anus, vagina, and urinary tract. The access ports not-so-well-known to the general public are: transdermally, which means through the skin; intravenous, which is through the veins; intramuscularly, or into the muscle; subcutaneous through the fat; and inhaled, which is through the lungs or mucous membranes. If we as a medical community can find so many different ways to get into the body, how do we know what other ways there are to get into our souls and spirits? Not to mention, how many ways are there to do the reverse, that is, to enter into the spirit realm?

God warns us over and over in his Word of the "cursed thing." These are literally demonically contaminated objects, and unfortunately they are all over our homes. I was shocked when I learned of these things. "These are objects to which demons cling. Anything used in the worship of Satan or in serving Satan is legal ground for demons. In other words the demons have a right to cling or use such objects."[186] Scripture tells us: *The graven images of their gods shall ye burn with fire: thou shalt not desire the silver or gold that is on them, nor take it unto thee, lest thou be snared therein: for it is an abomination to the Lord thy God. Neither shalt thou bring an abomination into thine house, lest thou be a cursed thing like it: but thou shalt utterly detest it, and thou shalt utterly abhor it; for it is a cursed thing* (Deuteronomy 7:25–26; KJV).

Now I know what you are thinking: I don't worship Satan, and I don't have any pentagrams in my house! We are not talking just about pentagrams. We are talking about items others have made, dedicating them to idols (demons) and/or placing a special "blessing or spell" on them and then you buying them and bringing them into your home. Ever been out of the country? Or bought one of those gag voodoo dolls at the gift store? Ever bought a souvenir at one of those places, you know, the one with the poor soul manning the booth, who with broken English, hands you your purchase and says "special"? Many statues and statuettes you buy in other countries are images of their demon gods. You in a sense paid tribute to these idols by purchasing them; you placed them in a special place of honor in your home, so everyone could see your treasure from your vacation. You now have a graven image of a demon god in your living room. This is a cursed object. Did you give a demon the right to be in your home? He lives there now; he has an honored place. I know this sounds ridiculous to us, but we are called by God to be separate! Following Jesus isn't just going to church on Sunday; it is about being totally committed to him. I know that thing cost you money, good money, you earned it, it was a token of your vacation. But are you willing to have your house defiled by it? Or you? This is what God meant by *thou shalt not desire the silver or gold that is on them, nor take it unto thee, lest thou be snared therein…Neither shalt thou bring an abomination into thine house, lest thou be a cursed thing like it.*

Following is a list of some "unlikely" familiar or cursed objects. Again, you may not be worshipping the evil one, but he is an intelligent deceiver. He wants these things in your home so he can get an attachment to you or your kids. A thief is always looking for a way in:

> Common familiar objects include: any occult object used in the practice of the occult arts, any Rock and Roll [CDs], tapes, posters, T-shirts, etc. [many rock stars have signed a contract with Satan in exchange for fame and money], any material from occultic role-playing fantasy games, any artifact of Eastern religions such as the little statue of gods people buy as souvenirs while traveling, any rosaries or objects used in the practice of Catholicism, any article used in the practice of Masonry, any literature or tapes, [CDs], on the occult or pagan, or new age religions.[187]

The list can go on.

For my Catholic readers, it is in love that I say this, because I was raised Catholic and am named after my parents' favorite nun; are not Mary and the saints dead people? When you pray to the saints or Mary you are expecting a dead person to make intercession for you to God on your behalf. The mother of God was a human, just like you and me. Although favored, she lived and died just as we did, and so did the saints. This practice is strictly forbidden in the Bible. It is in a sense necromancy (communing with the dead). Isaiah tells us: *Why consult the dead on behalf of the living?* (Isaiah 8:19; NIV). We already have a mediator for us! One who is constantly before the throne of God making intercession on our behalf! *For there is one God, and one mediator between God and men, the man Christ Jesus; Who gave himself a ransom for all, to be testified in due time* (1 Timothy 2:5–6; NIV). For more complete information on the Catholic Church I highly recommend the book *A Woman Rides the Beast* by Dave Hunt.[188] It is a thorough documentation of the Catholics Church's decrees, beliefs, and history. Again I say this to inform, not condemn. The information is available to all willing to follow God's Word.

Many of these objects must be denounced, repented of and destroyed; others need only be anointed with oil and spoken to out loud, stating that you are severing any demonic ties through witchcraft. Make no assumptions, make no mistake, use the Word as your guidebook; this is very real, not hocus-pocus!

As Christians we need to be keenly aware of entrance points. I think in this dispensation of the last days we need to identify as many portals as possible and ask the Holy Spirit to reveal these portals so we can protect ourselves. I remember as a young Christian I thought the God of the Old Testament was rather fierce, scary, and vengeful, and to be honest, over-the-top. I mean really, kill all the animals, men, women, and children, burn everything, don't take anything, sounds wasteful and harsh. But then my sister set me straight. She explained to me it was for the Jews' protection. God was being a very loving and protecting Father, protecting his beloved chosen people from these very evil and real portals! If you do your homework, these people and animals weren't even *people* and clean animals in God's eyes. They were half human and hybrid animals. If your child was playing in the toilet, you would do the obvious and tell him, "No, dirty!" You would strip the clothes off of the child and put him in the tub, and clean him up. Same principle! Or, do you tell your fifteen-year-old to go try a little Meth so he can get it out of system? No! One hit and he'll be hooked! The God of the Old Testament is the God of the New Testament; they cannot be separated. He is one, he is Holy and undefiled, he is love, protection, the same yesterday, today, and tomorrow.

If you have any form of a pentagram in your possession, or other cursed object, please renounce, repent, and destroy it (preferably with fire)! No longer attach yourself with an unholy umbilical cord.

Yoga

Let's face it. How many of us have taken a yoga class? "It is just exercise," we tell ourselves, and God requires our bodies move. The problem with yoga is that it is an access point.

> In India, the pentagram represents the elements of the five lower chakras of kundalini yoga. These elements are symbolized by the square, circle, triangle, oval and a wisp in the shape of an elongated letter "s." The elements correspond with the five levels of consciousness in the manifest universe below the Abyss. Indian mystics believe the fifth element is a reflection of three additional elements, combined as one, which are above the Abyss and therefore above man's conscious awareness. [189]

It is very hard for Christians today to see anything other than gray, but this is very black and white. Why would you want to do exercise which has its roots founded in ancient idol worship? Could it be a doorway into your life? Yoga is Hinduism; you cannot separate the two! The purpose of yoga is an actual link or yoke with the god Braham. It is supposed to arouse and control your Kundalini force. The word *Kundalini* means "coiled." It is the name of a Hindu goddess *symbolized by a snake;* she has three and a half coils and is asleep with her tail in her mouth. She resides at the tail of the spine, and when uncoiled she brings healing, psychic ability, strength, and power. I don't know about you, but anything which has to do with a Satanic snake uncoiling in my spine (which is the central nervous system pathway), offering me "healing, psychic power, and strength" sounds like Intelligent Deception to me.

Each position or posture of yoga is an act of worship to the sun god (the Baal of the Bible). In her book *Prepare for War,* Dr. Rebecca Brown, MD talks about the different types of yoga presented in the Western hemisphere;

> Hatha yoga, which is supposedly only physical exercise. Kundalini yoga, which is used heavily in the medical field, and promises healing of the mind and body. Tantra yoga is also used by the medical field and is becoming very popular amongst top executives of the large corporations. Tantra yoga is pure Satanism right down to the human sacrifices. The beginners of Tantra yoga usually do not realize what they are getting into. All sorts of sexual perversions are common in this type of yoga. There are many other types of yoga. Four main types are used within Hinduism: Karma yoga, Bhakti yoga, Jnana yoga and Raja yoga. Each of these four are supposed to be used by people of different "natures"... Yoga is specifically for the purpose of opening up the practitioner to the entrance of demons.[190]

The practice of yoga gives rise to other occultic or secret knowledge type of practices. And of course many seem to be completely harmless. Actually they seem like they are extremely helpful in our age of high stress and improper care of the "temple." They are: meditation, visualization, and imagination. For some yoga may not be a snare, just as alcohol or drugs may not be attractive to others even though they have "tried it." But beware; if yoga works well for you, what else will Satan bring your way which may be a huge snare or trap for you? Ask yourself what is the next logical step…an energy body work session after yoga at the gym, or someone suggests biofeedback in class? Intelligent Deception is sneaky, clever, works beneath the surface. This is why God clearly warned the Israelites to "abstain from all that is evil"! Remember, all of these counterfeits do actually work. This is why people are so drawn to them, but the Bible continually warns it is hurtful to God when you do these things.

Eastern Meditation

This is not only misunderstood, but very dangerous. Meditation in the Eastern religions involves "mind blanking," "allowing your mind to empty out," and "releasing the negative." This all sounds very good when you are trying to relax and let go of anxiety and stress, but the Bible tells us a very different story. Again, we see Satan's slither marks all over this one. The Bible does indeed tell us to meditate: *This book of the law shall not depart out of thy mouth; but thou shalt meditate therein day and night, that thou mayest observe to do according to all that is written therein: for then thou shalt make thy way prosperous, and then thou shalt have good success* (Joshua 1:8; KJV).

The Bible never tells us to blank our minds; instead meditation according to scripture is very active in nature, never passive. We are to read and ingest the Bible, we are to marinate in it, thinking on it continually. Thinking is an action verb. This does not have anything to do with mind blanking! A blank mind is one of the most dangerous places! Practicing occultists know this is an open doorway for all sorts of evil spirits. A blank mind, contrary to what is being taught, is an uncontrolled mind. God commands us to control our every thought! If you do not control your mind Satan will! *You will guard him and keep him in perfect and constant peace whose mind [both inclination and its character] is stayed on You, because he commits himself to You, leans on You and hopes confidently in You* (Isaiah 26:3; AMP). We have learned in previous chapters we are to *take every thought captive* (2 Corinthians 10:5; NIV). Captivity does not sound passive.

Much mediation is taught in which you reach deep into your subconscious or even unconscious mind, opening yourself up to and communicating with your "higher consciousness"...Ummm, who is your higher conscious? And why would you want to blank your mind to talk with it? You can't get any higher thought than Jesus, and we have been promised in the Word we have the mind and thoughts of Jesus through the Holy Spirit. *But we have the mind of Christ* (1 Corinthians 2:16; NIV).

Mantras are also a way to mind blank or put oneself into a trance. Rapid repetitions are words that are forbidden in the Bible. *And when you pray, do not keep on babbling like pagans, for they think they will be heard because of their many words* (Matthew 6:7; NIV).

"A mantra is the rapid repetition of a series of words or sounds. It has two purposes. The first is to produce a mystical state, which is actually a trance in which the mind is blanked out. This in turn places the person into direct contact with the spirit world. Secondly, the mantra is supposed to actually 'embody' a spiritual being. As the words are spoken, the being comes into existence and enters the person using the mantra. Mantras are a direct doorway opening up the person to the entrance of demons." [191] This is the dinner bell for demons! "Come and get it…a veritable buffet of human ignorance!"

Meditation, according to Dr. Rebecca Brown, is also very addictive; it is an escape from pain and reality. It gives a demonic high very similar to recreational drugs. Meditation: just say "NO!"

Visualizations and Imaginations

You can't pick up a self-help book without a section on visualization. Think yourself rich, thin, smart…whatever! Yes the Bible tells us *as a man thinks so is he* (Proverbs 23:7; NIV). But it doesn't tell us to visualize and focus our attention on objects. This is what hypnotists do. This is what the T-touch seminar I went to focused on: "Imagine you are tree…your roots are going deep into the earth,"…yada, yada. The more you think on a thing, the more you "release the power" of that thing. Satan capitalizes on this. He knows visualization puts us into direct contact with the spirit world. Ever been to a séance? You are told to concentrate on whomever you want to bring forth. Visualizations are the language of the spirit.

Advanced visualizations create a link, or a continual open door to our bodies. Biofeedback is another form of open door. These links are kept open by demonic spirits and will be very important when we study astral projections. Ask anybody who plays role-playing games like *Dungeons and Dragons* how much they have to *visualize* their character in order to advance in the game. These characters are often demons who help them to advance to the next level or get more power over the other players. The better you are at visualization, the more contact you have with the spirit world.

The Bible tells us to cast down vain imaginations:

> Because when they knew and recognized him as God, they did not honor and glorify him as God or give him thanks. But instead they became futile and godless in their thinking [with vain imaginings, foolish reasoning, and stupid speculations] and their senseless minds were darkened. Claiming to be wise, they became fools [professing to be smart, they made simpletons of themselves]. And by them the glory and majesty and excellence of the immortal God were exchanged for and represented by images, resembling mortal man and birds and beasts and reptiles...Because they exchanged the truth of God for a lie and worshiped and served the creature rather than the Creator. (Romans 1:21–23, 25; AMP)

Our senseless minds were darkened; we exchanged God for images of man, birds, beasts, and reptiles, all lies. Satan is no stranger to these three things: meditation, visualization, and imaginations... this is how he created his ambitious "I Wills." This is how he continually see's himself...this is how God said he had sin enter into his heart. This is how God says he has "foolish reasonings and stupid speculations."

> Casting down imaginations, and every high and lofty thing that exalteth itself against the knowledge of God, and bringing into captivity every thought to the obedience of Christ. (2 Corinthians 10:5; KJV)

Astral Projection

This is weird, and to be honest when I first heard of it and began to research it, I was utterly shocked. Not only at the vast amount of information, but at the "ease of use" of this devil's parlor trick.

Countless how-to books, CDs, etc., all promising astral projection in minutes! This is dangerous, dangerous stuff. What is astral projection? It is in a nutshell an OBE, or an Out of Body Experience, coined by New Agers and occultists. I also had a difficult time believing it could be done…ignorance!

> In astral projection the conscious mind leaves the physical body and moves into the astral body to experience. In astral projection you remain attached to your physical body by a "**silver umbilical type cord**." Some people are able to see the cord when astral projecting. To astral project, as with all out-of-body experiences, one must feel totally relaxed.
>
> Astral projection (or astral travel) is an out-of-body experience achieved either awake or via lucid dreaming or deep meditation. People who say they experience astral projection often say that their spirit or astral body has left their physical body and moves in another dimension known as the spirit world or astral plane. The concept of astral projection has been around and practiced for thousands of years, dating back to ancient China. It is currently often associated with the New Age movement. [192]

Astral projection can only come about with the help of a demonic force. These individuals have learned to separate their spirit bodies from their physical bodies through meditation, mind blanking, and other occultic techniques. They do not physically die unless that "link or cord" created by a demonic force is cut.[193] *For as **the body without the spirit is dead**…* (James 2:26; NIV). New Agers who practice this abomination call this link the "silver cord." Believe it or not, Solomon wrote about it in Ecclesiastes when he talked about death: *[Remember your Creator earnestly now] before the silver cord [of life] is* *snapped apart, or the golden bowl is broken, or the pitcher is broken at the fountain, or the wheel broken at the cistern [and the whole circulatory system of the blood ceases to function]. Then shall the dust [out of which God made man's body] return to the earth as it was, and the spirit shall return to God who gave it* (Ecclesiastes 12:6–7; AMP).

Dr. Rebecca Brown states: "Solomon was learned in the Eastern religions and practices. In fact, he fell in his later years into idol worship with his foreign wives. I have no doubt he probably experienced astral projection. He states in the book Ecclesiastes that he had tried everything. I think the 'wheel broken at the cistern' refers to the wheel of reincarnation. Eastern religions believe this wheel of reincarnation can only be broken when the spirit gains unity with God, which they call Brahman in Hinduism."[194] With this being said, the golden bowl and the pitcher may also be references to other occultic beliefs of death.

Astral projection can and is being done by many people today. I relate a story of astral projection in Chapter 14: Near Death Experiences: NDEs. The Bible talks about the Holy Spirit with capitalization, our spirit and evil spirits with a lowercase "s." We are a triune being with many "rooms" in each of our temples. Only the Holy Spirit should be allowed to separate our spirit from our bodies, as in open visions of heaven. As Paul states he did not know whether he was out of body or in the body when he saw the three levels of heaven, and it did not matter to him. Astral projection is a *self-controlled* out-of-body experience without the control or consent of the Holy Spirit. It is a counterfeit spirit that is in control of the situation. *For the word of God is quick and powerful and sharper than any two edged sword, piercing even to the dividing asunder of soul and spirit* (Hebrews 4:12; NIV). Why would God have to divide the soul and spirit? Unless there was an unholy link made?

Do you know the pictures of witches on broomsticks flying

through the air? This was a visual symbol of astral projection. The implications and serious ramifications for astral projection are seemingly endless. Now the human spirit has none of the encumbrances of physicality. This means the human spirit can function in the "spirit realm." It can do whatever evil spirits do. This means it can appear in ghost form to someone, and it can physically inflict damage to someone's home or personal body without the victim ever even knowing what or who was there. It can also "inhabit" another person's body, or even an animal, if there is an open door way for them to get in!

In her book *He Came to Set the Captives Free,* Rebecca Brown, MD explains her experiences of helping a high level satanic priestess leave the cult and accept Jesus. In the process the self-professed witch explained many of the things the cult did and what powers were available to the witches just by asking a demon to come in and inhabit them. One of them was astral projection. The former witch relates a tale of astral projection directed towards a particular doctor she did not like:

> The intern was a different matter. He was not a Satanist, but not a Christian either. He already disliked me, but was bound by the rules of his training program to care for me.
>
> I made his life miserable even as he made mine miserable. I astral-projected into his apartment and wrote all over his walls very impolite messages with a black marking pen, then signed my name to it. I threw dishes at him when he was home and several times unplugged his refrigerator so that all the food in it spoiled.
>
> Every time he tried to bring anyone to see the messages on the walls one of my demons would tell me ahead of time and I would have the demon completely clean the wall

> before anyone else could see the writing. He quickly learned that he couldn't say anything to anyone else about what was going on because they thought he was going crazy.[195]

The book goes on to describe many incredible works of the devil. Witches inhabit animals and use their bodies to spy on or attack their unsuspecting targets. As we just saw, they act as ghosts and invisibly attack people or sabotage property. And they even inhabit other witches and declare an all out fight to the death. There is no honor among thieves, and there is a lot of in-fighting amongst the demons and witches for positions of power. Spooky stuff, and you thought astral projection was just a fun perk to deep meditation!

OUIJA BOARDS

The popular board game company Parker Brothers manufactures and sells a cardboard game with letters of the alphabet and a plastic planchette. Now board games sound very benign, and the company maintains its game is strictly for entertainment purposes only. But in actuality it is a spiritual tool much like the pentagram to open a door or link to the spiritual realm. It is another counterfeit of the Intelligent Deceiver. Precursors of the Ouija board date back as far as 1200 BC. The use of the board is for divination, which means contact with spirits or entities for the use of obtaining and discovering insight, wisdom, and to communicate with spirits of the dead. This is a direct copycat, perversion of the Holy Spirit's gifts of wisdom, knowledge, prophecy, and discerning of spirits. Why would you go to a cardboard and plastic game for false answers when you could go to the Almighty God for real answers? God calls us stupid when we go to wood idols for spiritual help, and cardboard is a paper product, which comes from trees! Do you think the Word is for us today?

Divination is strictly forbidden in the Bible!

> Let no one be found among you who sacrifices his son or daughter in the fire, who practices divination or sorcery, interprets omens, engages in witchcraft, or casts spells, or who is a medium or spiritist or who consults the dead. Anyone who does these things is detestable to the Lord, and because of these detestable practices the Lord your God will drive out the nations before you. You must be blameless before the Lord your God. The nations you dispossess listen to those who practice sorcery or divination. But as for you, the Lord your God has not permitted you to do so. (Deuteronomy 18:10–14; NIV)

This is a very strong warning! The word *detestable* means worthy of being hated, causing or deserving intense dislike.[196] This is God talking! He says he hates it! Why would you want the Lord of Hosts hating what you do?

Use of the Ouija board leads to possession. At first it seems like harmless communication, but with whom? If the devil is a liar and the father of liars, and you are trying to contact your dead husband Fred, or whoever, what makes you think you are talking to Fred? Could it be a demonic spirit pretending to be Fred? This type of spirit is mentioned in the Bible. It is called a "familiar spirit." Whether we like it or not, we have spirits watching us, inhabiting us, and copying us. In other words they are "familiar" with us and our behaviors! They know us better than we do, so when a familiar spirit masquerades as your late husband Fred, you can bet they will put on a pretty good show. They will know your pet name, the time you first kissed, they will tell you some tidbit of information you will be ripe to receive after they have finished mind raping you. The next step is possession. You have opened the mental door; they are now able to come waltzing in. You have put out the welcome mat, lit up the neon "open" sign and left the door wide open. This particular form of divination is called "necromancy," which means communing with the dead. God really hates this because he knows you are not talking to your dead husband, and you certainly are not talking to God! Why go to your dead husband for answers about the future when the Bible clearly says you can go to God instead? He probably didn't have the answers in this life, why would he have the answers in the next? Stop grieving the Holy Spirit!

Familiar spirits according to Strong's Concordance are described as a source of defilement, abominable, and vain. If you were a necromancer in the Old Testament you were to be cut off from your own people or put to death by stoning (see Leviticus 20:6 and 27). If we still lived under Old Testament law, how often do you think you would be pulling the Ouija board off the shelf and using it for fun and entertainment to contact some dead and gone relative? Yeah, didn't think so! Just because we don't stone people to death for playing with a Ouija board, doesn't mean God changed his mind about what he thinks is the appropriate punishment.

Crystals and Crystal Balls

"Gaze into the crystal ball and tell me what you see." Crystal balls, crystals, and other rocks and gemstones are becoming increasingly used for "balancing" spiritual energy. Many are considered portals into the spirit realm as well as "links" to a specific spiritual energy force. The use of crystals is not new; you can find evidence of their use dating back to early paganism. But who created the stones? Could there have been an original God-given use for these minerals before Satan got his hands on them and corrupted them for his purpose? There is some intriguing evidence in the Bible suggesting certain stones were in fact representative of the twelve tribes of Israel and if we go back even further to before the fall of Lucifer, God gave him a gift of the breast piece; the breastplate of the priests was encrusted with stones.

> This is what the sovereign Lord says: "You were the model of perfection, full of wisdom and perfect in beauty. You were in Eden, the garden of God, every precious stone adorned you: Ruby, topaz, emerald, chrysolite, onyx and jasper, sapphire, turquoise and beryl. Your settings and mountings were made of gold; on the day you were created they were prepared." (Ezekiel 28:12–19; NIV)

I have often asked myself why God would specifically name certain stones, and why only nine of the twelve stones represented the tribes of Israel were mentioned in this text. Upon investigation, the Holy Spirit told me to count how many planets there are in our solar system: nine! Even though various astrological trains of thought disagree on which gemstone is associated with what planet, it is intriguing to again see a correlation of the planets and stars associated with Satan and his New Age movement! Author's note: Current scientists are now saying Pluto is not a planet. They say it isn't large enough to be classified as a planet, but it is not a moon, so what do you call it?

Exodus 28:15–30 describes and gives specific instructions for the making of the breast piece. This breastplate was encrusted with twelve mineral stones and was used for making decisions. *Whenever Aaron enters the Holy Place, he will bear the names of the sons of Israel over his heart on the breast piece of decision as a continuing memorial before the Lord. Also put the Urim and Thummim in the breast piece, so they may be over Aaron's heart whenever he enters the presence of the*

Lord. Thus Aaron will always bear the means of making decisions for the Israelites over his heart before the Lord (Exodus 28:29–30; NIV).

The twelve stones representing the twelve tribes of Israel are as follows: Sardonyx, Chrysolite or Topaz, Rock-Crystal, Emerald or Garnet, Lapis Lazuli or Sapphire, Diamond, Amber or Jacinth, Agate, Amethyst, Beryl, Malachite, Ring-Stone.[197] The various stones and tribes to which they are ascribed is still debated to this day.

In the early history of the Israelites you had to have a priest. This priest went to God for remission of sins and answers to questions. We don't have to have a human priest any longer; we have Jesus as our perfect priest. Through him we can find forgiveness of sin and communicate with God. I truly believe the use of crystals and crystal balls is Satan's way of trying to impersonate the role of Jesus. He wants us to commune with him instead. When we study the function and role of the breastplate and the Urim and Thummim, we see it was used for getting answers from God and making decisions. I ask you, what is the purpose of a crystal ball? Or a crystal or other minerals used in the occult? For getting answers to questions and making life decisions! Yeah, the Intelligent Deceiver wants a piece of that action; it will help him fulfill his "I wills."

> The earliest reference to Urim and Thummim in the Hebrew Bible is when Aaron carries them with him as high priest (see Exodus 28:30). Many scholars believe Urim and Thummim were the 12 stones that resided in the breastplate (with other precious stones) of the Jewish high priest ceremonial clothing when he officiated in the tabernacle or temple.[198]

In the Old Testament times the Hebrews did not have the blood bought luxury of direct conversation with Christ as we do today. So

God gave them his ordained way of communication until the time of the Messiah came to pass.

> Urim and Thummim (Hebrew: םי.מ·ו·תֻו םי.ר·וא, Arabic: ميمتو ميروا), typically translated as "lights and perfections" or "revelation and truth," were a *scrying* medium or divination process used by ancient Hebrews (usually Israelites) in revealing the will of God on a contested point of view or other problem...
>
> According to the teachings of Judaism, a small parchment with God's holy name, the *Tetragrammaton*, inscribed on it was slipped into an opening under the Urim and Thummim on the high priest's breastplate, which caused the breastplate to "glow" and thereby "transmit messages" from God to the Children of Israel.
>
> Some scholars have suggested "the" Urim and Thummim consisted of two crystals, but the precise nature of the medium is unknown. According to the Hebrew Bible, stones used for "an" Urim and Thummim were kept in the breastplate of Aaron, the brother of Moses.
>
> There is some evidence that Urim and Thummim were/was used as a lot that provided "yes" or "no" answers, depending upon whether the Urim or the Thummim came into play, as manipulated by a Hebrew oracle. There is also evidence that the medium was used as an ordeal to establish a person's guilt or innocence.[199]

So we see from studying the Hebrew scholars that the Urim and Thummim was a method of not only of talking with God, but seeking answers from God. Again, something good God ordained, corrupted by the Intelligent Deceiver.

So why the crystal, which is not one of the stones ascribed to Lucifer in Ezekiel 28? According to Wikipedia: "The earliest crystal balls were made from beryl, later being replaced by rock crystal. The druids used beryl for scrying, while the Scottish called them 'stones of power.'" Scrying is a form of divination; you are asking a rock for answers. Wasn't there something in the Bible about talking to useless idols made of stone and wood, who could not talk? Fascinatingly, Jesus is called the Rock; we find Satan carves a rock to worship.

Interestingly, the Hebrew name etymologically indicates rock-crystal was a "flashing, brilliant" stone.[200] This early Hebrew description certainly fits with Satan's overall view of himself!

According to practicing mediums:

> All crystal and gemstones are living organisms. Crystals have a life energy of their own. They are living in some manner of the word as they slowly grow in clusters. They are part of the Mineral Kingdom most are grown in nature. Crystals vibrate to their own frequency. The frequency they send out will determine which crystal you will chose at a certain point in your life. You do chose different crystals as your needs change. Many crystals are as old as our planet. Some people think of them as Record Keepers of the planet. Some crystals supposedly come here from off planet such as moldavite or other celestial crystals.[201]

Fry, commenting on the Ancients' use of crystals in general, stated:

> Legends occasionally mention crystals that could render invisibility (such as the one Apollonius of Tyana used before the Roman Emperor) and even cause weightlessness. They

> even used crystals to discover how to enter and escape time by negotiating a ninety degree angle phase shift. Was it all in the size and shape? Or did it involve mental forces and special "live" qualities within the crystal? [202]

Fry continues to comment on the crystalline structure of our world:

> It is a literal fact that most of our planet is made up of crystals of specific shapes. The present energy problems will be a thing of the past when we start using the wondrous potential of these shapes. Even the food we eat must be converted to tiny crystalline shapes before it can pass through the tissue walls. The ancient Central American word for blood was chalchuihatl, and it literally meant, "water of precious stones."[203]

Just as the Jews had their specific instructions for using the breastplate and the Urim and Thummim, so does Satan require specific rituals as well for using his corrupted tools to the spirit realm.

Crystals are indeed fascinating rocks, and many jewels and gemstones were used by the high priests for making crucial decisions for the tribes of Israel. But what is it about crystals that seem to be so mesmerizing and powerful? When you study crystals from a scientific standpoint they are an astounding creation indeed. In fact we use crystal technology all the time. Without it I would not be able to type on a computer, tell time, etc. Crystals are a type of transducer; they are a device for transforming one type of energy to another. The study of using crystal technology is called piezoelectricity. The problem with the occultic form of crystal use is they believe they are power sources. This is untrue; crystals in and of themselves do not contain power, but they may be correct in the fact they can transform energy, whether spiritual or physical or information.

Crystal Skulls

The very first questions that comes up are, "Where did these skulls come from?" and "Why do they exist?" There are countless hypotheses that they are the legacy of some higher intelligence. Many believe they were created by extraterrestrials or beings in Atlantis. Yet another theory maintains that these skulls together contain a history of mankind.

The most obvious theory links these to Mayans, although the Aztecs are a more formidable candidate for this, since a lot of their artwork as well as religious symbols featured skulls. In addition, they were the finest known crystal sculptors. Perhaps the skulls found in Mayan ruins were Out Of Place ARTifacts (OOPARTS).

What's more, some believe that, "The ancient Crystal Skulls are the computers of the ancients, they contain important information that help humanity to pass through its current series of challenges to take us into a Golden Age...They were a powerful tool for healing the body, mind, and spirit, by ancient civilizations such as the Mayans or the Atlanteans."[204]

There has been much speculation that these skulls are somehow linked to the "Year Zero" or December 21, 2012, the date at which the Mayan calendar ends.

When working on the Mitchel-Hedges skulls, according to some psychics who performed experiments on some of the skulls:

> Psychometry and scrying provided glimpses of the past and wonderful scenarios of ancient ceremonies. A connection with the fabled Atlantis was also brought out during one of the sessions...During my personal research with the

> skulls…while working with the skulls, performing scrying, I was using various colors and sounds. I placed the skull on a small light box and alternated several colors over the light source opening. After recording my sessions over a period of several weeks, I began a review of the results. I was shocked to learn that when I used a certain color over the light source it seemed to activate a time period. Researching my results further, I determined that each time I used the same color blue, for example, that I would revert to the same time frame. I could almost pick up where I left off at the end of the previous session that I used the particular color. The energy that these skulls produce is staggering. Are they indeed holding the knowledge of mankind?…Without ancient documentation, psychometry may be the only tool that can be utilized to obtain the information. Our research continues daily.[205]

These crystal skulls have been equated to "science out of place" again. Possibly ancient computers, but again I ask you, using what we have learned about Intelligent Deception, could it be something made by the giants or fallen angels? Another clue to our clouded genetic past?

Enoch 8:1 talks about the fallen angels teaching their wives and giant offspring about all manner of sorcery, divinations, implements of war, and even *the use of stones of every valuable and select kind.*[206]

This is all pretty fascinating stuff, but now that we have the high priest Jesus Christ, we no longer need a breastplate of rocks. Since he is brilliance incarnate, we no longer need an Urim and Thummim, whatever they may be, for making decisions. We can always go straight to the Father for answers and help in making decisions through Jesus Christ; we have also been given the Holy Spirit to help us.

If you have been a victim and duped by Intelligent Deception, and are currently using crystals or other gemstones of any type for any reason, renounce, repent, and destroy. Why talk to a rock, when you can go to the creator of the rock for all of the answers to your problems? Satan wants you to talk to him, not to God; this is blatant false idol worship. There is nothing wrong with owning gemstones and wearing them as jewelry; however, if these gemstones have been dedicated to the service of Satan, then you have been yoked to the evil spirit realm operating in your presence. I would strongly recommend destroying these trinkets of trickery!

Salt and Oil

Both salt and oil are spoken of in the Bible. Both have spiritual significance; both have been used and corrupted by the Intelligent Deceiver.

> In the Bible, salt symbolizes a vital part of God's covenant with His people: "And every oblation of thy meat offering shalt thou season with salt; neither shalt thou suffer the salt of the covenant of thy God to be lacking from thy meat offering: with all thine offerings thou shalt offer salt." (Leviticus 2:13); Elisha purified a spring by casting salt into it (2 Kings 2:19–22); In The Sermon On The Mount, Jesus referred to his disciples as "the salt of the earth" (Matt. 5:13); There are also many historical references to the destructive nature of salt.
>
> After the destruction of Carthage, the Romans scattered salt all over the surrounding countryside to make it barren forever. Abimelech did the same to the conquered city of Shechem (Judges 9:45). Lot's wife was turned into a pillar of salt when she looked back to watch the destruc-

tion of Sodom and Gomorrah (Gen. 19:26), and the word Sodom itself, is a derivative from the ancient Hebrew word for salt.[207]

The use of salt in the Bible was always symbolic, NOT ritualistic. Salt was an eternal covenant, meaning two parties would enter into an agreement and each would take salt from his pouch and mix it together, then break bread and dip the bread in the salt. You could never separate the two different salt grains from each other once mixed, so it was a symbol of eternal covenantship. Salt is used in many *occult rituals*. Salt comes in a crystalline form, therefore it represents crystal energy. Salt is also referred to as bitter. Salt is used in its corrupted form of self-knowledge, a symbol for knowledge and wisdom—Intelligent Deception!

Oil is symbolic of the blood of Jesus. Both Saul and David were anointed with oil; the vessels of the tabernacle were anointed and consecrated with oil. God tells Moses how to make the holy anointing oil in *Exodus:*

> Take the following fine spices: 500 schekels of liquid myrrh, half as much (that is 250 shekels) of fragrant cinnamon, 250 shekels of fragrant cane, 500 shekels of casia—all according to the sanctuary shekel—and a hin of olive oil. Make these into a scared anoint oil, a fragrant blend, the work of a perfumer. It will be the sacred anointing oil. Then use it to anoint the Tent of Meeting, the ark of the Testimony, the table and all its articles, the lamp stand and its accessories, the altar of incense the alter of burnt offering and all its utensils, and the basin with its stand. You shall consecrate them so they will be most holy, and whatever touches them will be holy. (Exodus 30:22–29; NIV)

This particular oil was sacred; it was only to be used by Aaron and his sons and the generations of priests to follow. Anyone caught using the oil for any other purpose was to be cut off from the people.

Olive oil is used throughout the Bible to anoint the sick. Since oil is symbolic of the blood of Jesus, it is used as a symbolic covering of Jesus' blood in the spirit realm. Just as the blood of the Passover lamb was put on the doorpost and lintels to keep the Lord's death angel from killing the first born in Egypt, the oil can be used in the same way. It is wise to anoint ones home or possessions against the enemy's envoys with a little oil.

The Intelligent Deceiver corrupts the anointing oil by attaching spells and incantations to the oil, promising things such as increased psychic power, higher spiritual vibrations, lottery luck, and others. Anytime salt and oil are mixed and a scripture passage is invoked it is being used in so called "white magic." White magic is a lie; it is impossible to do good with evil.

Spells, Curses, and Incantations

If God has prayer, then spells, curses, and incantations are Satan's counterfeit to it. We have prayer journals; witches have their book of shadows, which is much like a cookbook of recipes for curses, spells, and incantations.

There is a saying: "What is the difference between a precious child of God and a witch? The witches study harder!" Sad but true. Witches "practice" their craft, and they learn new spells, study ancient rituals, and meditate on false doctrine. If they really knew of the power available to them through Jesus and were not blinded by the deceiver, they would abandon their craft immediately, and I am convinced would be incredible fruitful saints for Jesus!

Prayer is conversing with God; the intercourse of the soul with God, not in contemplation or meditation, but in direct address to him. Prayer may be oral or mental, occasional or constant, ejaculatory or formal. It is a "*beseeching the Lord*" (Exodus 32:11; KJV); "*pouring out the soul before the Lord*" (1 Samuel 1:15; KJV); "*praying and crying to heaven*" (2 Chronicles 32:20; KJV); "*seeking unto God and making supplication*" (Job 8:5; KJV); "*drawing near to God*" (Psalms 73:28; KJV); "*bowing the knees*" (Ephesians 3:14; KJV). [208]

To pray in Strong's Concordance is "*Palal*, verb form; to pray, intervene, mediate, judge, meditate. If it is between two humans it is always a judgment. *Palal*; is interceding for or, on behalf of. *Tepillah*, noun; make a request, *Deesis*; is a wanting need, asking entreaty, supplication."[209]

It is difficult to open scripture without finding a reference to prayer. Prayer is a conversation. Conversations take place with language and words. The spoken word is probably one of the most misunderstood but powerful forms of energy available to humans today. The Bible is constantly reminding us of the evil of our tongues. Why would God do that? Remember the old childhood saying, "Sticks and stones may break my bones, but names will never hurt me?" I hated that statement, because names did hurt! They stay with you for life; they form our very concepts. In fact, words are the utmost in creative power! *And God Said, let there be…* (Genesis 1:3; NIV). There is something genius, inspired, productive, and inventive about spoken words. The Bible tells us we will either live by the words of our mouths or die by them. What a powerful statement!

James, Jesus' brother gives a whole discourse on the tongue: *Likewise the tongue is a small part of the body, but it makes great boasts. Consider what a great forest is set on fire by a small spark. The tongue is also a fire, a world of evil among the parts of the body. It corrupts the whole person, sets the whole course of his life on fire, and is itself set on fire by hell* (James 3:5–6; NIV).

Wow! It can set the whole course of your life! Isn't that interesting? Do you think if it can do this, that maybe, just maybe it could harm others as well? He goes on to say our speech can be lit by the very fires of hell! That doesn't sound real positive to me. God tells us on the Day of Judgment we will be held accountable for every idle word. Ouch!

So what are prayers? Prayers are praises, blessings, inquiries, requests, interventions, supplications, etc. to God. You are *invoking* the God of the Universe to act on your behalf. It is conversation with God, through Jesus. Jesus is our mediator, and no man can come to the Father but through him. If you have a good dad, and you have a problem or want to ask him a question, and you have a good relationship with him, your dad will do the best he can to give you your request or answer your question. Why do we think God, our heavenly father would do any less?

God equates prayer and praises in the Psalms as sweet incense in his nostrils. He also promises us he hears our every prayer. Jesus taught us how to pray with the Lord's Prayer; it is a specific guideline or outline on *how* we should pray, not an exact repetitive prayer. A portion of the Lord's Prayer says, *Your kingdom come, your will be done on earth as it is in Heaven* (Matthew 6:10; NIV). What is in heaven? No sickness, no poverty, salvation, etc. God wants this for us now on earth! He gives us specific instructions not to babble on and on as the pagans do: *When you pray, do not keep on babbling like pagans, for they think they will be heard because of their many words… Do not be like them, for your father knows what you need before you ask him* (Matthew 6:7–8; NIV). God warns us not to use vain repetitions. I can't help but think that vain repetitions also started at the Tower of Babel.

So if Jesus spent so much time talking about the power of our tongues (words) and gave us specific instructions on how to pray, made a public example of himself praying to God, talked endlessly about communion and relationship, and gave Paul words to the effect that we should "pray without ceasing," and talked of the power available to us through prayer—do you think maybe an Intelligent Deceiver who wanted to exalt himself above God and counterfeit his every move would maybe want to corrupt this member of our bodies and set our very lives and the lives of others on fire to achieve his evil scheming purpose? I would bet so! Prayer simply put, is asking for God's will in our lives and the lives of others. Casting spells is invoking an evil spirit to act on your behalf to exert one's own will in the lives of others. So in order for us to be aware of the schemes and wiles of this devil, let's do a little word study on corrupted prayer!

The following are from the Encarta Dictionary:[210]

Spell: Words with magical power, paranormal, a word or series of words believed to have magical power, spoken to invoke the magic, also to influence somebody or something.

Incantations: The ritual chanting or use of supposedly magic words.

Curses: Evil prayer, a malevolent appeal to a supernatural being for harm to come to somebody or something, or the harm that is thought to result from this.

Hex: a curse or bringer of bad luck or misfortune.

Let's compare this to the word *blessing* and *bless.*

Blessing: God's help, religious act to invoke divine help, prayer before meal of thanks, expression of approval, something fortunate.

Bless: make holy, protect, wish well, confer personal benefit on, thank.

God always gives three predictable answers to prayers:
Yes.
Not yet.
I have something better in mind!

When you study Wicca, they say what goes around, comes around, but even they admit so-called "white magic" ("good") can turn to gray magic. In other words, if you sent out a spell for money to come your way and your aunt dies the next day leaving you an inheritance, this so-called white spell turned gray because black magic caused the death of your loved one without you being aware of its power. Somehow, the white and black mixed to become gray. What this tells me is it was black to begin with! I don't know about you, but God doesn't work that way. He doesn't mix oil and water. In his kingdom there is no such thing as good magic and bad magic; it is just awesome, holy, pure power. God even promises us if something does go wrong, it is not because of him, it is because of Satan and his evil works, and God can work it for our good! I sure like the way God operates better!

In the end, all of the witchcraft, clairvoyants, sorcerers, psychics, etc. are just hungering for power. They have been promised "secret knowledge." It grieves me when I realize these poor souls have been duped by a malicious, vindictive, narcissistic copycat! The holy scriptures are replete with a "mysterious knowledge hidden from the powers and principalities of this world" and "power" is available to anyone who is filled with the Holy Spirit. Why go for the super-expensive knock-off, when you can have the free original?

> Although I am less than the least of all God's people, this grace was given me: to preach to the Gentiles the unsearchable riches of Christ, and make plain to everyone the administration of this mystery, which for ages past was kept hidden in God, who created all things. His intent was that now, through the church, the manifold wisdom of God should be made known to the rulers and authorities in the heavenly realms. (Ephesians 3:8–10; NIV)

> I pray that out of his glorious riches he may strengthen you with power through his spirit in your inner being, so that Christ may dwell in your hearts through faith. And I pray that you, being rooted and established in love may have power, together with all the saints to grasp how wide and long and high and deep is the love of Christ, and to know this love that surpasses knowledge—that you may be filled to the measure of all the fullness of God. (Ephesians 3:16–19; NIV).

God's "secret knowledge" was Jesus, who died for our sins. He paid a heavy fine to redeem us from Satan, who was holding us ransom, and still makes us believe he can still hold us even though the ransom has been paid. This secret knowledge is Jesus Christ crucified and raised from the dead. The "power" is in his Holy Spirit through this incredible love—this love surpasses all of our foolish earthly wisdom and intellect which Satan and his fallen angels are constantly trying to poison us with. If you have ever experienced

God's awesome power, how can you settle for a puny demonic parlor trick, which compromises your soul and eternity? Power and secret knowledge can be yours through Christ!

COVENANTS

Covenants are one of Christianity's foundations of faith. They are in effect promises made by God with his people. This is also an area that Satan corrupts, perverts, copies, and mocks.

The very idea Christians can covenant with their Almighty God is so repugnant to Satan he had to institute his own *versions* of covenants, in other words, making a deal with the devil, selling your soul to the devil, making a blood pact, etc., in exchange for your allegiance. It is a binding contract. The Intelligent Deceiver knew the ramifications of a covenant, and wanted it as part of fulfilling his "I wills."

What is a covenant? The Hebrew word *berit,* which translates covenant, is mentioned over three hundred times in the Old Testament. It is of a "binding agreement, or relationship usually drawn up with a solemn vow."[211] This "phenomenon" is unique; it involves a very solemn bonding between God and his people; its very heart and soul is of intimacy. This covenant was not without conditions from the person or people involved. Themes of gratitude, obedience, and exclusive loyalty were often the responsibility of the involved parties. Each of these covenants was accompanied by a solemn oath, usually incorporating a symbolic ritual, which was legally binding.

The very first covenant we see God make is to Noah in Genesis 8–9. It is still in effect today, and we can see the "evidence" of this intimate contract visible in our skies today, the rainbow. In this binding contract we see God bless Noah, his sons, and all humankind.

He places all plants and animals under human command, forbids eating meat with the blood still in it, and forbids murder. He commands humankind to practice capital punishment for murderers, and promises he will never again destroy all life on earth by flood. Then as a final sign for all of the ages that he will never flood the earth again, he makes the rainbow.

As we can see from this list Satan has perverted and made a mockery of every single one of these promises. We saw how he came in and cursed Noah's grandson Caanan, with a curse that is still in effect to this very day. We see he has made us to worship the earth instead of commanding it. Many cultures eat meat with blood in it, and also drink the blood of animals. Not to mention, in satanic rituals this one covenant condition is continually violated! Satan was a murderer from the start, so he is the father of murderers; he not only murders but condones and demands human sacrifice as offerings to his deity. Satan is the punishment for murderers, as they will share in his agony in hell. Satan is continually flooding and destroying God's peoples whenever and however he is allowed to. Satan's covenant signs are also binding, and visible to the trained eye.

The Abrahamic Covenant is found in Genesis 12–17. In this covenant, God promises: to make of Abraham a great nation and to bless those who bless him and curse those who curse him, to give Abraham's descendants all the land from the river (or *wadi*) of Egypt to the Euphrates, to make Abraham a father of a great many nations, and to give Abraham and his male descendants circumcision as the permanent sign of this everlasting covenant.

Satan had to get his claws into this one as well; any nation who curses Israel is cursed. Satan loves to make a mockery of this covenant promise by cursing Israel; it is called anti-Semitism. The Holocaust was but a grim reminder of what Satan thinks of God's chosen people. The second promise is still being fought over today, fighting continues all throughout the Promised Land, and there is constant haggling over borders and boundaries. We see the other promise of making Abraham a father of great many nations being corrupted in the prophecies of the Whore of Babylon (corruption of order at the tower of Babel). And lastly circumcision; the cutting of flesh is often a sign required of Satan by his followers of a blood pact with the evil one.

There are many more examples of covenants in the Bible: Lot, Jacob, Mosaic, Ark of the Covenant, Israel, Davidic, national, personal, and of course the New Covenant.

The New Covenant has to do with the spilling of innocent blood for remission of sin and a total fulfillment of the law. The crucifixion was the solemn oath of God who promised us a savior, fulfilled in all of the ritual symbolism of each station of the cross. The New Covenant is dependent upon our belief and obedience and loyalty to Jesus as the Messiah.

This one covenant is constantly made a mockery of by the horrific practice of human sacrifice as well as animal sacrifice. From ancient Babylonian times to the present, humans still practice human sacrifice. Words cannot express the barbaric demonic influence of the torture and deaths Satan "requires" of his covenant followers. Many children are dedicated to Satan at birth either knowingly by their parents or unknowingly tricked for a number of reasons. Many children are also purposefully bred for the one purpose of being sacrificed at a black mass for Satan. Many times practicing witches, warlocks, and Satanists are tortured, murdered, and offered if they do not obey this condition of their oath.

Don't believe this is still going on? Don't be so naïve. Satanists (witches) are not stupid; they know how to get their victims and get rid of the evidence. Here is an excerpt from a book called *He Came to Set the Captives Free*, a true account of a former high priestess and bride of Satan:

> The silence was one of fear. Each one was afraid that he or she might be chosen to be the sacrifice. At that moment Satan was no longer a glory to anyone, no longer an honor. A ripple of relief went through the crowd when the victim was dragged kicking and screaming through a side door and up onto the stage. The main Easter sacrifice is always a man. Occasionally additional sacrifices of women, children or animals are made, but the ceremony centers around the sacrifice of a man. Often a hitch hiker is picked up some days before the ceremony and carefully guarded until the time of the meeting. In the eyes of Satan and the crowd, that man becomes Jesus and Satan's supposed victory over Jesus at the cross is celebrated…Eventually the body was severed from the head and ground up, and portions mixed with drugs and other substances. Those who wanted more power ate some of the mixture.[212]

The shedding of innocent blood has very potent symbolism in the scriptures: *For the life of a creature is in the blood, and I have given it you to make atonement for yourselves on the altar; it is the blood that makes atonement for one's life…None of you may eat blood* (Leviticus 17:11; NIV).

What makes up the blood that it is given such significance by our God? The components and functions of blood are many, and truly without it we are dead. When I was an ER nurse we used to have a saying; "If you had a hole in the pipes (active bleeding), it wouldn't be long before your patient would crash and die." In other words, you could manually pump the heart, zap it, breathe for the patient, whatever, but if you didn't plug the hole, it would be to no avail.

In the beginning God told us he gave Adam the "breath of life." This "breath" is very literally transported in the blood. Blood's primary job is for gas transportation and exchange. A healthy human has an oxygen saturation of 98 percent or better. Other components of blood are red blood cells, white blood cells, plasma, platelets, and hemoglobin. In addition to carrying oxygen it carries sugar, amino acids, fatty acids, hormones, and aids in the removal of wastes. It also regulates PH, body temperature, and hydraulic functions. Most adults have about five liters or seven percent of their body weight in blood.

Blood for pagans is symbolic of energy, power, and life force; it is also a way of earning the gods' favor:

> Sacrifice is a form of communication with a deity for similar purposes. The word itself means "to make holy." As distinct from prayer, sacrificial offerings include objects of value and symbolic significance that are given to the gods to earn their favor…Historians, however, have often regarded blood sacrifice as the most powerful way to appease the gods…
>
> Participants in blood sacrifice rituals experience a sense of awe, danger, or exaltation because they are daring to approach the gods who create, sustain, and destroy life. The buildup of tension prior to the blood sacrifice gives way to a festive sense of triumph and relief. Morale is strengthened by the ritual killing because the group has itself performed the godlike act of destruction and is now capable of renewing its own existence. The underlying philosophical assumption is that life must pass through death.

According to ancient rites of sacrifice, the sacrificial animal or human should be of high value. The gods would be offended by a sickly or inferior offering.[213]

In the next quote we see how the Aztecs viewed blood sacrifice:

The Aztecs believed that the "vital energies" of one person could be transferred to another person through drinking the blood and eating the flesh. The gods also craved flesh and blood, so human sacrifice benefited both Aztecs and their ever-hungry deities.[214]

These "vital energies," "powers," and "life forces" may hold the key to the spiritual realm for many neopagan practitioners. The aborigines' ritualistic dances employ painting one another with blood.

In other cultures:

...the blood was considered to have the power of its originator and after the butchering the blood was sprinkled on the walls, on the statues of the gods and on the participants themselves. This act of sprinkling blood was called *bleodsian* in Old English and the terminology was borrowed by the Roman Catholic Church becoming *to bless* and *blessing*. The Hittite word for blood, *ishar* was a cognate to words for "oath" and "bond," see Ishara. The Ancient Greeks believed that the blood of the gods, *ichor*, was a mineral that was poisonous to mortals.[215]

Another equally scary scenario for the nature witches or individuals that practice witchcraft without the protection of a coven is the following dialogue:

> Then a friend suggested what seemed the perfect solution—blood donation! I'd been giving blood for several years and the thought just never had occurred to me before. So the next time I went in to donate, I approached it as ritual sacrifice for a particular purpose, and both the process and results seemed to be much improved. *Since then I've gone to donate blood many times, each time with a prayer for healing for the recipient of my blood, and a request for aid from the deity that seemed most appropriate.*[216]

I would hate to be the recipient of this person's blood since she had placed a "special blessing" on her donation! We must remember to cover ourselves symbolically with the precious blood of Jesus, as protection in our debased world.

The blood covenant of Christ is the power and triumph over Satan and his minions. The blood symbolizes life; it also covers a multitude of sins and perfects and makes us whole and pure in the eyes of our holy God. The Intelligent Deceiver wants to covenant; do not partake of an unholy agreement.

Jesus only requires belief. Worship comes as a natural by-product of belief, and conversely Satan demands worship and adoration with the impetus of severe penalty. Learn from the example of the wisest man to ever live; King Solomon. King Solomon had everything. Born a son out of the sin of King David and Bathsheba, he found favor with God when God asked him what he wanted and he asked for wisdom. God added to him fame, skill, riches, peace, etc. But Solomon really loved the ladies, and even though God warned Solomon to stay away from marrying foreign wives because he knew they would lead him into false idol worship, he did it anyway. He built a high place for Chemosh; he worshipped Ashtoreth, Molech, and others. As a consequence of his disobedience, his kingdom was ripped to shreds and later divided (see 1 Kings 11–12).

Solomon became entangled in the occult, and he ended up losing everything. The one thing Solomon did conclude after all his wisdom and stupidity was one thing: *Now all has been heard; here is the conclusion of the matter: Fear God and keep his commandments, for this is the whole duty of man. For God will bring every deed into judgment, including every hidden thing, whether it is good or evil* (Ecclesiastes 12:13–14; NIV).

Chapter Twelve

GHOSTS

Who doesn't have fond memories of sitting around a campfire or watching someone with a flashlight telling a haunting tale in a tent out in the woods? Ghost stories have been around for eons, intriguing us with mystery, frightening us into thinking we will be the next victim of scare tactics from beyond the grave, romancing us with the thought of a love unfinished, waiting an eternity in limbo for consummation. Most people view ghosts as disembodied spirits of human beings caught in-between our world and the next; unable to pass on into eternity without first finishing the business of this world, they are caught in "limbo." Or are they?

Why the mystery? Why the intrigue? What does the Bible have to say about ghosts and haunting spirits? Could people be stuck between two worlds, caught in a vortex of revenge, grief, unforgiveness, confusion and strife, tied to their homes, certain objects, or places of death? Caught in an invisible dimensional prison? Or, what if *they wanted you to believe* they were the spirits of the dead?

Just flip on the boob tube at any time throughout the day and you will see countless television programs on ghosts: Ghost Hunters, T.A.P.S., Psychic Detectives, A Haunting, Most Haunted Places, Paranormal State, etc. We as a culture have become fascinated with the un-dead. It is no longer an American cultural taboo to talk about the ghost or poltergeist in your house, or the encounter you had as a small child with an imaginary friend who told you to do things to your cat or dog when your parents weren't watching. In fact it is quite cool and tricked-out to be able to have such a true encounter, and quite possibly you have *the sight.*

So what do the ghost hunters and self-proclaimed psychic detectives claim ghosts are? According to the experts, as humans we reside in a physical body, and then upon death there is an energy transformation. In spirit form, they express themselves as energy, such as magnetic fields; they are able to control spatial temperature, such as making a certain room several degrees colder. They have the ability to move about through hard physical structures such as walls, doors, etc., because they are no longer bound to the physical laws of this tri/quad-dimensional world. They are able to navigate through quantum physics via the atomic pathways. Scientifically they "capture" their images on film as cloudy vapors, images of light, dark shadowy forms and balls of light that no longer subscribe to the laws of gravity. As a spiritual entity, they seem to communicate through the *emotions* of others, sometimes, through physical speech and telepathy. They also evidently have the ability to move matter since they are in a different atomic energy particle pathway; in other words they can move objects at will.

According to the experts there are different types of haunting, such as a residual haunting, which is more of a smell or memory of a spirit. Also there are actual spirits that choose physical interaction with humans. These are called poltergeists, which means noisy spirit, the prankster type. And then of course the mean ones, you know, the ones who scratch and bite, make a smelly vapor in the hallway or basement and haunt our sleep. All of these ghosts seem to have some pretty interesting physical, spiritual, and emotional characteristics.

According to the **Kentucky Paranormal Research Center** there are different types of hauntings:[217]

INTELLIGENT OR TRADITIONAL HAUNTINGS

This type of haunting is what most people think of when they hear the word ghost. These types of hauntings are very rare. An intelligent or traditional ghost is kind of like Casper in the sense that it interacts with people. The most common belief is that the ghost is connected to the site or people in some way.

Some reasons the ghost may be tied to the site or people:

1. Died as a result of a traumatic event, murder, car accident, etc.
2. Due to unfinished business.
3. The spirit may have died suddenly and not realized he/she died.
4. The living loved ones are so emotionally distraught they can't let go.
5. The spirit is emotionally connected to their loved ones.
6. They cannot rest due to an injustice done to them.
7. Fear of the other side or judgment.

These ghosts are generally associated with physical activity like slamming, opening, closing, unlocking doors and windows, voices, and sounds. A strong presence, a scent, or touch may be experienced. People rarely see a manifestation of the ghost in the form of an apparition or mist.

Residual Haunting

A residual haunt is believed to be activity of reoccurring or traumatic actions from past events that leave an imprint on the environment.

This type is probably the most common type of haunting. Because its characteristics are similar to the intelligent haunting, people often mistake it for an intelligent/traditional haunting. Like intelligent haunts, some examples of activity are phantom footsteps, sounds, images, and scents. One major difference between this haunting and the intelligent/traditional haunting, is that this type of haunting is not considered to be that of a ghost, and there is no interaction with the living.

It is believed that this activity is the dissipation of stored energy from the site. The theory is the energy is stored or absorbed by the site due to repetitive or traumatic events of the energy expended while performing such actions. Similar to a tape player, the energy is stored in the magnetic field of the environment. Over time the energy builds up and is discharged showing a replay of the event, and then the cycle starts again. Some suggest that atmospheric conditions such as storms may initiate the playback. There is also a quantum physics theory which relates the energy as light particles that are dormant until they are stimulated by an outside variable under the proper conditions. Researchers have observed that the energy tends to diminish over periods of time until eventually it is either exhausted, or the level is so low that it is not experienced again.

Portal Hauntings

Portals aren't really a new concept, as we've seen them in a lot of sci-fi flicks. But in the real world, portal hauntings are considered controversial as there is little known and the idea is mostly theory or speculation. Portals are thought to be doorways to another world or dimension in which entities travel through. It's speculated that portals are not limited to one location, region or limited to sacred ground. Typically places that experience a wide array of different types of anomalous activity such as glowing balls of light, odd creatures, strange shapes, or unexplained mists or fog, are suspected to have a portal in which these energies are traveling back and forth.

Contrary to what you may think, the Bible actually has many references to ghosts, contacting ghosts, and ghost-like appearances. Let's just name a few: Saul contacts Samuel from the dead via the witch of Endor (see 1 Samuel 28:6–19), Moses and Elijah interact with Jesus on the mount of transfiguration (see Matthew 17:1–8), and the disciples thought Jesus to be a ghost when he walked on water (see Mark 6:49). After the resurrection, Jesus appeared to Mary Magdalene (see John 20:10–18), and he appeared to his disciples and walked and talked with the two on the road to Emmaus (see Luke 24:13–40). And the most descriptive request of all, the story of the rich man and Lazarus (see Luke 16:19–31).

Now the really strange thing is in Luke 24:36–39, Jesus actually describes certain characteristics of a ghost: *While they were still talking about this, Jesus himself stood among them and said to them, "Peace be with you." They were startled and frightened, thinking they saw a ghost. He said to them, "Why are you troubled, and why do doubts rise in your minds? Look at my hands and my feet. It is I myself! Touch me and see; a ghost does not have flesh and bones, as you see I have"* (Luke 24:36–39; NIV).

Why would Jesus say that? Most translations do not use the word *ghost,* but *spirit* instead. According to Vine's Dictionary, *spirit* has eight different meanings: air or breath, the invisible intangible fleeting quality of "air," wind, wind's direction, element of life, a man's disposition or temper, God's Spirit, the Holy Ghost or Spirit, the third person of the Trinity, non-material beings, such as angels. In the Greek, the word *pneuma,* spirit and ghost are renderings of the same word. The Old Testament word *gawa'* means "to die" or "breathe your last," or "give up the ghost." But in the Hebrew the word *ob* means spirit of the dead, necromancer; pit.[218] The word usually represents the troubled spirits or spirits of the dead. So if we were to look at the word *ghost* here, as the disciples and King Saul would have understood it, I believe they would have thought it to be a spirit of the dead. The Bible is also very clear about the warnings of necromancy, which is contacting the dead; practitioners were to be put to death (see Deuteronomy 13). Many people believe we cannot fight what we cannot see, but the Bible actually warns us, and tells us exactly that; we fight against things we cannot see all the time.

So as Christians, what should we make of this ghost and haunting business? Can man live in between both worlds? The Bible is very clear the spirit goes to one of two places only! It is very plain, very straightforward; there are no gray areas. If you believe in Christ as your savior, your physical body is left behind and your spirit is immediately ushered into the presence of Christ in heaven (see Philippians 1:21–23; 2 Corinthians 5:8). Jesus told the thief on the cross he would be with him in paradise that very day. Option two is much less attractive. If you do not believe in Jesus as your Lord and savior, and your name is not written in the Lamb's Book of Life, your spirit is immediately deposited into a place of torment, to await further sentencing on the Day of Judgment (see 1 Thessalonians 4:13–18). This place is what we call hell; it is not limbo, caught between two worlds, trapped in between dimensions, etc. Nowhere in the Bible is such a place mentioned, and there is no way out.

Let's go to another informative story in Luke 16:19–31. This story is an actual event, because Jesus tells us names; parables do not use names. The story of Lazarus and the rich man gives us so much information about heaven and hell in such a simplistic manner, it can easily be overlooked. Basically Lazarus has an illness and is reduced to begging for food. Somebody drops him off at the gate of a rich man, and he just wants to eat the crumbs from his table. The rich man pays him no never mind, and he dies. Then the rich man dies and each is sent to his eternal abode. Lazarus goes to heaven, and the rich man goes to hell. (Not because he was rich, but because the Pharisee's in that time equated wealth with righteousness, and we all know wealth can't buy your way into heaven.) The rich man can "see" Lazarus in paradise, and vice-versa. He makes a strange request of Father Abraham (keep in mind both of these people are dead, and communicating to each other): *He answered, "Then I beg you, father, send Lazarus to my father's house, for I have five brothers. Let him warn them, so that they will not also come to this place of torment." Abraham replied, "They have Moses and the prophets; let them listen to them." "No, father Abraham," he said, "but if someone from the dead goes to them, they will repent." He said to him, "If they do not listen to Moses and the Prophets, they will not be convinced even if someone rises from the dead"* (Luke 16:27–31; NIV).

Isn't it interesting, a dead man in hell, requesting another dead man in heaven (paradise) go back and warn his father and five brothers to repent. Obviously, the rich man cannot do the deed himself, otherwise I think he would have. He asks Abraham to send Lazarus in his stead! Abrahams reply is quite plain, "If your family doesn't listen now to Moses and the Prophets, they certainly aren't going to listen to a ghost!" This story tells us that no human soul can return from hell to try to give us a message from the other side. It also tells us God will not allow human spirits from heaven to go back to earth and warn us. It is intrinsically implied if they did nobody would listen! This is different than someone being "raised from the dead" (resurrection) and coming back to life.

So this again leaves us with a question: Why did Jesus mention the characteristics of a ghost? No body, no bones. If we translate *ghost* to the word *spirit*, we again have two options. *Man's spirit* has been taken out of the equation; it can only go to heaven or hell. *It is not trapped* in between worlds. This leaves us with our other two options: good spirits or evil spirits, for spirit bodies seem to have extra-dimensional properties. If we look at what God said about the disembodied spirits of the dead, we have to assume he is talking of demons, who are, as we have learned, the disembodied spirits of giants, angel-human hybrids, who have no place in heaven and seek to torment and possess human beings. Why else would a good and loving God choose such a harsh penalty of death to necromancers? Remember, demons have all of the qualities and characteristics of angels. They are able to navigate outside of our known dimensions. They also have the past experience of being in a humanoid body, living on this earth. Their evil prince is the Prince of Darkness. They are called to do his bidding, to deceive, destroy, torment, kill, steal, and lie. *Satan and his demons can impersonate anything and anybody.* We know from the Bible demons can move objects and do physical harm to the human body, as in the example of the Seven Sons of Sceva: *...Then the man who had the evil spirit jumped on them and overpowered them all. He gave them such a beating that they ran out of the house naked and bleeding* (Acts19:16; NIV). Ghosts are yet another form of Intelligent Deception. Ghosts are deceiving spirits, demons! Not human in any way, shape, or form.

Familiar spirits are spoken of in the Bible extensively. When you look at the word *familiar* it is rather spooky. "Familiar from the Latin: *familiaris* of a family."[219] Webster's defines it as "closely intimate, well versed or acquainted, well known or remembered, common, presumptuous."[220] In many Wiccan circles or occultist practices a *familiar* is a spirit guide or demon that attends to and guides a person, especially a witch or wizard.

The Bible tells us to test the spirits! If you have ghosts or are experiencing ghostly happenings in your house, ask them straight out what god they serve. According to scripture if they deny Jesus as the Son of God and that he died for our sins and rose on the third day—then I think you can safely say you have a demonic manifestation going on instead of your late husband Fred. Demons can say the name of Jesus; they just can't admit he is Lord, was crucified and died for our sins, and rose on the third day. This is a valid test; use it.

My Ghost Story

When I was in college, I took a class on Life after Death, Near Death Experiences (NDEs). Yes, it was a bona fide, in the catalog, accredited course (your tax dollars at work). I was extremely excited to take this class as I had read many of the popular book titles on the subject. My professor was attempting to run the class in a parapsychology manner and was doing his own research in the area. We would assemble in a circle and share paranormal experiences each of the class members had experienced. I did not feel the need to divulge my unusual experiences, but true to my nature, my burning question for the professor was: Why does all the literature just focus on the positive life after death experiences? It seems *everybody* goes to heaven, or sees *the light*, and no one goes to a fiery hell. His response was that people who have had a negative death experience do not divulge this information for obvious embarrassing reasons, but most all people have a *positive enlightened* experience. In many of our class sessions our professor would have us meditate and try to contact "the spiritual realm" (basically a séance). I always felt a little creeped-out by this and would usually keep my eyes open and watch other people. This professor stated he had a long-distance girlfriend who would *visit* him on a regular basis by blowing on his neck or twirling his hair. He claimed she had been severely abused as a child and as a result developed the ability to separate from her body while the abuse was happening, and go to a happy place (astral projection). Again I felt a little creepy, but I was so hungry and interested in the paranormal I did little to protect myself.

Word definition: Creeped-Out: Holy Spirit Conviction!

Shortly after classes started I began to have a recurring dream. To preface this, a dear friend's father, who was my high school teacher, had committed suicide. In my dream, I would be with his son and daughter and we would be going to a red carpet event. Each time in the dream the son did not have a ticket to get into the event and we would leave him outside while we enjoyed the show. The dream became repetitive, and disturbing. The thought of leaving him outside while we enjoyed the privilege of going into the show was unbearable, so I chose to sleep in another bedroom in the trailer house I shared with my roommate who was away for the summer months. The dream stopped, but I started to experience a *presence* in the bedroom. I felt as though someone was watching me all the time. This *presence* would be confined only to the bedroom, but I was able to sense it at the doorway down the hall watching me in the living room. This *presence* would literally jump up and down like a spoiled child, and throw a temper tantrum. I was starting to get scared. I actually remember trying to talk to it. I asked it who it was and what it wanted, no reply. I told it to go away and leave me alone, but it did not. I started to spend a lot of time over at my boyfriend's house, and I told him about it. He thought my cheese had slid off of its cracker! So in desperation, I went to see my professor. I was a little sheepish, because I had not participated in class much, and we mostly talked about life after death experiences, not ghosts, but I figured he would be open to the conversation. Boy was he ever! And he even had answers to my questions; imagine that! My professor: "This dream is a conflict between the son and his father who committed suicide. You have been *chosen* as the go-between because you can see their unresolved issues from an objective viewpoint. The presence you feel is just frustrated; he is trying to contact you, and you are not listening. It is the spirit of the father; he wants you to help him resolve his issues so he can progress to the next level of the afterlife."

I asked my professor why he (*the presence*) had confined himself to the bedroom. He replied, "Well he knows you, he is being respectful of your space. After all this isn't even your bedroom, but he knows how to get your attention." I walked away wanting desperately to believe his plausible explanation, but thank God, I didn't. I just felt deep down something was amiss, and maybe my involvement in the class had opened a door to something I should not have had any business in. When I went home that night, the *presence* was extremely strong, and mad! It stood only about four feet tall and it threw a temper tantrum in the doorway like you wouldn't believe! I was really getting scared! This wasn't my high school teacher! Why was I so gullible, so ignorant? I slept in my bedroom that night, and the next morning as I was getting into my car, I *saw* it. It moved the curtain aside and was staring out of the bedroom window at me. It looked like a gray, skeletal, skinny, hairless, evil-faced old man. It just stared at me. I felt extreme frustration and evil intent sent my way in a truckload of hate. What was I thinking? Connie, you dummy! This is a demon! Get rid of it! I began to pray, I repented of my stupid involvement with the class, and anything I might have done to bring it out. Then I looked right at it and told it to leave. This was my house, and it could not stay, and it better be gone by the time I got back from school. When I got home that evening it was gone. But I will never forget the face, the temper tantrums, and my own naïve foolishness. How close once again I had come to demonic possession!

Familiar spirits are mentioned specifically sixteen times in the Old Testament. *When men tell you to consult mediums and spiritists, who whisper and mutter, should not a people inquire of their God? Why consult the dead on behalf of the living?* (Isaiah 8:19; NIV).

All sixteen times familiars are mentioned, it is in the context of mediums producing the spirits, the most famous being King Saul and the witch of Endor, producing the dead spirit of Samuel the High Priest in 1 Samuel 28. The funny thing about this particular encounter is it really scared the tar out of the witch! She had never seen an apparition quite like this one before. It wasn't her usual familiar spirit; this was real! There is a lot of controversy over whether or not God brought back Samuel from the dead, but why bother mentioning it if he didn't? What would be the purpose in bringing a fake? The scriptures call him Samuel by name. If all scripture is God-breathed, then you would be calling God a liar by saying it wasn't Samuel! Saul, was the only living person to actually see and talk to a real dead human spirit brought back from the grave! It is a very sad and grave situation, because Saul was held *very accountable* for this information:

> He said to her, "Perceive for me by the familiar spirit and bring up for me the dead person whom I shall name to you."…And when the woman saw Samuel, she screamed and she said to Saul, "Why have you deceived me? For you are Saul!" The king said to her, "Be not afraid; what do you see?" The woman said to Saul, "I see a god, (terrifying superhuman being) coming up out of the earth!"…And

> Samuel said to Saul, "Why have you disturbed me to bring me up?...and tomorrow you and your sons shall be with me among the dead." (Isaiah 8:8, 12, 15, 19; NIV)

So the Witch at Endor tells us she saw a terrifying superhuman being which would be consistent with an angel bringing Samuel up from out of the earth. Her reaction and descriptive use of the word *god* tells me that normally God's good angels are not in the business of bringing forth dead individuals, and this was definitely not her usual spirit guide, familiar, or helper. Saul consulted a medium, and for it, he was given a death sentence by God through Samuel. God really does have a just sense of irony—Saul who could no longer hear from God, due to disobedience to the Lord, now seeks a mistress of necromancy and the ghost of Samuel for answers. So God does just as he asks and stirs Samuel up from his rest to give Saul one last prophecy, his death sentence! God, who demanded witchcraft be a capital crime, and being the judge, gave Saul just what God said should be done! Death! We as Christians have an unjust view of a just God; we see him as all loving, but never as a corrective father! If he had let Saul get away with this crime, he wouldn't be much of a God. He has to be true to his character; he has to punish the crime just as he had commanded the Israelites to do!

A demon or impersonator of any sort would not be bringing Saul a prophetic message from God. Saul understood this; he was so distraught he fainted! This incidence is a good example also of the consequences witchcraft can have on our families and others. Saul wasn't the only one to die. Three of his sons died the next day, and the Bible tells us many of the Israelites fell slain.

This incidence is very different from the ghostly encounters many people have. I for one believe ghosts (spirits) haunt people and houses, but I don't believe for a second they are the dead spirits of humans caught between realms! Don't you believe it either! These are demonic spirits *masquerading* as dead humans. Humans they most likely tormented in life. Humans they were intimately acquainted (familiar) with. Now they come forth with their filthy lies and dress up in period appropriate clothes and appear before you as an innocent child killed by an evil stepmother or some such nonsense (you just happen to be able to corroborate this information with the local town archives). Wake up! These are tricks and taunts and traps laid out just especially for you!

Many of us want to believe our loved ones come back from the dead to give us little tokens of their affections. We want to believe that so badly! But remember familiar spirits can take on the looks and characteristics of anyone! In order for you to trap the bee, you have to bait it with honey! This is very dangerous ground you are walking on, and the demonic influences will take full advantage of your grief, loss, and loneliness. This is not to say God will not intervene in some cases and leave you with the hope of his love, but it is always a very different scenario.

The other possibility besides a demonic spirit haunting your home may be witches carrying out their spells and haunts by astral projection. As we learned from a previous chapter, astral projection allows the human spirit to project and act just as any other spirit would. This may be one explanation for apparitions or objects that move out of place or physical harm perpetrated upon their victim.

Let's take a closer look at what ghosts and haunted places conjure up for us in our emotions. There is a popular program on cable that depicts groups of people being left overnight in world famous most haunted places. These individuals are given video cameras and left to record what they see and their reactions. Now whether or not most of this is staged remains to be proven, but what you end up seeing is not spirits or objects moving or moaning, etc. What you end up with is a bunch of scared, emotionally wrought people who claim to have *felt* something. Rarely is anyone *not* scared out of their wits. When you talk to people who have encountered ghosts or unusual happenings in their home or elsewhere, fear is the number one emotion, followed by intense emotions of panic, hair standing on end, and unexplained emotional urges to harm others, repetitive nightmares, etc. As a result of frequent encounters, fears mount, tension builds, people become sleep deprived, and then Satan, who roams about as a roaring lion seeking whom he may devour, really puts the spurs to a person when they are at their weakest point.

At this point they have questioned whatever it is they have believed in, spiritually speaking, in the past. They are unable to function in society due too extreme spiritual, mental, and physical stress, and Satan and his lying minions are able to torture beyond repair those they have deceived into believing another lie. After all, what acquaintances will believe them when they tell them their house is haunted? No, society labels you as a nut case, which is just what an intelligent con artist would want! Now you have to sell your dream house at an extreme loss because rumors have circulated someone was murdered in the house and now it is haunted. So Satan again has achieved poverty as an added bonus. Then you lost your job or got demoted and have lost face with your peers because you had an emotional break, and now receive judgment and scorn. And to top it off you have lost your faith, because God didn't rescue you, and the church certainly didn't have any answers for you when you came knocking out of desperation! And through the trauma you lost your spouse because they couldn't explain why they hated and resented you now, so you have a divorce to add injury to insult and have lost the love of your life. Your kids hate you and have resorted to drugs or cutting to escape from the hell and nightmares they are still experiencing in their young minds, and they are disillusioned and confused about this world that they now are a part of, and have to live with. And to top off this killer sundae with the cherry on top, you have intense thoughts of suicide, have taken up chain-smoking, and can't seem to break out of this downward spiral funk. You are still tormented at night with dreams and memories, and most likely have a host of demons taking a crack at your psyche. So let's see what was accomplished by this *benevolent, lost, poor soul* who was just confused about the fact they had died and were *trapped between worlds*, had nowhere to go and nothing to do but kick you out of your house and scare you to death. They killed your dreams and your future as well as your security; they stole your partner, children, finances and faith, and they destroyed your life. Yep, who else loves to live by the motto, "Steal, kill, and destroy"? Sounds like Satan to me!

So if we were to make an interesting assumption that a spirit or ghost were a demon who possessed powers beyond our intellect, and they quite literally become closely intimate, well-versed with our daily routines, were intensely territorial, knew the intimate details and history of the area since they are not under our time constraints and dimensions, and had the uncanny ability to lie and deceive without abandon, I would make the conclusion that ghosts, hauntings, and the like are nothing more than tormenting, disembodied demons *masquerading as dead humans.* They in all probability inhabited and tormented in the past, in order to torment, inhabit and steal your mental and emotional well being in this life! Intelligent Deception!

House Cleansings

Do you know the spiritual history of your house, property, and apartment? Demons are territorial; we know this from Daniel when his prayer was delayed by the evil prince of Persia. Demons want your real estate and most likely already inhabit it. It is very difficult to know what the spiritual history of land or buildings are. Not all real estate is built on old Indian burial grounds, but your land or building may have been used by someone who was into the occult, even briefly. It may have been used in ancient times as a ritualistic site or it may have been the sight of a war or particular battle. It may also have been the site for sexual debauchery, murder, torture, or any other lascivious behavior, opening the doorway for territorial demons. Such activity *feeds* demonic entities. The spiritual gurus call this "*negative energy.*" Christians call it what it is: *sin*!

Objects, such as furnishings, antiques, tribal artifacts, and the like, may have been used in an unholy ritual; they may have only been in a room where spiritual debauchery took place. Either way, they can contain a sort of *spiritual resonance*; they may even be the hiding place or container for demons to enter your household. Remember the powerful container, the Ark of the Covenant? It too was just a piece of furniture, but it housed the Most High, with all of his power and glory! Why wouldn't a demonic spirit also want to clothe itself with a piece of furniture and pretend to wield his pitiful power from a picture, dresser, statue, etc.?

The Lord always gives us an example in scripture of how to deal with territorial spirits and past atrocities committed on ground. He tells us to bless the land, and consecrate the land with the blood of Christ. *In fact, the law requires that nearly everything be cleansed with blood* (Hebrews 9:22; NIV). I do this with every home I buy. We pray over the house and land and cleanse it with the blood of Jesus (not literal blood); we anoint the house and land with olive oil. The blood of Jesus is the only *charm* you need to ward off evil spirits…all others are just attractants and open doors.

Don't believe all the bunk about ghosts needing their space and resolving their unresolved issues! The Bible tells us to test the spirits: *Dear friends, do not believe every spirit, but test the spirits to see whether they are from God, because many false prophets have gone out into the world. This is how you can recognize the Spirit of God: Every spirit that acknowledges that Jesus Christ has come in the flesh is from God, but every spirit that does not acknowledge Jesus is not from God. This is the spirit of the antichrist* (1 John 4:1–3; NIV). They are demons, bent on generations of destruction! They hate you! And if they need to make rocking chairs move, and books to fly off shelves, and wear bonnets and frolic through the garden to make you believe their lie, then what an easy target! If you are living with this lie it can be broken easily through the power and blood of Jesus Christ. If you are a victim of this deception ask the demonic ghost if Jesus is the Son of God who came in the flesh. If they do not answer you, then you know this is not some angel sent by God. The Bible is very clear demons cannot answer this question. You do not need a spiritist, psychic, or a medium or even a priest. You can take authority over this demonic presence yourself and cast the demon(s) out. If you are a weak Christian, or have little knowledge in this area, seek out a strong Charismatic or Pentecostal pastor or elder who does not have the fear which is now implanted in you. Make sure the individual is strongly rooted in the Word, and has the power and anointing of the Holy Spirit. Also make sure you are not being charged money for a house deliverance; those that do are not to be trusted. All hauntings and ghosts can be rid of through the power of Jesus. HE came to set the captives free and conquer the hold of Satan once and for all. Don't put up with another lie of the deceiver!

Chapter Thirteen

REINCARNATION OR TRANSMIGRATION OF THE SOUL

Reincarnation is a very popular idea, and becoming more and more accepted in our mainstream culture. I can see why. Through a series of deaths and rebirths into another life form we eventually tire of physical pleasures and attain a life of spiritual bliss, nirvana, governed by karma. There are no repercussions for sin or wrongdoing; you simply get a do-over until you get it right. No chance for eternal judgment, a very attractive concept of the afterlife. The word *reincarnation* simply means "to be made flesh again" or "reappearance of something in a new form."[221]

According to Wikipedia:

> Reincarnation and transmigration of the soul is primarily an eastern religious tenant, such as Hinduism (includes Yoga), but also includes Greek philosophy, Paganistic and New Age movements, Jewish Mysticism, Native American Philosophies, and some sects of Occultic Christianity.

> Reincarnation is the core of the doctrine of Spiritism, a tolerant religious movement started in France in 1857. According to Spiritists souls will reincarnate to perfect themselves toward communion with God. The evolution of the soul is one of the main laws of the universe; it cannot be truly stopped; only delayed. Spirits have new chances to learn and evolve by reincarnating into new bodies. Forgetfulness of the past, including previous lives, is a gift through which souls get a chance to overcome their past, paying their debts to their enemies and themselves, and acquiring newer experiences for the future. [222]

Many prominent and successful individuals believe they have lived past lives: Henry Ford, General Patton, Edgar Cayce. In fact Henry Ford is quoted as saying:

> I adopted the theory of Reincarnation when I was twenty-six. Religion offered nothing to the point. Even work could not give me complete satisfaction. Work is futile if we cannot utilize the experience we collect in one life in the next. When I discovered Reincarnation it was as if I had found a universal plan. I realized that there was a chance to work out my ideas. Time was no longer limited. I was no longer a slave to the hands of the clock. Genius is experience. Some seem to think that it is a gift or talent, but it is the fruit of long experience in many lives. Some are older souls than others, and so they know more. The discovery of Reincarnation put my mind at ease. If you preserve a record of this conversation, write it so that it puts men's minds at ease. I would like to communicate to others the calmness that the long view of life gives to us. [223]

Many people claim to have vivid memories of past lives. They recall people, names, events, places; even some children claim to have these memories. How can they? Could there be a second, third, or infinite chances for us to move toward spiritual bliss, to get it right? What does the Bible have to say about reincarnation? Does the Bible contradict itself in certain stories of individuals coming back to life (e.g., Elijah, Moses, etc.)?

Well let's look at scripture. *And just as it is appointed for (all) men once to die, and after that the (certain) judgment* (Hebrews 9:27; AMP). I wish I could put, "end of chapter"! But I think you would be wanting for more. It is appointed for man one time to die. Not twice, three, four, five, six—once to die, and after that the *judgment.* No do-overs; it's heaven or hell for you. But, you say what about Lazarus, Mary and Martha's brother who was raised from the dead. He obviously died twice. And Jairus's daughter in Matthew 9:18–26 and a widow's son in Luke 7:11–15? Yes, all of them died and returned to life, normal, healthy, and functioning, not zombies. But reincarnation is different; it is dying and completely taking on a new human, animal, or vegetative form. I can assure you, all of these people did die, and they did not go on to live life as a goat, a flower, or Henry Ford! But each was judged according to what they had been shown in life and death. Do not be so eager for such an opportunity such as reincarnation promises; our Creator holds each of us accountable for the information he has shown or given us.

This concept of many do-overs and no penalty for our crimes, sins, or carnal pleasures is totally refuted in the next chapter of Hebrews:

> For if we go on deliberately and willingly sinning after once acquiring the knowledge of the Truth, there is no longer any sacrifice left to atone for (our) sins (no further offering to

> which to look forward). (There is nothing left for us then) but a kind of awful and fearful prospect and expectation of divine judgment and the fury of burning wrath and indignation which will consume those who put themselves in opposition (to God). How much worse (sterner and heavier) punishment do you suppose he will be judged to deserve who has spurned and (thus) trampled underfoot the Son of God and who has considered the covenant blood by which he was consecrated common and unhallowed, thus profaning it and insulting and outraging the (Holy) spirit (who imparts) grace (the unmerited favor and blessing of God)? (Hebrews 10:26, 27, 29; AMP)

So if we go on willfully sinning, after knowing the truth of Christ, our punishment would be much, much heavier. In other words, if we were actually given the chance for a do-over, for reincarnation, we actually would be given a harsher punishment in the end if we ever did reach *spiritual enlightenment.* This *spiritual enlightenment* we would realize is that we messed up so badly by not acknowledging the truth all around us, we really would burn however many times hotter in hell by the number of times we were reincarnated. God is mercy and grace, not karma! By *not allowing us to be reincarnated* he actually saves us from a more severe form of torment in hell if we reject him! Sounds weird, but this is our God. There are no do-overs!

There are some very curious passages of scripture dealing with what looks like reincarnation. In fact the advocates of reincarnation adamantly insist this is proof of reincarnation in the Bible! If we go to Matthew 11:10–14 it talks about John the Baptist and his prophetic role: …*and if you are willing to accept it, John himself is Elijah who was to come (before the kingdom)* (Matthew 11:14; NIV); and its corresponding verse: *Behold, I will send you Elijah the prophet before the great and terrible day of the Lord comes* (Malachi 4:5; NIV). Then: *The disciples asked him, "Then why do the scribes say that Elijah must come first?" He replied, "Elijah does come and will get everything restored and ready. But I tell you that Elijah has come already, and they did not know or recognize him, but did to him as they liked. So also the Son of Man is going to be treated and suffer at their hands." Then the disciples understood that he spoke to them about John the Baptist* (Matthew 17:10–14; NIV). So what does this mean? This is the mainstay of all arguments for reincarnation in the Bible. Elijah obviously did come back and become John the Baptist, but nobody recognized him! He did not talk of his past life as Elijah; he did not do the great miracles Elijah did. Likewise, few recognized Christ as the Messiah! John the Baptist was a type and shadow of Christ. All throughout scripture we have types and shadows of Christ woven intricately throughout scripture. Jesus also goes on to tell of the great price Elijah/John the Baptist paid as a result of this so-called reincarnation: *I tell you the truth: Among those born of women there has not risen anyone greater than John the Baptist; yet he who is least in the kingdom of heaven is greater than he* (Matthew 11:11; NIV).

Here is the clincher, Satan often uses scripture just like this. This is truth right? If you knew nothing else about scripture and didn't know how to look things up for yourself, you would be convinced God is truly contradicting himself and reincarnating one of his own, wouldn't you? Come on, admit it, this is one great argument! Let me ask you one question; how did Elijah die? Do you even know? The Bible tells us he didn't die! Go with me to 2 Kings 2:10–11. Apparently Elisha, Elijah's protégé asks for a double portion of his special spirit of faith, and Elijah gives us a clue he knows what is about to happen: *"You have asked a difficult thing," Elijah said, "yet if you see me when I am taken from you, it will be yours—otherwise not." As they were walking along and talking together, suddenly a chariot of fire and horses of fire appeared and separated the two of them, and Elijah went up to heaven in a whirlwind* (2 Kings 2:10–11; NIV). Elijah DIDN'T DIE! He was taken up to heaven just as Enoch was; Elijah got his *one chance* to die when he was John the Baptist! God doesn't do reincarnation!

Another very curious passage in Revelation about two witnesses: *And I will give power to my two witnesses, and they will prophesy for 1,260 days, clothed in sackcloth... These men have the power to shut up the sky so that it will not rain during the time they are prophesying; and they have power to turn the waters into blood and to strike the earth with every kind of plague as often as they want* (Revelation 11:3, 6; NIV). After which the beast comes out and kills them, and they lie in the street for three days while everyone declares an international holiday with gift-giving and celebrations, and then at three and half days God's breath of life enters them and they come to life again! Many scholars believe these two witnesses are Elijah and Moses because of the similarities to their previous ministries; Moses called plagues upon Egypt and turned the water to blood, and Elijah called fire from the heavens in his showdown with the prophets of Baal. Interestingly they also appeared with Christ at the Mount of Transfiguration. This appearance in the gospels makes sense chronologically because Herod had John the Baptist killed *before* the Mount of Transfiguration.

I actually happen to believe these two are the witnesses, but I do not think this is a case of reincarnation. They are simply raised from the dead, and not in the way we would typically think of it. They obviously transcend our physical bodies, because it says in Revelation 11:5 anyone who tries to harm or kill them basically gets killed by fire coming out of their mouths! I can't do that; can you? Yeah, so they are operating in a completely different set of dimensions than we are! The other reason I say they might be the two witnesses is this: Why did Satan want Moses' body when he died? Ever pondered that? *But even the archangel Michael, when he was disputing with the devil about the body of Moses...* (Jude 1:9; NIV). And also: *(The Lord of Moses) He buried in Moab, in the valley opposite Beth Peor, but to this day no one knows where his grave his* (Deuteronomy 34:6; NIV). So God himself buried Moses, and obviously there was a dispute between Michael and Satan over his body. Intriguing, isn't it? Could it be God resurrects Moses' body in the End Time scenario?

"Reincarnation means that you keep paying for your sins over and over and over again. After all this time, work, and energy, where is the hope of eternal life? And even more than that, the real you stopped existing somewhere in a past lifetime, so who is it that finally merges with a 'force' out in the cosmos somewhere? Doesn't sound real appealing to me."[224]

So from our study of the scriptures what can we make of all the claims by the thousands upon thousands of people who claim to have been reincarnated? I mean, some are truly convinced they were a soldier killed in World War I, or a famous singer from a past era, or Cleopatra, or Billy from Milwaukee, Wisconsin, or some famous yogi. The claims are further justified by hypnotic regression. Remember our discussions of the deceitfulness of demons? How they are able to possess, oppress, and suggest? What makes you think they aren't possessing you, and suggesting to your willing mind the story of someone who they were *familiar* with? Hypnosis is an open doorway into your subconscious mind. Every time you open this door, demons have a legal right to come in and inhabit your temple. You don't think they can tune you into your frequency? Why not? You believe you were Cleopatra for goodness sake! Don't be deceived! Learn to recognize the wiles of the devil! Reincarnation is just another lie created by Intelligent Deception! You will die! You will choose your destination, of that you can be sure. You do not get any chances for do-overs, so choose wisely!

Chapter Fourteen

NEAR DEATH EXPERIENCES: NDES

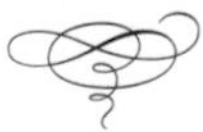

Does the Bible comment on Near Death Experiences? A resounding yes! In fact many of the disciples and apostles were privy to this experience. The title of Near Death Experiences is unfortunate and misleading, because most would assume you are *near death*, when in fact a more descriptive title would be "Brought Back to Life After Death Experiences" or simply "Resurrected." *Resurrected* means to come back to life after apparent death or to bring somebody back to life.[225]

In order to determine in today's society if someone is dead, we speak in terms of *clinical death*. Modern medicine has developed machines to assess one's life or lack thereof. For a medical doctor to pronounce death for legal records he needs one thing, no determinable heartbeat. We can actually keep people "alive" artificially with the use of machines if one is clinically brain dead, while keeping their heart and lungs pumping and receiving adequate oxygen. But once the machine is turned off, death is inevitable. The brain can only live a few minutes without oxygen. Without the brain stem telling the heart to beat, it is like unplugging your computer from the power source.

As a nurse with a background in cardiac and emergency medicine, I have personally been a part of a team of professionals who brought back people from the dead, sometimes on a nightly basis. These "codes" are graphic, emotional, and intensely charged, ordered chaos, as many people begin a myriad of machine and drug protocols to help bring the victim back to the realm of the living. Science has managed to recapture the breath of life. Most people brought back to life are too sick and *out of it* to begin talking about their experience, not to mention that when people die in a hospital setting most of the time they are only dead for few minutes until we bring them back. All the while we are pumping life-giving oxygen into them and acting as an artificial heart and circulating it for them. When I was a nurse you certainly didn't have time to sit down with the patient and discuss his or her "death experience"!

So what does the scripture say about resurrections? Should we be bringing humans back to life? Why has the occult got a hold of the idea and perverted it for their own gain? Could some famous NDEs be demonic hoaxes or something even more abominable to God? The problem with many of the NDE books, websites, and other organizations is they all seem to point to a *universal death experience,* which is anything but biblical! Many of those experiencing NDEs say they see a bright light, are surrounded by friends and family, they have a tunnel experience, and they may have a "life review session." Some are said to come back with psychic or healing abilities. Let's see how these collective experiences stand up to the resurrectees of the Bible. We'll examine who had NDEs in the Bible and what insight they brought back from the *other side.*

The scriptures give quite a long discourse on the resurrection of the dead in 1 Corinthians 15:12–58. Here is a small portion of this scripture: *But if it is preached that Christ has been raised from the dead, how can some of you say that there is no resurrection of the dead? If there is no resurrection of the dead, then not even Christ has been raised. And if Christ has not been raised, our preaching is useless and so is your faith…But Christ has indeed been raised from the dead,…for since death came through a man, the resurrection of the dead comes also through a man…The last enemy to be destroyed is death* (1 Corinthians 15:20, 21, 26; NIV).

Pretty profound stuff. Resurrection of the dead is definitely a God thing. It was meant to destroy the enemy; death. Who is death? Satan brought death upon us in the Garden of Eden when he introduced sin. Spiritual death is not knowing and understanding who God is. It is the opposite of eternal life. John 17:3 tells us what eternal life is: *And this is eternal life: (it means) to know (to perceive, recognize, become acquainted with, and understand) You, the only true and real God, and (likewise) to know Him, Jesus (as the) Christ (the anointed one, The Messiah), Whom you have sent* (John 17:3; AMP).

When Jesus summoned his twelve disciples, he gave them power and authority to *cure the sick, raise the dead, and drive out demons* (see Matthew 10:8). This was revolutionary thinking to them! Even after Jesus sent out the seventy-two messengers, they came back incredulous and joyful of their new adventures and power! *"Lord, even the demons submit to us in your name"* (Luke 10:17; NIV). The Bible actually mentions many people coming back to life again, many Jesus himself resurrected, and the Bible records that both Peter and Paul raised the dead. According to the Old Testament both Elijah and Elisha brought two different women's sons back to life. *The Lord heard Elijah's cry, and the boy's life returned to him and he lived* (1 Kings17:22; NIV). *Just as Gehazi was telling the king how Elisha had restored the dead to life, the woman whose son Elisha had brought back to life came to beg the king for her house and land. Gehazi said,*

"This is the woman, my lord the king, and this is her son whom Elisha restored to life." The king asked the woman about it, and she told him everything (2 Kings 8:5; NIV). There is even a very weird tale of a man who died and was brought back to life by touching Elisha's bones! *Elisha died and was buried…Once while some Israelites were burying a man, suddenly they saw a band of raiders; so they threw the man's body into Elisha's tomb. When the body touched Elisha's bones, the man came to life and stood up to his feet* (2 Kings 13:20–21; NIV). None of the Old Testament accounts record anything of their Near Death Experience.

The most famous is probably Lazarus, whom Jesus raised from the dead after he had been in a tomb, completely embalmed, and wrapped tightly in linens for four days. Even Lazarus' sister Martha, who believed Jesus could bring him back from the dead, didn't really want him too, because she was sure her brother was going to be rather smelly! (See John 11:38–44.) The scriptures again do not record his NDE! But it must have been quite a story as the chief priests plotted to kill Lazarus after his resurrection in John 12:10. Jesus again raises a widow's son in Luke 7:14–15. He raises Jairus' daughter and commands her parents not to tell about it: *Her parents were astonished, but he ordered them not to tell anyone what had happened* (Luke 8:56; NIV). This didn't imply he didn't expect them to talk about her death experience, but it was not the appropriate time in his ministry for word like this to get out.

Peter resurrected a woman in Joppa (see Acts 9:40). All he said was "*Tabitha, get up,*" and he presented her to the believers. And again in Acts, Paul resurrects a young man after he fell asleep in one of his sermons and fell out of a three story window to his death! *Paul threw himself on the young man and put his arms around him. "Don't be alarmed," he said. "He's alive." Then he went upstairs again broke bread and ate* (Acts 20:9–12; NIV). I betcha that kid never fell asleep in church again!

When Jesus died on the cross Matthew writes: *At that moment the curtain of the temple was torn in two from top to bottom, the earth shook and the rocks split. The tombs broke open and the bodies of many holy people who had died were raised to life. They came out of the tombs, and after Jesus' resurrection they went into the holy city and appeared to many people* (Matthew 27:52–53; NIV). Wow what a verse! You don't see this depicted in any movies! These people were dead, dead…I mean there is no excuse that they were in a coma or some such nonsense; they had been embalmed, wrapped in linen, and sealed in tombs. The subsequent earthquake caused by Jesus' death broke the tombs open. What I find fascinating about this verse is that these people were just hanging around for three days! They didn't go into the city until after Jesus was resurrected, and then they appeared to many people! They did appear to the centurion and those guarding Jesus, as is related in verse 54. Can you imagine? Why do you think they got the biggest stone and put a seal on it and posted a guard at the tomb?! The centurion and those other guards had to report the other tombs opened and dead people came to life again. The chief priests and Pharisees knew about this and didn't want to take any chances with Jesus coming back to life again.

In all of these instances of biblical resurrections the Word does not record what the resurrectees saw, experienced, or heard. Bummer. But the Word does allude to the fact that these people did say something, and it must have been powerful and marvelous or the chief priests and Pharisee's wouldn't have found them to be much of a threat. We do have a couple of other possible NDEs, one being Paul who wrote about it 2 Corinthians:— *I know a man in Christ who fourteen years ago was caught up to the third heaven. Whether it was in the body or out of the body I do not know—God knows. And I know that this man—whether in the body or apart from the body I do not know, but God knows—was caught up to paradise.*

He heard inexpressible things, things that man is not permitted to tell (2 Corinthians: 12:2–4; NIV). Most scholars believe Paul was talking about a personal experience he had fourteen years prior when he was stoned and left for dead in Acts 14:19–20. We do not know if he died and came back or not. He may simply have had an open vision of heaven. The other most quoted NDE is the stoning of Stephen, but the Bible is quite clear he had an open vision of heaven and of Jesus *before* they began to stone him to death (see Acts 7:54–60).

The other possible NDE was Jonah. Jonah was swallowed by the great fish, and was inside of if for three days and three nights. He prayed to God: *But you brought my life up from the pit, O Lord my God. When my life was ebbing away, I remembered you, Lord and my prayer rose to you to your holy temple* (Jonah 2:6–7; NIV). The reason why scholars say he most likely died was because Jonah was a model of the coming Christ, who also died and descended to the depths of the earth and was there three days and three nights.

So when we begin to study NDEs (resurrections) from the biblical perspective, we know the raising of the dead is of God! We begin to understand it was meant as a slap in the face of Satan to conquer his death plan (eternal misunderstanding and wrath of God). What we need to learn now is, is Satan going to try to imitate this maneuver of God? You better bet he wants a part of this action, as it will help him fulfill his "I will" goals. The Intelligent Deceiver has his hand mucking up the waters in the matter.

When you begin to study NDEs you find their "experiences" fall into three separate categories: heaven, hell, universal heaven. That is, those who have a true revelatory visit to heaven and meet Jesus; those who go straight to hell and have the hell scared out of them, resulting in repentance and acceptance of the Lord Jesus Christ as their savior (many seem to end up being preachers); and then those who have this feel-good experience, a vague, "all go to heaven" idea.

God is cool, call him by any name you chose, how you live your life isn't important, you don't have to be saved, "God is pure love, man!"

The first group of NDE-ers is what I call the Heaven Group. They are totally aware of their sinfulness, their gratitude to Jesus for saving them to eternal life is apparent, and many come back with truly uplifting stories of the life we can look forward to in heaven.

The second group is worth studying tremendously as it is terrifying; this is the Hell Group. They all come back with an immediate and urgent need to know Jesus, as soon as possible. Not one wants to ever go back to that place or have any other human go there, no matter how much they may despise them. The following is an excerpt from a MD's point of view of a man dying in a doctor's office. The doctor was performing CPR and other life saving measures:

> Each time he regained heartbeat and respiration, the patient screamed, "I am in Hell!" He was terrified and pleaded with me to help him…
>
> Then I noticed a genuinely alarmed look on his face. He had a terrified look worse than the expression seen in death! This patient had a grotesque grimace expressing sheer horror! His pupils were dilated, and he was perspiring and trembling—he looked as if his hair was "on end."
>
> Then still another strange thing happened. He said, "Don't you understand? I am in Hell. Each time you quit I go back to Hell! Don't let me go back to Hell!"…
>
> After several death episodes he finally asked me, "How do I stay out of Hell?" I told him that I guessed Jesus Christ would be the one whom you would ask to save you.
>
> Then he said, "I don't know how. Pray for me." Pray for him! What nerve! I told him I was a doctor, not a preacher…

I knew I had no choice. It was a dying man's request. So I had him repeat the words after me as we worked—right there on the floor.[226]

The following is a quote that pretty much sums up most of the last group, the Universal Heaven Group:

> God is really only concerned about what is within us, our heart and spirituality, not our sexual preference. The way to heaven is through love for everyone unconditionally. We do not go to heaven by worshipping Jesus, or by believing in his name, or by believing in the cross, or by accepting him as our Savior. *We grow to heaven by creating heaven within us by practicing the unconditional love of Jesus for everyone no matter who they are.* [227]

The NDE subculture is saturated with unbiblical ideas and principals. Our enemy has his slither marks all over it! If the above statement were true, Jesus suffered and died for nothing! Remember what the Bible teaches about testing the spirits? *Dear friends, do not believe every spirit, but test the spirits to see whether they are from God, because many false prophets have gone out into the world. This is how you can recognize the Spirit of God: Every spirit that acknowledges that Jesus Christ has come in the flesh is from God, but every spirit that does not acknowledge Jesus IS NOT from God. This is the spirit of the antichrist* (1 John 4:1–3; NIV). John tells us very plainly to "test these testimonials." The above testimonial totally flunks this test! Let's take a look at what some of the NDE researchers have surmised from their findings:

> Of all the theological explanations for the near-death experience (NDE), the Doctrine of Universal Salvation, also

> known as Universalism, is the most compatible with contemporary NDE accounts. Universalism embraces the idea that God is too good to condemn humankind to Eternal Hell and that, sooner or later, all humanity will be saved. Interestingly, a belief in Universal Salvation can be found in virtually all the world's major religions (Vincent, 2000, pp. 6–8). It is particularly essential to Zoroastrianism, the religion of the Magi (Vincent, 1999, pp. 9–10 and 46–47). [228]

Did you catch that? We can all be saved—sooner or later! This is simply Gnosticism repackaged for the twenty-first century! This is the New Age Movement in a nutshell, and the epitome of Satanism. This particular researcher also says good works are basically the message of the New Testament, and this is what will get you out of the *punishment phase* of your eternal *vibrations*:

> Restorative Universalism includes a judgment ("life review" in NDE terminology), followed by punishment for some but eventual universal salvation for all. I present an analysis of New Testament verses supporting the theologies of "Jesus Saves," Predestination, Good Works, and Universal Salvation, which reveals Salvation by Good Works to be supported by the greatest number of verses, followed by verses advocating Universal Salvation for All. [229]

This is a scathing irreverence toward the power and sacrifice of Jesus. This is directly contradicting the message of Jesus Christ. Why would he have to come to earth and be tortured and crucified for us if this were the case? But then again we are dealing with an enemy whose native tongue is lies. Following are some more false ideas from the NDE subculture regarding the nature of hell. We will tackle some of these false teachings and *doctrines of demons* in more detail in the hell section:

> Hell is a psychological condition which represents the hellish inner thoughts and desires within some souls. In hell, souls become uninhibited and their hellish condition is fully manifested. No demons are there to inflict punishment. Each soul acts out their own anger and hatred by warring and tormenting others. (Emanuel Swedenborg)
>
> Hell refers to levels of negative thought-forms that reside in close proximity to the earth realm. It is where we go to work out, or remain within, our hang-ups, addictions, fears, guilt, angers, rage, regrets, self-pity, arrogance, or whatever else blocks us from the power of our own light. (Dr. PMH Atwater)
>
> What people call hell is really a spiritual time-out condition in which souls reflect and work out the things that blocked them from the power of their own light. (Dr. PMH Atwater)
>
> An extreme neglect of spiritual matters on earth can result in an earthbound condition. This is the condition people often associate with ghosts. (Dr. Michael Newton)[230]

These NDE researchers and the poor souls who died and had an "experience" are being deceived. I have absolutely no doubt some experienced physical death. You have to remember any kind of physical trauma to the body is an assault from evil, and an open door to deceiving spirits, this includes death. Jesus himself said death was our enemy. I believe many of the deceived NDE-ers were taken on a "trip" with fallen angels and demons. I do believe many of them saw the heavens, but as we have learned, Satan and his angels can appear as angels of light, men, or any other form they may chose. They also have access to the heavens, and they are called the powers and principalities of the air mentioned so many times in the Bible.

Many of the false NDEs can be explained by a phenomenon called astral projection or an OBE, an Out of Body Experience. This is a difficult concept for many Christians to understand because we haven't been taught what it truly involves. Astral projection is a human's ability to separate his spirit body from his physical body and act as a spirit. Witches, Eastern religions, New Agers, and even certain Roman Catholics (called bilocation [Modern Catholic Dictionary][231]) practice this *technique.* This practice is not only evil, God looks at it as an abomination in his Word, unless the Holy Spirit is in control and wills the situation, for purposes such as open visions of heaven.

NDEs or resurrections have been taken over by a jealous fallen angel who wishes nothing more than to ruin mankind with his lying, deceit, and especially his area of expertise; death. None of this is off-limits to the realm of Intelligent Deception. Be on your guard and very wary of the trap of NDEs. Examine each testimony; test the spirits according to scripture as given by Jesus to John. Study your Bible, but do not close yourself off to the miraculous power of God's gift of resurrection!

CHAPTER FIFTEEN

PROPHECY, VISIONS, AND DREAMS

Chaos, misunderstandings, mysticism, and the occult all follow prophecy, visions, and dreams, but our Holy Bible has more stories on these three areas than on anything else. These spiritual planes have become literal "no-no's" for many Christians, but yet it was the way in which the Almighty spoke to his children. Most of the Old Testament is a collection of books from the major and the minor prophets. Close to fifty percent of our Bible deals with these three realms. Our most celebrated stories are about men who were able to interpret dreams, see visions, and had a front row view of the future of our planet. We have major areas of study of prophecy including eschatology (the study of end-time prophecies) and others. Where did it go wrong? How did God's forgotten language of talking to his people get so scrambled and mixed up with the occult? Is there any hope of "wading through the muck" to find the truth?

In this section we need to define these realms, we need to separate truth from corruption, and we need to have clear understanding of what God expects from his children *now* in regard to these spiritual realms.

Many of the prophets were considered weird, or "a bit off" in the Bible. They did things and said things that were against the mainstream of popular culture in their time. But on the flip side, many were brought to powerful positions and were loved and respected by many. However it was a dangerous occupation, they all seemed to walk a very precarious line of favor with whatever king or ruler happened to be in power at the time.

Let's define prophet. *Nabi* means a true prophet, one commissioned, enlightened, and equipped by God as his spokesman or "mouthpiece."[232] Wow, so if you are a prophet, God is using *your mouth, your voice, your language to speak his mind*! According to Bible teacher Derek Prince, prophecy has three main purposes: to edify, exhort, and comfort. This is confirmed by the apostle Paul: *But everyone who prophecies speaks to men for their strengthening, encouragement, and comfort* (1 Corinthians 14:3; NIV).

Prophecy is one of the nine gifts of the spirit; Paul tells us we should desire this gift. *Follow the way of love and eagerly desire spiritual gifts, especially the gift of prophecy* (1 Corinthians 14:1; NIV). So this scripture tells us the gift of prophecy is still for us today. We are ALL to eagerly desire it! When you begin to study the prophets, you begin to realize they operated in many different capacities of the Holy Spirit, not just prophecy.

Christians today become very uncomfortable when we talk about the gifts of the Spirit. They squirm in their chairs, wince, get angry; it does not fit into their theological way of thinking. "…in fact entire segments of the body of Christ have written off these supernatural aspects of God's Kingdom and His workings in the Church today because of fears about being deceived and led astray."[233] Remember our discussion on witchcraft? Practicing witchcraft are the gifts of the Spirit corrupted. However, many Christians out of this well-founded, albeit unbiblical fear, have written off the gifts completely, which is exactly what Satan wanted to accomplish; he has rendered us powerless. It's like someone inviting you to your own birthday party where there will be lots of presents to open, but you won't go because, heaven forbid, someone might have a cold there, and you could catch it. So you don't get any birthday presents because you were afraid. How dumb is that? The gifts go to waste, you have no fun, and the host is ticked-off because of your unfounded, foolish fear.

So prophecy is primarily an inspired hearer and speaker (mouthpiece) for God. So why use people? If God wanted to talk to us, why doesn't he just talk to us? Well it's not like he hasn't tried! When God commissions Isaiah to be his mouthpiece he tells Isaiah exactly what he is going to run into as a prophet. *He said, "Go and tell this people: Be ever hearing, but never understanding; be ever seeing, but never perceiving. Make the heart of this people calloused; make their ears dull and close their eyes. Otherwise they might see with their eyes, hear with their ears, understand with their hearts, and turn and be healed"* (Isaiah 6:9–10; NIV). People do not want to hear! It's just like the Chicken Little nursery rhyme; until the sky actually falls on your head, you are not gonna believe it! God does use his creation for his purpose and his pleasure. If you owned a mule and didn't use him for anything, what is the point of keeping the thing around? People were created to have a purpose; God chooses to use us as his vehicle for showcasing his power! He can use our mouths, to speak his thoughts.

Visions

"Visions are defined as revelations from God, it takes into its realm; sight, appearance, and vision as a faculty of the body, it can also be seen and heard."[234]

The problem today with *visions* is that they also have lost favor with the Christian crowd. Take for instance this passage from my Vine's Expository Dictionary under additional notes on visions: "Once Christ had finished his life's work, there was no longer any need for visionary communication from God to human beings since the Holy Spirit is now given to all believers as their means of discerning Gods' will for their lives through the words of Scripture."[235] Umm, I think this is awfully presumptuous. Where does it say in the scripture we are not to use the gifts of the Holy Spirit anymore? Where does it say God changed his form of communication with his people? Or, that God changed himself and his character period? If I am not mistaken, Jesus was finished with his "life's work" when Paul was still receiving his visions, as well as John, Peter, and all of the rest of Christ's disciples and apostles *after* he ascended to heaven. When did this time period end, with the book of Revelation? Can you imagine if John thought this way? "Well, Jesus is gone on to heaven, I will just sit here and wait for him. All these weird dreams I have been having must be something I ate!" No, I think this is a very cunning tactic of the Intelligent Deceiver. "Let's make Christians believe this stuff is not for their use anymore! Powerless, stupid humans, don't even know they have a revelatory gift freely available to them!" (wicked laughter) Wake up!

Let's see what the prophet Joel had to say about it. Remember he was God's mouthpiece; God was using Joel's voice to portray his thoughts! *And afterward, I will pour out my Spirit on all people. Your sons and daughters will prophesy, your old men will dream dreams, your young men will see visions. Even on my servants both men and women, I will pour out my Spirit in those days. I will show wonders in the heavens and on the earth, blood and fire and billows of smoke. The sun will be turned to darkness and the moon to blood before the coming of the great and dreadful day of the Lord* (Joel 2:28–31; NIV). Now I don't know about you, but I haven't seen the sun turned dark yet or the moon to blood or any of this other stuff. This is a time period marked from the day of Pentecost to the future day of Jesus' second coming. So we are still in this time frame! This verse is also quoted in Acts: *"And it shall be in the last days," God says, "that I will pour forth My Spirit on all mankind; and your sons and your daughters shall prophesy, and your young men shall see visions, and your old men shall dream dreams* (Acts: 2:17; NIV). Most biblical scholars can agree we are definitely in "the last days."

Visions are in the realm of actual visual sight as well as "insight," seeing with your spiritual eyes. They are called "seers." Samuel was a seer; he beheld visions from God and communicated them to the people. Seers are prophets, but not all prophets are seers. "The Old Testament uses two words primarily to refer to a seer: *ra'ah* and *chozeh. Ra'ah* literally means 'to see,' particularly in the sense of seeing visions. Other meanings include 'to gaze,' to look upon, and to perceive. *Chozeh* literally means a 'beholder in a vision' and can also be translated as 'gazer or stargazer.'"[236] The Encarta Dictionary has a much different take on it from the original Hebrew: "it means the ability to predict the future, occultist—somebody with supposed supernatural powers."[237]

The word *seer* has a negative connotation in Christian circles because it has been so misused and corrupted by the Intelligent Deceiver. He has come in and confused the meanings of the word, caused chaos. Can occultists "see" into other realms? You better bet they can! The power is very real; it's just used for all the wrong purposes, and to glorify the wrong "god," not to mention the "gift" is also a cheap knock-off. Seers can either have waking visions or dreams, but their gift is primarily visual.

Occultists usually take two different routes to access this counterfeit power: hallucinogenic drugs or years of disciplined meditation by studying the "ascended masters." Either way, seer activity in the Bible just seems to "show-up" for our prophets. They didn't have to go smoke something, or take a pill, or chew on an herb, and they didn't have to manipulate their physical body into chants and mantras meditating themselves into an altered state of mind for days on end, following the ancient sage's prescription for seeing into the other dimension, nor did they use a crystal ball. Holy Spirit power is much different in manifestation than occultic power, although it is copied in some forms.

Dreams

Everybody has dreams. Webster's Dictionary defines them as "images or ideas occurring in the mind during sleep,"[238] and in the Greek the word *onar* indicates divine presence and intention. [239] "*Enupnion* stresses a surprise quality that is contained in the dream."[240] These type of dreams are not like the ordinary fragmented, fanciful dreams of normal sleep, which are usually difficult to recall. Quite the contrary, these dreams will wake you up, stick with you, you will remember them, and you may even be very disturbed by them. The disturbing aspect is to be separated from nightmare type dreams; even though prophetic dreams may be frightening you will definitely know the difference.

Prophetic dreams and visionary dreams can happen to *anyone.* Many non-believers and also pagans throughout the Old and New Testaments had prophetic dreams. Pilot's wife had a very disturbing dream before Pilot was to judge Jesus. *While sitting on the judgment seat, his wife sent him a message, saying, "Have nothing to do with that righteous Man; for last night I suffered greatly in a dream because of Him"* (Matthew 27:19; NIV). The magi also apparently *all* had the same dream Herod was after them in Matthew 2:12. Other famous non-believers or pagans have had prophetic dreams, such as the cupbearer and baker Joseph was jailed with, several Pharaohs, and King Nebuchadnezzar being the most well-known and studied. Other well-known prophetic dreams experienced by those close to God were Jacob's Ladder, Joseph and the sun, moon, and eleven stars bowing before him, Daniels' revival of evil dream, Zechariah's lamp dream, and many others. Many were given divine dreams, but the pagans seem like they were not given the power to interpret them. Daniel and Joseph were both given the ability to interpret dreams. In some cases angels interpreted dreams for humans, and in others the dreams became self-explanatory.

To date I have only had the experience of one prophetic dream. I awoke in the middle of the night, and the dream was so fresh in my memory, so vivid, it was unlike any other dream I have ever had. I am a little slow sometimes, but I knew this dream had a meaning. I asked God to reveal the meaning…nada, zip, nothing. Believe me, it is no fun to have a prophetic dream and not know what it means. The dream made absolutely no sense to me, and I chalked it up to one of those "guess not" experiences. Weeks went by and life went on, and one afternoon out of the clear blue (I actually sat down to a cup of coffee and turned on Oprah) and Bam! There it was. I was urgently asked by the Holy Spirit to pray for a fellow believer who was going through a very difficult split from her husband, who just so happened to be a very *gifted* shaman. After about fifteen minutes of prayer the interpretation of the dream flooded my mind. I can even remember asking God about a certain aspect of the dream. The answer came immediately. I have to say it was truly one of the most exhilarating and disturbing experiences of my life.

Dreams are also an area corrupted by Satan. There are a gazillion dream interpretation books on the shelves of bookstores, and I gotta tell ya, some are just downright funny! You gotta know by now if

God does it, Satan's gonna copy it. I mean if you have a dream about putting fish in the toaster, there is some practicing occultist who will be more than happy to interpret it for you. "Will that be credit card or cash?" Although we can't go back to the Old Testament practice of putting magicians and sorcerers to death if they cannot interpret a dream, we certainly have the ability to avoid the shysters and wait on God for the answer.

Nightmares, recurring nightmares, and night terrors I believe to be in the realm of the demonic. What better way for demons to disrupt normal restorative bodily functions than to disrupt your sleep? Demonic activity is also more prevalent in the dark or during nighttime. Demons hate us, and want to terrorize us; we shouldn't think the father of liars wouldn't want to hinder our walk with God while we sleep any more than in another area. Take control of these evil spirits and follow Jesus' teachings on getting rid of them.

Why sleep? You can bet God has our undivided attention. We are not distracted by television, worries, and the normal everyday "busyness of our lives." The mind is in a state of reception and rejuvenation. What better time to communicate a divine message? Do not be afraid of the realm of dreams, God has spoken to us while we have been asleep since the beginning of time.

"The Holy Spirit uses three different avenues of visionary revelation to speak into our lives: dreams, visions and trances."[241]

Dreams occur during the sleep cycle, visions occur while we are awake.

> Trances are a stunned state wherein a person's body is overwhelmed by the Spirit of God and his mind can be arrested and subjected to visions or revelations God desires to impart. The New Testament Greek word for trance is *ekstasis*, from which our English word "ecstasy" is derived.[242]

The word *trance* would send most Christians through the roof, and many are very right to think this way. Trances are often associated with New Age philosophies and practices; in fact deep meditation does produce a trance-like state. But before we get off on what Satan has corrupted, let's go to the scriptures and get a clearer understanding. The Bible is very clear that many of the prophets did in fact experience this unique method of God communication. Paul had a trance experience: *Then when I came back to Jerusalem and was praying in the temple (enclosure), I fell into a trance (ecstasy)* (Acts 22:17; AMP). And Peter experienced a trance: *I was in the city of Joppa praying: and in a trance I saw a vision* (Act 11:5; NIV). In the Old Testament Baalam also experienced trances (see Numbers 24:4, 16). There are other words used when speaking of trances in the scriptures: falling down, falling as dead, a deep sleep, amazement and astonishment, as well as others. A trance evidently gets the physical body and all its worldly trappings out of the way, so the spirit is caught up into the spiritual realm and told spiritual things. It is a much clearer, cleaner connection to God. These trances may well have been OBEs, or Out of Body Experiences brought on by the Holy Spirit.

> Trance is from Latin "transīre": *to cross, pass over* and the multiple meaning of the polyvalent homonym "entrance" as a verb and noun provide insight into the nature of trance as a threshold, conduit, portal and/or channel. An intransitive usage of the verb "trance" now obsolete is "to pass," "to travel" is cognate with shamanic journeying and vision quests.[243]

Trances are easily simulated and brought on by a variety of occultic methods, but as we see in the scriptures, none of the prophets did anything to bring a trance about. In fact they seem quite dumbfounded about the whole process; they couldn't tell you if they were in the body or out of it! This is where our Intelligent Deceiver has mimicked yet another Holy Spirit function. The occult encourages trances; hypnosis is a form of a trance, and many Eastern religions perform elaborate meditations and chants to bring about a trance-like state. Mind-altering drugs and alcohol can produce trances or what is known as stupor. Demonic influences can cause trance-like states, and the medical profession calls these mental illnesses or catatonics.

When I was a nursing student I did my first ER rotation in a small college town hospital, and a young woman was brought into the facility by her landlord. She was in her early twenties; she was dressed like a hippy, no make-up, and I could remember thinking to myself, "Wow, that poor girl is being tormented to death." The look on her face was frozen terror, her eyes were in a fixed stare, she could barely walk, and was very stiff, she could not speak, and tears just streamed from her fixed gaze. She made no gesture she could understand what anyone was saying to her, and she made no attempt to communicate to anyone in anyway. It was creepy. We gave her all kinds of psych drugs and committed her, but this was not the answer to her problems. In reading her chart I found she had a history of depression, attempted suicide, and catatonia. It was very obvious she was "spiritually away" on a very haunting and horrible trip. I have no doubt it was a demonic presence brought on by some unseen open door in her poor tormented life. The woman's fixed gaze and demeanor have often haunted my memory, and when I think of her, I often pray for her, and wonder what ever happened to her.

Catatonics are actually worshiped and thought to be gods in places in India. According to the Maya concept in Hinduism these people have reached such an advanced level of "self realization," they no longer need the physical world! And yet millions of people in our country are trying to do just that...self-realize and check out of this world!

These trance trips can be brought on by a variety of methods such as: hypnosis, possession, channeling, altered states of consciousness, meditation, concentration, music, chanting, and even through scientific methods of altering brain waves (biofeedback). Christians should be very wary. The trance realm has been so corrupted by Satan, we should never try to bring about an ecstatic state on our own volition. This is strictly a Holy Spirit move, and not to be tried by our own power and will!

A crossover phase of visions and dreams are our modern-day premonitions. I believe many premonitions are just a form of dreams or visions and prophecy. Joseph, Mary's husband, was given a premonitory dream about Mary; this is classified as prophecy in the biblical text. Premonitions according to Encarta are strong feelings, without a rational basis, that something is going to happen, an advance warning about a future event. The word premonition does not occur in biblical text, and this may be due more to linguistic nuances and the evolution of language.

Precognition, on the other hand, is a form of Intelligent Deception. It involves various aspects of "secret knowledge" promised by the great liar. "*Precognition* (from the Latin præ-, 'prior to,' + cognitio, 'a getting to know') denotes a form of extra-sensory perception wherein a person is said to perceive information about places or events through paranormal means before they happen. A related term, *presentiment,* refers to information about future events which is said to be perceived as emotions. These terms are considered by some to be special cases of the more general term clairvoyance."[244] Both precognition and presentiment are corrupted forms of the Holy Spirit gift of knowledge.

As believers in this day and age, we need to be very aware of the many ways God communicates, reveals, enlightens, warns, and encourages his children. We also need to be very aware of the Intelligent Deceiver's ways of corrupting this communication and instead speaking his lies and deceits into our souls. Again God has not *hidden* anything from you. He isn't keeping this information a secret. He gave us his Word, a whole text on spiritual matters. We just need to be more diligent in our studies, and not be ignorant of the wiles and schemes and the devil.

Chapter Sixteen

DINOSAURS

No discussion on the paranormal would be complete without mentioning something about one of the most elaborate disinformation campaigns on our planet: dinosaurs. The other is the study of cryptozoology, which is the study of animals that elude our study due to superior camouflage.

Many Christians today have no clue where dinosaurs fit into their belief system. In fact I questioned it for years. I believed God created them, sort of…I kind of thought maybe they all got wiped out at the flood. Confusion reigned. And why wouldn't it? We are constantly bombarded with the "fact" our earth is "millions of years old." No wait—now they say "billions of years old." I thought a "fact" was supposed to be based on evidence, statistics, truth. At least this is what the dictionary says a "fact" is. The problem with dinosaurs is the facts change literally on a daily basis. We even have programs on the Discovery Channel of what the earth will look like in a couple billion years of evolution, when the dinosaurs will again reign. What? I thought we were all supposed to evolve into some sort of super-brainy alien looking thing. I must be watching the wrong stuff. Confusion reigns. What a great way for Intelligent Deception to deceive the babes in Christ. Kids love dinosaurs. Plant doubt and confusion and tell out-and-out lies, and wrap it all up in a great big, pretty package. Voila! Kids grow to adulthood; they perpetuate and actually study what they have been told.

Again, if you are a Bible-believing human and really believe all scripture is God breathed, then this would be the logical starting point for "fact finding." "But," you say, "the Bible does not mention dinosaurs." You are correct, no word in the Bible translates to dinosaur, but then again, why would it? We didn't invent the word *dinosaur* until 1841, thousands of years after they were written about. No, the Bible doesn't speak about dinosaurs, but it does talk quite a bit about dragons. And it does happen to mention two very unusual creatures we no longer see on a daily basis; they are the behemoth and the leviathan. Now I know what you are thinking. "My Bible commentary calls those things a hippo or an elephant, and the leviathan is a crocodile." Yeah, this is exactly what my Bible commentary says too. But they were only giving their opinion; the commentary is not "God breathed." And I have to tell you, when you read about the behemoth and the leviathan, and the description used, did the commentators ever go to a zoo and actually look at a hippo, elephant, or crocodile? What the Bible describes is nothing like any of those creatures. It's like comparing a horse to a cow. Yeah, they both got four legs, a big head, two big ears, and a tail, but they aren't even a close match!

So let's do just that. Let's go see what God himself actually says about the behemoth and the leviathan:

> Look at the behemoth, which I made along with you and which feeds on grass like an ox. What strength he has in his

> loins, what power in the muscles of his belly! His tail sways like a cedar; the sinews of his thighs are close-knit. His bones are tubes of bronze, his limbs like rods of iron. He ranks first among the works of God, yet his Maker can approach him with his sword. The hills bring him their produce, and all the wild animals play nearby. Under the lotus plant he lies, hidden among the reeds in the marsh. The lotuses conceal him in their shadow; the poplars by the stream surround him. When the river rages, he is not alarmed; he is secure, though the Jordon should surge against his mouth. Can anyone capture him by the eyes, or trap him and pierce his nose? (Job 40:15–24; NIV)

Now the first thing I noticed in this God-given biology lesson is the Lord says he made the behemoth along with man, and the behemoth was one of the first animals God made. Now we know God is no liar; his Word always matches up. This is why the Bible is the only book on the planet which can lay claim to this wonderful statement the Word is "infallible." *And God said, "Let the water teem with living creatures"* (Genesis 1:20; NIV). This was his first animal type creation, fishes on day five. He then went on to create the birds and flying creatures to round out the day. Day six he makes livestock, creeping things, wild animals, and man. The word *first* in the above selected text is also translated as; ""chief," in the "Hebrew *ray-sheeth'.* From the same as the *first,* in place, time, order or rank (specifically a *firstfruit*): - beginning, chief (-est), first (-fruits, part, time), principal thing." [245]

But does this passage prove the behemoth was a dinosaur? He is obviously a gigantic herbivore who lives in the Jordan River. No one but the Lord seems to be able to capture or kill the creature except the Lord. This is definitely not a description of an elephant or a hippo; we kill and capture them all the time, even though they are both incredibly strong and fearsome creatures. We know for a fact dinosaurs did exist; we have fossil evidence to support this "fact." Fossils can only be produced by incredibly immense, fast pressure, e.g., a worldwide flood. But what if we have been lied to by the deceiver? What if not all of these creatures died in the deluge? We know the fishes of the sea did not die, and the Bible states this creature was not even rattled by raging waters. Could it have survived? Could Noah have put two baby behemoths on his ark? Is there any other historical evidence to suggest not all dinosaurs (dragons) were killed in the deluge?

There is in fact a wide range of physical evidence to suggest dinosaurs lived and walked among men. We have the tracks along with footprints in Arizona. I am no dinosaur expert, but when you have actual, visual fossilized tracks they argue far better than some scientist who says it would be impossible. We have pottery and cave drawings and temples with artwork depicting creatures that look exactly like dinosaurs walking around with men! How would the artists know what they looked liked and acted like if they weren't eyewitnesses? Most all cultures have dragon myths and legends. Are you telling me all cultures, even ones far removed from any outside influence, would make up similar stories? I was mad when I started to research this subject; I could not believe how much physical evidence is out there, which never appeared or was mentioned in any of my school textbooks or lectures.

> According to evolutionists, the dinosaurs "ruled the Earth" for 140 million years, dying out about 65 million years ago. However, scientists do not dig up anything labeled with those ages. They only uncover dead dinosaurs (i.e., their bones), and their bones do not have labels attached telling how old they are. The idea of millions of years of evolution is just the evolutionists' story about the past. No scientist was there to

see the dinosaurs live through this supposed dinosaur age. In fact, there is no proof whatsoever that the world and its fossil layers are millions of years old. No scientist observed dinosaurs die. Scientists only find the bones in the here and now, and because many of them are evolutionists, they try to fit the story of the dinosaurs into their view.[246]

The following is an excerpt from a scientific journal quoting Dr. Schweitzer at Montana State University:

> When Schweitzer first found what appeared to be blood cells in a *T. Rex* specimen, she said, "It was exactly like looking at a slice of modern bone. But, of course, I couldn't believe it. I said to the lab technician: 'The bones, after all, are 65 million years old. How could blood cells survive that long?'" Notice that her first reaction was to question the evidence, not the paradigm. That is in a way quite understandable and human, and is how science works in reality (though when creationists do that, it's caricatured as non-scientific).[247]

So what could our possible land vertebrate candidates be for the behemoth? Many creation scientists believe the most likely answer is a sauropod, a type of a brontosaurus looking creature. The other less likely candidates are a giant monitor lizard and a Mushrushu, an extinct legendary creature talked about in apocryphal literature as the Bel dragon.

Mokele-mbembe: The Living Dinosaur!

In the jungles of central Africa countries of Congo, Cameroon, and Gabon are reports of an animal with a long neck, a long tail, and rounded shape tracks with three claws. The closest known animal that has these characteristics is a sauropod dinosaur. When some of the local people of the Likouala region would draw in the dirt or sand a representation of Mokele-mbembe they drew the shape of a sauropod dinosaur. Then when they were shown a picture of a sauropod dinosaur they said that picture is Mokele-mbembe. Mokele-mbembe means "one that stops the flow of rivers." French priests in the region called it "monstrous animal."

Its body size is somewhere between the size of a hippopotamus and an elephant. Its length has been reported to be between five to ten meters (sixteen to thirty-two feet). The length of the neck is between 1.6 to 3.3 meters (five to ten feet). The length of the tail is between 1.6 to 3.3 meters (five to ten feet). The reports out of Cameroon have reported Mokele-mbembe to be up to seventy-five feet in length.

There have also been reports of a frill on the back of the head. The frill is like the comb found on a cock (male chicken). There have also been reports of it having a horn on its head.

Mokele-mbembe lives in the pools and swamps adjacent to the rivers of the Likouala swamp region of the People's Republic of the Congo on the continent of Africa. It uses the lakes as a crossing path to go from one river to another river. The pygmies of the Likouala swamp region report that the essential diet of Mokele-mbembe consists of the malombo plant. Since it only eats plants the Mokele-mbembe is classified as an herbivore.

Mokele-mbembe lives most of the time underwater except when it eats or travels to another part of the swamp. It has been reported that Mokele-mbembe does not like hippopotamuses and will kill them on sight, but it does not eat them. Hippopotamuses cannot be found where Mokele-mbembe lives.

It has been reported that Mokele-mbembe will overturn boats

and kill the people from the boats by biting them and hitting them with its tail, but it does not eat the people.[248]

Mokele-mbembe means "one that stops the flow of rivers," an attention grabbing, descriptive name, which would fit God's description in Job: *When the river rages, he is not alarmed; he is secure, though the Jordon should surge against his mouth* (Job 40:23; NIV). This animal is thought to still be alive! Many reports come in from the Congo area, but no film has been taken of the animal. The Congo is a most dire swampland covering close to fifty thousand acres. How did this animal survive, and we not know about it? Easy, we know that giant squids exist, but we still can't catch the darn things. Animals are very good at evading their prey. God made them that way.

If this dinosaur is still alive, what about others? Yep, you guessed it, there are plenty of reports and scientific evidence to prove animals originally thought extinct occasionally wash up on beaches or end up in some fishermen's net. Why are the original dinosaurs so intensely large? One fact I learned is that reptiles continue to grow until they die. If prior to the flood the oldest man lived to be over nine hundred years old, imagine how big your pet iguana would become if his life were also extended beyond our current life spans? It's an intriguing concept.

The other contender for the right to be called a behemoth is the Mushrushu, although a very unlikely candidate. This animal is not a good match for God's description of his behemoth. Most likely this animal did exist, but it may have been a fallen angel hybrid animal, since it was the object of worship by pagans.

> The Ishtar Gate of the ancient city of Babylon dates to the reign of Nebuchadnezzer II, around 580 BC. The bas-reliefs which decorate the gate include two known animals—the lion and the wild ox—and one unknown animal, a dragon.

> Originally the word for this animal was read as *sirrush*, but now *mushrushu* is the accepted form. If the mushrushu ever were a living animal, it apparently is now extinct.
>
> Some cryptozoologists suggest the mushrushu is the same animal as the biblical behemoth and the "dragon" which King Nebuchadnezzar kept in the temple of the god Bel according to the story in the apocryphal tale of Bel and the Dragon. In that tale Nebuchadnezzar confronted Daniel with the Bel dragon. Daniel killed it. [249]

So if we have compelling evidence for behemoths being created by God, and they may have actually been dinosaurs (dragons), why would Satan want anything to do it? Why is Satan called the great dragon, great serpent, that leviathan of old? We will find out in our next Bible text; one of the most detailed descriptions (an entire chapter) of an animal may be a figure of speech relating characteristics of our archangel enemy: Satan. An easy way of describing it would be if I called someone a "cow." Now I would not mean they were a literal cow, but I may be describing the way they chew their food like cud, or emit methane, or walk clumsily along, or how they bellow across the room. See my point?

> Can you pull in the leviathan with a fishhook or tie down his tongue with a rope? Can you put a cord through his nose or pierce his jaw with a hook? Will he keep begging you for mercy? Will he speak to you with gentle words? Will he make an agreement with you for to take him as your slave for life? Can you make a pet of him like a bird or put him on a leash for your girls? Will traders barter for him? Will they divide him up among the merchants? Can you fill his hide with harpoons or his head with fishing spears? If

you lay a hand on him, you will remember the struggle and never do it again! Any hope of subduing him is false; the mere sight of him is overpowering. No one is fierce enough to rouse him. Who then is able to stand against me? Who has a claim against me that I must pay? Everything under heaven belongs to me? I will not fail to speak of his limbs, his strength, and his graceful form. Who can strip off his outer coat? Who would approach him with a bridle? Who dares open the doors of his mouth ringed about with his fearsome teeth? His back has rows of shields tightly sealed together; each is so close to the next that no air can pass between. They are joined fast to one another; they cling together and cannot be parted. His snorting throws out flashes of light; his eyes are like the rays of dawn. Firebrands stream from his mouth; sparks of fire shoot out. Smoke pours from his nostrils as from a boiling pot over a fire of reeds. His breath sets coals ablaze, and flames dart from his mouth. Strength resides in his neck; dismay goes before him. The folds of his flesh are tightly joined; they are firm and immovable. His chest is hard as rock, hard as a lower millstone. When he rises up, the mighty are terrified; they retreat before his thrashing. The sword that reaches him has no effect, nor does the spear or the dart or the javelin. Iron he treats like straw and bronze like rotten wood. Arrows do not make him flee; slingstones are like chaff to him. A club seems to him but a piece of straw; he laughs at the rattling of the lance. His undersides are jagged potsherds, leaving a trail in the mud like a threshing sledge. He makes the depths churn like a boiling caldron and stirs up the sea like a pot of ointment. Behind him he leaves a glistening wake; one would think the deep had white hair. Nothing on earth is

> his equal—a creature without fear. He looks down on all that are haughty; he is king over all that are proud. (Job 41:1–34; NIV)

Who then is able to stand against me? Who has a claim against me that I must pay? Everything under heaven belongs to me? This kind of boastfulness and arrogance may well be attributes of an actual creature, but they are also an uncanny likeness to Lucifer's claims before his fall.

His eyes are like the rays of dawn. Again we see another remark with an uncanny familiarity. Oh how you have fallen, Son of the Morning Dawn. When studying legends of leviathans and sea monsters, they all say the monster had a very interesting shining countenance quality in his eyes. Metaphorical, I am sure, but still uncanny.

Nothing on earth is his equal—a creature without fear. He looks down on all that are haughty; he is king over all that are proud. He is without fear…of God? He looks down on the haughty or boastful and he is king over pride. Sound like anyone we know? So why does God use metaphors like this? If you try to describe a tree to someone who has been blind from birth, they still wouldn't get it. But if you describe to them something they can relate too, then they are able to understand. We have a hard time understanding Satan…a fallen archangel. It boggles our mind why any created being, in the perfect presence of the Almighty, would think they could overthrow such a king. But when God describes him in a way we can relate to, a sea serpent with amazing ferocity, it brings it down to our level. It opens up our minds for a better understanding of the enemy. I think Satan was rather "dissed" by God's metaphor, calling him a serpent. So why not use this tactic against the creator, and create a confusion regarding dragons, dinosaurs, and the like, and get his people to question God's undying word? Intelligent Deception!

Notice how God's description of the leviathan is nothing like a crocodile. We capture and wrestle crocs all of the time. In fact we had a rather famous celebrity, the Crocodile Hunter, Steve Irwin, who even had his newborn baby in with a crocodile. Does this sound like the creature mentioned above? Also crocodiles do not breathe fire, and they have a soft underbelly, easily penetrated by a spear or javelin. I didn't write it; God did, and he is not a liar. I think he knows his creation quite well. There is another interesting metaphorical note regarding the leviathan and the behemoth. According to the book of Enoch, he saw these two great creations and likened them to church-leviathan, and state-behemoth! (Enoch 59:7)[250]

Satan didn't stop with the dinosaurs either. He went on to lie about the Ice Age animals and cave men as well. Most of the evidence for a young earth twenty-five thousand to ten thousand years old or less is very compelling and very well done in regards to scientific method.

The opposite reaction to the Ice Age is that there was no Ice Age. Why do I say that? I mean, didn't they make a popular kids animated movie about the Ice Age? So it must be true! Let's look at a popular Ice Age mammal, the wooly mammoth. Let's think about this logically…can mammoths survive on eating snowballs? Mammoths most likely consumed over a ton of food a day. Ever been to the North Pole? No green vegetation grows there. The mammoths they are finding have been flash frozen in the ice, and they aren't even wooly! Wait, how can that be? Wouldn't they freeze to death without a thick wooly coat? After all, it does get to fifty below zero on a consistent basis at the poles. And, scientists tell us they still have green, tropical vegetation in their stomachs. Wait a minute…how can an oversized elephant live on snowballs, without hair, at fifty below, and still have green undigested veggies in their bellies, when we know grass doesn't grow in subzero temperatures?

The answer is surprisingly simple when we actually stop to look at the facts and think a little. What if there was no Ice Age? What if it was a well thought out lie, again perpetrated on a public who is taught not to question theories or use critical thinking? What if instead, the earth was just like it is now, frozen only at the poles, warm at the equator? What if instead these animals did live on a continent near the equator, where we actually find lush tropical vegetation, and they had no need of a wooly coat? Now what if say, at the flood, a great cataclysmic change happened and the poles shifted? Meaning we still have North and South Poles, frozen wastelands, but due to the earth shifting on its axis the land mass that was in the Pacific Ocean is now at the North Pole. Fast, cataclysmic, instant freeze, this is why we find flash frozen non-wooly mammoths with tropical vegetation in their stomachs. When we stop to actually think things through, we can find acceptable alternative theories that match up with hard facts.

The Bible actually talks about cave men! Again, we find it in the Book of Job. Job is having a pity party and in a sense comparing himself to these "wild men," who were nothing more than social outcasts. *Haggard from want and hunger, they roamed the parched land in desolate wastelands at night. In the brush they gathered salt herbs, and their food was the root of the broom tree. They were banished from their fellow men, shouted at as if they were thieves. They were forced to live in the dry stream beds, among the rocks and in holes in the ground. They brayed among the bushes and huddled in the undergrowth. A base and nameless brood, they were driven out of the land* (Job 30:3–8; NIV). Evolutionists would like us to believe these social outcasts were our forefathers. Ever asked yourself why the "missing link" is still missing?

We live in the Information Age; there is absolutely no reason you can't hop on-line and conduct your own research into any of these areas. Stop taking the garbage and lies that are constantly being shoved down your throats by non-believers. We have been asked to be *separate* from the world. So be separate! *See to it that no one takes you captive through hollow and deceptive philosophy, which depends on human tradition and the basic principles of this world* (Colossians 2:8; NIV).

Cryptozoology

What about this weird sci-fi area called cryptozoology? Not only do you find information on real-life animals that are rare and even more rarely seen, but you also get these macabre descriptions and reports of mythological creatures such as vampires, werewolves, chupacabra, and others. Most recently the television program *Monster Quest* is investigating these phenomena.

Cryptozoology (from Greek: κρυπτός, *kryptós*, "hidden"; ζον, *zôon*, "animal"; and λόγος, *logos*, "knowledge" or "study" – *c.f.* zoology) is the search for animals believed to exist, but for which conclusive evidence is missing. The field also includes the search for known animals believed to be extinct. [251]

Does the Bible explain these creatures, or are they truly a figment of our imagination? The answer again is surprising. Yes, the Bible does talk about some of these creatures, and yes, some are the figment of our imaginations.

The most famous story of a man taking on the characteristics of an animal occurs in the book of Daniel. In our modern vocabulary we call it lycanthropy.

"*Lycanthropy* (Gr. *XiNos,* wolf, *etvOponros,* man), a name employed (1) in folk-lore for the liability or power of a human being to undergo transformation into an animal; (2) in pathology for a form of insanity in which the patient believes he is transformed into an animal and behaves accordingly."[252]

The account told in the Bible was to be a humbling experience for a great and mighty king: King Nebuchadnezzar. First he had a disturbing prophetic dream, which again could only be interpreted for him by Daniel. There was a condition in the dream that if the king acknowledged God's sovereignty, at the end of the seven years of animal-like behavior he could have his kingdom back. "*Let him be drenched with the dew of heaven, and let him live with the animals amongst the plants of the earth. Let his mind be changed from that of a man and let him be given the mind of an animal, till seven times pass by for him...* "(Daniel 4:15–16; KJV). One year later it happened just as the Lord had said it would. *Immediately what had been said about Nebuchadnezzar was fulfilled. He was driven away from people and ate grass like cattle. His body was drenched with dew of heaven until his hair grew like the feathers of an eagle and his nails like the claws of a bird. At the end of that time, I, Nebuchadnezzar, raised my eyes toward heaven, and my sanity was restored* (Daniel 4:33–34; KJV).

The Lord tells us this particular event was a mental lapse from sanity; he actually changed Nebuchadnezzar's mind from a man to an animal. Seven years this king went around acting like an ox... grazing, lying down in the wet grass, no physical hygiene. Some scholars believe this one event turned king Nebuchadnezzar from a pagan to a believer in God due to the fact he was indeed restored to his kingdom and ended the whole chapter with his praises and worship of the true God. One note I would like to bring to your attention...King Nebuchadnezzar was an arrogant pagan, he worshiped many deities, was a cruel king, and consulted mediums and witches continually. Even though this episode of changing his mind to that of an animal was allowed by God as a humbling experience, his instrument could have been Satan. The king had many open doorways into his life, and this kind of behavior was a manifestation of evil darkness.

That being said, let's move on to this business of the second definition of lycanthropy, the ability of a man to turn into an animal: "the liability or power of a human being to undergo transformation into an animal." Werewolves, vampires, and other wer-animals can be explained by total abandonment of self to worship of one evil being: Satan.

According to one encyclopedia:

> The term lycanthropy properly speaking refers to metamorphosis into a wolf (see Werwolf), it is in practice used of transformation into any animal...Lycanthropy is often confused with transmigration; but the essential feature of the wer-animal is that it is the alternative form or the double of a living human being, while the soul-animal is the vehicle, temporary or permanent, of the spirit of a dead human being. The vampire is sometimes regarded as an example of lycanthropy; but it is in human form. [253]

The myths and legends concerning these mythical creatures, and the glamorization of Hollywood, takes away from the real danger lurking behind Satanism. Talk to any high level witch who has left and renounced her worship of Satan, and they will tell you of the wer-animals. Even amongst witches they are the "undesirables."

A former self-proclaimed "bride of Satan," one of the top witches in the country came out of Satanism and told her story in a book called *He Came To Set The Captives Free.* Here is her explanation of wer-animals:

> These people were known werewolves and were always withdrawn, always watchful and always menacing. They were there as humans and did not turn into their other forms unless

> Satan so ordered and then usually only for disciplinary purposes. We did not touch them or talk to them. They belonged to Satan exclusively; they were totally sold out to him and were feared and disliked by everyone else in the cult. They were primarily guards and disciplinarians, used by Satan and his demons to ensure that the rest of us obeyed all orders.[254]

According to this former witch, wer-animals were demon-possessed humans which were 100 percent "sold out to Satan." They were used as instruments of discipline, which always resulted in death. These beasts would tear apart humans, and were even feared among the Satanists. Quite literally they are the hounds of hell.

Much has been done by the Intelligent Deceiver to perpetuate disinformation about his "evil beasts." We see computer games, comic books, role-playing games, movies, even night clubs glorifying these creatures. We see a growing trend of body modification by our "Goth-youth" to alter their teeth into fangs, tattoo and surgically alter their bodies into shapes of lizards and other animals, all in the name of "self-expression." Dangerous? Again we are playing with an intelligent enemy whose very existence thrives on deception, lies, entanglement, and possession.

What does the Bible have to say about all of this? Again, when you are aware of the terminology of the Holy Spirit, you can discover a great many truths hidden in the text. Terms like werewolves and vampires do not exist in the Bible, but we find the Holy Spirit goes to great lengths to distinguish between two different types of beasts, one clearly of God, and the other clearly of evil. The terms are: wild beast and evil beast. God says *the wild beasts of the field are mine* (Psalm 50:11; KJV). Also in scripture we see the term "evil beast." *And I will rid evil beasts out of the land* (Leviticus 26:6; KJV). Paul was talking about the Isle of Crete when he wrote about the Cretians:

> One of themselves, even a prophet of their own, said, The Cretians are always liars, evil beasts, slow bellies (gluttons). This witness is true. Wherefore rebuke them sharply, that they may be sound in the faith; Not giving heed to Jewish fables, and commandments of men, that turn from the truth. Unto the pure all things are pure: but unto them that are defiled and unbelieving is nothing pure; but even their mind and conscience is defiled. They profess that they know God; but in works they deny him, being abominable, and disobedient, and unto every good work reprobate. (Titus 1:13; KJV)

Paul said one of the prophets of Crete actually told him of the vileness of the island of men, he actually called them "evil beasts." These men were obviously involved in witchcraft and idol worship. You don't become an evil beast by walking with Jesus. In the above segment of scripture, these men were claiming they were walking and professing the Lord, but their actions proved they were not. This is where we get our demeaning phrase, "You Cretan!"

If demons have the ability to change their appearance to an angel of light, then we can assume they have the ability to change our appearance as well. American Indians commonly refer to this as *shape shifting* or *skinwalkers.* We see this trait exemplified in the Harry Potter movies as one of the professors turns herself from a cat to a witch and back again.

Egyptian hieroglyphics portray all sorts of man-beasts, many with a dog head and human body. The Israelites were the Egyptian captives for four hundred years; they would have learned many of the pagan rituals and traditions.

When Ezekiel is taken to a vision of the temple of Jerusalem to behold what kind of "unseen activity" was going on in the Lord's temple, this is what he saw: *And he said to me, "Go in and see the wicked and detestable things they are doing here." So I went in and looked, and I saw portrayed all over the walls all kinds of crawling things and detestable animals and all the idols of the house of Israel* (Ezekiel 8:9–10; KJV). Now what Ezekiel saw was satanic worship, pictures of demons, idols, and possibly wer-animals.

Griffons, satyrs, fauns, and other creatures: One of the questions I have always asked is; could the fallen angels also have experimented and genetically altered animals? After all, bestiality is a grave sin, punishable by death as commanded by God. What if the legends and myths have an element of truth to them? Take for instance the griffon. Greek literature is resplendent with great fear and well-mapped routes indicating griffons were along those trade routes, and they were guardians of gold. Griffons interestingly have a head of an eagle, a body of a lion, and yes, two wings. They are fiercesome, and their description is surprisingly consistent with a seraphim or cherubim crossing with a lion. Both of those angels have the face of an eagle and wings. Modern scientists attribute griffons to nothing more than the ancients seeing dinosaur skeletons of a protoceratops, but this does not explain the wings, or even the body of a lion. "In antiquity it was a symbol of divine power and a guardian of the divine. Some writers describe the tail as a serpent, in the manner of a chimera." [255]

The Flying Creatures—Phoenixes and Chalkadri

"And I looked and saw other flying creatures, their names Phoenixes and Chalkadri, wonderful and strange in appearance, with the feet and tails of lions, and the heads of crocodiles; their appearance was of a purple color, like the rainbow; their size nine hundred measures. Their wings were like those of angels, each with twelve, and they attend the chariot of the sun, and go with him, bringing heat and dew as they are ordered by God." [256]

In the book of Jasher, which is quoted in Joshua and 2 Samuel, there are strange stories of creatures whose lower half is that of a man and the upper half is a bear, and something described as a keephas and ducheepthath. There are stories of a beast with the upper half of a man and the lower a beast, and of a woman with lots of arms each ten cubits long.[257]

Vampires are another of the strange bat/human hybrid beings that evoke strong emotions of erotica, power, and immortality. Former Satanists report there is such a thing as a vampire cult. When on the path to *spiritual enlightenment* Satanists find themselves at a crossroads if they wish to gain more power and hidden knowledge. They must choose between becoming a vampire or a wer-animal, or becoming stagnant in their power. Many fear the intense physical pain involved in becoming a wer-animal and choose vampirism. Former vampires describe the "rush of drinking blood" as intoxicating and addictive; they even describe a supernatural growth of fangs, which occurs in a state of arousal, just as a man would get in an erection, their canines "grow." Many of the universal legends regarding vampirism are true according to former Satanists. They do sleep in coffins, cannot tolerate sunlight or garlic, as garlic is a blood purifier, and they prey on the helpless and homeless, as well as believe to become a total vampire you experience a physical death, rise on the third day, and are forever immortal. [258]

Do these strange creatures exist? Yes, they just don't want you to believe they do. People who are heavily involved in the occult know they exist. Whatever these creatures are they are results of man's attempt at provoking God; they are abominable animal/human hybrids, angel/animal hybrids, or demonically possessed humans capable of shape shifting—Don't be ignorant of the schemes and wiles of the devil; this is Intelligent Deception.

Part Three

The Abodes of the Dead:

Hell and Heaven

INTRODUCTION

I decided to end this book with two chapters on the afterlife. Number one because we are going to be spending eternity in one or the other, and two, because there are so many non-biblical myths and false teaching about both places. Stop the average person on the street and ask them where they are planning to spend their afterlife and most will tell you heaven. This is alarming, as the Bible is clear that the road to heaven is narrow, difficult, and has a small gate. And yet few people want to go to hell, but correspondingly they refuse to do what is necessary to stay out of hell.

I explore both paths, as both seem to have equal disinformation campaigns perpetrated by the Intelligent Deceiver.

CHAPTER SEVENTEEN

HELL

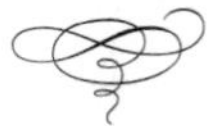

Someone once said; "Hell is the ultimate expression of free will." I believe this statement to be correct. We choose where we are to go when we die. As you can probably surmise from other areas in this book, I believe the original Hebrew and Greek word of God is inerrant. The Word tells us we can choose life or death (see John 10:10), and as we have already learned God did not create death, Satan did. We have only two choices for our eternal abode, and we are the ones who decide where we will reside based on a very simple choice, believe in Jesus as our savior or not.

No one goes to hell because of sin. Let me repeat and quantify that statement. No one goes to hell because of sin: all mankind sins, but we can choose to go to hell *because we refused the payment in full for our sin*, the ultimate torture, crucifixion, and sacrifice of Jesus Christ on the cross, who rose again on the third day in triumph. If we refuse this payment, we are doomed, not because of sin, but because of our refusal.

So does hell actually exist? What does the Bible say about it? Are there different levels or torments that exist in hell? Who was hell created for? Why would an "all loving God" *send* anyone there? What does it look like? Is there any way out? Could there be a purgatory or limbo? Where is hell, do we have an actual location?

In recent years, preaching fire and brimstone from the pulpit have become passé, out of vogue. The current thinking is preaching nothing but love and forgiveness, don't mention evil, and don't even bring up our own need for salvation…love, love, love. This is an unbalanced approach to the throne of God. I can honestly say from my own experience, I could not understand the love of God until I understood the evilness of my own heart, and the sheer knowledge there was a fifty-fifty chance I could go to hell literally scared me straight! Not to mention we do currently have a 100 percent death rate in this world! I was petrified of hell when I was in my teens and early twenties, and even though I sinned plenty, the knowledge there could be such a place always kept me running back to Jesus.

Let's address people's prevailing conceptions and presumptions about hell. After all, isn't hell just a place you get to go to and just party with the devil, do whatever you want? How about Satan looks like a guy dressed in red tights, with a horny head and a forked tail? Oh, I know, since you served this master so well in this life, you now get to serve with him in his kingdom, and learn even more hidden knowledge and dark arts? Or, hell is only where the really "bad" people go, like the murderers, thieves, and child molesters, and of course people like Hitler and Sadam Hussein. Then there are those who really don't believe hell exists at all, that we actually create our own hell in some other unknown dimension of our psyche.

Contrary to what the television tells us, popular literature and the latest guru, we have a book in our possession which describes this "place." It tells us where it is located, what we will find there, who it was created for, how many people will go there, what creatures live there and more. In fact there are over 150 scripture verses describing this place we call hell.

This book has attempted to better equip you and inform you of a creature capable of intelligent deception. A creature and an enemy not only rebellious toward his Maker but also inexplicably tied and bent on our very destruction, he knows we serve a just, vengeful God. This God of ours made a special place of torment, despair, and punishment for this being and his band of rebellious angels. This place is so hideous, so beyond the scope of anything an evil angel could possibly imagine a "loving God" would even think to create. It is a terrible, horrible place of punishment, a just reward for a crime against the Most High, the Most Powerful Being in all of creation. It is a place to experience the wrath of God for an arrogant being who caused God's loving people to be corrupted, his creation to suffer, lament, and groan. Great and terrible is the judgment of Almighty God.

We have this preconceived notion no loving God could send his creation to a place as awful as hell. "Hell seems disproportionate, a divine overreaction."[259] This is a false notion; if that is the case, then wouldn't you think the converse is true: sending Jesus to die on the cross and to endure one of the most horrible and gruesome deaths humans can think of, is a "divine overreaction" to our sin? It tells us we do not understand a God who loves his creation so much he would sacrifice his own son as a payment so we would not have to go to this awful place for eternity. However, many *choose* to not believe this; they instead *choose* to turn their back on an open invitation, and instead "follow" Satan to his demise. God will honor your free will choice! That is how consistent his character is, whether he wants you in heaven with him for himself or not, he will honor your decision. Hell is not a divine overreaction!

This concept is foreign to us because we put people in places for their own good, against their wishes because we have the power to do so. You are correct, you have that right, but there is a higher right, in God's eyes: It is called free will. This free will was given with the knowledge you could choose how you lived your life, whether right or wrong, without interference from a powerful being who has the ability to restrict this free will. You can't make a puppy love you, no matter how much you care for it, restrict its movement, etc. It has to choose to love and stay with you. Nothing is more frustrating than trying to get something or someone to love you when they choose not to. This is how God feels with us. He will give you the best of everything, if you will but choose to love and follow him, but if you refuse, he will honor your decision. *Say to them, "As surely as I live, declares the Sovereign Lord, I take no pleasure in the death of the wicked, but rather they turn from their ways and live. Turn! Turn from your evil ways! Why will you die, O house of Israel?"* (Ezekiel 33:11; KJV).

The scriptures tell us hell was created by God for the devil and his fallen angels. *Then shall he say to those at his left hand, Be gone from me, ye cursed, into the eternal fire, prepared for the devil and his angels* (Matthew 25:41; KJV). And in 2 Peter: *For God did not [even] spare angels that sinned, but cast them into hell, delivering them to be kept there in pits of gloom till the judgment and their doom* (2 Peter 1:4; KJV). We blame God for everything the devil does and did. We don't understand why God in his infallibility doesn't just wipe out Satan from this earth and start over without a fallen angel. We do not understand God. Instead we blame God, we injure the Most High with our self-righteous, "Well if I was God, I would do it differently." Would you? We do not understand an unchanging character. God could not and will not allow Satan to go unpunished. He has prepared a special place of doom and torment for him and his angels. Hell is not the devil's domain; it is not his kingdom which is so often portrayed. He doesn't want any part of his future imprisonment! He just wants you to go there with him for all eternity!

God has a plan, a place, and a future for Satan. He will not allow him to go unpunished. He plans on confining and tormenting him for all of eternity. This is how strongly God feels about Satan and his debauchery. He cannot tolerate an evil unpunished! God has allowed Satan the added torment of knowing what his future entails; it is a cruel anticipation. *Then the devil who had led them astray [deceiving and seducing them] was hurled into the fiery lake of burning brimstone, where the beast and false prophet were; and they will be tormented day and night forever and ever (through the ages of the ages)* (Revelation 20:10; AMP). All of his intelligent deception will get him nowhere but a fiery pit. This pit, we will learn, is the lowest of dungeons or levels of punishment. He will be tormented unceasingly for all of eternity. This is not a slap on the hand, a light duty prison. This is very real, and the scariest thing of all is we have the free will choice to follow him there.

Before we go on, let's take a look at the different names the Bible uses to describe hell and its differing levels of punishment. There are four different names used for the abodes of the dead: Sheol, Hades, Gehenna, and Tarturus.

Sheol literally means grave, or to die.[260] Contrary to popular belief, Sheol is more of a neutral word to describe death. It is the abode of the dead and is used to describe a place where the righteous and the unrighteous are contained awaiting judgment. We find most of references in the Old Testament, before Christ's resurrection, referring to Abraham's bosom and also to hell. We will delve further into this concept of Abraham's bosom (paradise) later.

Hades: "this word is a genuine dynamic equivalent for the Hebrew term Sheol" in early Christian Greek.[261] We often ascribe the word Hades to the Greek god of the underworld in classical mythology. In the Bible however Hades is often used in the context of divine judgment and punishment over the unrighteous. It is sometimes translated as "hell" and the "grave." God uses this word to describe his Divine Judgment. We see Hades used in the context of judgment in Luke 16:23 when describing Lazarus and the rich man, and also in Revelation 20:13–14.

Gehenna is sometimes translated as "hell" in the Bible. Gehenna was originally a garbage dump in a deep valley outside of Jerusalem, and was called the Valley of Slaughter. Fires burned continually to consume the refuse, and the many bodies of criminals who were dumped there. Tradition tells us brimstone (sulfur) was added to the dump to keep the fires continually burning.[262] See also Jeremiah 7:30–33.

Before Gehenna became a dump, pagans offered their children as burnt offerings to the god of Molech (Baal) (see 2 Kings 23:10).

Gehenna continually burned; it was extremely foul, putrid, and vile, reeking of death. Jesus referred to Gehenna as a place where sinners were punished after death. *You serpents! You spawn of vipers! How can you escape the penalty to be suffered in hell (Gehenna)?* (Matthew 23:33; AMP). Jesus equated hell with a burning, rotting, foul garbage pit. We can understand that.

Tartarus is an interesting word; it is used specifically as an ultimate punishment.[263] It is used for the dark abode of the wicked dead and is the place of eternal punishment for the fallen angels. *For if God did not spare angels when they sinned, but sent them to hell, putting them into gloomy dungeons (Tartarus) to be held for judgment* (2 Peter 2:4; AMP).

> I beheld…a desolate spot, prepared and terrific. There too, I beheld seven stars of heaven bound in it together, like great

> mountains, and like a blazing fire. I exclaimed: For what species of crime have they been bound, and why have they been removed to this place?...These are those of the stars which have transgressed the commandment of the most high God; and are here bound, until the infinite number of the days of their crimes be completed. From thence I afterwards passed on to another terrific place; Where I beheld the operation of a great fire blazing and glittering, in the midst of which there was a division. Columns of fire struggled together to the end of the abyss, and deep was their descent. But neither its measurement nor magnitude was I able to discover; neither could I perceive its origin. Then I exclaimed: How terrible is this place, and how difficult to explore!...Enoch, Why art thou alarmed and amazed at this terrific place, at the sight of the place of suffering? This, he said, is the prison of the angels; and here are they kept forever. (Enoch 21:1–6)[264]

So we have physical death which is Sheol, Hades which is divine judgment, then hell is described as Gehenna, a putrid burning pit, and Tartarus eternal torment, all descriptive of a place of eternal punishment originally created for Satan and his fallen angels who sinned by corrupting mankind.

There seems to be a final level of hell often overlooked and it will come after the final White Throne Judgment. Hell will actually be relocated! The Bible tells us it will be thrown into the eternal lake of fire. This has to happen because God promises to create a new heaven and a new earth, and he promises to literally bring the New Jerusalem to earth and live with us on earth (see Revelation 21). So I'm thinking God doesn't want hell to be at the center of his new earth.

> Then I saw a great white throne and him who was seated on it. Earth and sky fled from his presence, and there was no place for them. And I saw the dead, great and small, standing before the throne, and books were opened. Another book was opened, which is the book of life. The dead were judged according to what they had done as recorded in the books. The sea gave up the dead that were in it, and death and Hades gave up the dead that were in them and each person was judged according to what he had done. Then death and Hades were thrown into the lake of fire. The lake of fire is the second death. If anyone's name was not found written in the book of life, he was thrown into the lake of fire. (Revelation 20:11; NIV)

The Bible says so much more about hell than just the meanings of those four words. In Bill Wiese's book, *23 Minutes in Hell* he lists scriptures which describe a place where there is:

Desolation, no life
Humiliation and shame
A physical location in the center of the earth where there is:
    No hope, mercy, peace, purpose, rest.
A Bottomless Pit
Foul odors/stench
Prison
Pits
Physical bodies in hell
Demons that torture
Darkness
Degrees of punishment
Destruction

Eternal separation (from God)
Fear
Fire that eternally burns
Profanity
Thirst, the absolute absence of water
Torment
Worms
Wrath
Weeping and gnashing of teeth[265]

The above list of torments, like weeping and gnashing of teeth, require eyes and teeth. Foul odors require olfactory senses (nose and nasal cavity). Darkness requires sight. Torment and torture speaks of having a body with emotions. Thirst requires a tongue, mouth, and sensory feedback loops telling your brain you are thirsty. Prison bars or pits cannot keep a free-floating spirit encased. All of this is better described in the following true story found in the Bible.

One of the most profound and descriptive stories Jesus tells about hell is found in Luke 16:19–31. Keep in mind this is an actual account of a place called Abraham's bosom (paradise) and a geographically physical location called hell. There are three people in this story, all once living, breathing humans who existed on our planet: a beggar named Lazarus, a rich man, and our patriarch Abraham. Of the three, two are living in peace, rest, and eternal goodness; the other is still in hell, experiencing the same torment day in and day out for all of eternity. We can safely assume the rich man has been in hell for over two thousand years, and is still suffering under our feet as we speak. This is the story as Jesus told it:

> There was a rich man who was dressed in purple and fine linen and lived in luxury every day. At his gate was laid a

> beggar named Lazarus, covered with sores and longing to eat what fell from the rich man's table. Even the dogs came and licked his sores. The time came when the beggar died and the angels carried him to Abraham's side. The rich man also died and was buried. In hell, where he was in torment, he looked up and saw Abraham far away, with Lazarus by his side. So he called to him, "Father Abraham, have pity on me and send Lazarus to dip the tip of his finger in water and cool my tongue, because I am in agony in the fire." But Abraham replied, "Son, remember that in your lifetime you received your good things, while Lazarus received bad things, but now he is comforted here and you are in agony. And besides all this, between us and you a great chasm has been fixed, so that those who want to go from here to you cannot, nor can anyone cross over from there to us." He answered, "Then I beg you father, send Lazarus to my father's house, for I have five brothers. Let him warn them so that they will not also come to this place of torment." Abraham replied, "They have Moses and the prophets, let them listen to them." "No father Abraham," he said, "but if someone from the dead goes to them, they will repent." He said to him, "If they do not listen to Moses and the prophets, they will not be convinced even if someone rises from the dead." (Luke 16:19–31 NIV)

First, notice angels came to carry Lazarus to Abraham's side, and the rich man was buried and just went straight to hell. The next thing we notice, the rich man has *physical capabilities;* he can look up, indicating he has a body of some sort, and he can see Abraham and Lazarus far off in the distance. Next he can talk to them, so he must have a mouth, vocal cords, and some sort of air to pass over his voice box to produce speech. The next thing we notice is that he is absolutely parched; so much so, even a small drop of water on the tip of his tongue would provide a split second of relief from his agony, so he has a tongue. Next he is tormented by fire, but not completely burned up, so he has the physical sensation of flesh burning continually. There is a great chasm fixed between them so neither can cross over and "visit each other" or escape to the other side. The next thing we see is the rich man still has all of his mental capabilities: he can think, he has regrets, and he remembers his family, especially his five brothers, and he does not wish for them his fate. The one thing we find absent in this passage is an absolute lack of complaining about why he was there, and no mention of "get me out." Instead we see a settled "I deserve this" type of resolve in his thinking. There is no mention of "this isn't fair, I did some good things, I was well liked and a good person in life," nothing, just a request to ease his perpetual thirst, and to warn his family of their fate.

I find the lack of water in hell interesting because it indicates our very separation from God's love. Jesus was described as the living water, rivers of living water, and drink from the well that never runs dry. This perpetual thirst, the dryness, heat, and suffocation of hell tells us we have no idea how much of God is in everything on our planet. Earth is mostly water, our bodies are mostly water, no wonder we cannot survive eternity without the real living water. In a prophecy about Jesus the Old Testament prophet Zechariah says *As for you because of the blood of my covenant with you, I will free your prisoners from the waterless pit* (Zechariah 9:11; NIV).

The Location of Hell

How do we know where hell is located? The Bible is quite clear that hell is a bottomless pit. In order for something to be "bottomless" it can't be measured. Enoch stated he could not find its measurements. *Columns of fire struggled together to the end of the abyss, and deep was their descent. But neither its measurement nor magnitude was I able to discover; neither could I perceive it origin.*[266] I am no science wiz, but if hell is in the shape of a sphere, (assuming it is in the middle of the earth) does a sphere have a bottom? If you are in the center of a sphere in the middle of the earth, no matter what direction you are able to go to would be up, thus it is truly "bottomless."

The Word tells us over and over again hell or the "pit" is at the center of the earth…*in the lowest parts of the earth* (Psalm 139:15; NIV)…*for they are all delivered unto death, to the nether parts of the earth* (Ezekiel 31:14; KJV). Jesus describes where he will go after he is crucified and before he arises: to the belly of the earth. *For as Jonah was three days and three nights in the belly of a huge fish, so the Son of Man will be three days and three nights in the heart of the earth* (Matthew 12:40; NIV). And in Ephesians: *He [Jesus] also first descended into the lower parts of the earth* (Ephesians 4:9; AMP). Now why would Jesus go down to the heart of the earth, to hell? To kick Satan's butt? No, remember Satan isn't confined to hell yet.

This is a great place to explain one of the mysteries of the afterlife, and show how great God's sacrifice for us was. In the story of Lazarus and the rich man, we learned the rich man could see Lazarus in Abraham's bosom. This was what Jesus called paradise. Remember the thief on the cross? Jesus said to him, *"Today you will be with me in Paradise"* (Luke 23:43; NIV). That verse bugged me for years, because the way I understood it, Jesus went down to hell for three days, and I had falsely assumed he was fighting the devil, but this wasn't the whole story at all! Paradise was once at the center of the earth, it was divided from the torments of hell by the great fixed chasm we learned about in Luke. Jesus went there and preached to all the righteous people in paradise, the "holding place" awaiting Jesus' blood which would redeem them forever. Now they had a high priest who atoned for their sins, now they could be brought into the presence of a Holy, Almighty God. Jesus went down to Abraham's bosom (Paradise) and cleaned it out, and took all of these departed souls to heaven. Paradise and heaven are two different places. Does Paradise still exist? No, there is no need for a "holding place" any longer. Jesus' death and resurrection were what was needed to provide an entrance for us to be with God forever! As sinners the righteous dead could not be with an almighty, righteous God in heaven until their sins were atoned for through the blood of Christ. This is why the huge curtain was ripped in two separating the Holy of Holies from normal people. We have free access now to the throne room of God!

It is important to note here this was not purgatory or limbo. These people were not being punished for their sins; they had believed in God, and had followed his laws and commandments as laid out in the Old Testament. They just did not have a savior to allow them into the courts of heaven yet. As for purgatory or limbo, there is absolutely no reference, no mention, no allusions to the "opportunity for belief after a preliminary period of punishment."[267] Remember in the story of Lazarus and the rich man they were not allowed to cross back and forth.

So what does hell really look like? What kind of haunts and terrors await those who choose to go there? We have already established the fact we will have some form of a body and mind and of course spirit down there, with all of its capacities, and possibly even a "heightened" level of senses down there. Jesus taught us it was better to lose a body part on earth if it was causing you to sin than to lose your whole body in hell...*than for your whole body to go to Hell* (Matthew 5:30; NIV). We are told hell is a place of utter darkness: ...*before I go to the place of no return, to the land of gloom and deep shadow, to the land of deepest night, of deep shadow and disorder, where even the light is like darkness* (Job 10:21–22; NIV). "Where even the light is like darkness." I would imagine the only light is from fire and burning brimstone. The next thing unbelievers have to look forward to is shame and humiliation. *Now they bear their shame with those who go down to the Pit* (Ezekiel 32:24; NIV). Just as Adam and Eve were stripped of their covering in the Garden of Eden, so we can imagine God would have the same punishment in mind for Satan and his angels, in hell.

Hell is referred to as a prison, complete with chambers, and locked away…*is the way to hell, descending to the chambers of death* (Proverbs 7:27; NIV). *They will be gathered together, as prisoners are gathered in the pit, and will be shut up in the prison* (Isaiah 24:22; NIV). In her disturbing book a *Divine Revelation of Hell*, Mary K. Baxter describes her experience of being taken to hell by Jesus in order to come back and warn the populace at large there is indeed a place of utter torment and desolation people go to when they do not believe in Jesus. (I highly recommend this book. It is the type of book that haunts you, you cannot get the images out of your head, and it spawns in you a great desire to evangelize your neighbors.)

> The cell was completely bare except for the woman in the rocking chair…
>
> "Back on earth," said Jesus, "this woman was a witch and a worshiper of Satan. She not only practiced witchcraft, but she taught witchcraft to others…Many times," said the Lord, "I called on her to repent. She mocked Me and said, 'I enjoy serving Satan. I will keep on serving him.' She rejected the truth and would not repent of her evil. She turned many people away from the Lord; some of them are in hell with

> her today. If she had repented, I would have saved her and many of her family, but she would not listen.
>
> "Satan deceived this woman into believing that she would receive a kingdom of her own as her reward for serving him. He told her she would never die, but would have a life with him forever. She died praising Satan and came here and asked him for her kingdom. Satan, the father of lies, laughed in her face and said, 'Did you think I would divide my kingdom with you? This is your kingdom.' And he locked her in this cell and torments her day and night."[268]

This woman was a practicing witch, she must have been very proficient at shape-shifting, and now is doomed for all of eternity to endure the pain of her beloved black arts. Stories like these help us to better understand the underworld. It helps us to understand there are differing degrees of torment, there are cells, and pits certain individuals are confined too. And probably the biggest lesson: we aren't partying with the devil! We will have no freedom, no reign, no life, no purpose, no mercy, no hope, and no rest, just one torture after the next, forever!

The next thing mentioned in the scripture is an oddity to our current thinking: worms. Worms are mentioned over nineteen times in scripture, and they all pertain to worms eating our flesh *in the afterlife!* Three times they are mentioned in the book of Mark in reference to the fact they don't die! *...and be thrown into hell, where their worm does not die* (Mark 9:48; NIV). *The worm should feed sweetly on him* (Job 24:20; KJV)...*the maggot is spread under you and worms cover you* (Isaiah 14:11; NIV). Ehhwww! It is hard for us to imagine such a place, but believe it or not, modern science has found worms that seem to thrive in incredible heat upon the surface of the earth. In the depths of the ocean, where we usually think of deep dark and cold, there are hot volcanic vents that reach temperatures of upwards of seven hundred degrees! In these hot gaseous vents they have found colonies of living creatures, tube worms reaching up to three feet, crabs and other creatures that seem to thrive in these boiling, noxious waters. God can do anything, and if he chose to have worms devour the fallen angels' flesh in hell, then I guess it goes without saying they would devour our flesh as well.

There are other stories of people who have died and come back to life (NDEs, resurrectees) and others who have had open visions who come back and report other creatures in hell. Some have said spiders, worms, scorpions, snakes, and other gigantic hairy ferocious creatures.[269] Fear is a recurring theme for lost souls in hell. It makes sense the creatures we fear now on earth would be a part of eternal torment.

Demons and indescribable creatures are also part of the tortures of hell. *For the dark places of the earth are full of the haunts of cruelty* (Psalm 74:20; NIV). *That day will be darkness, and not light…It will be as though a man fled from a lion only to meet a bear, as though he entered his house and rested his hand on the wall only to have a snake bite him* (Amos 5:18–19; NIV). There are many insinuations in scripture to being ripped, torn, shredded, whipped, broken, beaten, eaten, bitten, and clawed while enduring the mental and spiritual tortures in hell. In his book *23 Minutes in Hell*, Bill Weise describes his experience in hell:

> As I looked at the walls, I saw that they were covered with thousands of hideous creatures. These demonic creatures were all sizes and shapes. Some of them had four legs and were the size of bears. Others stood upright and were about the size of gorillas. They were all terribly grotesque and disfigured. It looked as though their flesh had been decompos-

> ing and all their limbs were twisted and out of proportion. Some displayed immense, long arms or abnormally large feet. They seemed to me to be the living dead. There were also gigantic rats and huge spiders at least three feet wide and two or three feet high. I also saw snakes and worms, ranging from small to enormously large.
>
> The fiendish creatures lined the tunnel walls as well. They were distinctly wicked. Their eyes were cauldrons of evil and death. Everything was filthy, stinking, rotten and foul. There was one other distinguishing aspect about these creatures—they all seemed to possess a hatred for mankind. They were the epitome of evil.[270]

If the torments described so far don't frighten you then the next one should. Fire is another recurring theme, I can't think of a worse fate than to burn alive. Nothing is more painful in life than to have the flesh burned from your bones. The fire that is described in hell is unlike any fire we are aware of on the crust of the earth. Fire here requires oxygen and a combustible material here to burn, and when the material or energy runs out, so does the fire. No, the fire described in hell never goes out. Unlike the Holy Fire of God, which possesses a strange property of non-consumption, as in the burning bush Moses was witness to, this fire does consume and cause physical anguish and pain.

> *Let burning coals fall upon them; let them be cast into the fire, into deep pits, that they rise not up again.* (Psalm 140:10; NIV)

> *He shall be tormented with fire and brimstone.* (Revelation 14:10; NIV)

> *Sodom and Gomorrah… They serve as an example of those who suffer the punishment of eternal fire.* (Jude 7; NIV)

> *They will throw them into the fiery furnace, where there will be weeping and gnashing of teeth.* (Matthew 13:42; NIV)

> *…because I am in agony in this fire.* (Luke 16:24; NIV)

> *On the wicked he will rain fiery coals and burning sulfur; a scorching wind will be their lot.* (Psalm 12:6; NIV)

"Some scientists have reported that the core temperature at the center of the earth is approximately twelve thousand degrees." [271]

Fire is but one level or degree of punishments, as are the pits and cells and the lake of fire. God tells us in his Word there will be degrees of punishments; we are also held accountable for what we know and reject. In the parables Jesus talks in riddles and stories; they are not easy to understand. In fact he outright tells people, "They hear but do not understand." I believe Jesus does this for good reason—mercy. God is a merciful God. Just as he would not allow Lazarus to come back from the dead as a ghost and warn the rich man's brothers—he knew they wouldn't believe him, and this disbelief would add to their punishment, more rejection justice.

God doesn't want one soul to go to hell, and he certainly doesn't want to add to their already harsh sentence. It is a cruel irony so many choose to reject the Word. For this reason there are levels of hell, levels of torment. For those wanting justice for wrongs committed to them or their loved ones, they can rely on God; he will be the ultimate avenger. Nothing goes unseen, nothing unpunished if there is no repentance. The Bible tells us *He will reward each according to his works* (Matthew 16:27; NIV). And in Zechariah: *Just as the Lord of hosts determined to do to us, according to our ways and according to our deeds, so He has dealt with us* (Zechariah 1:6; NIV). And in Matthew: *Therefore you will receive greater condemnation* (Matthew 23:14; NIV). This implies there is a degree of lesser condemnation. We also see a greater condemnation for those who lead children astray. *But if anyone causes one of these little ones who believe in me to sin, it would be better for him to have a large millstone hung around his neck and to be drowned in the depths of the sea* (Matthew 18:6; NIV).

Fire, brimstone, a lake of fire. This lake of fire is where Satan will ultimately end up; it seems to be the worst of the punishments. *And the beast was taken, and with him the false prophet that wrought miracles before him, with which he deceived them that had received the mark of the beast, and them that worshiped his image. These both were cast alive into a lake of fire burning with brimstone* (Revelation 19:20; NIV).

Some will share in the fate of Satan and his evil angels. *And whosoever was not found written in the book of life was cast into the lake of fire* (Revelation 20:15; NIV). A sobering thought.

I love what God writes about the fate of Satan. Satan has an eternity of shame to be paraded in front of men. Whoever he embodies as his final world leader will have no tomb. In other words, he won't get a kingly burial. He will be covered with the dead, he will be trodden underfoot, he will be laughed at and mocked. I think it is safe to say whatever evils he has perpetrated upon man, it will all come full circle with all the power and might of a vengeful, wrathful God.

> But you are brought down to the grave, to the depths of the pit, Those who see you stare at you, they ponder your fate: "Is this the man who shook the earth and made kingdoms tremble, the man who made the world a desert, who

> overthrew its cities and would not let his captives go home?" All the kings of the nations lie in state, each in his own tomb, But you are cast out of your tomb like a rejected branch; you are covered with the slain, with those pierced by the sword, those who descend to the stones of the pit. Like a corpse trampled underfoot, you will join them in burial for you destroyed your land and killed your people. (Isaiah 14:15–21; NIV)

How many people will go to hell? Unfortunately the Bible tells us many will choose to follow Satan to his demise, and only a few will choose life with Jesus. The Word tells us our hearts (minds) are wicked beyond belief. *Enter through the narrow gate. For wide is the gate and broad is the road that leads to destruction, and many enter through it. But small is the gate and narrow the road that leads to life, and only a few find it* (Matthew 7:13; NIV). This verse should put some holy fear and trembling into our hearts. Have you checked your life lately? Following Jesus with all of your heart? Clean? He flat tells us many of us won't make it!

These are but a few of the judgments the Almighty God saw fit to impose upon Satan and his band of fallen angels. He feels very strongly capital punishment for all of eternity is to be inflicted on this evil fallen being who has caused so much loss of life, pain, and strife for mankind, nature and angels, and of course God himself.

Our culture spends far more time contemplating and planning their weekend than they do preparing for their eternities. If I planned on spending 7.5 minutes somewhere, I wouldn't think about it, plan for it, but if I was planning to spend the rest of my eternal life somewhere I would want to know where I was going, what I will be doing, what kind of the things I will encounter, etc.

I hope if you are a believer this gives you some background for a physical hell. If you are one who doesn't believe in the existence of hell, let me ask you a simple question. Are you willing to gamble your very life on your opinion?

> Hell from beneath is excited about you, to meet you at your coming…They all shall speak and say to you: "Have you also become as weak as we?" (Isaiah 14:9–10; NIV)

Chapter Eighteen

HEAVEN

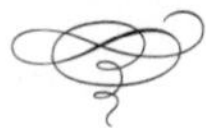

Heaven for believers is a place of eternal rest and communion with God. No more tears, heartache, death, depravity, frustration…no more curse. But yet heaven is one of the most misunderstood places, cloaked in myths, and false presumptions and preconceived notions and traditions, it is little wonder nobody is excited about going there, much less spending an eternity there.

The word *heaven* actually means "the place of everlasting bliss."[272] We know of three heavens in the Bible. Paul refers to the third heaven (2 Corinthians 12:2), which implies a first and second. The three heavens, along with scriptural examples, are:

1. The earth's atmosphere: Genesis 1:20 (where birds fly)
2. The cosmos beyond earth's atmosphere: Genesis 1:14 (where the stars are)
3. The abode of God: Psalm 11:4

Many people believe when you die and go to heaven you get to sit on your own fluffy cloud in the midst of the sky and play a harp all day and night. How boring is that? And who gave us that idea, I wonder…Or, you just go to sleep for all eternity. I like to sleep as much as the next guy, but if that is all there is…no thank you! Many believe heaven is what you create in your own psyche as the happiest time you spent here on earth. I'm sorry, but even my most precious memories would get boring living them over and over again. Some believe you just become this airy, ethereal, spirit substance and do nothing but spiritual stuff all eternity, like sing continual hymns and have nothing but an eternal church service. I am not much of a corporate churchgoer myself; I prefer home Bible studies, so this thought is not very appealing to me. Or, you don't retain your identity, you don't remember anything of this life, and you just get to go float about basking in your lack of earthly desires (because you are now so spiritual), one with the all-universal force. Sorry that is Buddhism, not Christianity! Christians attribute a lot of false presumptions to this place called heaven. Many believe their children, newborns who died and could not accept Jesus, did not go to heaven. Many believe there will be no animals or recognizable physical things in heaven because this would be "sacrilegious and totally unspiritual."

Christians have some really odd, off the wall ideas about our eternal abode, which is to say the least very sad and disturbing. You have to ask yourself, why we don't know more about where we are going, and who is creating all of these false ideas and assumptions, allowing us to believe heaven would be such a boring place we must find an alternative to our eternal choices? We spend so much time researching our next car or computer or cell phone purchase, and we don't spend very much time contemplating or researching where we are going to spend our eternities.

Let's say you just got a permanent job placement in China, and on the way you will have a layover in LAX for two hours. How much time will you spend studying the LAX airport versus life in China? Exactly, none! But historically this is not what we do; we instead spend all of our time studying the airport in which we spend a very short time, and none studying about our future home and destination! This little "trip" we call life is what decides our final destination.

Thankfully for us, we have a "destination brochure" in our hands, and a travel agent who is out of this world! It is called the Holy Bible, and Jesus, and it describes for us our future destination in words beyond belief! The Bible has so much to say about those who choose the way of life, those who accept the payment for their sins, Jesus Christ crucified and resurrected, those blessed few who now get to go be with their savior in heaven forever! The Bible speaks of heaven in terms of compensation. With that statement, I want you to look at your world around you…yes the earth. Does creation not shout with all her might at the wonder and creativity of our God? Is it not beautiful beyond words: the mountains, fertile planes, diverse wildlife, plant life, unique humans, the incredible food, the pure waters, the oceans, the deserts, the sky, the stars? I want you to remember it, because even in its cursed and fallen state this planet we call earth is God's taste! Earth is a shadow or foretaste of heaven. *For God so greatly loved and dearly prized the world that He [even] gave up His only begotten (unique) Son, so that whoever believed in (trusts in, clings to, relies on) Him shall not perish (come to destruction, be lost) but have eternal (everlasting) life* (John 3:16; AMP). God loves this world. As much as it may nauseate some of you, this fantastic world is his creation, and according to his Word he plans on resurrecting this fallen, dead world and bringing his holy city down to it, the New Jerusalem, and dwelling here! This fact alone, the new heavens and the new earth will change our perspective of heaven quite drastically. Would you like to take a tour?

First we need to slay a few false dragons in regards to heaven, and the Bible says it is sharper than a two-edged sword, so I think it will be our weapon of choice for the task at hand. If you have read this entire book, you know Satan has his claws into everything of God's because of his ambitions to be "like God." One day, Satan will be permanently locked away in the lake of fire, so he can no longer deceive the nations. But until that day comes, we need to be aware of his deceptions and heaven is one he continually lies to people about, and mocks the Creator of his Holy Abode.

As I said earlier, we only have two choices for our eternal abode, heaven or hell, but unfortunately many people falsely assume if they are "good" they will go to heaven. We learned earlier, you could be considered morally perfect on this earth and still not make it into heaven. There is only *one way*, and it is believing in Jesus as your savior! All other paths lead to eternal hell and judgment. That being said, let's go slay some sacred cows of tradition.

"Heaven is spiritual, God is spirit, therefore none of the things we would recognize here on earth will be in heaven, no physical body, no houses, no food, no animals, no friends, no family, no spouses, no children,"...yada, yada, yada! Where does it say that in the Bible?

Let's dissect this statement and see where we went wrong according to the scriptures. The Bible actually talks about heaven in physical terms, not just spiritual. Heaven itself is described as "a place." A "place" connotes physicality. If the God of the universe, the universe which is also a "place," describes heaven as a place, I have to take him at his word. You will see from the following text, he did not say ethereal, spiritual, airy, nothingness.

> Do not let your hearts be troubled (distressed, agitated). You believe in and adhere to and trust in and rely on God; believe in and adhere to and trust in and rely also on Me. In My Father's house there are many dwelling places (homes). If it were not so, I would have told you; for I am going away to prepare a place for you. And when I go and make ready a place for you, I will come back again and will take you to Myself, that where I am you may be also. And [to the place] where I am going, you know the way. (John 14:1–4; AMP)

This passage of scripture gives us so much information about heaven and the sheer physicality of it! It is exciting! Heaven is God's dwelling place, besides within us. Since God is omnipresent he is everywhere, but it is obvious he likes to concentrate a certain aspect of himself in a specific place. Jesus describes for us what heaven is like; it has many homes. We all know what a home is. It is a physical structure, a place where we eat, sleep, play, work, worship, have a family, entertain friends, cultivate gardens, raise livestock, house our pets, etc. A home…guess what? God created home life on earth as a model after his home life. Are we not created in his image? We see this reflected in the model of Eden: lavish gardens, abundance of wildlife, abundance of food, companionship, etc. Jesus goes on to say, *If it were not so, I would have told you…for I am going away to prepare a place for you.* This excites me even further. Jesus himself says he is going there personally to prepare a place for me, and he tells us if it were a different way he would have told us himself! Ever wonder why Jesus was a carpenter? I think he really enjoys making houses and furniture for his children! Three times in this passage, Jesus calls heaven a *place.* The Encarta Dictionary defines *place* as an area or portion of space, somebody or something can occupy, it also has locality, a geographic locality, e.g. a town, country, or region, a square or street, and a dwelling. Vine's Expository Dictionary defines *place* in the Greek, "*topos:* refers to 'place' as a heavenly destiny prepared by Jesus for his followers, and to heaven itself."[273] I know this is going to make people mad, and I can just hear them say, "Sacrilegious! A physical place is not spiritual!" But I didn't write the Bible, God did; so take your argument up with him.

You just can't get around the solidity of the word *place.* If heaven is a physical place, then how do we explain leaving our physical bodies on this planet and going and living a physical existence in the next place? Well, thankfully the Bible explains this too. *But our citizenship is in heaven. And we eagerly await a Savior from there, the Lord Jesus Christ, who, by the power that enables him to bring everything under his control, will transform our lowly bodies so that they will be like his glorious body* (Philippians 4:20–21; NIV). Again, we see a physical body we are familiar with (lowly bodies) get to be transformed to a "glorious body." Halleluiah!

1 Corinthians tells us of this mystery of our physical mortal bodies and our spiritual (glorified) bodies. *If there is a natural body, there is also a spiritual body…I declare to you, brothers, that flesh and blood cannot inherit the kingdom of God, nor does the perishable inherit the imperishable. Listen, I tell you a mystery: We will not all sleep, but we will all be changed…For the perishable must clothe itself with imperishable, and the mortal with immortality* (1 Corinthians 15:44–54 NIV).

This is a strange passage, as it attempts to describe to us our mortal bodies can't be in heaven, but they will be changed and clothed with an imperishable, immortal body. Jesus is the fountain of youth, folks. We get to turn in our diseased, disfigured, battered, old, wrinkly, weak bodies for a new body suit! All throughout scripture it is consistent that a spirit likes to be housed. Even God, who is without argument a Spirit, chooses a dwelling place.

What does this glorious body look like and function like? We get a clue from the resurrected body of Christ, *his* glorious body.

Whenever Jesus appeared to his disciples after his resurrection he appeared in human flesh and body form, but with some rather startling and amazing bonus features:

> While they were still talking about this, Jesus himself stood among them and said to them, "Peace be with you." They were startled and frightened, thinking they saw a ghost. He said to them, "Why are you troubled, and why do doubts rise in your minds? Look at my hands and my feet. It is I myself! Touch me and see; a ghost does not have flesh and bones, as you see I have." When he had said this, he showed them his hands and feet. And while they still did not believe it because of joy and amazement, he asked them, "Do you have anything here to eat?" They gave him a piece of broiled fish and he took it and ate it in their presence. (Luke 24:36–43; NIV)

This passage gives us a lot of information about our possible glorious new bodies. First Jesus just appeared…did he walk through a wall? Just materialize? We don't know, but the text seems to suggest an element we are not capable of in our mortal bodies, and his hyper dimensionality. Jesus seems to be operating in hyperspace or all ten or more dimensions. Wouldn't that be cool, to walk through matter? The disciples thought he was ghost, as they mean "spirit" in the context of the text, because they knew Jesus did indeed die, and was buried. This is where he clarifies their doubts, and shows them an aspect of his deity; he read their minds and saw doubt. The Bible talks about only God being able to know the hearts and minds of man. I think this unique feature is only the domain of God, and will not be a feature of our new heavenly bodies. *I the Lord search the heart and examine the mind…* (Jeremiah 17:10; NIV). A spirit doesn't have flesh and bones; he even had them touch him. Obviously his body was quite real to the touch; Jesus also retained the scars of his crucifixion as he showed them his feet and hands. And to make doubly sure he had erased their doubts he was indeed living flesh, he asked for food and ate in their presence.

Our glorious new bodies may have a type of real flesh and bone, display hyper-dimensional capabilities, retain our likeness, retain our memories, and still require food. Author Randy Alcorn talks about the physicality of the human form in heaven in his book, *Heaven.* "God did not create Adam as a spirit and place it inside a body. Rather, he first created a body, *then* breathed into it a spirit. There was never a moment when a human being existed without a body."[274] The added benefit we are told elsewhere is there will be no more disease, sickness, death, sadness, or tears! *He will wipe every tear from their eyes. There will be no more death or mourning or crying or pain, for the old order of things has passed away* (Revelation 21:4; NIV). What an incredibly personal and physical message; *He will wipe every tear from their eyes…*Can you imagine Jesus wiping your tears? In order for him to do this you must have eyes and tear ducts and emotions.

Another clue supporting an actual glorious body is found in the story of the Mount of Transfiguration. Jesus' *face shone like the sun, and his clothes became as white as the light* (Matthew 17:2; NIV). Why would you need clothes if you were but a spirit? His face shone like the sun; Moses had the same countenance when he came off the mountain after receiving the Ten Commandments. Our faces may too reflect the glory of our Lord. Also of note Elijah and Moses were also with Jesus on the Mount, and the disciples recognized them!

How did they do that? I know none of them had ever seen Elijah or Moses since Elijah was taken to heaven many, many centuries before and so Moses had died as well, but yet they recognized them! This means we retain our individual identities and names. What makes you, you? It is not only your physical body, but your mind, emotions, personality, and spirit.

If we have glorified physical bodies, which require clothing, food, rest, and we express emotions, speak, and think, then what will we do in heaven? The idea of an eternal church service is not what the scriptures describe of our holy abode. The sheer idea of worship continually to some people is repulsive. Many God-fearing people are not into singing and worship as we know it from our church services, not to mention this is an area where much dissention among churchgoers breeds discontent and causes churches to split. The argument? We should be singing old hymns versus new contemporary worship songs. Since we know those kinds of sinful, self indulgent ideas won't be in heaven, what will worship look like?

True worship comes from the heart, a heart of sheer adoration and awe. I can honestly tell you, I can't sing a lick, and I do not feel my heart bursting with compulsory worship when I sing in church. I feel the closest in worship and adoration when I view an incredible mountain range backed against a sky emblazoned with golds, purples, reds, and oranges. Or when I see wildlife, or horses gallop and frolic, glorying in their God-given strength and beauty, this is when I feel my limbs and voice moved to giving God ultimate heartfelt glory and praise. Will we not experience those things so much more in heaven, and our worship come from a place of such utter compulsion and sheer joy, worship is no longer a dreaded thirty- to forty-five-minute chore in church on Sunday but a continual bursting forth of grateful emotion? Ever tasted a meal so good you can't wait for the next bite? Do you not say with loaded mouth, to the cook "this is wonderful"? Do you not groan and make a weird expression of "yummmm," while your mouth is full? This will be our compulsory praise in heaven; it will be as natural as breathing here on earth.

Heaven is referred to in terms of a city and a country. *Instead, they were longing for a better country—a heavenly one. Therefore God is not ashamed to be called their God, for he has prepared a city for them* (Hebrews 11:16; NIV). If we are going to have houses built for us, then we would need a heavenly address. The very idea of such "worldly" civics such as cities or a country is abhorrent to many people's "spiritual" idea of heaven. But the scriptures give us such incredible detail about our future country and city, they defy imagination. Jesus even goes so far as to give us the exact measurements of this new city, and indeed it is huge!

> And he carried me away in the Spirit to a mountain great and high, and showed the Holy City, Jerusalem, coming down out of heaven from God. It shone with glory of God, and its brilliance was like that of very precious jewel, like a jasper, clear as crystal. It had a great, high wall with twelve gates, and with twelve angels at the gates. On the gate were written the names of the twelve tribes of Israel. (Revelation 21:10; NIV)

The chapter goes on to describe the Holy City: It was a cube twelve thousand stadia in length, width, and height. The wall was 144 cubits thick, it was made of jasper, the city street of purest transparent gold. The foundations were decorated with every precious jewel and stone: jasper, sapphire, chalcedony, emerald, sardonyx, carnelian, chrysolite, beryl, topaz, chrysoprase, jacinth, and amethyst. Each of the twelve gates was made of a single pearl.

There is a lot of controversy over the book of Revelation being a purely symbolic book, and if this is what you believe that's okay. I just happen to believe there are too many extremely specific qualities and measurements for everything to be just symbolic. Take for instance the argument over the actual size of the New Jerusalem. In our current measurements, twelve thousand stadia equals roughly fourteen hundred miles high, wide, and deep. That means the city would take up three-quarters of the United States. Proponents of the symbolic interpretation say this city would be too heavy for the crust of the earth and would violate our current atmosphere. I think they are missing a huge piece to the puzzle and they are not taking into consideration this gigantic cubed city is beyond our known dimensions. Factor in at least six more dimensions according to quantum physics and it works. Not to mention, we are talking about God here! Did you forget God's argument with Job in Job 38:4–5? Where were you when I laid the foundations of the earth? Or hung the earth on nothing? Kinda puts our silly arguments into perspective.

Christians have a tradition that Peter will meet them at the pearly gates of heaven, and look at the Lamb's book of life and open the door for them. But scripture specifically states there are *twelve* pearly gates, each one named after a disciple and the gates are always open. So this is false tradition. As we went over before with the story of Lazarus and the rich man, most likely one of the first people we will see will be our model father Abraham, since we will reside in "his bosom," and hopefully make our way to the throne of God.

The next noted feature of this city is its river, The River of Life, and Tree of Life:

> Then the angel showed me the river of the water of life, as clear as crystal, flowing from the throne of God and of the Lamb down the middle of the great street of the city. On each side of the river stood the tree of life, bearing twelve crops of fruit, yielding its fruit every month. And the leaves of the tree are for the healing of the nations. No longer will there be any curse. The throne of God and the Lamb will be in the city, and his servants will serve him. They will see his face, and his name will be on their foreheads. (Revelation 22:1–4; NIV)

A river of water flowing from the throne of God to where? Down the middle of the street, and presumably out of the city, forming other streams, lakes, ponds, etc. On each side of the river was the Tree of Life, each side, and it says tree as singular, which is interesting. The tree does produce fruit every month. Fruit is for eating, and the next line is the leaves are for the healing of nations. This is an interesting term, because we have the idea all will be completely healed in heaven. This may be a grace issue for those who accepted Jesus on this earth, but did not live the best life possible for Jesus. Maybe these individuals will need to work on their inner healing as the eons pass. The Bible is unclear on this area, and it is a mystery we will know when we get there.

Again, we see the solidity of heaven and the New Jerusalem. Notice the next verse; we will serve Him, *his servants will serve him.* To serve suggests the idea of work. Certainly we will have rest and reward, but we will also work. Work was created by God. Adam and Eve both had jobs in the Garden of Eden. The work in heaven will not be dull and tedious, unfulfilling, ambition driven, a daily drone and grind, working for cursed dollars, just to make ends meet. Instead our work will be exciting, fulfilling, helpful, service oriented, exploratory. I can just imagine what work I will be doing in heaven. I can't wait for the job title and the promotion.

The Bible says we will be given robes of righteousness, crowns of glory, and positions of authority, according to our works here on earth. The Bible also describes our tithes and offerings are kept in detailed accounts in heaven and we are storing our treasure up there. So this means we may have some system of markets, goods, and services, otherwise why the storing of wealth? The Bible also says *that the kings of the earth will bring their splendor into it* (Revelation 21:24; NIV). This verse alone describes a hierarchy. And they will bring their tithes and offerings to the throne of God. Over and over again we see the original model of earth before the corruption of sin and the curse of death on mankind was a model of the original heaven. We see written in Revelation and Isaiah themes of nations, rulers, civilizations, and cultures. This original heaven will still be our new earth's model of government rulership by God and Jesus, followed by a hierarchy of human kings and subjects. It will be godly business as usual.

R. Alcorn writes in his book *Heaven*; "We're told there are scrolls in Heaven, elders who have faces, martyrs who wear clothes, and even people with 'palm branches in there hands' (Revelation 7:9). There are musical instruments in the intermediate Heaven (Revelation 8:6), horses coming into and out of Heaven (2 Kings 2:1; Revelation 19:14), and an eagle flying overhead in Heaven (Revelation 8:13). Perhaps some of these objects are merely symbolic with no corresponding physical reality. But is that true of all of them?"[275]

We are taught there will be no humans given in marriage, or the concept of husband and wife in heaven. *At the resurrection people will neither marry nor be given in marriage; they will be like the angels in heaven* (Matthew 22:30; NIV). This is a difficult statement because I cannot imagine myself not being married to my husband in heaven.

But if you read the statement carefully, it doesn't say in heaven, it says at the resurrection! This means not until after the new heavens and the new earth! So I could be wrong, you have to judge for yourself, but I believe we will still be married in the sense of relationship with our spouses in heaven. But our ultimate goal will not be to be married to people, but to Jesus! Jesus, all throughout scripture portrays himself as the bridegroom and his church (people) are his bride. This is why the heresy of Jesus being married on earth to Mary Magdalene is such a lie! Jesus could not or would not marry on earth; he was keeping himself pure for his bride the church! This is an area which is difficult to understand and Satan has his lies and deceptions marring up the surface. This may be why angels do not marry either; they too are part of the church, and may be a portion of the bride. This may explain the horrible punishment the fallen angels will endure for "coming unto the daughters of men, and taking them as their bride" (see Genesis 6).

Are there animals in heaven? I was always taught animals have no soul, and therefore are not candidates for heaven. However, this did not sit well with me, since I am one of those crazy horse and dog people. I love animals. I always wanted to be a vet, but God had another path chosen for me. Growing up in remote and rural Montana, human friends were always a long ways away and I spent most of my day with my pets and horses. I have had every critter as a pet or under my care at one point or other in my life, from domestic to wild, and I have had the unique experience of seeing the unconditional love of God, glimpsed in their eyes.

What kid has not asked where their beloved pet has gone after they have passed? Even wise King Solomon asked the same question in Ecclesiastes: *As for men, God tests them so that they may see that they are like the animals. Man's fate is like that of the animals; the same fate awaits them both: As one dies, so dies the other. All have the same breath;*

man has no advantage over the animal...Who knows if the spirit of man rises upward and if the spirit of the animal goes down into the earth? (Ecclesiastes 3:18–21; NIV).

Does the Bible address animals in heaven? Yahoo! It does! For those of you who find this repulsive, it's okay; let me show you some scriptures that may shock you. *Delight yourself also in the Lord, and he will give you the desires and secret petitions of your heart* (Psalm 37:4; NIV). Well, you say, "This scripture doesn't say anything about animals." Maybe it doesn't for your heart, but mine screams please let me have my beloved horse back when I get to heaven! It has been a secret petition of mine since the day he died, and I hope to be riding this great steed in the battle of Armageddon. Many people forget God created all the diverse wildlife and domestic animals for our and his pleasure. If the God of the universe delights in his creation, would it not go against his nature to do away with animals in heaven?

God uses animals as similes all throughout scripture, even going so far as calling Jesus the Lamb of God. Romans 8:19–23 describes the suffering all creatures must endure until the coming of our Lord and the renewal of all things. Isaiah speaks of a time in God's eternal kingdom when animals will no longer hunt and eat each other, or harm humans. *The wolf will live with the lamb, the leopard will lie down with the goat, the calf and the lion and the yearling together; and a little child will lead them. The cow will feed with the bear, their young will lie down together, and the lion will eat straw like the ox. The infant will play near the hole of the cobra, and the young child put his hand into the viper's nest. They will neither harm nor destroy on all my holy mountain* (Isaiah 11:6–9; NIV). Many scholars say this will be on the new earth only, but is it? Is not heaven the original model for the earth? God even created animals before humans. He made them lower than us, and he gave us authority over them, and don't get me wrong, they were not made in the likeness and image of God as we were.

If animals were not important to God, why would he be the first to slay animals and shed innocent blood for the covering of sin? (see Genesis 3). Innocent animals were good enough to atone for sin for thousands of years before Christ became the ultimate, perfect sacrificial Lamb. Contrary to popular thought, God did not delight in the sacrificial system of the Old Testament. He found it abhorrent. But it was the only way for us humans to understand the gravity of our sins, an innocent creation had to die and shed its blood for our evil and sinful nature. If you had to slay your favorite pet lamb, that cute cuddly doe-eyed lamb, to atone for lying and gossiping at work, would you be so careless with your words next time? It would bring home the message strongly that sin is ugly, deadly, and costly.

If animals were not important to God, why did he save only eight humans and two of every kind of beast on earth from the wrath of his judgment flood? After the flood he made a covenant to *all* living creatures of every kind on the earth…with the covenantal sign of the rainbow. R. Alcorn points out the repeated emphasis on animals in those verses.[276] *"I now establish my covenant with you and with your descendants after you and with every living creature that was with you—the birds, the livestock and all the wild animals, all those that came out of the ark with you—every living creature on earth. I establish my covenant with you: Never again will all life be cut off by the waters of a flood; never again will there be a flood to destroy the earth"* (Genesis 9:9–11; NIV). God not only established a covenant with man, but also with animals!

For every animal of the forest is mine, and the cattle on a thousand hills. I know every bird in the mountains, and the creatures of the field are mine (Psalm 50:10–11; NIV). All animals are owned by God; we are only the caretakers. We are told everything that has breath will praise the Lord.

Praise the Lord from the earth, you great sea creatures and all ocean depths...wild animals and all cattle, small creatures and flying birds... Let them praise the name of the Lord, for his name alone is exalted; his splendor is above the earth and the heavens (Psalm 148:7,10,13; NIV). Even from the earth, animals evidently praise God their creator.

Then I heard every creature in heaven on earth under the earth and on the sea, and all this is in them, singing: "To him who sits on the throne and to the Lamb be praise and honor and glory and power for ever and ever!" (Revelation 5:13; NIV). Did you catch that? Every creature *in heaven*! Is this "living creatures" like the cherubim, or animals? The same word "creature" is used of all of God's created animals in the scriptures. If you think this is bizarre, wait until you hear what author Randy Alcorn has to say:

> The most striking example of animals praising God in Heaven is often overlooked because of word selection in our Bible translations. We're told eight times in Revelation of "living creatures" in the intermediate Heaven: Day and night they never stop saying: "'Holy, holy, holy is the Lord God Almighty, who was and is and is to come'...The living creatures give glory, honor and thanks to him who sits on the throne" (Revelation 4:8–9). The word translated "living creatures" is *zoon*. Throughout most of the New Testament the word is translated "animal" and is used to indicate animals sacrificed in the Temple and wild, irrational animals (Hebrews 13:11: 2 Peter 2:12; Jude 1:10). In the Old Testament, the Septuagint used *zoon* to translate the Hebrew words for animals including the "living creatures"

> of the sea (Genesis 1:21: Ezekiel 47:9)…In virtually every case inside and outside of Scripture, this word means not a person, not an angel, but an *animal*…Somehow we have failed to grasp that the "living creatures who cry out Holy, holy, holy" are animals—living breathing intelligent and articulate animals who dwell in God's presence, worshiping and praising him.[277]

Of course we know these living creatures are the cherubim and seraphim, but nonetheless, they are called "creatures."

Boy, that will cook your noodle, won't it? We have to remember people sinned, animals didn't. Another interesting word study to do regarding animals is the word *nephesh.*

> When God breathed a spirit into Adam's body, made from the earth, Adam became *nephesh*, a living being or soul (Genesis 2:7). Remarkably, the same Hebrew word, *nephesh*, is used for animals and for people. We are specifically told that not only people, but animals have the "breath of life" in them (Genesis 1:30, 2:7, 6:17, 7:15, 22). Am I suggesting that animals have souls? Certainly they do not have human souls. Animals aren't created in God's image, and they aren't equal to humans in any sense. Nonetheless there is a strong biblical case for animals having non-human souls. I didn't take this seriously until I studied the usage of the Hebrew and Greek words *nephesh* and *psyche*, often translated "soul" when referring to humans. (*Nephesh* is translated *psyche* in the Septuagint.) The fact that these words are often used of animals is compelling evidence that they have non-human souls.[278]

All throughout scripture we see the horses of heaven. Many scholars point out in the language of the prophets they were only describing modes of transportation they had no way of describing in their pre-technological language. If this were the case then why didn't they say "like a horse, or like a chariot"? No, they used the word horse. *The armies of heaven were following him, riding on white horses and dressed in fine linen, white and clean* (Revelation 19:14; NIV).

Also remember King Nebuchadnezzar who acted like an ox for seven years? God specifically told us he gave him the mind of an animal. *"Let him be drenched with the dew of heaven, and let him live with the animals amongst the plants of the earth. Let his mind be changed from that of a man and let him be given the mind of an animal, till seven times pass by for him…"* (Daniel 4:15–16; NIV). Could this be what separates us from animals; their simple God created mind, versus our complex mind, instead of the idea of a soul-less creature?

The fact is we are just like Solomon; we don't know whether animals souls go to heaven or not, but the Bible gives us some pretty interesting and compelling verses for us to chew on, and I for one, can't wait to get up there and find out what creatures live and worship our God.

What about children? I am also one of those wild, wacky people that think heaven is full of the lost souls of children. When you ponder the sheer numbers of children, babies, and fetuses which have left this earth due to the curse brought on by Satan (disease, trauma, war, famine, abortion), you can't help but believe these children have found their true home in heaven.

Many people, especially parents, direct their anger and fury toward the Almighty when they lose a child. Who do you think is behind this misplaced anger? These parents lose their faith and are overwrought with grief and guilt, and wonder whether their innocent child is in the arms of God. Satan always lies about the abode of God and his children; he doesn't want people to know just how good and faithful God is. It goes against his goals of being worshiped like God. So what does the Bible have to say about it?

Suffer the little children to come unto me…for of such is the kingdom of God. Verily I say unto you, Whosoever shall not receive the kingdom of God as a little child, he shall not enter therein (Mark 10:14–15; KJV). The word *kingdom* here means the "realm of God."[279] Jesus is talking about heaven here. Are children born in sin? Yes, the Bible is very clear all mankind is tainted with sin, but children seem to receive a special escape clause for a short period; it is called the age of accountability. Just as we have laws not trying children as adults, so does the Almighty. We see this in 1 Samuel: *Now Samuel did not yet know the Lord; The word of the Lord had not yet been revealed to him* (1 Samuel 3:7; NIV). In this passage the boy Samuel was living with the priest Eli, and God called to Samuel in the middle of the night. Samuel thought it was Eli calling him. So in this passage, God decides the age at which he reveals himself to children. I think it would be very hard to attach a generic age of accountability to children as each is in such unique circumstances and each child matures at differing rates. We must remember God is a good God and merciful. Even fetuses can be filled with the Holy Spirit as we saw with John the Baptist. *…he shall be filled with the Holy Ghost even from his mother's womb* (Luke 1:15; NIV), and: *As soon as the sound of your greeting reached my ears, the baby in my womb leaped for joy* (Luke 1:44; NIV).

We can only assume these children grow up in heaven being taught the principles of God in a perfect environment.

The Bible also tells us we will be reunited with relations, this includes lost children and loved ones, and we will also retain our nationalities and language. *After this I looked and there before me was a great multitude that no one could count, from every nation, tribe, people and language, standing before the throne and in front of the Lamb. They were wearing white robes and were holding palm branches in their hands* (Revelation 7:9; NIV).

It will be a fascinating day to see all people from every culture, every color of skin, every era of time, gathered to praise God.

We have to remember this short life span is literally *a placement exam for eternity*. We have a manufacturer's error wired into our DNA called sin, due to the curse and Intelligent Deception. God has a quality control problem on his hands; we are seconds, not worthy of the high standards God himself requires in his pure holy nature. This is where Jesus comes in; Jesus inspects each and every one of us, he examines our hearts, the source of the problem, and he asks each one of us if we would like to be made pure and perfect without blemish, and to live in and inherit a kingdom beyond our understanding. In order for us to be made whole, we have to ask the master to come into our hearts and fix our quality control problem. Because of our free will we often forget we do not belong to ourselves, we were purchased with a price, we were made by a creator to whom we owe our very existence. God uses our life to determine if we are fit for use in his kingdom. Life on earth is just the factory floor. We have true eternal life to look forward to, our real vocations, our real home, in eternity with Jesus.

Hope to see you there!

> *No eye has seen, no ear has heard, no mind has conceived what God has prepared for those who love him.* (1 Corinthians 2:9; NIV)

EPILOGUE

A summary of this much information is a hard concept, even for me. Satan's strategies continually morph with what society allows as acceptable behavior, and he takes full advantage of our ignorance of the Word. Suffice it to say the best way to go about this battle is to realize and come to terms with the fact we are indeed in a *continual unseen battle*, fighting superior beings with superior knowledge.

After my first encounter, I thoroughly thought my "demons coming out of the closet experience" was over, and I would never have such experiences again. Instead, I have found the battle progressive, and the fight going into areas, and into such depths, as I could never have imagined.

I think for many Christians out there, understanding we have indeed been called to fight is half the battle. The other half is preparation and knowledge on your part, and the other factor is realizing who you are in Christ. Without this knowledge, you leave yourself open for fear, anxiety, and poor morale; all are crippling to any good foot soldier.

The other aspect of any good military strategy is to realize what your particular rank is. Are you called to leadership? Are you a spy, gathering intel? Are you a weapons specialist (i.e. operate in many giftings of the Holy Spirit)? Are you the guy that sounds the battle cry, or stands in the gap in prayer and supplication for reinforcements to the troops? Identify your calling, and do it.

Many make the mistake of charging into battle with the enemy unprepared, or trying to take ground God did not call you to take (e.g., walking into a coven meeting and preaching to practicing witches; this is suicide unless you have been specifically called to do so).

All battles are being fought for spiritual ground—souls. It could be yours or someone else's. Battles are fought from full attacks to retreats. And many Christians need to learn how to take stock and reload (refresh), learn new strategies, or call in reinforcements. We are always engaging in battle whether we realize it or not. Many of my most memorable battles have been in a dream state, when I am confronted by a demon and use a spiritual gift such as tongues or even just the name of Jesus to confront and command submission from the entity.

The other most important strategy we must literally engrain and tattoo on our conscious minds is to *TEST THE SPIRITS!* Both good and bad, this is where we fail miserably. The test is easy; ask the entity whether Holy Spirit or evil spirit to identify itself, and what and whom it serves, and if Jesus died on the cross for our sins and rose on the third day. It's a simple pass or fail test, and you will always know what you are dealing with. Remember we are dealing with deceiving spirits, especially elevated to new heights of lies, ruses, frauds, and trickery. If they choose to appear as your loving deceased Aunt Dora, or a beautiful, benevolent, light-bearing alien creature, or a prankster spirit playing a practical joke, just ask them to take the test; Jesus bought this privilege for us at the cross.

Even though we are battling in the spiritual unseen realm, many of our battles will have a physical manifestation. Satan uses the weakness of the human vessel to tackle our defenses. In other words, he will use other humans to hurt us, with words or deeds, eliciting a physical retaliation on your part. He wins this one every time. We cannot fight a spiritual being with our physical bodies, we are simply too weak. Instead we need to learn how to fight with the spirit and the tools and gifts God has provided us: his Word, Holy Spirit gifts, love, forgiveness, etc. Remember demonic spirits need to be fed and cared for, and they thrive on sin and rebelliousness from you. They count on your verbal retaliation to your enemy, or your undermining of a coworker who has hurt you; the ways are countless. Instead the word tells us to speak well of our enemies and forgive those who needlessly use and abuse us. This is deadly poison or an exploding grenade to a demonic spirit bent on your destruction.

Also remember God's holiness. It is another area of misunderstanding and contention. We have been lied to by the popular media and cowardice teachings of certain religions. God is supremely holy! Nothing unholy can touch or defile him. This area of understanding is of utmost importance to us, because without it, we would not be able to understand why the enemy works so hard at filthiness and defilement and degradation of the requirements of the purity and holiness of God. Many people believe God is all-forgiving and will allow "small sins" to go unpunished; this is a lie straight from the father of liars, Satan. All sin, whether a small white lie or stealing pencils at work to gossiping about people, are sins. Your "good deeds" are not good enough to allow you to go heaven. God cannot stand sin, which is why he gave us Jesus.

Holiness and purity are difficult concepts to understand in our current society. We often forget to stay within this sterile field; we are deceived and led astray, and walk away from holiness and purity, and we again become contaminated Christians. God cannot tolerate this contamination. We have to again repent and be made clean, and keep ourselves holy and pure, and free of this contamination. Satan's job is to contaminate us and make us unclean; our job is to stay within the bounds of the sterile field, and when we fail, recognize it and ask for another autoclave job! Stay within the purity field! *Do not defile yourself with detestable practices!*

Finally, understanding your enemy and how he operates with a devious, cunning intent will help you to avoid the many pitfalls and snares he has set up for the ignorant Christian. Now you will be able to walk the minefield with confidence and assurance with each step you will not fall a victim or a prey of the enemy. KNOW THINE ENEMY! Do not be intelligently deceived!

NOTES

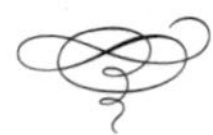

1. *Amplified Version of The Holy Bible,* (Michigan: Zondervan, 1987).
2. King James Version Gift & Award Bible, Revised (Michigan, Zondervan, 2002).
3. *The Life Application Bible, New International Version* (Wheaton: Tyndale House Publishers & Michigan: Zondervan Publishing House, 1991).
4. W.E. Vine, *Vine's Concise Dictionary of the Bible* (Tennesse: Thomas Nelson Publishers, 2005"earnestly" (*spoudios*) 108
5. *Rose Book of Charts, Maps, and Time Lines* (California: Rose Publishing, 2005), 54-56.
6. W.E. Vine, *Vine's Concise Dictionary of the Bible* (Tennessee: Thomas Nelson Publishers, 2005), 12, Anointed one-*mashiach* (4899), 167, Guardian-*epitropos*-2012, 52, Cherub-*cheroubim*-3742.
7. David E. Flynn, *The Stones of Fire & Pre-adamite Civilization,* David Flynn, http://www.mt.net/~watcher/stones.html
8. W.E. Vine, *Vine's Concise Dictionary of the Bible* (Tennessee: Thomas Nelson Publishers, 2005), 02 violence-*chamas*-2555
9. ibid., 174, heart-*leb*-3820.

10. "**Lucifer**." *Encyclopædia Britannica.* 2009. Encyclopædia Britannica Online. 17 Feb. 2009 <http://www.britannica.com/EBchecked/topic/350594/Lucifer>.
11. Rabbi Nosson Scherman, *The Chumash, Bereishis/Genesis* (New York: Mesorah Publications, ltd., 1995).
12. W.E. Vine, *Vine's Concise Dictionary of the Bible* (Tennesse: Thomas Nelson Publishers, 2005), 103, Dragon-*drakon* 1404.
13. Philip D. Morehead, *The New American Webster Handy College Dictionary* (New York: Penguin Books, 1995), 212-Drag.
14. W.E. Vine, *Vine's Concise Dictionary of the Bible* (Tennesse: Thomas Nelson Publishers, 2005), 333, seducing-*planao*-4105 and 85, deceiver-*planos*-4108.
15. Dr. Ed Murphy, *The Handbook for Spiritual Warfare* (Tennesse: Thomas Nelson Publishers, 2003), 30.
16. James Strong, LL.D., S.T.D., *The New Strong's Exhaustive Concordance of the Bible* (Tennesse: Thomas Nelson Publishers, 1990), Hedge-7753.
17. Faustus Scorpius, Inspiration of the Daimon Samyaza, The Covenant of Samyaza, Copyright 1991, Graeme Wilson, www.necronomi.com/magic/satanism/samyaza.txt.
18. *Encarta Dictionary*, Word Program-insight.
19. Chris Ward, D. Min., The Origin of Demons, Chris Ward, http://www.logoschristian.org.
20. W.E. Vine, *Vine's Concise Dictionary of the Bible* (Tennesse: Thomas Nelson Publishers, 2005), 74. Crafty-panourgia-3834, dolos-1388.
21. Libronix Digital Library System, Logos Software 3, *Harpers Bible Dictionary*, 245.

22. W.E. Vine, *Vine's Concise Dictionary of the Bible* (Tennesse: Thomas Nelson Publishers, 2005), 250, Naked-*'erwah*-6172.
23. Charles Frances Hunter as told by Roland Buck, *Angels on Assignment* (Pennsylvania: Whitaker House, 1979), 44-45.
24. James Strong, LL.D., S.T.D., *The New Strong's Exhaustive Concordance of the Bible* (Tennessee: Thomas Nelson Publishers, 1990), Hebrew and Greek, G5459, H5397,H784
25. Charles & Annette Capps, *Angels, Knowing Their Purpose, Releasing Their Power* (Oklahoma,Harrison House, 1994), 134.
26. W.E. Vine, *Vine's Concise Dictionary of the Bible* (Tennesse: Thomas Nelson Publishers, 2005), 239, Mighty-*geburah*-1369, *ischus*-2479.
27. ibid., 16, Archangel-*archangelos*-743.
28. Richard Laurence, LL.D. Archbishop of Cashel, *The Book of Enoch the Prophet* (Oklahoma, Artisan Publishers, 1980), Enoch 20:1-7.
29. Chris Ward, Angelic Ranking, Chris Ward, http://www.logoschristian.org/thrones/.
30. Matthew Bunson, *Angels A to Z* (New York: Three Rivers Press, Random House,, 1996), 262-4, Seraphim.
31. James Strong, LL.D., S.T.D., *The New Strong's Exhaustive Concordance of the Bible* (Tennessee: Thomas Nelson Publishers, 1990), Eyes-3788.
32. Moses Maimonides, *Guide for the Perplexed*, Friedländer tr. [1904], www.sacred-texts.com.
33. W.E. Vine, *Vine's Concise Dictionary of the Bible* (Tennesse: Thomas Nelson Publishers, 2005), 52, Cherub-*cheroubim* -3742.

34. James Strong, LL.D., S.T.D., *The New Strong's Exhaustive Concordance of the Bible* (Tennessee: Thomas Nelson Publishers, 1990), Beasts-*Zoon*-2226.
35. *New International Version* (Michigan: Tyndale House Publishers and Zondervan Publishing House, 1988), 2307, Commentary on living creatures.
36. Stephen D. Renn (Editor), *Expository Dictionary of Bible Words* (Massachusetts: Hendrickson Publishers, 2005), Wheel- 'ophan-212.
37. Matthew Bunson, *Angels A to Z* (New York: Three Rivers Press, Random House, 1996), *Ophanim*, 203-4, *Galgal*, 116.
38. Stephen D. Renn (Editor), *Expository Dictionary of Bible Words* (Massachusetts: Hendrickson Publishers, 2005), 837, Principality/Rule-*mashal-4910.*
39. James Strong, LL.D., S.T.D., *The New Strong's Exhaustive Concordance of the Bible* (Tennessee: Thomas Nelson Publishers, 1990), Chief- *arche*-746-747.
40. ibid., Fall- na phal-5307.
41. Chuck Missler, Mark Eastman, *Alien Encounters* (Idaho: Koinonia House, 2003), 363.
42. William Whiston, A.M. (Translator), *Josephus, The Complete Works* (Tennessee: Thomas Nelson Publishers, 1998), 1.3.73.
43. Richard Laurence, LL.D. Archbishop of Cashel, *The Book of Enoch the Prophet* (Oklahoma: Artisan Publishers, 1980), Enoch 7.
44. ibid., Enoch 8.
45. Faustus Scorpius, Inspiration of the Daimon Samyaza, The Covenant of Samyaza, Copyright 1991, Graeme Wilson, www.necronomi.com/magic/satanism/samyaza.txt.
46. Ref. Steve Quayle, BUFO Paranormal & UFO Radios, 2003, http://www.burlingtonnews.net/redhairedmummiesunitedstates.html.

47. Stephen Quayle, *Genesis 6 Giants, The Master Builders of the Prehistoric and Ancient Civilizations* (Montana: End Time Thunder Publishers, 2005), Inside Cover.
48. ibid., 384.
49. ibid., 59.
50. Chuck Missler, Mark Eastman, *Alien Encounters* (Idaho: Koinonia House, 2003), 240.
51. ibid.
52. ibid., 241-2.
53. Richard Laurence, LL.D. Archbishop of Cashel, *The Book of Enoch the Prophet* (Oklahoma: Artisan Publishers, 1980), Enoch 15.
54. Rev. George H. Schodde, Ph.D., *The Book of Jubilees* (Oklahoma: Artisan Publishers, 1980), 10:1-5.
55. Faustus Scorpius, Inspiration of the Daimon Samyaza, The Covenant of Samyaza, Copyright 1991, Graeme Wilson, www.necronomi.com/magic/satanism/samyaza.txt.
56. Stephen Quayle, *Genesis 6 Giants* (Montana: End Time Publishers, 2005), 215.
57. ibid., 145.
58. Rabbi Nosson Scherman, *The Chumash, Bereishis/ Genesis* (New York: Mesorah Publications, 1995), 43-44, Commentary.
59. ibid.
60. ibid.
61. Chuck Missler, Mark Eastman, *Alien Encounters* (Idaho: Koinonia House, 2003), 284.
62. ibid.
63. Paul S. Taylor of Eden Communications, Where did Easter get its Name?, Christian Answers Network, http://www.christiananswers.net/q-eden/edn-t020.html.

64. Wikipedia, Constantine I, http://en.wikipedia.org/w/index.php?title=Constantine_I&printable=yes
65. Paul S. Taylor of Eden Communications, Where did Easter get its Name?, Christian Answers Network, http://www.christiananswers.net/q-eden/edn-t020.html.
66. Royce Carlson, The Pagan Origins of Easter, Zenzibar-Royce Carlson, http://www.zenzibar.com/Articles/easter.asp.
67. Jerry Wilson, The Easter Page, Jerry Wilson, http://wilstar.com/holidays/easter.htm.
68. Royce Carlson, The Pagan Origins of Easter, Zenzibar-Royce Carlson, http://www.zenzibar.com/Articles/easter.asp.
69. Fredrick A. Larsen, The Starry Dance, The Star Project, http://bethlehemstar.net/dance/dance.htm.
70. Wikipedia, Halloween, http://en.wikipedia.org/wiki/Halloween.
71. Faustus Scorpius, Inspiration of the Daimon Samyaza, The Covenant of Samyaza, Copyright 1991, Graeme Wilson, www.necronomi.com/magic/satanism/samyaza.txt.
72. Wikipedia, Superstring-Theory, http://en.wikipedia.org/wiki/Superstring_theory.
73. Rebecca Brown MD, *Prepare for War* (Arizona: Whitaker House, 1987), 108.
74. Chuck D. Pierce and Rebecca Wagner Sytsema, *Protecting Your Home From Spiritual Darkness* (California: Regal Books, 2004), 20.
75. James Strong, LL.D., S.T.D., *The New Strong's Exhaustive Concordance of the Bible* (Tennessee: Thomas Nelson Publishers, 1990), 20, Greek 1139 *daimonizomai.*
76. ibid., 126, 7069 *qanah.*
77. Dr. Chuck Missler, *Learn The Bible in 24 Hours* (Tennessee: Thomas Nelson Publishers, 2002), 84.

78. ibid., 83-4.
79. Dr. Caroline Leaf, *Who Switched Off My Brain?* (Switch on Your Brain Publishing, 2007), 124.
80. James Strong, LL.D., S.T.D., *The New Strong's Exhaustive Concordance of the Bible* (Tennessee: Thomas Nelson Publishers, 1990), 46, Greek *katadunasteuo.*
81. Stephen D. Renn (Editor), *Expository Dictionary of Bible Words* (Massachusetts: Hendrickson Publishers, 2005), 370-1, fear- yare'-3372.
82. ibid., 705, Overcome- gud-1464.
83. Philip D. Morehead, *The New American Webster Handy College Dictionary,* (New York: Penguin Books, 1995), 483.
84. Henry W. Wright, *A More Excellent Way* (Pleasant Valley Publications, 2005), 18.
85. Rebecca Brown MD, *He Came to Set the Captives Free* (Arizona: Whitaker House, 1986), 161.
86. Rebecca Brown MD, *Prepare for War* (Arizona: Whitaker House, 1987), 139.
87. Mary K. Baxter or Dr. T.L. Lowery, *A Divine Revelation of Heaven* (Pennsylvania: Whitaker House, 1998), 86.
88. *101 Scientific Facts & Foreknowledge*, Eternal Productions, www.eternal-productions.org * 1-877-370-7770.
89. James Strong, LL.D., S.T.D., *The New Strong's Exhaustive Concordance of the Bible* (Tennessee: Thomas Nelson Publishers, 1990), G2380, thuo, A primary verb; properly to *rush* (*breathe* hard, *blow*, *smoke*), that is, (by implication) to *sacrifice* (properly by fire, but generally); by extension to *immolate* (*slaughter* for any purpose): -kill , (do) sacrifice, slay.
90. Paul Scanlon, *If God Doesn't Have Your Thinking, He Doesn't Have You,* Abundant Life Ministries, http://www.alm.org.uk/media/articles/paul/index.php.

91. Henry W. Wright, *A More Excellent Way* (Pleasant Valley Publications, 2005), 145.
92. Henry W. Wright, *A More Excellent Way* (Pleasant Valley Publications, 2005), 145.
93. Dr. Caroline Leaf, *Who Switched Off My Brain?* (Switch on Your Brain Publishing, 2007), 108.
94. Henry W. Wright, *A More Excellent Way* (Pleasant Valley Publications, 2005), 145-6.
95. ibid., 145.
96. Francis S. Collins, *The Language of God* (New York: Free Press, A Division of Simon and Schuster, 2006), 18.
97. Wikipedia, DNA, http://en.wikipedia.org/wiki/DNA.
98. Henry W. Wright, *A More Excellent Way* (Pleasant Valley Publications, 2005), 244-5.
99. ibid., 243.
100. National Institute of Drug Abuse, Methamphetamine Addiction: Cause for Concern, Hope for the Future, 2007, http://www.nida.nih.gov/pdf/tib/meth.pdf.
101. Henry W. Wright, *A More Excellent Way* (Pleasant Valley Publications, 2005), 180.
102. Wikipedia, Virus, http://en.wikipedia.org/wiki/virus.
103. ibid., virus.
104. Wikipedia, Antiobiotics, http://en.wikipedia.org/wiki/Antibiotics.
105. Wikipedia, Black Death, http://en.wikipedia.org/wiki/Black_Death.
106. James Strong, LL.D., S.T.D., *The New Strong's Exhaustive Concordance of the Bible* (Tennessee: Thomas Nelson Publishers, 1990), Greek *Pharmakeia* 5331, 5332.
107. Richard Laurence, LL.D. Archbishop of Cashel, *The Book of Enoch the Prophet* (Oklahoma: Artisan Publishers, 1980), Enoch 8:3-4.

108. Dr. Caroline Leaf, *Who Switched Off My Brain?* (Switch on Your Brain Publishing, 2007), 127.
109. Dr. Chuck Missler, *The Book of Genesis: A Commentary* (Idaho: Koinonia House, 2004), CD-Notes.
110. Chuck Missler, Mark Eastman, *Alien Encounters* (Idaho: Koinonia House, 2003), 150-3.
111. Dr. Chuck Missler, *The Book of Genesis: A Commentary* (Idaho: Koinonia House, 2004), CD-Notes.
112. ibid.
113. Francis S. Collins, *The Language of God* (New York: Free Press, A Division of Simon and Schuster, 2006), 1-2.
114. Dr. Chuck Missler, *The Book of Genesis: A Commentary* (Idaho, Koinonia House, 2004), CD-Notes.
115. ibid.
116. Dr. Chuck Missler, *Prophecy 20/20* (Tennesse: Thomas Nelson Publishing, 2006), 11.
117. ibid., 13.
118. Wikipedia, Astronomy, http://en.wikipedia.org/wiki/Astronomy.
119. Wikipedia, Astrology, http://en.wikipedia.org/wiki/Astrology.
120. Chuck Missler, Mark Eastman, *Alien Encounters* (Idaho: Koinonia House, 2003), Tower of Babylon Steps Planets.
121. E. Raymond Capt, *The Glory of the Stars* (Oklahoma: Artisan Publishers, 1976), 4.
122. Wikipedia, Alchemy, http://en.wikipedia.org/wiki/Alchemy.
123. Wikipedia, Days of the Week, http://en.wikipedia.org/wiki/Days_of_the_week.
124. Dr. Chuck Missler, *Signs in the Heavens* (Idaho: Koinonia House, 1999),CD-Notes.
125. ibid.

126. ibid.
127. Matthew Bunson, *Angels A to Z* (New York: Three Rivers Press, Random House, 1996), 38, Baraqyal.
128. Wikipedia, Kabbalah, http://en.wikipedia.org/wiki/Kabbalah.
129. Matthew Bunson, *Angels A to Z* (New York: Three Rivers Press, Random House, 1996), 36, Baal.
130. David E. Flynn, UFOs Aliens & Antichrist: The Angelic Conspiracy & End times Deception, David Flynn, http://www.mt.net/~watcher/angelicconspiracy.html.
131. ibid.
132. Wikipedia, Baal, http://en.wikipedia.org/wiki/Baal.
133. Niel Freer, Breaking the Godspell: Thoughts on the Work of Zecharia Sitchin, Zecharia Sitchin, http://www.ufoevidence.org/topics/ZechariaSitchin.htm.
134. Wikipedia, Babylonian gods, http://en.wikipedia.org/wiki/Babylonian_Gods#Babylonia_and_Assyria.
135. Wikipedia, Dingir, http://en.wikipedia.org/wiki/Dingir.
136. *The Book of Jasher*, Translated into English from Hebrew, 1810 (Oklahoma: Artisan Publishers, 1988), 4:18.
137. Ellie Crystal, Popol Vuh, Ellie Crystal, http://www.crystalinks.com/popolvuh.html.
138. Chuck Missler, Mark Eastman, *Alien Encounters* (Idaho: Koinonia House, 2003), 300.
139. Stephanie Relphe, Death Thoughts: Mind Control Victims & Alien Abductees, Metatech- Stephanie Relphe, http://www.metatech.org/death_thought_mind_control_victim.html.
140. Chuck Missler, Mark Eastman, *Alien Encounters* (Idaho: Koinonia House, 2003), 257.
141. Jim Wilhelmsen, Cattle Mutilations: A "Mining" for Resources; Food & Construction Elements, Jim Wilhelmsen, http://www.echoesofenoch.com/cattle_mutilations.htm

142. Wikipedia, Atlantis, http://en.wikipedia.org/wiki/Atlantis
143. Plato, *Critias atlanti,* Wikipedia, Atlantis, http://en.wikipedia.org/wiki/Atlantis
144. Richard Laurence, LL.D. Archbishop of Cashel, *The Book of Enoch the Prophet* (Oklahoma: Artisan Publishers, 1980), Enoch 8.
145. ibid., Enoch 10:11.
146. Stephen D. Renn (Editor), *Expository Dictionary of Bible Words* (Massachusetts: Hendrickson Publishers, 2005), 212-3, Corruption-7843, 1015, Violence-2555.
147. David Hatcher Childress, *Technology of the Gods* (Illinois: Adventures Unlimited Press, 2000), 159-60.
148. Faustus Scorpius, Inspiration of the Daimon Samyaza, The Covenant of Samyaza, Copyright 1991, Graeme Wilson, www.necronomi.com/magic/satanism/samyaza.txt.
149. Stephen Quayle, *Genesis 6 Giants* (Montana: End Time Thunder Publishers, 2005), 81.
150. E. Raymond Capt, *The Great Pyramid Decoded: God's Stone Witness* (Oklahoma: Hoffman Printing, 2003), 11, 49-51.
151. ibid., 12.
152. ibid., 59.
153. Joesph A. Seiss *A Miracle in Stone: The Great Pyramid,* [1877], John Bruno Hare, http://www.sacred-texts.com/earth/ams/ams06.htm.
154. Wikipedia, Hyksos, http://en.wikipedia.org/wiki/Hyksos.
155. Joesph A. Seiss *A Miracle in Stone: The Great Pyramid,* [1877], John Bruno Hare, http://www.sacred-texts.com/earth/ams/ams06.htm.
156. E. Raymond Capt, *Stonehenge and Druidism* (Oklahoma: Hoffman Printing, 1979), 60.
157. Dr. Chuck Missler, *Monuments, Sacred or Profane?* (Idaho: Koinonia House, 1991), CD-Notes.

158. Wikipedia, Great Pyramid, http://en.wikipedia.org/wiki/Great_Pyramid.
159. Joesph A. Seiss *A Miracle in Stone: The Great Pyramid*, [1877], John Bruno Hare, http://www.sacred-texts.com/earth/ams/ams06.htm.
160. David E. Flynn, The Pyramids of Egypt and Mars, David Flynn, http://www.mt.net/%7Ewatcher/pyramid.html.
161. ibid.
162. E. Raymond Capt, *The Great Pyramid Decoded: God's Stone Witness* (Oklahoma: Hoffman Printing, 2003), 58.
163. Wikipedia, Sphinx, http://en.wikipedia.org/wiki/Sphinx.
164. Hancock's *Fingerprints of the Gods*, 1995, 375 (Hancock and Bauval, *Keeper of Genesis*, published 1997 in the U.S. as *The Message of the Sphinx*). (*op. cit.*, p.189)
165. William Whiston, A.M. (Translator), *Josephus, The Complete Works* (Tennessee: Thomas Nelson Publishers) 1.2.3.
166. Biblefacts.org, The Great Pyramid, Biblefacts.org, http://biblefacts.org/myth/pyramid.html.
167. Stephen Quayle, *Genesis 6 Giants* (Montana: End Time Thunder Publishers, 2005), 154, 163.
168. ibid., 165-166.
169. David E. Flynn, The Pyramids of Egypt and Mars, David Flynn, http://www.mt.net/%7Ewatcher/pyramid.html.
170. ibid.
171. E. Raymond Capt, *Stonehenge and Druidism* (Oklahoma: Hoffman Printing, 1979), 63.
172. ibid., 59.
173. Dr. Chuck Missler, *The Mysteries of the Planet Mars* (Idaho: Koinonia House, 1996), CD-Notes.
174. Lambert Dolphin *The Red Planet: Mars the Mysterious*, Koinonia House,http://www.khouse.org/articles/1997/19/

175. ibid.
176. Richard Hoagland, Redundant Geometry, Richard Hoagland, http://www.enterprisemission.com/message.htm.
177. David E. Flynn, The Zodiak, Cherubim & the Sphinx, David Flynn, http://www.mt.net/~watcher/newun.html.
178. ibid.
179. Dr. Chuck Missler, *The Mysteries of the Planet Mars* (Idaho: Koinonia House, 1996), CD-Notes.
180. ibid.
181. James Strong, LL.D., S.T.D., *The New Strong's Exhaustive Concordance of the Bible* (Tennessee: Thomas Nelson Publishers, 1990), H7293, rahab ,*rah'-hab,* From H7292, *bluster* (*blusterer*): - proud, strength.
182. Wikipedia, Coven, http://en.wikipedia.org/wiki/Coven.
183. Rebecca Brown MD, *Prepare for War* (Arizona, Whitaker House, 1987), 172.
184. Chris Ward, Angelic Ranking, Chris Ward, http://www.logoschristian.org/thrones/.
185. Diane Vera, The Rising gods of the Modern West, The Church of Azazel, http://www.angelfire.com/ny5/dvera/CoAz/belief/risingGods.html#Lilith.
186. Rebecca Brown MD, *He Came to Set the Captives Free* (Arizona: Whitaker House, 1986), 278-280.
187. ibid.
188. Dave Hunt, *A Woman Rides The Beast* (Oregon: Harvest House Publishers, 1994).
189. Diane Vera, The Rising Gods of the Modern West, The Church of Azazel, http://www.angelfire.com/ny5/dvera/CoAz/belief/risingGods.html#Lilith.
190. Rebecca Brown MD, *Prepare for War* (Arizona: Whitaker House, 1987), 124, 192-197.

191. ibid., 124-5.
192. Ellie Crystal, Astral Projection, Ellie Crystal, http://www.crystalinks.com/astralprojection.html.
193. Rebecca Brown MD, *Prepare for War* (Arizona: Whitaker House, 1987), 259-6.
194. ibid., 261.
195. Rebecca Brown MD, *He Came to Set the Captives Free* (Arizona: Whitaker House, 1986), 87.
196. *Encarta Dictionary*, Word Program - detestable.
197. Jewish Encyclopedia, Breastplate of the Priests, http://www.jewishencyclopedia.com/404#404/breastplate.
198. Jewish Encyclopedia, The Urim and Thummin, http://www.jewishencyclopedia.com/view.jsp?artid=52&letter=U&search=Urim%20And%20Thummin.
199. ibid., Urim and Thummin
200. ibid., rock crystal.
201. Ellie Crystal, Gemstones, Ellie Cyrstal, http://www.crystalinks.com/gemstones.html.
202. ibid.
203. ibid.
204. Mendak, The 13 Crystal Skulls, Mendak, http://www.mendhak.com/80-the-13-crystal-skulls.aspx.
205. ibid.
206. Richard Laurence, LL.D. Archbishop of Cashel, *The Book of Enoch the Prophet* (Oklahoma: Artisan Publishers, 1980), 8:1.
207. David Tocher, The Lore of Salt, http://www.curezone.com/foods/salt/lore_of_salt.htm.
208. Eastons Bible Dictionary, Prayer, http://eastonsbibledictionary.com/p/prayer.htm.
209. James Strong, LL.D., S.T.D., *The New Strong's Exhaustive Concordance of the Bible* (Tennessee: Thomas Nelson Publishers, 1990), 7878-pray.

210. *Encarta Dictionary*, Word Program – spell/incantation/curse/blessing.
211. Stephen D. Renn (Editor), *Expository Dictionary of Bible Words* (Massachusetts: Hendrickson Publishers, 2005), 217–19, Covenant-1285.
212. Rebecca Brown MD, *He Came to Set the Captives Free* (Arizona: Whitaker House, 1986), 72-4.
213. Encyclopedia of Death and Dying, Sacrifice, http://www.deathreference.com/Py-Se/Sacrifice.html.
214. ibid.
215. Wikipedia, Blood, http://en.wikipedia.org/wiki/Blood.
216. Althea Whitebirch, Blood Sacrifice, The Pagan Library, http://www.paganlibrary.com/editorials/blood_sacrifice.php.
217. Kentucky Paranormal Research Center, www.kypinvestigations.com.
218. Stephen D. Renn (Editor), *Expository Dictionary of Bible Words* (Massachusetts: Hendrickson Publishers, 2005), 923, Spirit- ru ach-7307.
219. Wikipedia, Familiar Spirit, http://en.wikipedia.org/wiki/Familiar_spirit.
220. Philip D. Morehead, *The New American Webster Handy College Dictionary* (New York: Penguin Books, 1995), 255-familiar.
221. Encarta Dictionary. Word Program, Reincarnation.
222. Wikipedia, Reincarnation, http://en.wikipedia.org/wiki/Reincarnation.
223. Wikipedia, Reincarnation, Henry Ford, http://en.wikipedia.org/wiki/Reincarnation#Henry_Ford.
224. Steve Russo, *What's the Deal with Wicca?* (Minnesota: Bethany House Publishers, 2005), 111.
225. *Encarta Dictionary*, Word Program—resurrected.

226. A Doctors Tesitmony about a Patient who died, Testimonies. Com.au., http://www.testimonies.com.au/topics/hell_experiences_1.htm.
227. Kevin Williams, The NDE and Spirituality, Near Death Experiences and the Afterlife, http://www.near-death.com/ Kevin Williams' research.
228. ibid.
229. Ken Vincent, Ed .D., NDEs and Universal Salvation, Near Death Experiences and the Afterlife, http://www.near-death.com/experiences/origen021.html.
230. ibid., multiple quotes.
231. Modern Catholic Dictionary- Bilocation, http://www.catholicreference.net/index.cfm.
232. Stephen D. Renn, (Editor) *Expository Dictionary of Bible Words* (Massachusetts: Hendrickson Publishers, 2005), 765, Prophet-4396.
233. Jim W. Goll, *The Seer* (Pennsylvania: Destiny Image Publishers, 2004), 18-19.
234. Stephen D. Renn, (Editor) *Expository Dictionary of Bible Words* (Massachusetts: Hendrickson Publishers, 2005), 1016-18, Visions.
235. Stephen D. Renn, (Editor) *Expository Dictionary of Bible Words* (Massachusetts: Hendrickson Publishers, 2005), 1018, additional notes on visions.
236. Jim W. Goll, *The Seer* (Pennsylvania: Destiny Image Publishers, 2004), 21-22.
237. *Encarta Dictionary*, Word Program - seer.
238. Philip D. Morehead, *The New American Webster Handy College Dictionary* (New York: Penguin Books, 1995), 213.
239. Stephen D. Renn (Editor), *Expository Dictionary of Bible Words* (Massachusetts: Hendrickson Publishers, 2005), 303, Dream- *onar*-3677.

240. Jim W. Goll, *The Seer* (Pennsylvania: Destiny Image Publishers, 2004), 59.
241. ibid., 60.
242. ibid., 64.
243. Wikipedia, Trance, http://en.wikipedia.org/wiki/Trance.
244. Wikipedia, Precognition, http://en.wikipedia.org/wiki/Precognition.
245. James Strong, LL.D., S.T.D., *The New Strong's Exhaustive Concordance of the Bible* (Tennessee: Thomas Nelson Publishers, 1990), H1060, b^{e}kor, From H1069; *firstborn*; hence *chief*: - eldest (son), first-born (-ling).
246. Ken Ham, Dinosaurs in the Bible, Answers in Genesis, http://www.answersingenesis.org/docs/2.asp.
247. David N. Menton, "Ostrich-osaurus" Discovery?, Answers in Genesis, http://www.answersingenesis.org/docs2005/0328discovery.asp.
248. Scott T. Norman, Mokelembembe: The Living Dinosaur, Scott T. Norman, http://www.mokelembembe.com/.
249. Philip R. "Pib" Burns, Mushrushu Stamps, Philip Burns, http://www.pibburns.com/cryptost/sirrush.html.
250. Richard Laurence, LL.D. Archbishop of Cashel, *The Book of Enoch the Prophet* (Oklahoma: Artisan Publishers, 1980), Enoch 59:7.
251. Wikipedia, Cryptozoology, http://en.wikipedia.org/wiki/Crytozoology.
252. Wikipedia, Lycanthropy, http://en.wikipedia.org/wiki/Lycanthropy.
253. Classic Encyclopdedia, 11th Ed., Encyclopedia Britannica [1911], Lycanthropy, http://www.1911encyclopedia.org/Lycanthropy.
254. Rebecca Brown MD, *He Came to Set the Captives Free* (Arizona: Whitaker House, 1986), 223-30.

255. Wikipedia, Griffin, http://en.wikipedia.org/wiki/Griffin.
256. Richard Laurence, LL.D. Archbishop of Cashel, *The Book of Enoch the Prophet* (Oklahoma: Artisan Publishers, 1980), 13-14.
257. *The Book of Jasher*, Translated into English from Hebrew, 1810 (Oklahoma: Artisan Publishers, 1988), 36:31, 61:14, 80:19.
258. Paraphrased and excerpted from *Interview with an Ex-Vampire* (Mark Productions, 2005). DVD, Bill Schnoebelen.
259. R.C. Alcorn, *Heaven* (Illinois: Tyndale House Publishers, 2004), 24.
260. Stephen D. Renn (Editor), *Expository Dictionary of Bible Words* (Massachusetts: Hendrickson Publishers, 2005), 460, 485 Hades-*sheol*, 7585.
261. ibid.
262. Wikipedia, Gehenna, http://en.wikipedia.org/wiki/Gehenna.
263. Stephen D. Renn, (Editor), *Expository Dictionary of Bible Words* (Massachusetts: Hendrickson Publishers, 2005), tartaroo-5020.
264. Richard Laurence, LL.D. Archbishop of Cashel, *The Book of Enoch the Prophet* (Oklahoma: Artisan Publishers, 1980), Enoch 21:1-6.
265. Bill Wiese, *23 Minutes in Hell* (Florida: Charisma House, 2006), Appendix A, 137-155.
266. Richard Laurence, LL.D. Archbishop of Cashel, *The Book of Enoch the Prophet* (Oklahoma: Artisan Publishers, 1980), 21:1–6.
267. Bill Wiese, *23 Minutes in Hell* (Florida: Charisma House, 2006), Appendix B, M. J. Erickson, 159.
268. Mary K. Baxter, *A Divine Revelation of Hell* (Pennsylvania: Whitaker House, 1993), 85.

269. ibid., previous two books, Wiese & Baxter, Creatures in Hell (see pages in endnotes 275, 277)
270. Bill Wiese, *23 Minutes in Hell* (Florida: Charisma House, 2006), 29–30.
271. ibid., 22.
272. James Strong, LL.D., S.T.D., *The New Strong's Exhaustive Concordance of the Bible* (Tennessee: Thomas Nelson Publishers, 1990), Greek, Heaven 2032, 3771, 3772.
273. ibid., 734, Place- maqom-4725.
274. R.C. Alcorn, *Heaven* (Illinois: Tyndale House Publishers, 2004), 57.
275. ibid., 427.
276. ibid., 373.
277. ibid., 375.
278. ibid., 374.
279. James Strong, LL.D., S.T.D., *The New Strong's Exhaustive Concordance of the Bible* (Tennessee: Thomas Nelson Publishers, 1990), Greek, Kingdom, G932